Edgar Allan Poe
A Bibliography of Criticism
1827–1967

EDGAR ALLAN POE
A Bibliography of Criticism
1827–1967

J. Lasley Dameron and Irby B. Cauthen, Jr.

A John Cook Wyllie Memorial Publication

Published for the Bibliographical Society of
the University of Virginia

By the University Press of Virginia
Charlottesville

THE UNIVERSITY PRESS OF VIRGINIA
Copyright © 1974 by the Rector and Visitors
of the University of Virginia

First published 1974

ISBN: 0-8139-0498-6
Library of Congress Catalog Card Number: 73-89824
Printed in the United States of America

MEMORIAE

IOHANNIS COOK WYLLIE

SACRVM

Contents

Preface

THIS bibliography of criticism on Edgar Allan Poe beginning in 1827 is designed to serve as a guide to the scholarly and critical work on Poe published up to 1968, the year first covered by the *Poe Newsletter* (now *Poe Studies*) in its annual listings of Poe criticism. This study is based primarily upon Irby B. Cauthen's master's thesis, "A Descriptive Bibliography of Criticism of Edgar Allan Poe, 1827–1941" (University of Virginia, 1942); and upon my *Edgar Allan Poe: A Checklist of Criticism, 1942–1960* (Charlottesville, Va.: Bibliographical Society of the University of Virginia, 1966). It is designed to be all-inclusive, although it is certainly not complete. For aid in locating additional criticism on Poe published between 1827–1967, one should consult two recently completed dissertations available on microfilm: John E. Reilly's *Poe in Imaginative Literature: A Study of American Drama, Fiction, and Poetry Devoted to Edgar Allan Poe or His Works* (Ann Arbor, Mich.: University Microfilms, 1966), and Ester F. Hyneman's *The Contemporaneous Reputation of Edgar Allan Poe with Annotated Bibliography of Poe Criticism, 1827–1967* (Ann Arbor, Mich.: University Microfilms, 1968). Professor Reilly recently announced his intent to include additional entries in a reworking of his dissertation, which is at present the most complete listing of Poe's treatment in creative literature.

Encyclopedic (and dictionary) essays on Poe, along with listings treating Poe in fiction, drama, and poetry, have been excluded except those entries which in the judgment of the compilers are important in understanding Poe's critical reception—especially literary appraisals appearing in print before 1909, the year when centennial estimates largely established Poe as a major American writer. No attempt is made to list all printings or reprintings, but reprintings of entries not readily available are noted when possible, particularly essays that have been collected and reprinted in a single volume.

All entries composed in English are annotated except those not verified or read and except very short articles (under three pages) whose titles accurately suggest their content. In some instances, annotations are quoted from various bibliographical sources like *PMLA, American Literature,* the *Cumulative Book Index,* and the *International Index to*

Periodicals. An attempt has been made to regularize the form of non-English entries to enhance the reader's use of this study, although in some instances complete bibliographical information was not provided by the source. Some critical reviews, especially reviews of book-length studies of Poe, are included and accompany annotations, but no attempt has been made to list these reviews in any particular order. The Index is designed primarily to serve as a title and subject index, focusing chiefly on the titles of Poe's works and matters of bibliographical and literary interest contained in annotations. Critics, editors, translators, and compilers—along with coauthors and coeditors—are indexed, however, in instances when their names appear in annotations and when their names are mentioned within entries that are not initially listed under their surnames.

The compilers acknowledge with gratitude the help of scholars and librarians here and abroad who have contributed materially to the compilation of this bibliography. Especially helpful have been Professors Eric W. Carlson, Charles Long, Burton Pollin, Carl L. Anderson, John E. Reilly, Floyd Stovall, W. T. Bandy, and Mrs. Tamara Miller. Among those contributing to the section of foreign language entries are Professors F. Lyra, Roger Forclaz, Rolando Anzilotti, Koh Kasigawa, Claude Richard, H. Tagiri, M. Mendelson, V. Trasheva, Roger Asselineau, Hans Galinsky, Georg Roppen, Harro H. Kühnelt, W. D. Wassenaar, Esteban Pujals, and Roberto Birindelli. Most importantly, the compilers wish to express their indebtedness to Professor Richard Beale Davis of the University of Tennessee and the late John Cook Wyllie, Librarian of the Alderman Library of the University of Virginia, who suggested and encouraged this study.

The library staffs of the following libraries ably assisted during all phases of this project: John Brister Library, Memphis State University; Alderman Library of the University of Virginia; Library of Congress, Washington, D.C.; and the libraries of Duke University, the University of North Carolina, and the University of Tennessee. Miss Mary Jane Urbanski and Mr. Edward F. Breslin, graduate students in English pursuing their studies at the University of Virginia, aided in the task of verifying entries located in the Alderman Library. Participating in the arduous compiling and preparation of the typescript were Mrs. Adriana Orr of Washington, D.C.; Mrs. Mary Stagg, Mrs. Ruby Jean Powell, and Mrs. Bonnie Kunzel, all of Memphis, Tennessee. Finally, the compilers gratefully acknowledge the permission of the *University of North Carolina Studies in Comparative Literature* to use entries from *Russian Studies of American Literature,* ed. Clarence Gohdes *et al.* (Chapel Hill: University of North Carolina Press, 1969).

My special thanks go to the National Endowment for the Humanities for awarding me two grants to work on this study and to the Memphis State University Foundation for its significant contribution in funding a summer's research at the University of Virginia. I wish moreover to thank Professor William Osborne, Chairman of the Department of English, Memphis State University, and Mr. Clark Neal, Director of Research Administration, also of Memphis State University, for their aid and guidance.

J. LASLEY DAMERON

December 1973
Memphis State University
Memphis, Tennessee

Abbreviations

ABC	American Book Collector	CEA	CEA Critic
		ChiR	Chicago Review
AgN	L'Age Nouveau Idées Lettres Arts	CJ	Classical Journal
		CL	Comparative Literature
AH	American Heritage		
AI	American Imago	CLAJ	College Language Association Journal (Morgan State College, Baltimore)
AION-SG	Annali Istituto Universitario Orientale (Naples, Sezione Germanica)		
		CUF	Columbia University Forum
AL	American Literature		
AN&Q	American Notes and Queries	Cweal	Commonweal
		DA	Dissertation Abstracts
AS	American Speech	DM	Dublin Magazine
AQ	American Quarterly	DUJ	Durham University Journal
Archiv	Archiv für das Studium der Neueren Sprachen		
		EA	Études Anglaises
ArQ	Arizona Quarterly	EI	Essay and General Literature Index
BB	Bulletin of Bibliography		
		EIC	Essays in Criticism (Oxford)
BBr	Books at Brown	EJ	English Journal
BNYPL	Bulletin of the New York Public Library	ELH	Journal of English Literary History
BPLQ	Boston Public Library Quarterly	ELN	English Language Notes
BSUF	Ball State University Forum	ES	English Studies
		ESQ	Emerson Society Quarterly
BuR	Bucknell Review		
BUSE	Boston University Studies in English	EUQ	Emory University Quarterly
		Expl	Explicator
CBI	Cumulative Book Index	FLe	Fiera Letteraria
CE	College English	GaR	Georgia Review

HR	Hispanic Review	MLR	Modern Language Review
HudR	Hudson Review		
II	International Index	MP	Modern Philology
JA	Jahrbuch für Ameri-kanstudien	MQ	Midwest Quarterly
		N&Q	Notes and Queries
Jour	Journal	NCF	Nineteenth-Century Fiction
JEGP	Journal of English and Germanic Philology		
		NEQ	New England Quar-terly
JHI	Journal of the His-tory of Ideas		
		NJHSP	New Jersey Histori-cal Society Proceed-ings
JSH	Journal of Southern History		
KHSR	Kentucky State His-torical Society Regis-ter	NMQ	New Mexico Quar-terly
		NRF	Nouvelle Revue Fran-çaise
KR	Kenyon Review		
L&P	Literature and Psy-chology (New York)	NS	Die Neueren Spra-chen
LCC	Library of Congress Catalogue	NYFQ	New York Folklore Quarterly
LCUP	Library Chronicle of the University of Pennsylvania	NYHSQ	New York Historical Society Quarterly
		NYRB	New York Review of Books
LCUT	Library Chronicle of the University of Texas		
		NYTBR	New York Times Book Review
Mag	Magazine	NYTM	New York Times Magazine
MASJ	Midcontinent Ameri-can Studies Journal		
		PAAS	Proceedings Ameri-can Antiquarian Soci-ety
MdF	Mercure de France		
MHM	Maryland Historical Magazine		
		PBSA	Papers of the Biblio-graphical Society of America
MHRA	Annual Bibliography of English Language and Literature, Edited for the Modern Hu-manities Research As-sociation		
		Person	The Personalist
		PMHB	Pennsylvania Maga-zine of History and Biography
MissQ	Mississippi Quarterly	PMLA	Publications of Mod-ern Language Associ-ation
MLN	Modern Language Notes		
MLQ	Modern Language Quarterly	PN	Poe Newsletter
		PQ	Philological Quarterly

PR	Partisan Review	TR	Table Ronde
PrS	Prairie Schooner	TSE	Tulane Studies in English
PULC	Princeton University Library Chronicle	TSL	Tennessee Studies in Literature
PW	Publishers' Weekly		
QR	Quarterly Review	TSLL	Texas Studies in Literature and Language
QRL	Quarterly Review of Literature (Bard College)	UCPMP	University of California Publications in Modern Philology
RDM	Revue des Deux Mondes	UKCR	University of Kansas City Review (also listed as UR, University Review, [Kansas City, Mo.])
RdP	Revue de Paris		
RES	Review of English Studies		
Rev	Review, Revue		
RLC	Revue de Litterature Comparée	UTQ	University of Toronto Quarterly
RLMC	Revista di Letterature Moderne e Comparate (Florence)	UTSE	University of Texas Studies in English
		UVaAB	University of Virginia Alumni Bulletin
RR	Romanic Review		
RSH	Revue des Sciences Humaines	UVaHS	University of Virginia Humanistic Studies
SA	Studi Americani (Rome)	UVaMag	University of Virginia Magazine
SAQ	South Atlantic Quarterly	UVaRec	University of Virginia Record
SatRL	Saturday Review of Literature (also SatR, Saturday Review)	VMHB	Virginia Magazine of History and Biography
SB	Studies in Bibliography: Papers of the Bibliographical Society of the University of Virginia	VQR	Virginia Quarterly Review
		WHR	Western Humanities Review
SLM	Southern Literary Messenger	WMQ	William and Mary Quarterly
SP	Studies in Philology	WWN	Walt Whitman Newsletter
SR	Sewanee Review		
SWR	Southwest Review	YCGL	Yearbook of Comparative and General Literature
TLS	Times Literary Supplement (London)		
TQ	Texas Quarterly	YR	Yale Review

YULG	*Yale University Library Gazette*	*YWES*	*Year's Work in English Studies*

* In section listing entries composed in English, the asterisk indicates works not read or verified.

F Foreign entry; indicates item not composed in English when appearing before a letter.

Checklist of Poe Criticism Composed in English
1827–1967

A

A1 A. "A Literary Causerie: Edgar Allan Poe." *Academy,* LXX (Jan. 13, 1906), 39–40.
Admires Poe's poetry.

A2 Abel, Darrel. "Coleridge's 'Life-in-Death' and Poe's 'Death-in-Life.' " *N&Q,* CC (May 1955), 218–20.
"Poe learned from Coleridge to use supernatural details in his portrayals of the semblance of life in a dead person." *AL.*

A3 ———. "Edgar Allan Poe, 1809–1849." *American Literature.* 4 vols. Woodbury, N.Y.: Barron's Educational Series, 1963, II, 208–24.
Interprets Poe's work as "the consummate literary expression of a South which never existed except as a romantic idea."

A4 ———. "Edgar Poe: A Centennial Estimate." *UKCR,* XVI (Winter 1949), 77–96.
Poe as critic was a competent judge of his contemporaries, composed a few poems of high quality, and masterfully created tales that stir the reader's sensibilities.

A5 ———. "A Key to the House of Usher." *Interpretations of American Literature.* Ed. Charles Feidelson and Paul Brodtkorb, Jr. New York: Oxford University Press, 1959, pp. 51–62.
Reprinted from *UTQ,* XVIII (Jan. 1949), 176–85.

A6 ———. "A Key to the House of Usher." *UTQ,* XVIII (Jan. 1949), 176–85.
"The Fall of the House of Usher" is a "consummate psychological allegory" which achieves unity through symbolic suggestions.

A7 ———. "Le Sage's Limping Devil and Mrs. Bullfrog." *N&Q,* CXCVIII (April 1953), 165–66.
"Sees a passage in Chapter III of Le Sage's *The Devil upon Two Sticks* as source for Hawthorne's 'Mrs. Bullfrog,' as well as Poe's 'The Man That Was Used Up.' " *AL.*

A8 Abernethy, Julian W. *American Literature.* New York: Maynard, Merrill, 1902.
Finds Poe a "lesser Coleridge" and commends him as an American author. See pp. 310–22.

A9   Abrams, M. H. *The Mirror and the Lamp: Romantic Theory and the Critical Tradition.* New York: W. W. Norton, 1958.

Comments on Poe's theory of the short poem, pp. 136–37 and *passim.*

A10   "Absens." "The University and Its Alumni." *UVaMag,* IX (Oct. 1870), 24–29.

Edgar Poe's name is "proudest and foremost upon our roll of honor."

A11   Adams, Percy G. "Poe, Critic of Voltaire." *MLN,* LVII (April 1942), 273–75.

Poe's blunder in charging that Voltaire is careless in designating the place in a scene from *Mort de César.*

A12   Adams, Richard P. "Romanticism and the American Renaissance." *AL,* XXIII (Jan. 1952), 419–32.

In attempting to expound upon Morse Peckham's proposed definition of romanticism as a "shift away from thinking of the universe as a static mechanism" to that of "dynamic organism," Adams finds Poe a negative romanticist who rejects the old static mechanistic world order but does not arrive "at a satisfactorily dynamic and organic metaphysic to replace it."

A13   Adams, Robert Martin. *Nil: Episodes in the Literary Conquest of Void during the Nineteenth Century.* New York: Oxford University Press, 1966.

Poe's "nothing does possess a remarkable variety of colorings and literary shadings; it has been imaginatively apprehended"; see pp. 41–50.

Reviewed:
Petersen, *PN,* I, 14–16.

A14   Adams, William Henry Davenport. *Wrecked Lives; or, Men Who Have Failed.* 2nd ser. New York: Pott, Young, 1880.

Poe's life and character are made the subject of a Griswoldian homily; see pp. 297–320.

A15   Adkins, Nelson F. " 'Chapter on American Cribbage': Poe and Plagiarism." *PBSA,* XLII (3rd quarter 1948), 169–210.

Poe's concern with plagiarism is related to his concept of imitation and originality and is an integral part of a touchstone or cardinal principle which he applied in his criticism with eminent success.

A16   ——. "Poe's Borrowings." *N&Q,* CLXVI (July 28, 1934), 67–68.

A possible source of Poe's "Song" ("I saw thee on thy bridal day") is a poem by Fitz-Greene Halleck.

A17   ——. "Poe's 'Ulalume.' " *N&Q,* CLXIV (Jan. 14, 1933), 30–31.

A poem by Willis Gaylord Clark influenced "Ulalume."

A18   Adler, Jacob H. "Are There Flaws in 'The Cask of Amontillado'?" *N&Q,* CXCIX (Jan. 1954), 32–34.
"Poe's use of a Frenchman with long residence and family history in Italy is a flaw." *AL.*

A19   Albee, John. "Poe and Aristotle." *Dial,* XXXIV (March 16, 1903), 192.
Poe as critic.

A20   Albright, Daniel. *An Account of the Discussion of Narrative Technique, from Poe up to James.* Chicago: Dept. of Photographic Reproduction, University of Chicago, 1956.
See pp. 3–47 for an expository discussion of Poe's theory of fiction.

*A21   ——. "An Account of the Discussion of Narrative Technique from Poe up to James." Diss., University of Chicago, 1956.

A22   Alderman, Edwin Anderson. "Edgar Allan Poe and the University of Virginia." *VQR,* I (April 1925), 78–84.
Discusses Poe's life at the university and the possible effect of the university on Poe.

A23   ——. "Poe and the University." *UVaAB,* 3rd ser., II (April 1909), 136–40.
This address was delivered in Cabell Hall at the University of Virginia on January 19, 1909.

A24   Alexander, G. W. "The Poetry of Charles Baudelaire." *UVaMag,* LXIX (Jan. 1909), 228–35.
There are passing references to Poe's influence on Baudelaire.

*A25   Alexander, Jean Avon. *Affidavits of Genius: French Essays on Poe from Forgues to Valéry.* Ann Arbor, Mich.: University Microfilms, 1960.

A26   ——. "Affidavits of Genius: French Essays on Poe from Forgues to Valéry." *DA,* XXII (Sept. 1961), 866.
French essays on Poe reveal a trend of evolution or discovery.

*A27   ——. "Affidavits of Genius: French Essays on Poe from Forgues to Valéry." Diss., University of Washington, 1960.

A28   Alfriend, E. M. "Unpublished Recollections of Edgar Allan Poe." *Literary Era,* VIII (Aug. 1901), 489–91.

A29   Allan, Carlisle. "Cadet Edgar Allan Poe, U.S.A." *American Mercury,* XXIX (Aug. 1933), 446–55.
An account of Poe's army and West Point career.

A30   Allen, Gay Wilson. "Edgar Allan Poe." *American Prosody.* New York: American Book Co., 1935, pp. 56–90.
One of the best essays on Poe's prosody. In minutely examining the

meter and rhyme of Poe's poetry, this critic compares Poe's theory and practice.

A31   Allen, Hervey. "Edgar Allan Poe." *Dictionary of American Biography.* Ed. Dumas Malone. New York: Scribner's, 1935.

A straightforward, chronological biography with a brief account of the personality of the man and of his fame.

A32   ———. "Foreword." *The Gold Bug,* by Edgar Allan Poe. Notes on the Text by Thomas Ollive Mabbott. New York: Doubleday, Doran, 1929, pp. vii–xxix.

Essay on the publication and sources of "The Gold Bug."

A33   ———. "Introduction." *The Book of Poe: Tales, Criticisms, Poems.* Ed. Addison Hibbard. Garden City, N.J.: Doubleday, Doran, 1929, pp. xi–xvii.

An appreciative introduction to Poe and a brief analysis of some of the serious problems in collecting Poe's works.

A34   ———. "Introduction." *The Complete Tales and Poems of Edgar Allan Poe.* New York: Random House, 1938, pp. v–viii.

Brief commentary on Poe's importance as a writer and on editing his work.

A35   ———. "Introduction." *Tales of Edgar Allan Poe.* New York: Random House, 1944, pp. vii–xii.

Briefly traces Poe's reputation as a writer and stresses his ability to project mystical vistas.

A36   ———. *Israfel: The Life and Times of Edgar Allan Poe.* 2 vols. New York: George H. Doran, 1926. Reprinted New York: Farrar and Rinehart, 1934, and by Rinehart, 1956.

A detailed biography, but not always accurate.

Reviewed:

J. W. Krutch, *SatRL,* III, 493–94.

TLS, May 5, 1927, p. 314.

T. S. Eliot, *Nation-Athenaeum,* XLI (May 21, 1927), 7, 219.

Sidney Cox, *SR,* XXXV, 241–43.

Stanley T. Williams, *YR,* XVI, 812–16.

Percy H. Boynton, *New Republic,* L (May 11, 1927), 340–41.

Viola Paradise, *Forum,* LXXVII, 958.

Padraic Colum, *Cweal,* VI (Aug. 24, 1927), 373–75.

Carl Van Doren, *Century Mag,* CXIII, 510–11.

Malcolm Cowley, *Dial,* LXXXIII, 168–71.

Theodore Morrison, *Independent,* CXVIII (Jan. 22, 1927), 106.

Killis Campbell, *SP,* 474–79.

Bookman, LXIV, 511–12.

Peter Quennell, *New Statesman,* XXIX (April 16, 1927), 16–17.

Killis Campbell, *AL*, VII, 220–24.

B. Dobree, *London Mercury*, XXXII, 493–94.

A37 ——. "Mr. Allen Replies." *SatRL*, III (Feb. 26, 1927), 618.
A letter to the editor answering James H. Whitty's critical commentary on Allen's *Israfel: The Life and Times of E. A. Poe.*

A38 ——. "Poe in Carolina." *North American Rev*, CCXVI (July 1922), 65–66.

A39 ——. "Poe in South Carolina." *Poetry*, XX (April 1922), 48–49.

A40 ——. *Selected Tales and Poems,* by Edgar Allan Poe. Introd. Hervey Allen. New York: W. J. Black, 1943.
Allen's introduction (22 pages) is primarily biographical; volume is reprint of 1927 edition.

A41 ——, and Thomas Ollive Mabbott. *Poe's Brother: The Poems of William Henry Leonard Poe.* New York: George H. Doran, 1926.
Includes a sketch of Henry Poe's life, pp. 19–36, and a text of his poetry together with some prose dealing with his brother Edgar, pp. 39–87.
Reviewed:
Independent, CXVIII (Feb. 19, 1927), 220.
Bookman, LXIV, 511–12.

A42 Allen, James L., Jr. "Stanza Pattern in the Poetry of Poe." *TSL*, XII (1967), 111–20.
Much of Poe's poetry reveals significant similarities of stanzaic pattern.

A43 Allen, James Lane. "Night Shadows in Poe's Poetry." *Continent Rev* (New York), V (Jan. 23, 1884), 102–4.

*A44 Allen, M. L. "Edgar Allan Poe and the British Magazine Tradition." Diss., Birmingham University, 1965.

A45 Allen, Mozelle Scaff. "Poe's Debt to Gautier, Pascal, and Voltaire." Diss., University of Texas, 1940.

A46 ——. "Poe's Debt to Voltaire." *UTSE,* No. 15 (1935), 63–75.
Evidence suggests that Voltaire did in some degree influence Poe.

A47 Allen, R. T. P. [Letter to the Editor.] *Scribner's Monthly*, XI (Nov. 1875), 142–43.
In letter concerning Poe at West Point and immediately afterwards, dated Farndale, Ky., Sept. 10, 1875, Academy graduate reports that in 1834 Poe worked in a Baltimore brickyard.

A48 Allibone, S. A. "Poe, Edgar Allan." *A Critical Dictionary of English Literature and British and American Authors*. Philadelphia: Lippincott, 1870.

Criticism of Poe's work is flattering, but the biography contains errors; see II, 1614–15.

A49   Almy, Robert E. "J. N. Reynolds: A Brief Biography with Particular Reference to Poe and Symmes." *Colophon,* NS II (Winter 1937), 227–45.

Discusses Reynolds's popularization of Symmes's theories of the construction of the earth and the effect of these theories on Poe's writings.

A50   Alterton, Margaret. "An Additional Source for Poe's 'The Pit and the Pendulum.' " *MLN,* XLVIII (June 1933), 349–56.

Juan Antonio Llorente's *History of the Spanish Inquisition* is source for Poe's method of handling Inquisition material.

*A51   ———. "Origins of Edgar Allan Poe's Critical Principles." Diss., University of Iowa, 1922.

A52   ———. *The Origins of Poe's Critical Theory.* Iowa City: University of Iowa, 1925. University of Iowa Studies, 1st ser., No. 9, April 15, 1925. Also appears in *University of Iowa Humanistic Studies,* II, No. 3 (1925).

Poe laid the foundation of his criticism in his reading from *Blackwood's,* scientific journals, Plato, Augustus Wilhelm von Schlegel, and the *Philosophical Transactions of the Royal Society of London.*
    Reviewed:
Killis Campbell, *MLN,* XLI, 208.
"H. B. C." *Rev. of English Studies,* III, 489–90.

A53   ———, and Hardin Craig, eds. *Edgar Allan Poe: Representative Selections.* New York: American Book Co., 1935.

Poe conceived of an analogy between the action of the forces of nature and the unified arrangement of a literary work. See "Introduction," pp. xiii–cxviii.
    Reviewed:
AL, VIII, 106–7.

A54   Amacher, Richard E. "Poe's 'The City in the Sea.' " *Expl,* XIX (May 1961), item 60.

Poe's poem demonstrates a self-contained structure.

A55   Anderson, Carl L. *The Swedish Acceptance of American Literature.* Philadelphia: University of Pennsylvania Press, 1957.

Poe was one of the "chief representatives of American literature" in Sweden in the years before 1920, *passim.*

A56   Anderson, David. "A Comparison of the Poetic Theories of Emerson and Poe." *Person,* XLI (Autumn 1960), 471–83.

"Emerson sought a union of truth and art; for Poe, art alone was the supreme goal."

*A57   Anderson, Don Max. *Edgar Allan Poe's Influence upon Baude-laire's Style*. Ann Arbor, Mich.: University Microfilms, 1955.

A58   ——. "Edgar Allan Poe's Influence upon Baudelaire's Style." *DA*, XV (1955), 2197–98.
A "community of expressive techniques and verbal associations through which similar or identical impressions are created supports the conclusion that Baudelaire's style originates in Poe's writings."

A59   ——. "Edgar Allan Poe's Influence upon Baudelaire's Style." Diss., University of Iowa, 1955.

A60   Anderson, William W. "Thomas Holley Chivers M.D., 1807–1858." *Annals of Medical History*, NS III (July 1931), 391–93.

A61   Anon. "American Fiction." *Edinburgh Rev*, CLXXIII (Jan. 1891), 31–65.
Of Poe's fiction and artistic accomplishments.

A62   ——. "The American Library." *Blackwood's Mag*, LXII (Nov. 1847), 574–92.
Denies Poe any boldness of imagination, but comments upon Poe's power of analysis and descriptive ability; see pp. 582–87.

A63   ——. "American Poetry." *Eclectic Mag*, XX (Aug. 1850), 567–69.
A critical discussion of Poe's art reprinted from *Fraser's Mag*, XLII (July 1850), 17–19.

A64   ——. "Ancient Letter of Poe Shows Origin of Gold Bug." Memphis *Commercial Appeal*, Nov. 15, 1925, sec. 4, p. 7.
Reproduces a letter by Poe to Richard Bolton concerning cryptography and a brief commentary on Richard Bolton's solving of an intricate "Cryptograph."

A65   ——. "The Art of Poe." *Christian Science Monitor*, Jan. 28, 1920, p. 14.
Poe has skill and artistry, but his morbid delineations are depressing.

*A66   ——. [Article on Mary Rogers.] New York *Evening Journal*, June 29, 1897, p. 27, col. 1.

A67   ——. "Autographs." *New-York Mirror*, XX (Jan. 1, 1842), 3.
On Poe's commentaries on signatures that are reproduced in *Graham's Magazine*.

A68   ——. "Autographs." *New-York Mirror*, XX (Jan. 1, 1842), 3.
Review of *Autography*.

A69   ——. "Baltimore's Tribute to Poe." Baltimore *Evening News*, Extra, Wednesday, Nov. 17, 1875.
A full account of the ceremonies of unveiling the Poe monument.

A70 ——. "Baudelaire and Poe," in "Musings without Method." *Blackwood's Mag*, CXCIII (March 1913), 417–19.
On Baudelaire's affinity with Poe.

A71 ——. "Beethoven Letter Fetches £1,250." London *Times*, Nov. 13, 1963, p. 6.
Selling of a Poe letter.

A72 ——. "A Bibliography of Edgar A. Poe." *Literary World*, XIII (Dec. 16, 1882), 457.
A brief but useful bibliography of Poe's writings and of some translations of Poe.

A73 ——. "Book Gives Origin of Poe Sculpture at Metropolitan Museum." New York *Evening Post*, Sept. 17, 1927, sec. I, p. 13.
Bas relief discovered in Museum was bought by Steele Mackaye Benefit Show.

A74 ——. "Born in Boston, Jan. 19, 1809: Edgar Allan Poe: Died in Baltimore, Oct. 7, 1849." Baltimore *Sun*, Jan. 17, 1909, 2nd sec., pp. 13–17.
Presents a series of articles on Poe's life, the history of the Baltimore memorial, and Poe's place in the history of English literature.

A75 ——. "Boston to Observe Centenary of Poe." Boston *Herald*, Jan. 17, 1909, News sec., p. 3.

A76 ——. "Cadet Edgar Allan Poe." *Army and Navy Jour*, XLVI, No. 22 (Jan. 30, 1909), p. 604.
On Poe's brief career at West Point.

A77 ——. "The Case of Poe." *TLS*, June 14, 1923, p. 397.

A78 ——. "The Centenary of Edgar Allan Poe." London *Daily Chronicle*, Jan. 8, 1909, p. 7.

A79 ——. "Centennial Memorial Section." Richmond *Times-Dispatch*, Jan. 17, 1909, sec. 3, pp. 1–4.
A profusely illustrated section of news stories concerning Poe, Richmond, and the University.

A80 ——. "Claimants for Poe's Birthplace." *Literary Digest*, XXXVIII (Jan. 30, 1909), 179–80.
A summary of the dispute over the city of Poe's birth.

A81 ——. "Concerning the Portrait of 'Edgar.' " *SLM*, II (Dec. 1940), 652.
A portrait of Poe at five years of age could be authentic.

A82 ——. "Correspondence of the Courier." Charleston *Courier*, Oct. 11, 1849, p. 3.
A notice of Poe's death.

A83 ———. "Criticism of Poe's 'Raven.'" *New-York Mirror*, II (April 26, 1845), 42–43.
Tongue-in-cheek criticism.

A84 ———. "Curious Alleged Plagiarism by the Late Edgar Allan Poe." *Literary World*, XII (Feb. 5, 1893), 102–63.
"To One in Paradise" is attributed to Tennyson.

A85 ———. "Current Notes of the Book World." Washington *Post*, Jan. 17, 1909, mag. sec., p. 6.
Some current prices on Poe items.

A86 ———. "Death of Edgar A. Poe." Baltimore *Evening Sun*, Oct. 8, 1849, p. 2.

A87 ———. "Death of Edgar A. Poe." Greenville *Mountaineer*, Oct. 19, 1849, p. 2.
A notice of Poe's death.

A88 ———. "Death of Edgar Allan Poe." *Literary World*, V (Oct. 13, 1849), 319.
An obituary with a short biographical sketch.

A89 ———. [Death of Edgar Allan Poe.] New York *Journal of Commerce*, Oct. 9, 1849, p. 2.
Announces Poe's death and praises his genius.

A90 ———. "Death of Edgar Allan Poe." *Wheler's Southern Monthly Mag*, I (Nov. 1849), 118.

A91 ———. *The Dedication Exercises of the Actors' Monument to Edgar Allan Poe, Sculptured by Richard Henry Park, and Unveiled in the Metropolitan Museum of Arts, New York City, May 4, 1885*. New York: T. L. Devinne, 1885.
Contains an "Introductory Address" (A. S. Sullivan), "Speech of Presentation" (Edwin Booth), "Speech Unveiling the Monument" (John Gilbert), "Song of the Free" (G. E. Montgomery), "Speech of Acceptance" (Gen. L. P. di Cesnola), "Commemorative Oration" (Wm. R. Alger), and a "Poem" (William Winter).

A92 ———. [Discussion of the Genesis of "The Raven."] *Athenaeum*, No. 2473 (March 20, 1875), p. 395.
"The Raven" was suggested by two poems by Tennyson: "No more," published in 1831, and "Anacreontic," published in the same year.

A93 ———. "A Dreamer of Things Impossible." *Academy*, LXI (Sept. 28, 1901), 263–64.
Tales such as the "Ms. Found in a Bottle" anticipate the "wonder-tales" of Jules Verne and H. G. Wells, while other tales anticipate Conan Doyle and Stevenson.

A94   ——. "The Dual Personality of Edgar Allan Poe." *Current Literature,* XLIII (Sept. 1907), 287–88.

A95   ——. "E. A. Poe, Lawyer, Ex-Football Star." New York *Times,* Dec. 1, 1961, p. 33.
Poe's great-nephew dies.

A96   ——. "E. A. Poe's New Work. *Tales of the Grotesque and Arabesque.* By Edgar A. Poe: 2 vols.—Philadelphia: Lea and Blanchard." *SLM,* VI (Jan. 1840), 126.
A brief notice.

A97   ——. "The Early Days of the Jefferson Society." *UVaMag,* LIX (Jan. 1899), 180–83.
Some references to Poe's relations with the society.

A98   ——. "Edgar A. Poe." *New World,* IV (June 4, 1842), 367.
Some remarks on the singularly pure and idiomatic style of Poe's writings.

A99   ——. "Edgar A. Poe." *Quarterly Jour and Rev,* I (Jan. 1846), 92–96.
Review of *The Raven and Other Poems* (1845).

A100   ——. "Edgar A. Poe." *Rural Repository* (Hudson, N.Y.), XXVII (July 26, 1851), 161.
Primarily a repetition of biographical facts.

A101   ——. "Edgar A. Poe and the Juleps." *Lippincott's,* IX (May 1872), 599.
A ridiculously false story of Poe's drinking a tumbler of brandy before breakfast and then admitting that he had already drunk thirteen juleps.

A102   ——. "Edgar A. Poe, Esq." Philadelphia *Saturday Courier,* July 25, 1846, p. 1.
Poe is a gifted genius.

A103   ——. "Edgar A. Poe Is Lecturing on Poets and Poetry at Richmond, Va." *Wheler's Southern Monthly Mag,* I (Oct. 1849), 98.
This news item is followed by statement that Poe "has joined the sons of temperance."

A104   ——. "Edgar A. Poe to the Rescue!" *Life in Letters. American Autograph Jour,* V (Feb. 1941), 667–77.
The reporting of a separate edition (Boston, 1849) of "X-ing a Paragraph."

A105   ——. "Edgar Allan Poe." *Academy,* LVII (Aug. 5, 1899), 137.
Declares that Poe was not a man void of "sweetness and light."

A106 ———. "Edgar Allan Poe." *Biographical Mag,* VII (May 1855), 211–20.
Defends Poe's character and elaborates on his "unique genius."

A107 ———. "Edgar Allan Poe." *Eclectic Mag,* NS XXI (March 1875), 303–6.
Finds reading Poe a sickening task. Reprinted from *SatR* (London), XXXVIII (Dec. 19, 1874), 802–3.

A108 ———. "Edgar Allan Poe." *Edinburgh Rev,* CVII (April 1858), 419 42.
A most scathing essay on Poe's character; has little to say about Poe's literary talents. Reprinted in *Eclectic Mag,* XLIV (July 1858), 388–98; *Littel's Living Age,* LVII (June 1858), 803–16; *Ladies Repository,* XIX (July 1859), 419–23; and introductory paragraphs appear in John R. Thompson's *The Genius and Character of Edgar Allan Poe* (Richmond: Garrett & Massie, 1929), pp. 51–52.

A109 ———. "Edgar Allan Poe." *Edinburgh Rev,* CCXI (Jan. 1910), 207–26.
Poe is the only American who is a "world-author."

A110 ———. "Edgar Allan Poe." *Harper's Weekly,* XIX (Dec. 11, 1875), 1001–2.
An account of the dedication of the Baltimore monument.

A111 ———. "Edgar Allan Poe." *Independent,* LXVI (Jan. 21, 1909), 157–58.

A112 ———. "Edgar Allan Poe." *Leisure Hour,* III (July 6, 1854), 427–29.

A113 ———. "Edgar Allan Poe." *Littel's Living Age,* CCLX (Feb. 20, 1909), 500–504.
Poe's "poems are essentially original in subject as in style."

A114 ———. "Edgar Allan Poe." New York *Herald,* Oct. 28, 1875, p. 4.
The unveiling of the Poe monument in Baltimore.

A115 ———. "Edgar Allan Poe." *Southern Rev,* XXII (July 1877), 126–49.
Concludes that "within his very definite limits," Poe is "unsurpassed."

*A116 ———. [Edgar Allan Poe.] *Talisman and Odd Fellow's Mag,* I (Sept. 1846), 105.

A117 ———. "Edgar Allan Poe." *UVaMag,* XLIX (Oct. 1887), 1–13.
Poe was a misfit in the American milieu.

*A118 ———. "Edgar Allan Poe." *Wiley Bulletin,* XXXIII (Winter 1950), 4–5.

"A brief account of the part played by publishers Wiley and Putnam in promoting Poe's books." *AL.*

A119 ——. "Edgar Allan Poe: A Genius of the Shadows." Birmingham (Eng.) *Daily Mail,* Jan. 19, 1909, p. 4.

A120 ——. [Edgar Allan Poe.] "A Great Man Self-Wrecked." *National Mag,* I (Oct. 1852), 362–65.

Poe is described as "one of the most popular and imaginative of our writers."

A121 ——. "Edgar Allan Poe: A Vindication." *St. James Mag,* XXXVIII (ser. III of vol. 2) (1875–76), 331–33.

A122 ——. "Edgar Allan Poe and His Poetry." *Glasgow University Mag,* No. 1 (Jan. 1878), pp. 8–10.

"Poe's genius is intensely lyrical."

A123 ——. "Edgar Allan Poe and His Writings." *Once a Week* (London), Nov. 4, 1871, pp. 404–10; Nov. 18, 1871, 447–50.

A124 ——. "Edgar Allan Poe and the Hall of Fame." *Current Literature,* XXXIX (Dec. 1905), 613–14.

A reporting of Poe's failure to gain admittance by a seven-vote margin.

A125 ——. "Edgar Allan Poe at Fort Monroe." *Tales of Old Fort Monroe,* No. 3 (Oct. 1957), n. pag.

From a monograph published by the Committee for the Fort Monroe Casemate Museum.

A126 ——. "Edgar Allan Poe: Centenary of a Great Poet, Astute Critic, and Original Story Teller." *Collier's,* XLII (Jan. 16, 1909), sec. I, 10.

A127 ——. "Edgar Allan Poe, 1809–1849." *Twelve American Writers.* Ed. William M. Gibson and George Arms. New York: Macmillan, 1962, pp. 191–94.

Poe "led toward symbolism and surrealism."

A128 ——. "Edgar Allan Poe on Cryptography." *Bookman,* XVII (March 1903), 4–5, 7.

Praise for Poe's "swift and unerring" skill in cryptography.

A129 ——. *The Edgar Allan Poe Shrine.* Richmond: The Old Stone House, 1923.

A130 ——. "Edgar Allan Poe Speaks." *Life,* LXXVI (Nov. 25, 1920), 964.

Verse.

A131 ——. *Edgar Allan Poe Special Number. Book News Monthly,* XXV (Aug. 1907), 783–854.

Contains six articles on Poe.

A132 ———. "Edgar Allan Poe's Career in Philadelphia." Philadelphia *Public Ledger,* Jan. 17, 1909, mag. sec., p. 1.

A133 ———. "Edgar Allan Poe's Great Balloon Hoax." Philadelphia *Public Ledger,* Jan. 17, 1909, mag. sec., p. 6.

A134 ———. "Edgar Poe and His Biographers." *Temple Bar,* LXVIII (Aug. 1883), 530–39.

A135 ———. "Edgar Poe in the Spirit World." *Herald of Light,* I, No. 3 (July 1857), 106–17.
  Edgar Poe returns from the "spirit-land" several times from 1853 to 1856.

A136 ———. "Edgar Poe's Cottage." New York *Herald,* June 10, 1883, p. 10.

A137 ———. "An Effort to Save the Poe Cottage." New York *Times,* Nov. 19, 1895, p. 1.

A138 ———. "Facsimile of Faculty Record." *UVaAB,* VI (Nov. 1899), between pp. 80 and 81.
  This concerns Poe's appearance before the faculty of the university to tell what he knew of student irregularities.

A139 ———. "A Failure." Boston *Daily Evening Transcript,* Oct. 17, 1845, p. 2.
  Comments on Poe's recitation and lecture at the Lyceum attributed to Cornelia Walter.

A140 ———. "The Fame of Edgar Allan Poe." *Munsey's Mag,* XII (Feb. 1895), 553–54.

A141 ———. "Famous Poe–Dickens Mystery Solved." *NYTM,* June 1, 1913, pp. 2, 9.
  Reprints the important *Saturday Evening Post* review by Poe of *Barnaby Rudge.*

A142 ———. "The Fate of the Gifted." *UVaMag,* IV (June 1860), 506–12.
  Discusses Poe in Griswoldian terms.

A143 ———. "Finding the Harmonic Equivalent of Edgar Allan Poe." *Newsweek,* VII (Feb. 15, 1936), 30.
  On Poe's works rendered into music.

A144 ———. "From Edgar A. Poe to Mr. John Allan." *SLM,* III (Jan. 1941), 22–29.
  Facsimile reproduction with some comments on letters from the Valentine papers.

A145 ———. "Genius and the Law of Libel." New York *Tribune,* Feb. 19, 1847, editorial page, col. 2.

Comments on the *Literati* articles that aroused English and the subsequent law suit.

A146 ——. "Ghost of Edgar Allan Poe." *Newsweek,* XII (Nov. 28, 1938), 27–28.

A147 ——. "Governor for Poe Day." Baltimore *Sun,* Jan. 14, 1909, p. 12.

Governor Crothers expresses hope that public schools will honor Poe.

A148 ——. "Greeley Pays Poe for Contributions to Tribune with Promissory Note." *Bruno's Weekly,* II (March 4, 1916), 526–28.

Horace Greeley's promissory note of Oct. 24, 1845, is printed here with a Poe letter to Thompson of Jan. 13, 1849.

A149 ——. "Halleck and Poe." *Round Table,* IX (Feb. 13, 1869), 101–2.

Poe compared to Fitz-Greene Halleck.

A150 ——. "Highways and Byways." *Chatauquan,* XXX (Feb. 1900), 453.

A presentation of some incidents from Poe's life.

A151 ——. "How Poe Must Have Looked." *Current Literature,* XLI (Sept. 1906), 287–90.

Reproductions of drawings from Oliver Leigh's *Edgar Allan Poe.*

A152 ——. "How the British Regard Poe—and America." *Literary Digest,* XXXVIII (Feb. 13, 1909), p. 255.

A condensation of British criticism at the centennial.

A153 ——. "Important Unpublished Poe Material." *Bodley Book Shop* (Brooklyn, N.Y.) *Catalogue,* No. 1 (1935), p. 38.

A copy of the 1859 *Poetical Works,* once owned by Augustine O'Neil, contains his recollections of the Poes at Fordham.

A154 ——. "Ingram for the Defence." Richmond *Standard,* June 5, 1880, p. 2.

A news story of Ingram's attack on Stedman.

A155 ——. [Introduction.] *Anastatic Printing as Described by Edgar Allan Poe in 1845.* Chicago: Silver Quoin Press, 1946, pp. [1–5].

Prefatory commentary on Poe's proposed "method of printing which is now so completely obsolete."

A156 ——. "Introduction." *The Raven and Other Poems,* by Edgar Allan Poe. New York: Effingham Maynard, 1899, pp. 3–6.

A three-page biographical introduction followed by brief critical comments by several critics of Poe.

A157 ——. "Ishmael of American Letters." *Current Literature,* XLVI (Feb. 1909), 172–75.

Poe should be included in the writer's Hall of Fame.

A158   ——. "Israfel in the Laboratory." *TLS,* Oct. 7, 1949, p. 648.
"Poetry, for Poe, was a branch of mechanics. There is never any calm and light, never any reflux of daily human affairs in his verse. Though there is not now 'the large-orbed wonder' his writings once excited in America and Europe, his 'music remains, and can move magically.' " *AL.*

A159   ——. "The Journal of Julius Rodman: A Newly Discovered Work by the Late Edgar A. Poe." *Mirror of Literature,* Nov. 3, 1877, pp. 9–10.
This reports Ingram's discovery and quotes extensively from the *Journal* itself.

A160   ——. [*Kai Yi:* A Possible Source for "The Raven."] *Academy,* LX (June 22, 1901), 525–26.
"Kai Yi" is a Chinese poet who flourished about 200 B.C. "The source" is quoted.

A161   ——. "Kit-Katicisms." *Kit-Kat,* V (April 1916), 39–46.
Biographical sketch introducing a series of articles on Poe by Landon C. Bell to appear in succeeding issues; see pp. 39–42.

A162   ——. "The Lady Editor Who Paid Poe Fifty Cents a Page." *Current Opinion,* LXII (March 1917), 204.
Poe is quoted in a letter to Mrs. Sarah Josepha Hale, editor of *The Opal* (March 31, 1844), that fifty cents per page "will be amply sufficient."

A163   ——. "Letters from the Poets." *Poems and Essays of Edgar Allan Poe.* New York: W. J. Widdleton, 1876, pp. cxxxiii–cxl.
Poets respond to an invitation to attend dedicatory ceremonies of a Poe monument in Baltimore.

A164   ——. "Letters of Edgar Allan Poe, 1845–1849." *BNYPL,* VI (Jan. 1902), 7–11.
Some letters to E. A. Duyckinck.

A165   ——. "The Life and Poetry of Edgar Poe." *Littel's Living Age,* XXXVI (April 16, 1853), 157–61.
Poe's genius was "allied to vice in its grosser forms," but he is the "most original imaginative writer America has yet produced." Reprinted from *Chambers' Journal,* XIX (Feb. 23, 1853), 137–40.

A166   ——. "The Life and Writings of Edgar Poe." *Hogg's Instructor,* I (Aug. 1853), 97–106.
Poe's character is sharply criticized; his art, especially his poetry, is generally praised. Reprinted in *Eclectic Mag,* XXXI (Feb. 1854), 263–72.

A167 ———. "Lines to the Bust of Poe." *UVaMag,* LXIX (Jan. 1909), 203.
Verse.

A168 ———. "Literariana: American." *Round Table,* IV (Dec. 15, 1866), 327.
Touches upon "the great omissions in the existing collections of Edgar Poe's writings."

A169 ———. "Literary Reputation in the Balance." *Bookman* (London), LXXII (Aug., Sept. 1927), 256–58, 297–300; LXXIII (Oct. 1927), 28–30.
Some answers to Alfred Noyes's "Edgar Allan Poe" appearing in the June number of the *Bookman,* 1927.

A170 ———. "Long Letter by Poe to Irving Revealed." New York *Times,* Jan. 12, 1930, pp. 1, 19.

A171 ———. "Lost Lenore." *Hearth and Home,* V (Aug. 23, 1873), 535.
"The Raven" is perhaps overrated, but it has been tremendously popular, living because of its truth.

A172 ———. "The Lounger." *Critic,* XLVI (April 1905), 291–307.
Commentary on a recent sale of a MS of "Ulalume" for $1,000, pp. 301–5.

A173 ———. "To Poe." *UVaMag,* LXI (March 1901), 352.
Verse (signed "Lucifer").

A174 ———. "Magazine Makers of America." *Scholastic,* XXXIII (Nov. 19, 1938), 6.
Poe is considered an important magazine editor.

A175 ———. "The Manuscript of Poe's 'Eulalie.' " *BNYPL,* XVIII (Dec. 1914), 1461–63.

A176 ———. "Memoir." *The Poetical Works of Edgar Allan Poe.* Edinburgh: William P. Nimmo, 1872, pp. 13–30.
"As a poet Poe is undoubtedly the most original that America has yet produced."

A177 ———. "The Memory of Poe." New York *Herald,* March 27, 1881, p. 8.
Printing of Poe's letters to J. E. Snodgrass along with editorial commentary.

A178 ———. "The Monument: Ceremonies of Dedication." *Poems and Essays of Edgar Allan Poe.* New York: W. J. Widdleton, 1876, pp. cxxvii–civ.
An account of the ceremonies dedicating a monument to Poe at Baltimore on November 17, 1875.

A179 ——. "More Pity for Poor Poe." New York *World,* May 5, 1885, p. 4.
Concerning the actors' monument in the Metropolitan Museum.

A180 ——. "Mother of Poet Poe Visited Portland." Portland (Maine) *Sunday Telegram,* Feb. 4, 1912, p. 20.
Elizabeth Arnold's theatrical appearances in Portland.

A181 ——. "The Murder of Mary Rogers: A Mystery That Was Never Solved—How Poe Preserved It in a Story." New York *Tribune,* Oct. 29, 1885, p. 5.

A182 ——. "The Mystery of Poe." *Nation,* CXIX (Dec. 10, 1924), 615–16.
An attack on Moore's criticism of Poe in *Conversations in Ebury Street.*

A183 ——. "New Analyses of Poe's Greatness." *Current Literature,* XLIX (Dec. 1910), 672–74.

A184 ——. "The New and Old Poe." *Critic,* VI (Jan. 31, 1885), 50–51.

A185 ——. "New Light on Poe's Tragic Love Affair with Sarah Helen Whitman." *Current Opinion,* LXI (Dec. 1916), 416.

A186 ——. "A New Manuscript of Poe's 'Politian.'" *Nation* LXXXV (Sept. 5, 1907), 205–6.
The discovery of an autograph copy of *Politian* which once belonged to Ingram.

A187 ——. "The New Poe." *Atlantic Monthly,* LXXVII (April 1896), 551–54.
A review of the Stedman-Woodberry edition of the *Works.*

A188 ——. "New Poe Letter Is to Be Sold." Richmond *News-Leader,* Oct. 5, 1935, "Football Extra," p. 4.
This letter from Poe to John Neal, dated Richmond, Sept. 4, 1835, concerns an exchange of the *Messenger* and *The Galaxy.*

A189 ——. "News for Bibliophiles." *Nation,* XCI (Nov. 25, 1910), 492.
A discussion of the publishings of Poe's tales.

A190 ——. "No. 7, The Raven and Other Poems." *Godey's Lady's Book,* XXXII (Jan. 1846), 48.
A brief notice.

A191 ——. "Note [to a Reprint of *Tamerlane*]." *Tamerlane and Other Poems,* by Edgar Allan Poe. Greenwich, Conn.: Privately printed at the Literary Collector Press, 1905, pp. v–viii.
An essay on the editions of *Tamerlane.*

A192 ——. "Notes about Men of Note." *New-York Mirror,* II (July 5, 1845), 201.

Poe is both industrious and eccentric.

A193 ——. "Notes on the Genealogy of the Poe Family." *Gulf States Historical Mag,* I (Jan. 1903), 281–83.

Reprints Poe's letter to William Poe of August 20, 1835.

A194 ——. "Obituary—Oct." *American Quarterly Register and Mag,* II (Dec. 1849), 493.

A195 ——. [Obituary of Edgar Allan Poe.] Washington *National Era* III (Nov. 1, 1849), 175.

With a brief biographical sketch of the noted author born in Virginia in 1811 (*sic*).

A196 ——. " 'Oh Tempora! Oh Mores!' An Unpublished Poem of Edgar Allan Poe." *No Name Mag* (Baltimore), I (Oct. 1889), 1–2.

A satire on a Mr. Pitts, a Richmond dry goods clerk, written by Poe when he was seventeen years old.

A197 ——. "On the Death of Edgar A. Poe." *UVaMag,* V (Dec. 1860), 124–25.

Verses reprinted from an unnamed periodical.

A198 ——. "The 150th Anniversary of Poe's Birth." *BPLQ,* XI (April 1959), 108–10.

Lists Poe materials on exhibit in the Boston Public Library in the spring of 1959.

A199 ——. "100 First Editions Found at Poe Museum in Virginia." New York *Times,* Nov. 26, 1962, p. 26.

Poe editions offered for sale.

A200 ——. "Original Poetry." *Broadway Jour,* I (Feb. 8, 1845), 90.

"The Raven" is quoted and briefly cited as original.

A201 ——. "Park Department Plans to Refurbish Poe Cottage." New York *Times,* March 31, 1965, p. 43.

New York City Parks Department opens bids for refurbishing Poe Cottage.

A202 ——. "Peoria in a Passion about Poets and Poe." New York *World,* Nov. 26, 1875, p. 5.

A satire in verse of the Baltimore monument dedication.

A203 ——. "Personalities" [Edgar Allan Poe]. *Independent,* XXVII (Jan. 28, 1875), 6.

A censure of Poe's character and personality.

A204 ——. "The Place of Poe in French Literature." *Ex Libris* (Paris), I (May 1924), 328–31.

A summary of criticism.

A205 ———. "Poe a Bricklayer in 1834?" *AN&Q*, III (June 1943), 36.
"A discussion of a 'short factual squib' from the *Century* of November 1875 asserting that the writer had been told that Poe worked in a brickyard in 1834." *AL*.

A206 ———. "Poe Again." Bristol (Eng.) *Times and Mirror*, Jan. 16, 1909, p. 20.

A207 ———. "Poe and Other Poets." *Academy*, LXXVIII (May 14, 1910), 467–71.
Poe, to this writer, "is essentially a pagan, almost as much as Emerson."

A208 ———. "Poe and Walt Whitman." *Andrews' American Queen*, IV (Nov. 13, 1880), 404.
Poe's "fame is much larger than his work."

A209 ———. "Poe Anniversary," "Poe in New York," "[Poe] at Columbia University." *Outlook*, XCI (Jan. 30, 1909), 227–29.
Reports of centenary celebrations.

A210 ———. "Poe as a Dramatist." *TLS*, Nov. 1, 1923, p. 725.

A211 ———. "Poe as a Tone Painter." *Literary Digest*, XXXIV (June 1, 1907), 881.
A reporting of an article by C. L. Moore in *The Dial* for May 16, 1907.

A212 ———. "The Poe Bust." *UVaAB*, IV (May 1897), 32.

A213 ———. "Poe Centenary." *BPLQ*, I (Oct. 1949), 151–55.
Discusses the Poe collection held by the Boston Public Library.

A214 ———. "The Poe Centenary." London *Times*, March 2, 1909, p. 10.
A reporting of the remarks of Conan Doyle, Whitelaw Reid, and others about Poe.

A215 ———. "The Poe Centenary." *UVaAB*, 3rd ser., II (April 1909), 131–36.
A brief description of the exercises.

A216 ———. "The Poe Centennial." *UVaMag*, LXIX (Jan. 1909), 248–50.

A217 ———. "Poe Exercises Begin." Baltimore *Sun*, Jan. 19, 1909, p. 9.
The Raven Society of the University of Virginia celebrates Poe's one hundredth birthday.

A218 ———. "Poe in Europe." *Bookman*, XXVIII (Feb. 1909), 528.
A statement about Poe's popular revival in Europe.

A219 ———. "Poe in the Hall of Fame." *Outlook,* XCVI (Nov. 12, 1910), 570–71.
Poe's election is here reported.

A220 ———. "Poe in the Hall of Fame." *World's Work,* XXI (Dec. 1910), 13713–14.
Poe's admittance to the Hall is reported.

A221 ———. "Poe Is Famous at Last." Baltimore *Sun,* Oct. 22, 1910, p. 2.
Announcing Poe's inclusion in the Hall of Fame of New York University.

A222 ———. "Poe Letters and Manuscripts Found in a Pillow Case." *Current Opinion,* LXX (June 1921), 823–24.
New letters reported by Geo. H. Sargent in the Boston *Transcript* along with the MSS of "Lenore," "Annabel Lee," and letters to Henry B. Hirst.

A223 ———. "Poe Memorial." *Critic,* III (May 9, 1885), 223.
On the actors' monument to Poe, designed by Richard H. Park.

A224 ———. "The Poe Memorial." *UVaAB,* IV (Nov. 1897), 87.
Concerning plans for a memorial at the University.

A225 ———. "The Poe Memorial Association of the University of Virginia." *UVaAB,* V (Nov. 1898), 82–83.

A226 ———. "Poe Memorial Exercises." *UVaAB,* VI (Nov. 1899), 65–74.
A reporting of the unveiling of the Zolnay bust.

A227 ———. "Poe Not Appreciated in His Own Land; So Declares Ibañez, the Famous Spanish Author." *State Service,* IV (May 1920), 411–13.

A228 ———. "Poe on Poe: The Timely Discovery of a Remarkable Letter from the Poet." Baltimore *American,* April 4, 1881, p. [4].
A letter from Poe to Dr. Snodgrass dated April 1, 1841, in which Poe, among other things, defends himself against Burton's charge of habitual drunkenness. See p. [2] for editorial commentary on the letter.

A229 ———. "Poe Remembered in the South." *Literary Digest,* LXXVII (June 30, 1923), 31–32.
A modeled scene representing Poe at Sullivan's Island is on exhibition at the Charleston (S.C.) Museum.

A230 ———. "The Poe Room at the University of Virginia." *Christian Science Monitor,* Jan. 15, 1916, p. 22.
A brief account of the room at 13 West Range.

A231 ———. "Poe, the Pathfinder—A German Poet's Worshipful Tribute." *Current Opinion,* LXII (Feb. 1917), 121–22.

A232 ——. "Poe the Poet: Recollections of Two Citizens Who Knew Him Well. . . ." Richmond *Sunday State,* Nov. 29, 1885, p. 1.
A firsthand account of Poe's early days in Richmond based on an interview with J. A. Clarke and David Bridges.

A233 ——. "Poe Was Weak, but Not Wicked." *UVaMag,* XXXVI (June 1897), 419–25.
Poe's faults are due to the influence of circumstances upon his sensitive and passionate nature.

A234 ——. "Poe's 'Affectation of Learning.' " *Critic,* I (March 26, 1881), 80.

A235 ——. "Poe's Cottage at Fordham: Poe and Posterity." *Current Opinion,* LIV (Feb. 1913), 140.
A reporting of the movement to save the Fordham cottage.

A236 ——. "Poe's Cottage Made Landmark." New York *Times,* March 8, 1966, p. 30.

A237 ——. [Poe's Disquisition on "The Poetic Principle."] Norfolk *Daily Southern Argus,* Sept. 17, 1849, p. 2.

A238 ——. "Poe's Earliest French Sponsor." *Literary Digest,* XL (April 23, 1910), 816.
A reporting of a news story concerning the death of Felix Tournachon ("Nadar") who was Poe's "earliest French translator."

A239 ——. "Poe's Father Lived in Hollis Street." Boston *Herald,* Jan. 14, 1909, p. 7.

A240 ——. "Poe's Little Cottage Now Houses Another Poet." *NYTM,* Aug. 29, 1915, pp. 3–4.
The residence in the Fordham Cottage of one Orville G. Victor, the "poet"-custodian of the museum.

A241 ——. "Poe's Parents on the Boston Stage." Boston *Herald,* Jan. 17, 1909. Editorial, Society, Finance sec., p. 8.

A242 ——. "Poe's Poetry." *TLS,* March 23, 1922, p. 188. Reviews Whitty's *Poems* and claims Poe owes a great debt to the English Romantic poets.

A243 ——. "Poe's Raven." *TLS,* Sept. 27, 1928, p. 692. Lists prices of Poe items for sale.

A244 ——. "Poe's *Tales* [New York: Wiley and Putnam]." *American Whig Rev,* II (Sept. 1845), 306–9.
Reviewer cites artistry and originality.

A245 ——. "Poe's Valentine." *Cweal,* XV (March 2, 1932), 481.
Poe sent a valentine to "Miss Louise Olivia Hunter" soon after Virginia's death.

A246 ———. "Poe's Works." *Southern Quarterly Rev*, XXIV (July 1853), 284.

Comments on the Redfield Edition.

A247 ———. [Review of] *Poe's Works.* Vol. III. *The Literati; New York; J. C. Redfield. Sartain's Union Mag of Literature and Art,* VII (Nov. 1850), 317.

A brief notice.

A248 ———. "The Poet Poe as a Soldier." *UVaAB,* VI (Feb. 1900), 109.

Concerning the discovery of Poe's army days.

A249 ———. "Poetry and Poets." *UVaMag,* XI (Jan. 1873), 175–83.

Discusses theories of poetry and contrasts Poe with other poets.

A250 ———. "The Poets of America." *Irish Quarterly Rev,* V (Sept. 1855), 572–76.

Praises Poe's verse but laments Poe's debased life.

A251 ———. "The Popularity of Poe." *Nation,* LXXXVIII (Jan. 21, 1909), 55–56.

Poe's style and avoidance of morality have made him popular.

A252 ———. "The Potency of Poe." *Literature* (N.Y. American ed.), IV (April 9, 1899), 301–2.

Briefly discusses Poe's influence and literary accomplishments.

A253 ———. [Review of] *Pym's Adventures and Discoveries [Arthur Gordon Pym].* *New-York Mirror,* XVI (Aug. 11, 1838), 55.

A254 ———. *"The Raven and Other Poems.* By Edgar A. Poe. New York and London: Wiley and Putnam." *The Harbinger,* I (Dec. 6, 1845), 410–11.

Reviewer finds that Poe's poems have "more of *effect,* than of *expression."*

A255 ———. " 'The Raven'—By Edgar Allan Poe." *SLM,* XXV (Nov. 1857), 331–35.

Sources of "The Raven."

A256 ———. "The Real Poe." *Outlook,* LXXII (Nov. 8, 1902), 581–82.

A literary notice of J. A. Harrison's edition of the *Works.*

A257 ———. "Religion of Edgar Allan Poe." *Current Opinion,* LXIX (Sept. 1920), 408–10.

A reporting of C. Alphonso Smith's article on "Poe and the Bible."

A258 ———. [Review of *Eureka.*] Boston *Daily Evening Transcript,* July 20, 1848, p. [2].

Sneers at Poe's "lavish ostentation of scientific lore," recognizes his talent, but doubts his sincerity.

A259　———. [Review of *Eureka*.] *Literary World*, III (July 29, 1848), 502.

A260　———. [Review of *The Raven and Other Poems* (1843).] *Athenaeum*, No. 957 (Feb. 28, 1846), pp. 215–16.

A261　———. "A Reviewer's Notebook." *Freeman*, V (April 19, 1922), 142–43.

Poe's critical essays were an expression of a natural gift and reflect a strong critical vein.

A262　———. "The Satanic Streak in Poe's Genius." *Current Literature*, XLVIII (Jan. 1910), 93–96.

A263　———. "Secret History of 'The Raven.'" *Current Literature*, XLV (July 1908), 58–59.

A264　———. "The Secret of Poe's Despair." *Golden Book*, XVIII (Sept. 1933), 258–59.

A facsimile and inexact transcription of Poe's letter to Eveleth of Jan. 4, 1848, in which he tells of Virginia's illness and death.

A265　———. "Set by Audubon Sold for $60,000." New York *Times*, May 25, 1966, p. 44.

U.S. military cadets attempt to purchase an edition of Poe poems.

A266　———. "Shadowed Lives." *Senior Scholastic*, XLVIII (March 25, 1946), 22.

Poe and Lanier lived unfortunate lives.

A267　———. "A Shrewd Doctor-Collector Acquired Original Raven Manuscript from Edgar Allan Poe." *Physicians' Times Mag*, II (July 1930), 78–79, 93.

On the purchase of the Raven MS (illustrated on pp. 78–79) by Dr. Samuel A. Whitaker of Phoenixville, Pa.

A268　———. [Review of] *Siope, A Fable. Baltimore Monument*, II (Dec. 2, 1837), 68.

A brief notice recognizing the individuality of Poe's style.

A269　———. *Some Edgar Allan Poe Letters*. Printed for members only: The Bibliophile Society. Boston, 1915.

Presents letters of Dr. Snodgrass and others along with biographical commentary.

A270　———. "Some Poe Questions." *Bookman*, XXXVI (Dec. 1912), 354–55.

Discusses Poe's writing of *Barnaby Rudge* and the abrupt ending of "The Mystery of Marie Rogêt."

A271 ———. "Some Twentieth Century Estimates of Poe." *American Rev of Reviews,* XXXIX (Feb. 1909), 225–27.

A compilation of centenary praise.

A272 ———. "Souvenirs of Poe's Last Visit to Richmond." *PULC,* XII (Winter 1951), 83–87.

Relics of Poe's last visit to Richmond in 1849 consist of a "daguerre-otype portrait of Poe, a manuscript of 'Annabel Lee,' and an auto-graph letter written by Poe," all belonging to Mrs. Alexander McMillan Welch of New York.

A273 ———. "Spectral Loves of Edgar Allan Poe." *Current Literature,* XLIV (Jan. 1908), 48–49.

A review of Macy's *Edgar Allan Poe.*

A274 ———. "Suggestion of Poe's 'The Raven' Traced to Charles Dickens' 'Barnaby Rudge.' " Pittsburgh *Post,* Jan. 15, 1911, sec. Two, p. 2.

A275 ———. "*Tales.* By Edgar A. Poe. London. 1845. Wiley and Putnam." *Littell's Living Age.* LXXIX (Nov. 15, 1845), 343.

Reviewer admires Poe's ingenuity but disparages the horrors and cruelties. First appeared in the London *Critic* (1845).

A276 ———. "*Tales* by Edgar A. Poe. New York. Wiley and Put-nam." *Graham's Mag,* XXVII (Sept. 1845), 143.

In this brief notice, reviewer cites Poe's tales as "among the most original and characteristic compositions in American letters."

A277 ———. "*Tales of the Grotesque and Arabesque.* By Edgar A. Poe. 2 vols. Lea and Blanchard, 1840." *Godey's Lady's Book,* XX (Jan. 1840), 46.

A brief notice.

A278 ———. "*Tales of the Grotesque and Arabesque.* By Edgar A. Poe. Two volumes. Lea and Blanchard, Philadelphia." *Burton's Gentleman's Mag,* VI (Jan. 1840), 58.

A very brief notice.

A279 ———. "Three Portraits Reveal Poe's Gift as Artist." New York *Times,* Sept. 22, 1930, pp. 1, 3.

Portraits of Mrs. Sarah E. Shelton, Virginia Clemm, and Poe himself.

A280 ———. "To Isadore." *Carolina Spartan* (Spartanburg, S.C.), Feb. 2, 1876, p. 1.

A printing of "To Isadore," ascribing it to Poe.

A281 ———. "A Travestie." *UVaMag* (Jefferson Monument Magazine), I (March 1850), 178–80.

A parody of "The Raven."

A282 ——. "A Tribute to Edgar Allan Poe." *Rainbow*, I (Nov. 1920), 4–5.

A283 ——. "Triumphavit." *UVaMag*, LX (Jan. 1900), 291.
Verse clearly descriptive of Poe.

A284 ——. "Typical Characteristics [of Poe]." *Round Table*, V (Jan. 5, 1867), 4–5.
Poe was really "an abandoned rake."

*A285 ——. "An Unpublished Letter from Edgar Allan Poe." *Quarto* (Oct. 1949), extra no. to accompany No. 19.
"Poe's letter is dated July 4, 1836, and is addressed to Lewis Cass, from whom an article was solicited for the *Southern Literary Messenger*. (The *Quarto* is an irregularly published folder issued by The Clements Library Associates of the University of Michigan.)" *AL*.

A286 ——. "An Unpublished Letter of Edgar Allan Poe." *Autograph*, I (Jan.–Feb. 1912), 41–43.
A Poe letter of Feb. 3, 1842, to F. W. Thomas is presented along with some critical commentary.

A287 ——. "An Unpublished Letter of Poe." *Dial*, XLIV (Jan. 16, 1908), 32–33.
A letter to Hastings Weld, coeditor of *Brother Jonathon* with N. P. Willis, from Poe ("Philadelphia, August 14, 1841") asking for a signature to use in the autography articles.

A288 ——. "Was Poe a Plagiarist?" *Family Herald*, LXXXIX (July 12, 1902), 122A.
Some verses by the Chinese poet Kia Yi as a source for "The Raven."

A289 ——. "Was Poe a Plagiarist?" *Munsey's Mag*, XIV (Jan. 1896), 505.
Thomas Holley Chivers as precursor of Poe.

A290 ——. "Wayward Genius." *Nation*, CXXI (July 8, 1925), 59–60.
Another attack on Poe, "our most outstanding embarrassing genius."

A291 ——. "West Point Gets Cadet Poe's Book." New York *Times*, July 8, 1966, p. 32.
Purchase of the 1831 edition of Poe's poems.

A292 ——. "When Edgar Allan Poe Wrote for 50 Cents a Page." New York *Times*, Jan. 28, 1917, p. 14.
Some letters from Poe to Mrs. Sarah J. Hale about contributions for *The Opal*.

A293 ——. "Why Poe?" *Puck*, VIII (Feb. 9, 1881), 381.
A query as to why actors should erect a monument to Poe.

A294 ——. "Wiley and Putnam's Library." *Democratic Rev*, XVI (Dec. 1845), 459.

Brief notice of the publication of *The Raven and Other Poems*, 1845.

A295 ——. "Wiley and Putnam's Library of American Books." *Godey's Lady's Book*, XXXI (Dec. 1845), 271.

A brief notice of the publication of Poe's *Tales*.

A296 ——. "The Woman Who Rejected Poe." Boston *Herald*, Jan. 17, 1909, Magazine sec., p. 5.

Mrs. Whitman gives her portrait to Brown University.

A297 "Arbute." "Do Painting and Poetry 'Mellow the Mind and Soften the Heart'?" *UVaMag*, IV (April 1860), 357–64.

A comparison of Poe and the English artist George Morland.

A298 Archibald, R. C. "Music and Edgar Allan Poe." *N&Q*, CLXXIX (Sept. 7, 1940), 170–71.

Seven additions to the musical compositions listed by Evans's *Music and Edgar Allan Poe*.

A299 "Argus." "New Light on Poe." *Critic*, XIX (Nov. 7, 1891), 254.

Points out some errors in William O'Leary Curtis's article "Edgar Allan Poe," *American Catholic Quarterly*, XVI (Oct. 1891), 818–33.

A300 Armes, W. D. "Poe and Plagiarism—Theory and Practice." *Transactions and Proceedings of the American Philological Society*, XXXVIII (Dec. 1907), xxxi.

Argues that the character Poe attributed to himself during the Longfellow war was a pose. (An abstract.)

A301 Arndt, Karl J. "Poe's *Politian* and Goethe's *Mignon*." *MLN*, XLIX (Feb. 1934), 101–4.

A few lines of *Politian* resemble some descriptive passages in *Mignon*.

A302 Arnold, John. "Poe's 'Lionizing': The Wound and the Bawdry." *L&P* (University of Hartford), XVII, No. 1 (1967), 52–54.

Poe is one of the first American authors to treat the "wounded alienate" as hero.

A303 Ashmore, Basil. "Introduction." *The Mystery of Arthur Gordon Pym*, by Edgar Allan Poe and Jules Verne. Devised and introduced by Basil Ashmore. Westport, Conn.: Associated Booksellers, 1961, pp. 7–9.

Pym is "nothing less than Poe's allegorical autobiography."

A304 Ashmun, Margaret, ed. *Modern Short Stories*. New York: Macmillan, 1914.

The short story per se began with Poe. See "Introduction," pp. xi–xxx. Poe's story "The Cask of Amontillado" is included in this collection, pp. 1–13.

A305   Astrov, Vladimir. "Dostoievsky on Edgar Allan Poe." *AL,* XIV (March 1942), 70–74.

"Dostoievsky's article on Poe in 1861 indicates an understanding of the American's unfettered imagination, psychological penetration, and mastery of realistic detail." *AL.* Reprinted in Eric Carlson, ed., *The Recognition of Edgar Allan Poe* (Ann Arbor: University of Michigan Press, 1966), pp. 60–62.

A306   Aswell, James R., ed. *Native American Humor.* New York: Harpers, 1947.

Contains Poe's "Never Bet the Devil Your Head," pp. 112–15—a condensed version.

A307   Auden, Wystan H., ed. *Edgar Allan Poe: Selected Prose and Poetry.* With introd. New York: Rinehart, 1950.

Emphasizes the significance of *Eureka* and *Pym* in the course of Poe's literary accomplishments. See "Introduction," pp. v–xvii; reprinted in Eric Carlson, ed., *The Recognition of Edgar Allan Poe* (Ann Arbor: University of Michigan Press, 1966), pp. 220–30.

A308   Auslander, Joseph. "Letter to Virginia Clemm." *Muse Anthology of Modern Poetry.* Ed. Dorothy Kissling and Arthur H. Nethercot. Poe Memorial Edition. New York: Carlyle Straub, 1938, pp. 174–75.

Verse.

A309   ———. "The Poet of Ravens and Lost Ladies." *Muse Anthology of Modern Poetry.* Ed. Dorothy Kissling and Arthur H. Nethercot. Poe Memorial Edition. New York: Carlyle Straub, 1938, pp. 116–29.

Biography.

A310   Austin, Henry. "Lilitha, Princess of Ghouls: Poe's Last Poem." *Southern Bivouac,* NS I (April 1886), 655–57.

A poor imitation of *Ulalume.*

A311   ———. "Pioneers of American Literature: V. Edgar Allan Poe." *Peterson's Mag,* NS VII (March 1897), 221–36.

Biographical and Poe's influence on English and continental authors.

A312   ———. "Poe as a Plagiarist and His Debt to Macaulay." *Literature* (American ed.), V (Aug. 4, 1899), 82–84.

A313   ———. "Poe Coming to His Kingdom." *Dial,* XXVII (Nov. 1, 1899), 307–8.

A reporting of the ceremonies at the University of Virginia on the anniversary of Poe's death.

A314   ——. "Preface." *The Gold Bug and the Black Cat,* by Edgar
Allan Poe. New York: R. F. Fenno, 1899, pp. 5–27.
   An appreciative commentary upon "The Gold Bug" and "The Black
Cat."

A315   ——. "Preface." *The Murders in the Rue Morgue and A Tale
of the Ragged Mountains,* by Edgar Allan Poe. New York: R. F.
Fenno, 1899, pp. 5–24.
   Critical appraisal and some discussion of the literary background of
"The Murders in the Rue Morgue" and "A Tale of the Ragged
Mountains."

A316   ——. "Preface." *The Mystery of Marie Rogêt,* by Edgar Allan
Poe. New York: R. F. Fenno, 1899, pp. 5–15.
   Poe handles the subject of "The Mystery of Marie Rogêt" with
delicacy and ingenuity.

A317   Axson, Stockton. "The Life and Art of Edgar Allan Poe."
Rice Institute Pamphlet, III (Jan. 1916), 79–100.
   In spite of his weaknesses, both personal and literary, Poe "did as
much, if not more, for beauty in America than any other literary
man of his day."

B

B1   B., F. "Placing Poe." *Christian Science Monitor,* XXVI (Nov.
17, 1934), 16.
   Discusses the Valentine letters in relation to Pope-Hennessy's biography.

B2   B., W. A. "Introduction." *Monsieur Dupin: The Detective Tales
of Edgar Allan Poe.* New York: McClure, Phillips, 1904, pp. iii–xiv.
   On the genesis of Poe's detective story, an artistic form wholly
original with Poe.

B3   Babler, O. F. "Czech Translations of Poe's 'Raven.'" *N&Q,*
CXCII (May 1947), 235.
   "Seven translations are listed between 1869 and 1946." *AL.*

B4   ——. "German Translations of Poe's 'Raven.'" *N&Q,*
CLXXIV (Jan. 1, 1938), 9–10.
   Ten German translations listed with a reprint of the translation
in each case of stanza 16 of "The Raven."

B5   Bacheller, Morris. "Edgar Allan Poe, the Most Original Genius of American Literature." *Munsey's Mag,* XL (Jan. 1909), 448–51.
Places emphasis on Poe's sensitivity and originality and compares him to Whitman and Emerson.

B6   [Bagby, George W.] "Editor's Table." *SLM,* XXXI (Nov. 1860), 393.
A brief comment on the success of the lectures on Poe being then delivered throughout the southern states by John R. Thompson, former editor of the magazine.

B7   Bagley, Carol L. "Early American Views of Coleridge as Poet." *Research Studies of State College of Washington,* XXXII (Sept. 1934), 292–307.
See pp. 304–6.

B8   Bailey, Elmer James. "Religious Thought in Edgar Allan Poe." *Religious Thought in the Greater American Poets.* Boston: Pilgrim Press, 1922, pp. 32–46.
Poe's religious tenets are vague and tend to be far more pagan than Christian in character.

B9   Bailey, James O. "The Geography of Poe's 'Dream-Land' and 'Ulalume.'" *SP,* XLV (July 1948), 512–23.
Poe may have drawn geographic details from his knowledge of John Cleves Symmes's theory of a hollow earth, which was widely known and reflected in the literature of Poe's day.

B10   ———. "Introduction." *Symzonia: A Voyage of Discovery* (*1820*), by John C. Symmes. Scholars' Facsimiles and Reprints. Gainesville: University of Florida, 1965, pp. [1–8].
Poe's use of *Symzonia;* see pp. [1–5].

B11   ———. "Poe's 'Palaestine.'" *AL,* XIII (March 1941), 44–58.
Presents parallels and differences between Poe's essay on "Palaestine" and Rees's *Cyclopaedia.*

B12   ———. "Poe's Stonehenge." *SP,* XXXVIII (Oct. 1941), 645–51.
Poe's essay is drawn almost entirely from the article on Stonehenge in Rees's *Cyclopaedia.*

B13   ———. "Sources of Poe's *Arthur Gordon Pym,* 'Hans Pfaall,' and Other Pieces." *PMLA,* LVII (June 1942), 513–35.
The significance of the novel *Symzonia* and George Tucker's *A Voyage to the Moon* as sources for Poe.

B14   ———. "What Happens in the 'Fall of the House of Usher'?" *AL,* XXXV (Jan. 1964), 445–66.
In the light of the narrator's explanations, what happens in Poe's story can be explained in terms of Poe's possible use of vampire lore.

B15   Bailey, Margaret Emerson. "Dove and Raven." *Atlantic Monthly,* CXXXII (Nov. 1923), 647–56.
   An account of Poe's relations with Mrs. Whitman.

B16   Baird, W. "Edgar Allan Poe." *Southern Mag,* XV (Aug. 1874), 190–203.
   "It is over the realm of shadows" that Poe reigns supreme.

B17   Baker, Harry T. "Coleridge's Influence on Poe's Poetry." *MLN,* XXV (March 1910), 94–95.
   "The indebtedness of Poe as a poet to Coleridge is greater and more specific than is commonly believed."

B18   ——. "Poe and Hazlitt." *Nation,* LXXXVII (Oct. 8, 1908), 335.
   Poe's criticism of Campbell's plagiarism from Blair is found expressed earlier in Hazlitt's *English Poets* (1818).

B19   ——. "A Source of 'The Raven.'" *Nation,* XCI (Dec. 22, 1910), 601–2.
   Dickens' *Barnaby Rudge* is emphasized as the source.

B20   Baker, Lawrence H. "Eerie Gloom and Melancholy Shroud / Poe in His Grave." Baltimore *Sun,* Feb. 3, 1924, Part II, sec. 5, p. 1.
   A news story about Poe's grave and Westminster churchyard.

B21   Balakian, Anna. "Influence and Literary Fortune: The Equivocal Junction of Two Methods." *YCGL,* No. 11 (1962), pp. 24–31.
   Poe "was to express the American version of German Romanticism in such a way as to effect the future of French poetry"; see pp. 26–27.

B22   Baldwin, Charles Sears. *Essays out of Hours.* New York: Longmans, Green, 1907.
   See Section III, "Poe's Fixing of the Short Story Form," pp. 148–61.

B23   ——. "Introduction." *American Short Stories.* New York: Longmans, Green, 1904, pp. 1–35.
   Poe perfected the short-story form; editor includes "The Fall of the House of Usher," pp. 155–76.

B24   Baldwin, Summerfield. "The Aesthetic Theory of Edgar Poe." *SR,* XXVIII (April 1918), 210–21.
   Poe antedates modern aestheticisms. He reconciles the Aristotelian and the Platonist and finds art a "transcendence of reality."

B25   Balz, Albert George Adam. "The Raven, A Melodrama." *UVaMag,* LXIX (Jan. 1909), 211–15.
   A review of Max Heinrich's *The Raven, A Melodrama.*

B26   Bandy, William T. "Baudelaire and Poe." *TQ,* I, Supplement (Feb. 1958), 28–35.
   Presents the facts and comments on the affinity between Baudelaire and Poe.

B27 ———. "An Imaginary Translation of Poe." *RLC,* XXXIII (Jan.–March 1959), 87–90.
"On *Les Contes d'Edgar Poe,* Paris, 1846, supposedly translated by Mme. Meunier." *AL.*

B28 ———. *The Influence and Reputation of Edgar Allan Poe in Europe.* Baltimore: F. T. Cimino, 1962.
Poe "has made a profound impression and had a decisive influence on some of the sharpest minds in Europe."

B29 ———. "Mallarmé's Letter to Mrs. Whitman: A Correction." *MLN,* LXV (Nov. 1950), 507.

B30 ———. "Mallarmé's Sonnet to Poe: The First Text?" *RLC,* XXXVII (Jan.–March 1963), 100–101.

B31 ———. "New Light on a Source of Poe's 'A Descent into the Maelström.' " *AL,* XXIV (Jan. 1953), 534–37.
"The Maelström: A Fragment," *Fraser's Magazine* (1834) was a source for Poe's story.

B32 ———. "New Light on Baudelaire and Poe." *Yale French Studies,* No. 10 (1953), pp. 65–69.
Evidence is strong that Baudelaire's 1852 essay on Poe was largely translated from a review of the Redfield edition of Poe's work in the *Southern Literary Messenger* for March 1850.

B33 ———. "Poe's 'An Enigma (or Sonnet), IV.' " *Expl,* XX (Dec. 1961), item 35.
Explains allusion.

B34 ———. "Poe's Secret Translator: Amédée Pichot." *MLN,* LXXIX (May 1964), 277–80.
Pichot, Poe's first translator and Baudelaire's contemporary, was editor of the leading French magazine specializing in Anglo-American literature.

B35 ———. "Poe's Solution to 'The Frailey Land Office Cipher.' " *PMLA,* LXVIII (Dec. 1953), 1240–41.
"Some corrections of Wimsatt's solution of the cipher." *AL.*

B36 ———. "A Source of Poe's 'The Premature Burial.' " *AL,* XIX (May 1947), 167–68.
"Mrs. Seba Smith's poem, 'The Life-Preserving Coffin,' along with its accompanying note, which appeared in the *Columbian Lady's and Gentleman's Magazine* for January, 1844, provides a more likely source for Poe's tale than those which have been previously suggested." *AL.*

B37 ———. "Were the Russians the First to Translate Poe?" *AL,* XXXI (Jan. 1960), 479–80.
First translations of "Poe's writings were French, not Russian."

B38   ——. "Who Was Monsieur Dupin?" *PMLA,* LXXIX (Sept. 1964), 509–10.

On the derivation of the name "C. Auguste Dupin."

B39   Barcus, Annie Edward. "Poe on Intemperance." *N&Q,* CLX (June 6, 1931), 405.

A moralistic sketch against intemperance from *Sterling's Southern Fifth Reader* (New York, 1866) is thought to be by Poe.

B40   Barcuse, Berry. "Beddoes and Poe." *SatRL,* IX (June 10, 1933), 643.

B41   Bardin, James C. "To the Verse of Poe." *UVaMag,* LXIX (Jan. 1909), 221.

Verse.

B42   Barge, Alfred. "Edgar Allan Poe, Mystic and Psychologist." *Anglo-French Rev,* III (May 1920), 344–51.

"Poe felt a continuous, if not a profound, interest in the writings of the mystics."

B43   Barhite, Jared. "Apostrophe to Edgar Allan Poe's Fordham, N.Y., Home." *Book-Lover,* V (June 1904), 746–47.

B44   Barnes, Dora M. "Edgar Allan Poe: Impressions of His Life and Work, and His Associations with Stoke Newington." *Edgar Allan Poe Centenary, 1849–1949.* Metropolitan Borough of Stoke-Newington. Edgar Allan Poe Centenary Commemoration. London: Inclusive Service, 1949, pp. 9–58.

Appreciative and biographical.

B45   Barr, Wm. A. "An Estimate of Poe." *UVaAB,* 3rd ser., II (April 1909), 183–84.

An "extract from a sermon delivered in the University Chapel, University of Virginia, January 17, 1909."

B46   Barrows, A. C. "Why Is Poe 'Rejected' in America?" *Dial,* XXVI (Feb. 16, 1899), 109–10.

Reprinted in *Literary World* (Boston), XXX (March 4, 1899), 77–78 with title "A Criticism of Poe."

B47   Bašić, Sonja. "Edgar Allan Poe in Croatian and Serbian Literature." *Studia Romanica et Anglica Zagrabiensia,* Nos. 21–22 (July–Dec. 1966), pp. 305–19.

Poe's importance in Serbo-Croatian literature begins in 1863, reaching a peak in the early 1900's and again in the 1950's.

B48   Baskett, Sam S. "A Damsel with a Dulcimer: An Interpretation of Poe's 'Eleonora.'" *MLN,* LXXIII (May 1958), 332–38.

Possible relationships between Coleridge's "Kubla Khan" and Poe's short story.

B49   Basler, Roy P. "Byronism in Poe's 'To One in Paradise.' " *AL,*
IX (May 1937), 232–36.
  Finds parallel between Poe and Byron verified by "Marginalia."

B50   ——. "The Interpretation of 'Ligeia.' " *CE,* V (April 1944),
363–72.
  " 'Ligeia' seems both aesthetically and psychologically more intel-
ligible as a tale, not of supernatural, but rather of entirely natural,
though highly phrenetic, psychological phenomena." Reprinted in
Basler's *Sex, Symbolism, and Psychology in Literature* (1948), pp.
143–59; and in Robert Regan, ed., *Poe: A Collection of Critical
Essays* (Englewood Cliffs, N.J.: Prentice-Hall, 1967), pp. 51–63.

B51   ——. "On Poe's 'The Valley of Unrest.' " *Readings for Liberal
Education.* Ed. Louis G. Locke *et al.* New York: Rinehart, 1953, pp.
127–28.
  Reprint from *The Explicator,* V (Dec. 1946), 25, and Basler's *Sex,
Symbolism, and Psychology in Literature* (1948).

B52   ——. "Poe's Dream Imagery." *Sex, Symbolism, and Psychology
in Literature.* New Brunswick, N.J.: Rutgers University Press, 1948,
pp. 177–201.
  Poe's poetry can be understood by examining his imagery in terms
of Freudian symbolism.

B53   ——. "Poe's 'Ligeia.' " *The Creative Reader.* Ed. Robert W.
Stallman and Reginald E. Watters. New York: Ronald Press, 1954,
pp. 286–94.
  Reprint from *CE,* V (April 1944), 363–72, and Basler's *Sex,
Symbolism, and Psychology in Literature* (1948).

B54   ——. "Poe's 'Ligeia.' " *PMLA,* LXXVII (Dec. 1962), 675.

B55   ——. "Poe's *The City in the Sea.*" *Expl,* V (Feb. 1946),
item 30.
  "The poem is a symbolic avowal (come hell or high water!) of
Poe's poetic creed."

B56   ——. "Poe's *The Valley of Unrest.*" *Expl,* V (Dec. 1946),
item 25.

B57   ——. "Poe's *Ulalume.*" *Expl,* II (May 1944), item 49.
  " 'Ulalume' may be read as symbolic of the human personality's
quest for fulfillment in love." *AL.*

B58   ——. "Two Interpretations of Edgar Allan Poe's 'Ulalume.' "
The Creative Reader. Ed. Robert W. Stallman and Reginald E. Watters.
New York: Ronald Press, 1954, pp. 861–62.
  Reprint from *Explicator,* II (May 1944), item 49, and Basler's
Sex, Symbolism, and Psychology in Literature (1948).

B59   Basore, John W. "Poe as an Epicurean." *MLN,* XXV (March 1910), 86–87.

Poe in "Mesmeric Revelation" is found to be "under the spell of Lucretius" and interested in Epicureanism.

B60   Bass, William W. "Edgar Allan Poe as Critic of Southern Writers and Literature." Diss., University of North Carolina, 1954.

Considers Poe primarily "as one interested in Southern writers and literature as he expressed himself through his critical writings."

B61   Bate, Walter J. "Edgar Allan Poe." *Criticism: The Major Texts.* New York: Harcourt, Brace, 1952, p. 351.

Poe's critical outlook is mainly significant as one of the more extreme examples of the romantic attitude.

B62   Bates, Katherine Lee. *American Literature.* New York: Macmillan, 1897.

Declares Poe's mind to be a "compound of poetry and mathematics" and cites his influence on Verne, Stockton, and Anne Katherine Green Rohlfs; see pp. 179–86, 292–99.

B63   Baudelaire, Charles. *Baudelaire on Poe.* Trans. Lois and Francis Hyslop, Jr. State College, Pa.: Bald Eagle Press, 1952.

See "Introduction," pp. 1–33, for a discussion of the backgrounds of Baudelaire's essays on Poe and on Poe's critical reception in France.

Reviewed:

J. B. Hubbell, *AL,* XXIII, 529–30.

F. Keene, *NYTBR,* Feb. 10, 1952, p. 18.

N. Joost, *Poetry,* LXXXI, 247–51.

B64   ——. "Edgar Allan Poe: His Life and Works." Trans. H. Curwen. *The Choice Works of Edgar Allan Poe.* London: Chatto & Windus, 1902, pp. 1–21.

Society has a "special anathema" for a writer of Poe's genius. An earlier edition appeared in 1899.

B65   ——. "Edgar Allan Poe: His Life and Works." Trans. H. Curwen. *The Works of Edgar Allan Poe.* London: John Camden Hotten, [1874?], pp. 1–21.

B66   ——. *The Mirror of Art.* Trans. and ed. Jonathan Mayne. Doubleday Anchor Books. Garden City, N.Y.: Doubleday, 1956.

Baudelaire either quotes from or refers to Poe in a few of these essays.

B67   ——. "New Notes on Edgar Poe." *The Recognition of Edgar Allan Poe.* Ed. Eric Carlson. Ann Arbor: University of Michigan Press, 1966, pp. 43–60.

Poe is symbol of alienated artist in a materialistic society. This Preface to *Nouvelles histoires extraordinaires par Edgar Poe* (Paris: Michael Lévy frères, 1857) was translated by Lois and Francis Hyslop, Jr.; see *Baudelaire on Poe* (1952).

B68 ——. "Poe—His Life and Works: 1852." *The Art of the Essay.* Ed. Leslie A. Fiedler. New York: Thomas Y. Crowell, 1958, pp. 549–59.

A translation of Baudelaire's essay depicting Poe as a writer struggling against an unsympathetic America.

B69 Baum, Paull F. "Poe's 'To Helen.' " *MLN,* LXIV (May 1949), 289–97.

Poe's poem is a boyhood idealization of Mrs. Jane Stith Stanard "combined with literary reminiscences and with the poignant memory of the poet's foster-mother."

B70 Bayless, Joy. "Another Rufus W. Griswold as a Critic of Poe." *AL,* VI (March 1934), 69–72.

The other Griswold is Rufus White Griswold, editor of the *New England Weekly Gazette,* of Hartford.

B71 ——. "Rufus W. Griswold: Poe's Literary Executor." Diss., Columbia University, 1940.

Published by Vanderbilt University Press in 1943.

B72 ——. *Rufus Wilmot Griswold: Poe's Literary Executor.* Nashville: Vanderbilt University Press, 1943.

See pp. 161–200 for an account of Griswold's activities as Poe's literary executor.

B73 Baym, Nina. "The Function of Poe's Pictorialism." *SAQ,* LXV (Winter 1966), 46–54.

Poe's pictorialism has a function that is both thematic and organic.

B74 Beach, Burton T. "Poe's New York Homes and Haunts." New York *Herald,* Magazine sec., Nov. 27, 1910.

B75 Beach, John W. "A Perfumed Sea." *CJ,* XXIX (March 1934), 454–56.

The epithet "A perfumed sea" in Poe's "To Helen" can be appropriately applied to the Mediterranean Sea.

B76 Beale, Robert Cecil. "Poe and the Short Story." *The Development of the Short Story in the South.* Charlottesville, Va.: Michie, 1911, pp. 12–24.

Credits Poe with contributing to the techniques of the modern short story.

B77 Beaver, Kate W. "Poe and the Hall of Fame." *Dial,* XXX (Jan. 1, 1901), 8.

B78   Beebe, Maurice. "Art as Religion: the Ivory Tower Tradition." *Ivory Towers and Sacred Founts: The Artist as Hero in Fiction from Goethe to Joyce.* New York: New York University Press, 1964, pp. 114–71.

Poe's Roderick Usher is "an ideal and complete prototype of the artist-as-God"; see especially pp. 118–31.

B79   ———. "The Fall of the House of Pyncheon." *NCF,* XI (June 1956), 1–17.

Hawthorne in *The House of the Seven Gables* and Poe in "The Fall of the House of Usher" utilize setting to achieve characterization and dramatic effect.

B80   ———. "The Universe of Roderick Usher." *Person,* XXXVII (Spring 1956), 147–60.

By comparing *Eureka* and "The Fall of the House of Usher," critic finds "a close analogy between Poe's cosmology and his theory of the short story." Reprinted in Robert Regan, ed., *Poe: A Collection of Critical Essays* (Englewood Cliffs, N.J.: Prentice-Hall, 1967), pp. 121–33.

B81   Beers, Henry Augustin. *A History of English Romanticism in the Eighteenth Century.* New York: Henry Holt, 1899.

Suggests comparison between Warton's "Verses on Sir Joshua Reynolds' Painted Window" and "To Helen," and Brockden Brown is seen as the forerunner of Poe and Hawthorne; see pp. 356, 403.

B82   ———. *A History of English Romanticism in the Nineteenth Century.* New York: Henry Holt, 1901.

Discusses relationships between Tieck, Poe, and Hawthorne, notes that Poe's "Raven" inspired Rossetti's "Blessed Damozel," and suggests a lineage from Poe to Swinburne to Arthur O'Shaughnessy; see pp. 162–63, 300–301, and 389.

B83   ———. *Nathaniel Parker Willis.* Boston: Houghton, Mifflin, 1885.

Discusses Poe's relationship with Willis; see *passim.*

B84   ———. *An Outline Sketch of American Literature.* New York: Chatauqua Press, 1887.

Concludes that the defect of Poe was "in character—a defect which will make itself felt in art as in life," pp. 212–21. Reprinted as *Initial Studies in American Letters* (New York: Chatauqua Press, 1891).

B85   Belden, Henry Marvin. "Observation and Imagination in Coleridge and Poe: A Contrast." *Papers, Essays, and Stories by His Former Students in Honor of the Ninetieth Birthday of Charles Frederick Johnson.* Hartford: Trinity College, 1928.

Finding both poets "romantics, poets of wonder and magic," the author proceeds to point out similarities and differences between them; see pp. 131–75.

B86   ——. "Poe and Coleridge." *Nation,* XC (Jan. 6, 1910), 11.
"Coleridge had preceded Schlegel as Poe's teacher."

B87   ——. "Poe's Critique of Hawthorne." "Appendix I." *PMLA,* XIV (1899), lxvii–lxix.
Poe was inconsistent in his attitude toward Hawthorne—an abstract of a paper read to MLA in 1898. See also Belden's "Poe's Criticism of Hawthorne," *Anglia Zeitsschrift für Englische Philologie,* NS XI (1901), 376–404.

B88   ——. "Poe's 'The City in the Sea' and Dante's City of Dis." *AL,* VII (Nov. 1935), 332–34.
Poe may have picked up suggestions from Dante.

B89   Belgion, Montgomery. "Introduction." *A Selection of Poems,* by Edgar Allan Poe. London: Grey Walls, 1948, pp. 7–18.
Proposes that Poe's poems tend to be "unfinished," yet they have a "transcendent value."

B90   ——. "The Mystery of Poe's Poetry." *EIC,* I (Jan. 1951), 51–66.
Poe's significant achievement in poetry is due to his careful attention to an arrangement of measures, alliteration, repetition and to words "in terms of sound and power of suggestion."

B91   Bell, Landon Covington. "A Defense of Edgar Allan Poe, *Kit-Kat,* V (April, June, Sept., Dec. 1916), 1–12, 69–82, 124–32, 175–84.
Defends Poe by quoting evidence against Griswold.

B92   ——. *Poe and Chivers.* Columbus, Ohio: Charles A. Trowbridge, 1931.
Examines the "merits of the charge of plagiarism" made by Chivers against Poe and concludes that the charge is not convincing.

B93   ——. "Two Poe Portraits." *UVaAB,* 3rd ser., XII (Jan. 1919), 106–7.

B94   Benét, Laura. "Introduction." *Edgar Allan Poe Stories: Twenty-eight Thrilling Tales by the Master of Suspense, Edgar Allan Poe.* New York: Platt & Munk, 1961, pp. [1–7].
Poe "himself typifies impetuous, romantic, sensitive, adventuresome and inquiring youth."

B95   ——. "Introduction." *Tales,* by Edgar Allan Poe. Great Illustrated Classics. New York: Dodd, Mead, 1952, pp. [1–8].
Biographical sketch.

B96	——. *Young Edgar Allan Poe.* New York: Dodd, Mead, 1941.
An out-and-out unrestrained, imaginative, romantic rendering of
Poe's life to the year 1841.

B97	Bennett, Arnold. "Poe and the Short Story." *Books and Persons, Being Comments on a Past Epoch, 1908–11.* London: Chatto,
1917.
Poe's philosophy of art is seen as pure Latin in origin, and declares
that his lyrics and short stories are not uniquely good; see pp. 84–87.

B98	Bennett, Hannaford. "Biographical Introduction." *Tales of
Mystery and Imagination,* by Edgar Allan Poe. London: John Long,
1905, pp. 5–8.

B99	Bennett, John. "On Poe's Raven: Reactions of One of Our
Still Younger Intellectuals." *SatRL,* IV (Sept. 10, 1927), 103.
In "The Bowling Green" there is a sketch of an attempt to read
"The Raven" to a young and curious child.

B100	Benson, Adolph B. "Scandinavian References in the Works
of Poe." *JEGP,* XL (Jan. 1941), 73–90.
Evaluates the accuracy of Poe's references to persons and things
Scandinavian.

B101	Benson, Eugene. "The American Critic." *The Season* (New
York), III (Sept. 2, 1871), 171.
Poe is a "technical critic" whose judgments are generally sound.

B102	——. "Poe and Hawthorne." *The Galaxy,* VI (Dec. 1868),
742–48.
Poe has an "intellectual conscience" and is a "realist" in method;
Hawthorne has a "moral" conscience and is an "idealist." Both have
imagination.

B103	Benton, Joel. *In the Poe Circle, with Some Account of the
Poe-Chivers Controversy, and Other Poe Memorabilia.* New York:
M. F. Mansfield and A. Wessels, 1899.
Essays on Chivers, "The Raven," Baudelaire, and a brief bibliography.

B104	——. "Poe's Opinion of 'The Raven,'" *Forum,* XXII (Feb.
1897), 731–33.
"It's the greatest poem that was ever written."

B105	——. "Was Poe a Plagiarist?" *Forum,* XXIII (May 1897),
363–72.
An inconclusive reviewing of the Poe-Chivers relationship.

B106	Benton, Richard P. "Current Bibliography on Edgar Allan
Poe." *ESQ,* No. 47 (2nd quarter 1967), pp. 84–87.
Checklist of items published 1963–66.

B107 ———. "Current Bibliography on Edgar Allan Poe." *ESQ,* No. 38 (1st quarter 1965), pp. 144–47.
Lists entries for years 1962–64.

B108 ———. "Is Poe's 'The Assignation' a Hoax? *NCF,* XVIII (Sept. 1963), 193–97.
Story is a hoax and inspired by the Byron-Guiccioli romance.

B109 ———. "Platonic Allegory in Poe's 'Eleonora.'" *NCF,* XXII (Dec. 1967), 293–97.
Poe's story may owe much to "Plato's conception of the twin Venuses" and the latter's theory of reminiscence.

B110 ———. "The Works of N. P. Willis as a Catalyst of Poe's Criticism." *AL,* XXXIX (Nov. 1967), 315–24.
Willis "served as a catalyst for two of Poe's central critical ideas."

B111 Bergel, Lienhard. "Benedetto Croce, Poe, and American Criticism." *Comparative Literature: Proceedings of the Second Congress of the International Comparative Literature Association.* Ed. Werner P. Friederich. Chapel Hill: University of North Carolina Press, 1959, II, 507–16.
Poe and Croce, although varying in some aspects of aesthetic thought, agreed on the "non-rational nature of art."

B112 Bettany, George T. "Introduction." *Tales of Adventure, Mystery and Imagination,* by Edgar Allan Poe. Ed. Bettany. London: Ward, Lock, 1890.
Praises Poe's method and Romantic subject matter, pp. iii–vi.

B113 Bewley, Sir Edmund Thomas. *The Origin and Early History of the Family of Poë or Poe.* Dublin: Ponsonby and Gibbs, 1906.
An attempt to trace Poe's ancestry from the early seventeenth century.

B114 ———. "The True Ancestry of Edgar Allan Poe." *New York Genealogical and Biographical Record* (New York), XXXVIII (Jan. 1907), 55–69.
Poe's ancestry "cannot be strictly traced further back than four generations."

B115 Bewley, Marius. "On the American Macabre." *View,* V (Oct. 1945), 7–8, 18, 20.
Characterizes Poe's use of the macabre; see especially p. 20.

B116 Beyer, T. P. "Edgar Allan Poe—A Tribute." *Methodist Rev,* XCV (July 1913), 536–43.
Advances a tolerant view of Poe's character and recognizes his art.

B117 Bezanson, Walter E. "The Troubled Sleep of Arthur Gordon Pym." *Essays in Literary History Presented to J. Milton French.* Ed.

Rudolf Kirk and C. F. Main. New Brunswick, N.J.: Rutgers University Press, 1960, pp. 149–75.

Pym's "literary worth depends almost entirely on Poe's central technique of dream recital."

B118   Bickerstaffe-Drew, Francis [John Ayscough]. "Of Some Americans." *Catholic World*, CXV (Oct. 1922), 41–55.

An essay on American fictionists; see pp. 49–51 for a comparison of Poe and Hawthorne.

B119   Biedy, H. Alois. *Mysteries of Poe's* Raven. New York: H. Alois Biedy and George Bollella, 1936.

Attempts to interpret theme, background, and symbolism.

B120   Bierly, Charles E. Eureka *and the Drama of the Self: A Study of the Relationship between Poe's Cosmology and His Fiction.* Ann Arbor, Mich.: University Microfilms, 1958.

B121   ——. "*Eureka* and the Drama of the Self: A Study of the Relationship between Poe's Cosmology and His Fiction." *DA*, XVIII (Jan. 1958), 228–29.

The "underlying theme of Poe's work is a concern with the nature of being," and *Eureka* "is a distilled autobiography of Poe's emotional and intellectual life."

B122   ——. "*Eureka* and the Drama of the Self: A Study of the Relationship between Poe's Cosmology and His Fiction." Diss., University of Washington, 1957.

B123   Bilks, Patrick S. "Sergeant Major Poe: January Nineteenth Marks Hundred and Twenty-fifth Anniversary of Birth of Edgar Allan Poe, One-time Soldier and Cadet." *Recruiting News* (War Department, Recruiting Publicity Bureau, U.S. Army, Governor's Island, N.Y.), XVII, No. 2 (Jan. 15, 1935), 4–5.

B124   Binford, Elizabeth Harrison. "One of Poe's Biographers." *Kit-Kat,* V (June 1916), 61–64.

On James A. Harrison.

B125   Birkhead, Edith. *The Tale of Terror.* New York: Russell & Russell, 1963.

Poe penetrated into "trackless regions of terror" and fashions, with laborious art, "an instrument admirably adapted to his purposes"; see pp. 197–220. Earlier printing London: Constable, 1921.

B126   Birss, John H. "Emerson and Poe: A Similitude." *N&Q,* CLXVI (April 21, 1934), 279.

Finds a similarity between "The Raven" and Emerson's "Woodnotes."

B127   ——. "Poe in Fordham: A Reminiscence." *N&Q,* CLXXIII (Dec. 18, 1937), 440.

B128 Bittner, William. *Poe: A Biography.* Boston: Little, Brown, 1962.

Attempts "to present the life of Poe in light of his associates, his times, and his peculiarities" and "to show how and why he wrote what he did."

Reviewed:

Bradbury, *The Listener,* LXX (Nov. 7, 1963), 763.

TLS, Jan. 23, 1964, p. 66.

Faverty, Chicago *Sunday Tribune Magazine of Books,* Dec. 9, 1962, p. 12.

Gold, *New York Herald-Tribune Books* (Oct. 14, 1962), p. 9.

Howard, *NCF,* XVIII, 97–98.

Mabbott, *AL,* XXXV, 95–96.

Moore, *SatR,* XLV (Oct. 13, 1962), 23.

Wilson, *VQR,* XXXIX, 340–41.

B129 ———. "Poe and the 'Invisible Demon.'" *GaR,* XVII (Summer 1963), 134–38.

In his stories Poe demonstrates a hazy connoisseurship of wines.

B130 Bixby, William Keeney. *Some Edgar Allan Poe Letters, Printed for Private Distribution from Originals in the Collection of W. K. Bixby.* St. Louis: W. K. Bixby, 1915.

Some letters from Poe to Snodgrass and Cornelius Mathews.

B131 Black, Ladbroke Lionel Day. *Some Queer People.* London: Low, 1931.

See chap. 7, pp. 136–52.

B132 Blackmur, Richard P., ed. *The Fall of the House of Usher and Other Tales.* With afterword. New York: New American Library, 1960.

Poe gives the reader a chance at a make-believe world. See "Afterword," pp. 375–83.

B133 Blair, Walter. "Poe's Conception of Incident and Tone in the Tale." *MP,* XLI (May 1944), 228–40.

Poe's theory and practice reveal his concern that "incident and tone work together from the start of the tale to its inevitable conclusion to achieve a unified effect."

B134 Blake, Warren Barton. "Commemorations of Edgar Allan Poe." *Dial,* XLVII (Sept. 1, 1909), 118–20.

A review of Woodberry's life of Poe, Didier's *Poe Cult and Other Papers,* and Harrison's *Last Letters of Edgar Allan Poe to Sarah Helen Whitman.*

B135 ———. "Edgar Allan Poe: A Centenary Outlook." *Dial,* XLVI (Feb. 16, 1909), 103–5.

A high appraisal of Poe's work.

B136   Blanch, Robert J. "The Background of Poe's 'Gold Bug.' " *English Record* (New York State English Council), XVI, No. 4 (April 1966), 44–48.

Discusses both literary and experiential sources.

B137   ———. "Poe's Imagery: An Undercurrent of Childhood Fears." *Furman Studies,* NS XIV (May 1967), 19–25.

Poe "carried over to maturity a wide range of his own childhood fears."

B138   Bledsoe, Thomas F. "On Poe's 'Valley of Unrest.' " *MLN,* LXI (Feb. 1946), 91–92.

"On the origin of the word *Nis* as Poe uses it in the earliest version of the poem." *AL.*

B139   Blesi, Marius. "Anna Cora Mowatt." Diss., University of Virginia, 1938.

Poe's relations with Mrs. Mowatt are discussed herein.

B140   Block, John. "Epitaph." *Muse Anthology of Modern Poetry.* Ed. Dorothy Kissling and Arthur H. Nethercot. Poe Memorial Edition. New York: Carlyle Straub, 1938, p. 193.

Verse.

B141   Block, Louis J. "Edgar Allan Poe." *SR,* XVIII (Oct. 1910), 385–403.

Recognizes Poe's attributes as a writer and critic, declaring "partisans and defenders" have overstated their judgments.

B142   Bode, Carl, ed. *American Life in the 1840's.* New York: New York University Press, 1967.

Includes passages from Poe's review of Longfellow's *Ballads and Other Poems* to illustrate the growing trend toward reading as pleasure. Reprinted as paperback, New York: Doubleday, 1967.

B143   Bohner, Charles H. "The Poe-Kennedy Friendship." *PMHB,* LXXXII (April 1958), 220–22.

Kennedy comments on Poe's character in a letter (1869) to G. W. Fahnestock of Philadelphia.

B144   Boll, Ernest. "The Manuscript of 'The Murders of the Rue Morgue,' and Poe's Revisions." *MP,* XL (May 1943), 302–15.

Poe's painstaking efforts to create flawless art are demonstrated in comparing the first manuscript of this story with the final form.

B145   Bolton, Reginald P. "The Poe Cottage at Fordham." *Transactions of the Bronx Society of Arts, Sciences, and History,* I, Part V (1922), 1–16.

Describes the cottage and gives its history. See also John Henry Boner's poem "Poe's Cottage at Fordham," pp. 15–16.

B146 Bonaparte, Marie P. "The Black Cat." *PR*, XVII (Nov.–Dec. 1950), 834–60.
Chapter from the author's *The Life and Works of Edgar Poe: A Psychoanalytical Interpretation* as translated by John Rodker (1949).

B147 ———. *The Life and Works of Edgar Allan Poe: A Psychoanalytic Interpretation.* Trans. John Rodker. London: Imago, 1949.
Poe's life and works demonstrate that he was a sado-necrophilist. Excerpt entitled "Morella" appears in Eric Carlson, ed., *The Recognition of Edgar Allan Poe* (Ann Arbor: University of Michigan Press, 1966), pp. 172–76.
Reviewed:
Joseph Linkin, *Psychology Rev*, XL, 183–86.

B148 ———. "Poe and the Function of Literature." *Art and Psychoanalysis.* Ed. William Phillips. New York: Criterion Books, 1957, pp. 54–88.
Editor reprints a significant chapter from Bonaparte's *Life and Works of Edgar Allan Poe* (1949).

B149 ———. "Psychoanalytic Interpretations of Stories of Edgar Allan Poe." *Psychoanalysis and Literature.* Ed. Hendrick M. Ruitenbeek. New York: Dutton, 1964, pp. 19–101.
Reprinted from Bonaparte's *Life and Works of Edgar Poe* (1949).

B150 Bond, Frederick Drew. "Poe as an Evolutionist." *Popular Science Monthly*, LXXI (Sept. 1907), 267–74.
Considers Poe a speculative thinker.

B151 ———. "The Problem of Poe." *Open Court*, XXVII (April 1923), 216–23.
Explains why Poe could not support himself and his family and why he had difficulty getting along with others.

B152 Bondurant, Agnes M. *Poe's Richmond.* Richmond: Garrett and Massie, 1942.
Concerned primarily with the "nature of early nineteenth-century Richmond."

B153 Boner, John H. "On a Portrait of Poe." *Chap-Book*, II (Nov. 1894), 3.
Verse.

B154 ———. *Poems.* New York: Neale, 1903.
Two poems on Poe; see pp. 17, 19.

B155 ———. "Poe's Cottage at Fordham." *Century Mag*, XXXIX (Nov. 1889), 84–85.
Verse. Also appears in *University of Virginia Magazine*, XXX (Jan. 1890), 337; *Book-Lover*, IV (March–April 1903), facing frontis-

piece; and in *Muse Anthology of Modern Poetry*, ed. Dorothy Kissling and Arthur H. Nethercot, Poe Memorial Edition (New York: Carlyle Straub, 1938), pp. 186–87.

B156   Booth, Bradford A. "The Identity of Annabel Lee." *CE*, VII (Oct. 1945), 17–19.

A critical evaluation of the poem.

B157   ——, and Claude Jones. *Concordance of the Poetical Works of Edgar Allan Poe*. Baltimore: Johns Hopkins Press, 1941.

See the introduction (pp. v–xiv) for some critical discussion of Poe's diction. Reprinted Gloucester, Mass.: P. Smith, 1967.

B158   Boughton, James Henry. [Poe and *Barnaby Rudge*.] New York *Times*, May 11, 1913, p. 287.

Declares that Poe could have written the *Barnaby Rudge* critique.

B159   Bowen, Edwin W. "Poe Fifty Years After." *Forum*, XXXI (June 1901), 501–10.

Critical opinions of Poe.

B160   Bowra, Sir Cecil M. "Edgar Allan Poe." *The Romantic Imagination*. Cambridge, Mass.: Harvard University Press, 1949, pp. 174–96.

Poe is an important figure in the history of the Romantic movement in spite of the fact that "he carried to an extreme conclusion certain ideas and aspirations which others pressed less rigorously"—as his emphasis upon the Beyond.

B161   Boyd, Andrew Kennedy Hutchison. "Edgar Allan Poe." *The Critical Essays of a Country Parson*. London: Longmans, Green, 1867, pp. 210–48.

Admires Poe's genius but disparages his character (a review of Griswold edition, 1856).

B162   Boyd, Ernest. "Edgar Allan Poe." *Literary Blasphemies*. London: Harper, 1927.

The legend of Poe and his rehabilitation; see pp. 163–85.

B163   Boyer, Philip A. "Introduction." *The Gold Bug*, by Edgar Allen [*sic*] Poe. Philadelphia: Franklin Publishing and Supply Co., 1921, 7–9.

Poe's "The Gold Bug" is unique as a "detective story" and has served as a model for Poe's imitators.

B164   Boynton, Percy H. "Edgar Allan Poe." *A History of American Literature*. New York: Ginn, 1919, pp. 173–89.

Poe "was a vigorous agent in the upbuilding of the American magazine, a stimulator of honest critical judgment, a writer of a few poems and a few tales of the finest but the most attenuated art."

B165 ———. "Poe and Journalism." *EJ* (College Edition), XXI (May 1932), 345–52.

Poe strove for journalistic effects which now undermine his fame.

B166 Braddy, Haldeen. *Glorious Incense: The Fulfillment of Edgar Allan Poe.* Washington, D.C.: Scarecrow Press, 1953.

Often inaccurate and impressionistic, this critic attempts to demonstrate Poe's rise to fame by surveying critical opinion of Poe since 1850 to 1950. Reprinted New York: Kennikot Press, 1963.

Reviewed:

Arlin Turner, *MLQ*, XV, 376–77.

Harold Blodgett, *ES*, XXXV, 175–76.

John Ostrom, *AL*, XXV, 508–9.

B167 ———. "Poe's Flight from Reality." *TSLL*, I (Autumn 1959), 394–400.

Poe's art "was a conscious attempt to transmit an experience of escape to the reader without involving that reader in any more of a psychological dilemma than the writer himself felt."

B168 Bradley, Sculley. "Poe on the New York Stage in 1855." *AL*, IX (Nov. 1937), 353–54.

G. H. Boker's *The Bankrupt* contains a reference to Poe and may be "the earliest American play to make use of the type of detective conceived by Poe."

B169 Bradley, William Aspenwall. "Edgar Allan Poe's Place in Literature." *Book News Monthly*, XXV (Aug. 1907), 789–92.

Poe "possessed of a positive original genius," has "contributed directly to the general development of modern literature."

B170 Bradshaw, Sidney Ernest. "Of Edgar Allan Poe (1809–1849)." *On Southern Poetry prior to 1860.* Richmond: B. F. Johnson, 1900, pp. 64–67.

Poe was "pre-eminently a lyrist."

B171 Brady, Charles A. "Lunatics and Selenophiles." *America*, XCIX (July 26, 1958), 448–49.

Trips to the moon by famous authors, including Poe.

B172 Bragg, Clara W. *Material by and about Poe to Be Found in the Library of Columbia University.* New York: Columbia University, 1909.

A bibliography which is now of little use.

B173 Brashear, Minnie M. *Mark Twain, Son of Missouri.* Chapel Hill: University of North Carolina Press, 1934.

Twain may have read a great deal of Poe.

B174   Breen, Edward J. "A Century of Poe." *Cweal,* XV (Dec. 9, 193,1), 156.

B175   Brenner, Edgar. "Another Poem Claimed for Poe." *Critic,* NS V (April 10, 1886), 183–84.
Of "Leonainie," the hoax poem with a retelling of the story of a dissipated young man's leaving the MS in payment for a room at a Richmond inn.

B176   Brenner, Rica. "Edgar Allan Poe." *Twelve American Poets before 1900.* New York: Harcourt, 1933, pp. 142–68.
Praises Poe's technical skill, his creation of emotional effect, but denies him "depth of feeling, variety of experience," and "broad philosophy."

B177   Brevard, Caroline M. "Edgar Allen [*sic*] Poe." *Literature of the South.* New York: Broadway Publ., 1908, pp. 67–82.
Appreciative essay on Poe's writings with some attention to his life and current critical opinion.

B178   Brewster, W. T. "Introduction." *Specimens of Modern English Literary Criticism.* New York: Macmillan, 1907, pp. ix–xxxiii.
Poe held to the artistic view of literature. Editor includes "The Philosophy of Composition," pp. 257–68.

B179   [Briggs, Charles F.] "Memoir of Edgar Allan Poe." *The Poetical Works of Edgar Allan Poe.* New York: J. S. Redfield, 1858, pp. xvii–xxx.
Poe is an enigma, and his works reflect a religion of the Beautiful.

B180   ——. "The Personality of Poe." *Independent,* XXIX (Dec. 13, 1877), 1–2.
"The author of 'The Raven' was not a pleasant person to know."

B181   [——.] [Poe.] *Holden's Dollar Mag,* IV (Dec. 1849), 765–66.
In the Griswold tradition, critic finds Poe's poetry mechanical and dwells upon a shocking scandal in regard to Poe's life.

B182   Brigham, Clarence S. "Edgar Allan Poe's Contributions to Alexander's Weekly Messenger." *PAAS,* NS 52 (April 1942), pp. 45–125.
"Reprints all of Poe's identifiable articles that appeared in *Alexander's Weekly Messenger* between December 6, 1839, and May 6, 1840: many of the articles are cryptograms solved by Poe." *AL.*

B183   ——. *Edgar Allan Poe's Contributions to* Alexander's Weekly Messenger. Worcester, Mass.: The [American Antiquarian] Society, 1943.
See especially the introduction, pp. 3–11.

B184 ———. *Poe's "Balloon Hoax."* Metuchen, N.J.: American Book Collector, 1932.

On the publication and reception of Poe's story.

B185 Brock, Henry I. "A First Night for Edgar Allan Poe." *NYTMS,* Nov. 11, 1923, p. 6.

B186 Broderick, John C. "Poe's Revisions of 'Lenore.' " *AL,* XXXV (Jan. 1964), 504–10.

Attempts to demonstrate through analysis that the final version of Poe's poem is poetically superior to other versions.

B187 Bronson, Walter C. *A Short History of American Literature.* New York: D. C. Heath, 1900.

Sees two men in Poe, "a man of analytic intellect and a man of poetic imagination"; his criticism is "of little interest," but in his best work Poe "was emphatically original"; see *passim.*

B188 Bronx Board of Trade. *In Commemoration of the One Hundredth Anniversary of the Birth of Edgar Allan Poe, Poet, Author, and Editor. This Pamphlet is Issued the Nineteenth Day of January, Nineteen Hundred and Nine.* New York: Printed pursuant to a resolution of the North Side Board of Trade, 1909.

Contains letters from various dignitaries: "The Poetry of Poe" by Arthur Hobson Quinn; "Richmond Associations" by J. H. Whitty; a biographical sketch, and reprints of some of Poe's poems and Poe's "Masque of the Red Death."

B189 Bronx Society of Arts and Sciences. *In Memoriam: Edgar Allan Poe, 1809–1849. January Nineteenth, Nineteen Hundred and Nine.* New York: Bronx Society of Arts and Sciences, 1910.

Proceedings of the society include an account of the opening of Poe's cottage at Fordham and the texts of addresses given during the Poe Centenary Exercises held at New York University.

B190 Brooks, Cleanth, and Robert Penn Warren. "Interpretation" [of "The Fall of the House of Usher"]. *Understanding Fiction,* New York: F. S. Crofts, 1943, pp. 202–5.

Poe's story creates in the reader the sense of nightmare but has no tragic impact.

B191 ———. "Ulalume—A Ballad." *Understanding Poetry.* New York: Henry Holt, 1938, pp. 358–62.

Poe's poem has little unity or meaning.

B192 Brooks, Van Wyck. *America's Coming-of-Age.* New York: B. W. Huebsch, 1915.

Poe's relation to his contemporary Gothicism is emphasized; see pp. 30–34. Reprinted New York: Doubleday, 1958.

B193 ——. *The Flowering of New England, 1815–1865.* New York: Dutton, 1937.

Discusses Poe's relationship to John Neal, Hawthorne, Emerson, Longfellow, and others; see *passim.*

B194 ——. *New England: Indian Summer, 1865–1915.* New York: Dutton, 1940.

Some mention of Poe's significance to Whitman, Harriet P. Spofford, Henry James, Frost, and Robinson; see *passim.*

B195 ——. "Poe." *A Chilmark Miscellany.* New York: E. P. Dutton, 1948, pp. 187–207.

This essay first appeared as "Poe in the South" in *The World of Washington Irving* (1944), pp. 337–61.

B196 ——. "Poe as Critic." *A Chilmark Miscellany.* New York: E. P. Dutton, 1948, pp. 303–09.

This essay first appeared as "Poe in the North" in *The World of Washington Irving* (1944), pp. 443–56.

B197 ——. Poe in the North." *The World of Washington Irving.* Cleveland: World Publishing, 1944, pp. 443–56.

Poe was not a great critic, for he was too much in the tone of his time, although he did compose "a few fine essays in the realm of literary theory or on single authors, Bryant, Mrs. Browning, Dickens, Hawthorne."

B198 ——. "Poe in the South." *The World of Washington Irving.* Cleveland: World Publishing, 1944, pp. 337–61.

Although Poe reflects much of the conventions of his time, he was both a conscious artist and a confirmed neurotic whose nightmares depicted in his work will endure the tests of time.

B199 ——. "The World of Washington Irving." *Atlantic Monthly,* CLXXIV (Sept. 1944), 141–48.

A reprint of a chapter from the author's *The World of Washington Irving.*

B200 ——, and Otto L. Bettmann. *Our Literary Heritage: A Pictorial History of the Writer in Amercia.* New York: E. P. Dutton, 1956.

See pp. 30–35 for a brief essay on Poe along with pictures and illustrations.

B201 Brophy, Brigid. "Detective Fiction: A Modern Myth of Violence?" *HudR,* XVIII (Spring 1965), 11–30.

Poe emphasized the "puzzle" feature of detective fiction along with his depiction of the "detective-hero-deliverer"; see pp. 24–27.

B202 Brown, Clarence A. "The Aesthetics of Romanticism." *The Achievement of American Criticism.* New York: Ronald Press, 1954, pp. 149–82.

See pp. 156–57 for a brief discussion of Poe's significance as a critic who advanced high standards of literary excellence.

B203 Brown, Glenora W., and Deming B. Brown. *A Guide to Soviet Russian Translations of American Literature.* New York: King's Crown Press, 1954.

Lists Russian translations of Poe published during the 1920's.

B204 Brown, Wallace C. "The English Professor's Dilemma." *CE,* V (April 1944), 380–85.

A critical analysis of Poe's "Annabel Lee" and "To Helen" reveals the superiority of the latter.

B205 Browne, Irving. "Concerning the New 'Poe.' " *Critic,* XXVI (Jan. 26, 1895), 66–67.

"Poe is to be admired in his works, not in his life."

B206 Browne, William H. "Poe's 'Eureka' and Recent Scientific Speculations." *New Eclectic Mag,* V (Aug. 1869), 190–99.

Eureka is a "prose poem . . . one of the boldest speculations conceived by the brain of a man."

B207 ———. "*The Works of Edgar Allan Poe.* Ed. John H. Ingram." *Southern Mag.* XVI (June 1875), 640–50.

Review is primarily biographical with a severe criticism of Griswold; Ingram's "conscientious pains" are complimented.

B208 Brownell, William C. "Poe." *American Prose Masters: Cooper —Hawthorne—Emerson—Poe—Lowell—Henry James.* New York: Scribner's, 1923, pp. 172–223.

Poe is "historically" an important figure, but his "lack of moral imagination accounts for the vacuity of his writings." Reprinted in Norman Foerster's *American Critical Essays* (New York: Oxford Press, 1930), pp. 235–92; and by Cambridge, Mass.: Harvard University Press, 1963.

B209 ———. "Poe." *Scribner's Mag,* XLV (Jan. 1909), 69–84.

Concludes that Poe's writings are largely "valueless."

B210 Browning, Elizabeth Barrett. *The Letters of Elizabeth Barrett Browning.* 2 vols. London: Smith and Elder, 1897.

Acknowledges receiving a volume from Poe and expresses appreciation of his dedication to her; see I, 249.

B211 ———. *Letters of Robert Browning and Elizabeth Barrett Browning, 1845–46.* New York: Harper, 1898.

See E. B. B.'s letter to R. B. of Dec. 1, 1845, and March 7, 1846.

B212   Bruce, Philip A. "Background of Poe's University Life." *SAQ,* X (July 1911), 212–26.
A discussion of the University of Virginia in its beginnings.

B213   ———. "Certain Literary Aspects of Poe." *SR,* XXII (Jan. 1914), 38–49.
"Keats, Shelley, and Tennyson preëminently, and, in a hardly less degree, Coleridge" influenced Poe's taste.

B214   ———. "Edgar Allan Poe." *The Virginia Plutarch.* 2 vols. Chapel Hill: University of North Carolina Press, 1929.
A biographical account; see II, 188–205.

B215   ———. "Edgar Allan Poe and Mrs. Whitman." *SAQ,* XII (April 1913), 129–40.
Discusses the relationship between Poe and Mrs. Whitman and Mrs. Whitman's staunch defense of Poe.

B216   ———. "Was Poe a Drunkard?" *SAQ,* XI (Jan. 1912), 3–21.
Admits an "infirmity," but pleads that it be judged without harshness.

B217   Bruce, W. C. "The Tardy Recognition of Poe and a Short Compend of Griswold's Charges." *UVaMag,* XVIII (Nov., Dec. 1878), 104–15.

B218   Bruno, Guido. "Poe and O. Henry." *Bruno's Weekly,* III (July 29, 1916), 874–75.

B219   Buchan, John. "Introduction." *Tales of Mystery and Imagination,* by Edgar Allan Poe. London: T. Nelson and Sons, 1910, pp. 1–9.
Poe was, morally and intellectually, "Emerson's extreme antitype."

B220   Buckingham, Joseph T. *Personal Memoirs and Recollections of Editorial Life.* 2 vols. Boston: Ticknor, Reed, and Fields, 1852.
David Poe takes offense to the author's comments on Elizabeth Poe's acting, I, 57.

B221   Buckley, James M. "Edgar Allan Poe." *Christian Advocate* (New York), LXXXIV (Jan. 14, 1909), 45–46.
On the circumstances of Poe's death.

B222   Buranelli, Vincent. *Edgar Allan Poe.* New York: Twayne, 1961.
Biographer adopts a balanced view between the Freudian and anti-Freudian approaches, emphasizing Poe's Romanticism, symbolism, and tonal quality.
    Reviewed:
Bradly, *AL,* XXXII, 532–33.
Hicks, *SatR,* XLIV (Aug. 12, 1961), 13.
Levine, *AQ,* XVII, 133–44.
Moore, *YWES,* XLII, 282.
Levine, *MASJ,* IV, 78.

B223 ———. "Judgment on Poe." *AQ*, XVII (Summer 1965), 259–60.

On scholarship and critical approaches to Poe.

B224 Burch, Francis F. "Clement Mansfield Ingleby on Poe's 'The Raven': An Unpublished British Criticism." *AL*, XXXV (March 1963), 81–83.

In 1850 Clement Mansfield Ingleby praises the poem for its "fine melody," music, but is not pleased with some of its diction.

B225 Burke, Kenneth. "The Principle of Composition." *Poetry*, XCIX (Oct. 1961), 46–53.

An essay on the "principles" of aesthetics relative to the writing of "The Raven" as revealed in Poe's "The Philosophy of Composition."

B226 Burkholder, Robert S. "A Popular Error concerning Poe." *South Atlantic* (Wilmington, N.C.), III (Aug. 1878), 373–75.

Poe was not dissipated at the University of Virginia.

B227 Burroughs, John. "Mr. Gosse's Puzzle over Poe." *Dial*, XV (Oct. 16, 1893), 214–15.

Gosse is apprised why Poe did not appear in a literary popularity poll.

B228 Burton, Richard. "The American Contribution." *Masters of the English Novel*. New York: Henry Holt, 1909, pp. 313–31.

Poe "created on native soil the tale of fantasy, sensational plot, and morbid impressionism."

B229 ———. "Poe." *Literary Leaders of America*. New York: Chautauqua Press, 1903, pp. 66–98.

Favorable criticism of Poe as poet, critic, and "a remarkable writer of short stories."

B230 ———. "Poe." *Muse Anthology of Modern Poetry*. Ed. Dorothy Kissling and Arthur H. Nethercot. Poe Memorial Edition. New York: Carlyle Straub, 1938, p. 184.

Verse.

B231 Burton, William E. [Review of *Arthur Gordon Pym*.] *Burton's Gentleman's Mag*, III (Sept. 1838), 211.

Finds *Pym* a "prudent attempt" to fool the reading public.

*B232 *Burton's Gentleman's Magazine and American Monthly Review*. Vols. I–VIII; July 1837–Dec. 1840. Philadelphia, C. Alexander. Microfilm copy, made in 1954 by University Microfilms, Ann Arbor, Michigan.

B233 Burwell, William M. "Edgar A. Poe and His College Contemporaries." *UVaAB*, 3rd ser., XVI (April 1923), 168–80. "From the Richmond *Times-Democrat*, May 18, 1884."

Personal recollections of Poe and the University.

B234   Butterfield, James. [Correspondence on "The Raven."] *Academy*, LXII (May 24, 1902), 521.

Poe blended a variety of sources in composing "The Raven."

B235   Butterfield, Richard, and Joseph Jackson. "Poe's Obscure Contemporaries." *AN&Q*, II (April 1942), 27–29.

On "Colonel" John Stevenson Dusolle, Thomas G. Spear, and others.

C

C1   C., A. "To Poe." *UVaMag*, LX (Oct. 1899), 1.
Verse.

C2   C., C. S. "Editorial Note." *Tales of Adventure, Mystery and Imagination*, by Edgar Allan Poe. London: Geo. Newnes, n.d., p. 2.

"Poe's creations . . . must be regarded as those of the one literary genius yet produced in America."

C3   C., W. H. [Cudworth, Rev. W. H.]. "Cryptography—MR [*sic*] Poe as a Cryptographer." Lowell, Mass., *Weekly Journal and Courier*, April 19, 1850, p. 2.

Poe as skillful cryptographer.

C4   ———. "Mr. Poe, as a critic." Lowell, Mass., *Daily Journal and Courier*, May 6, 1850, pp. 1–2.

Poe's criticism has considerable merit.

C5   Cabell, James Branch. "To Edgar Allan Poe, Esq." *Ladies and Gentlemen: A Parcel of Reconsiderations*. New York: McBride, 1934.

Believes Poe to be the only American literary genius; that Poe and Dickens have a certain similarity of style; and that Poe is actually a realist in his criticism of life and literature; see pp. 241–62.

C6   Cadman, B. Meredith. "Poe Music." *Etude Music Mag*, LVIII (March 1940), 159.

C7   Cain, Henry Edward, "James Clarence Mangan and the Edgar Allan Poe–Mangan Question." Diss., Catholic University, 1929.

C8   ———. *James Clarence Mangan and the Poe-Mangan Question.* Washington, D.C.: Catholic University Press, 1929.

"Apart from some similarities in the technique of the two men, there is no direct or indirect evidence to support the contention that one influenced the other."

Reviewed:

Margaret Alterton, *MLN*, XLV, 554–55.

Killis Campbell, *JEGP*, XXX, 456–57.

G. Bersch, *Litteraturblatt f. germ. und roman. Philologie,* LII (1931), 269–70.

C9   Cairns, William B. *A History of American Literature.* Rev. ed. New York: Oxford University Press, 1930.
A restrained survey of Poe's life and work; see especially pp. 412–28 for comments on Poe as poet, critic, and fictionist. First edition was published in 1912.

C10   ——. "Poe's Use of the Horrible." *Dial,* L (April 1, 1911), 251–52.
Believes that Poe used the horrible only when it was necessary to the development of the tale.

C11   ——. "Some Notes on Poe's 'Al Aaraaf.'" *MP,* XIII (May 1915), 35–44.
Poe's debt to Moore, Shelley, and Coleridge is admitted.

C12   Calcott, Emily Sinclair. "The Influence of Isaac D'Israeli on Edgar A. Poe." Diss., University of Virginia, 1931.

C13   Callow, James T. *Kindred Spirits: Knickerbocker Writers and American Artists, 1807–1855.* Chapel Hill: University of North Carolina Press, 1967.
A study of Poe's contemporaries, but Melville, Whitman, and Poe are not included.

C14   Cambiaire, Célestin P. *The Influence of Edgar Allan Poe in France.* New York: G. E. Stechert, 1927.
Poe's influence in France is far-reaching, especially his influence on French poets.
    Reviewed:
Killis Campbell, *MLN,* XLIII, 493–94.
"M. R." *SR,* XXXVI, 509.
A. J. Dickman, *PQ,* VIII, 96.
Victor Klemperer, *Deutsche Literaturztg* (1929), 808–10.
T. O. Mabbott, *SatRLit,* VI (May 31, 1930), 1093.
Y. G. Dantec, *RLC,* X, 375.

C15   ——. "The Influence of Edgar Allen [*sic*] Poe in France." *RR,* XVII (Oct.–Dec. 1926), 319–37.
Poe's influence on French poets and prose writers is discussed.

C16   ——. "The Influence of Edgar Allan Poe in France." Diss., University of Iowa, 1925.

C17   Cambon, Glauco. "Space, Experiment and Prophecy." *The Inclusive Flame: Studies in American Poetry.* Bloomington: Indiana University Press, 1963, pp. 3–52.

Poe was an influential innovator of poetry and poetic theory; see pp. 4–9.

C18   Cameron, Kenneth W. "Poe's 'Bells' and Schiller's 'Das Lied von der Glocke.' " *ESQ,* No. 19 (2nd quarter 1960), p. 37.

Suggests Poe may have read Schiller's poem in Madame de Staël's *Germany* (1813).

C19 ———. "Poe's 'The Bells'—A Reply to Schiller and Romberg?" *ESQ,* No. 38 (1st quarter 1965), pp. 2–73.

Andreas Romberg's musical version of Schiller's "Das Lied von der Glocke" may have influenced Poe.

C20   Campbell, Killis. "Bibliographical Note." *Poems,* by Edgar Allan Poe. Reproduced from the Edition of 1831. Facsimile Text Society Publication No. 35. New York: Columbia University Press, 1936, [pp. 1–8].

Bibliographical commentary on the 1831 edition.

Reviewed:

E. E. Leisy, *Southwest Rev,* XXI, 242–43.

D. K. Jackson, *AL,* VIII, 105.

C21 ———. "Bibliographical Notes on Poe." *Nation,* LXXXIX (Dec. 23, 1909), 623–24.

C22 ———. "A Bit of Chiversian Mystification." *UTSE,* No. 10 (1930), pp. 152–54.

The poem "The Departed," published in the *Broadway Journal* of July 12, 1845, over the signature "L." and attributed by Chivers to Poe, is really the work of Chivers.

C23 ———. "Contemporary Opinion of Poe." *PMLA,* XXXVI (June 1921), 142–66.

An examination of contemporary notices and reviews of Poe, concluding that Poe (1) as a poet was not held highly and indeed was most ignored until after the publication of "The Raven"; (2) as a short story writer had great local fame and was recognized nationally at the time of his death; (3) as a critic was best known, but as a fearless and caustic one, not always impartial; (4) had his early reputation abroad because of his poetry and romances. Reprinted in author's *Mind of Poe* (1933), pp. 34–62.

C24 ———. "Gleanings in the Bibliography of Poe." *MLN,* XXXII (May 1917), 267–72.

Bibliographical notes.

C25 ———. "Introduction." *Poe's Short Stories.* New York: Harcourt Brace, 1927, pp. ix–xxv.

Poe's stories are "his most important contribution to imaginative literature."

Reviewed:

H. S. V. Jones, *JEGP*, XVII, 440.

C26 ———. *The Mind of Poe and Other Studies.* Cambridge, Mass.:
Harvard University Press, 1933.

Includes "The Mind of Poe," "Contemporary Opinion of Poe," "The
Poe-Griswold Controversy," "The Backgrounds of Poe," "Self-
Revelation in Poe's Poems and Tales," "The Origins of Poe," and
"The Poe Canon." Reprinted New York: Russell & Russell, 1962.

Reviewed:

TLS, July 20, 1933, p. 498.

P. H. Boynton, *MP*, XXXI, 100–101.

E. E. Leisy, *Southwest Rev*, XVIII (Winter 1933), 2.

New Republic, LXXVI (Aug. 6, 1933), 27.

F. C. Prescott, *MLR*, XXIX, 464–66.

H. M. Jones, *JEGP*, XXXIII, 313–14.

John C. French, *MLN*, XLIX, 554–55.

F. M. Hopkins, *PW*, CXXIII (June 17, 1933), 1977–79 (on
Campbell's "The Poe Canon").

C27 ———. "Marginalia on Longfellow, Lowell and Poe." *MLN*,
XLII (Dec. 1927), 516–21.

Discusses a variety of matters relative to Griswold's editing, Poe's
use of sources in several of his short stories, and factual knowledge
of Poe's life.

C28 ———. "Miscellaneous Notes on Poe." *MLN*, XXVIII (March
1913), 65–69.

Discusses the origin of several of Poe's works and presents some
evidence relative to the dating of Poe's lectures.

C29 ———. "New Notes on Poe's Early Years." *Dial*, LX (Feb. 17,
1916), 143–46.

A discussion of the Ellis-Allan papers.

C30 ———. "News for Bibliophiles." *Nation*, XCIII (Oct. 19,
1911), 362–63.

Presents several unsigned items which he believes are Poe's.

C31 ———. "Poe." *A History of American Literature.* Ed. William
Peterfield Trent *et al.* 3 vols. New York: G. P. Putnam's, 1918, II,
55–69.

Emphasizes Poe's versatility, points out his strengths and limitations,
and acknowledges his influence.

C32 ———. "Poe and the 'Southern Literary Messenger' in 1837."
Nation, LXXXIX (July 1, 1909), 9–10.

"Poe was back in Richmond in 1837 . . . posing as the editor of
the *Southern Literary Messenger.*"

C33 ———. "Poe Bibliography." *A History of American Literature.*
Ed. William Peterfield Trent *et al.* 3 vols. New York: G. P. Putnam's,
1919, II, 452–68.
> The "Cambridge" history lists a fine bibliography of Poe's writings
> and works about Poe.

C34 ———. "The Poe Canon." *PMLA*, XXVII (Sept. 1912),
325–53.
> An attempt to determine the authenticity of Poe-ascribed items. Re-
> printed in author's *Mind of Poe* (1933), pp. 187–238.

C35 ———. "Poe Documents in the Library of Congress." *MLN*,
XXV (April 1910), 127–28.
> Calls attention to some letters in the Ellis-Allan papers.

C36 ———. "The Poe-Griswold Controversy." *PMLA*, XXXIV (Sept.
1919), 436–64.
> Griswold was not a good editor, and his biography of Poe is largely
> prejudiced. Reprinted in author's *Mind of Poe* (1933), pp. 63–98.

C37 ———. "Poe in Relation to His Times." *SP*, XX (July 1923),
293–301.
> Although the reflection of contemporary interests is quite vague in
> Poe, he "betrays the influence of his times in virtually everything he
> wrote." Reprinted as "The Backgrounds of Poe" in author's *Mind
> of Poe* (1933), pp. 99–125.

C38 ———. "Poe, Stevenson, and Béranger." *Dial*, XLVII (Nov. 16,
1909), 374–75.
> Concerned with the source of "whose heart-strings are a lute."

C39 ———. *Poems of Edgar Allan Poe.* New York: Ginn, 1917.
> Criticism and notes are excellent. Reprinted New York: Russell &
> Russell, 1962.
> Reviewed:
> *Dial*, LX (Dec. 1917), 595.
> C. Alphonso Smith, *MLN*, XXXIII, 172–75.

C40 ———. "Poe's Indebtedness to Byron." *Nation*, LXXXVIII
(March 11, 1909), 248–49.
> Poe was "under the Byronic spell during half-dozen years preceding
> 1830, and . . . this spell was not entirely broken before 1837."

C41 ———. "Poe's Knowledge of the Bible." *SP*, XXVII (July
1930), 546–51.
> A criticism of W. M. Forrest's *Biblical Allusions in Poe.*

C42 ———. "Poe's Reading." *UTSE*, No. 5 (1925), pp. 166–96.
> Examines Poe's opinions of his contemporaries and his reading of
> them.

C43 ———. "Poe's Reading: Addenda and Corrigenda." *UTSE*, No. 7 (1927), pp. 175–80.
Lists Shakespearean quotations in Poe and calls attention to several corrections that should be made in "Poe's Reading," *UTSE*, No. 5 (1925), pp. 166–96.

C44 ———. "Poe's 'Silence.'" *Nation*, XC (Jan. 20, 1910), 62.
Acknowledges that Henry Wilder Foote is correct in attributing a sonnet to Thomas Hood rather than to Poe.

C45 ———. "Poe's Treatment of the Negro and of the Negro Dialect." *UTSE*, No. 16 (1936), pp. 106–14.
There are few Negro characters in Poe's writings, and, although they are loyal, they are generally unprepossessing.

C46 ———. "Recent Books on Poe." *SP*, XXIV (July 1927), 474–79.
Comments on Mary Newton Stanard's *Edgar Allan Poe Letters . . . in the Valentine Museum*, Mary E. Phillips's *Edgar Allan Poe, The Man*, and Hervey Allen's *Israfel*.

C47 ———. "Some Unpublished Documents Relating to Poe's Early Years." *SR*, XX (April 1912), 201–12.
Another discussion of the Ellis-Allan papers which follows up his article in *MLN*, XXV (April 1910), 127–28.

C48 ———. "The Source of Poe's 'Some Words with a Mummy.'" *Nation*, XC (June 23, 1910), 625–26.
Sheppard Lee by Bird (Philadelphia, 1836) is the source.

C49 ———. "Three Notes on Poe." *AL*, IV (Jan. 1933), 385–88.
Concerned with the methods and material Poe employed in writing "The Fall of the House of Usher," "The Cask of Amontillado," and his review of Irving's *Astoria*.

C50 ———. "Unique Poe Items." *Literary Review*, New York *Evening Post* (March 5, 1921), p. 14.
Describes some Poe items in the University of Texas library.

C51 ———. "Who Was 'Outis'?" *UTSE*, No. 8 (1928), pp. 107–09.
Believes "Outis" to have been C. C. Felton.

C52 ———, ed. *The Complete Short Stories of Edgar Allan Poe*. Introd. Hervey Allen. New York: Sun Dial Press, 1943.
"Published in 1927 under title *Poe Short Stories*." CBI.

C53 Canby, Henry Seidel. "Edgar Allan Poe." *Classic Americans*. New York: Harcourt, Brace, 1931, pp. 263–307.
Largely based on Allen's *Israfel* and Krutch's *Edgar Allan Poe*. Critic emphasizes Poe's journalistic capacities and is generally unfavorable in regard to the merits of Poe's art.

C54 ——. *The Short Story in English.* New York: Henry Holt, 1909.

Discusses Poe's membership in the "school of romantic emotionalism"; see pp. 227–45.

C55 Cantrell, Clyde H., and Walton R. Patrick. *Southern Literary Culture: A Bibliography of Masters' and Doctors' Theses.* Ann Arbor, Mich.: Edwards Brothers, 1955.

Lists Poe entries through the summer of 1948.

C56 Caputi, Anthony. "The Refrain in Poe's Poetry." *AL,* XXV (May 1953), 169–78.

Poe may have viewed the refrain largely as a device to produce emotional excitement, but in the use of the refrain he was often effective.

C57 Cargill, Oscar. "A New Source for 'The Raven.'" *AL,* VIII (Nov. 1936), 291–94.

The "new source" is two poems by Bürger in William Taylor's *Historic Survey of German Poetry* (1830).

C58 Carley, C. V. "A Source for Poe's 'Oblong Box.'" *AL,* XXIX (Nov. 1957), 310–12.

"The story is probably based on newspaper accounts of the murder of Samuel Adams by John Colt." *AL.*

C59 Carlson, Eric W. "Charles Poyen Brings Mesmerism to America." *Jour of the History of Medicine and Allied Science,* XV (April 1960), 121–32.

"Includes some remarks on Poe." *AL.*

C60 ——. "Introduction." *Introduction to Poe: A Thematic Reader.* Glenview, Ill.: Scott, Foresman, 1967, pp. xv–xxxv.

Finds a consistent pattern of "artistic intention and philosophic implication" in Poe's work.

C61 ——. "Poe's 'Eldorado.'" *MLN,* LXXVI (March 1961), 232–34.

Interprets poem as "another expression of Poe's lifelong attachment to an absolute ideal."

C62 ——. "Poe's 'Ulalume,' 6–9." *Expl.* XI (June 1953), item 56.

The opening lines of Poe's poem reflect the speaker's grief.

C63 ——. "Symbol and Sense in Poe's 'Ulalume.'" *AL,* XXXV (March 1963), 22–37.

Poe achieves artistic unity through dramatic structure and symbolism.

C64 ——, ed. *The Recognition of Edgar Allan Poe: Selected Criticism since 1829.* Ann Arbor: University of Michigan Press, 1966.

Critical appreciation of Poe has been slow, and recent critics find him "a great forerunner exploring the real horrors and self-realization of modern man"; see "Preface," pp. vi–xi.

Reviewed:

Kesterson, *SSF,* V, 200–202.

Lehan, *NCF,* XXIII, 120–22.

Lehan, *VQR,* XLIII, lix.

Smithline, *Library Jour,* XCI, 6087.

Stovall, *AL,* XXXIX, 226–27.

Wilbur, *NYRB,* IX (July 13, 1967), 16, 25–28.

C65 Carlton, W. N. C. "The Authorship of *English Notes by Quarles Quickens* Reviewed." *American Collector,* I (Feb. 1926), 186–92.

Tries to disprove Poe's authorship of the *Notes.*

C66 Carnevale, Lena. "Consistency." *Muse Anthology of Modern Poetry.* Ed. Dorothy Kissling and Arthur H. Nethercot. Poe Memorial Edition. New York: Carlyle Straub, 1938, p. 192.

Verse.

C67 Carson, David L. "Ortolans and Geese: The Origin of Poe's *Duc De L'Omelette.*" *CLAJ,* VIII (March 1965), 277–283.

Relates Poe's story to certain aspects of Poe's experiences at the United States Military Academy.

C68 Carter, Boyd. "Poe's Debt to Charles Brockden Brown." *PrS,* XXVII (Summer 1953), 190–96.

Poe used certain incidents and elements in *Edgar Huntly* for his "Tale of the Ragged Mountains."

C69 Carter, H. Holland. "Some Aspects of Poe's Poetry." *Arena,* XXXVII (March 1907), 281–85.

Some not-too-critical impressions of the poetry.

C70 Carter, John F. "Poe's Last Night in Richmond." *Lippincott's,* LXX (Nov. 1902), 562–66.

The reminiscences of the doctor whose cane Poe took by mistake to Baltimore.

C71 Cary, Richard. " 'The Masque of the Red Death' Again." *NCF,* XVII (June 1962), 76–78.

Points out parallel in the *New York Expositor.*

C72 ———. "Poe and the Great Debate." *TSLL,* III (Summer 1961), 223–33.

Poe took part in the great debate over the nature of American literature during 1815–50.

C73   ——. "Poe and the Literary Ladies." *TSLL,* IX (Spring 1967), 91–101.

Poe ignored his self-ordained rules in reviewing volumes by poetesses.

*C74   Casale, Ottavio Mark. *Edgar Allan Poe and Transcendentalism: Conflict and Affinity.* Ann Arbor, Mich.: University Microfilms, 1965.

C75   ——. "Edgar Allan Poe and Transcendentalism: Conflict and Affinity." *DA,* XXVI (May 1966), 6693.

Poe "was not as divorced from transcendentalism as is sometimes alleged."

*C76   ——. "Edgar Allan Poe and Transcendentalism: Conflict and Affinity." Diss., University of Michigan, 1965.

C77   Cauthen, Irby B., Jr. "A Descriptive Bibliography of Criticism of Edgar Allan Poe, 1827–1941." Master's Thesis, University of Virginia, 1942.

A useful annotative bibliography.

C78   ——. "Lowell on Poe: An Unpublished Comment." *AL,* XXIV (May 1952), 230–33.

Lowell comments on Poe's personality in a letter to John H. Ingram (May 12, 1879).

C79   ——. "Music and Edgar Allan Poe." *N&Q,* CXCIV (March 1949), 103.

Four additions to Miss May Garrettson Evans's *Music and Edgar Allan Poe, A Bibliographic Study.*

C80   ——. "Poe's *Alone:* Its Background, Source, and Manuscript." *SB,* III (1950), 284–91.

"This poem, considered authentic, in Poe's earlier manner, derives in part from Byron's *Manfred.*" *AL.*

C81   Cecil, L. Moffitt. "Poe's 'Arabesque.' " *CL,* XVIII (Winter 1966), 55–70.

Poe's tales have an affinity with those of the *Arabian Nights* and create "an effect comparable to that produced by the arabesque in the graphic arts."

C82   ——. "Poe's Tsalal and the Virginia Springs." *NCF,* XIX (March 1965), 398–402.

Poe's description of the extraordinary water on the island of Tsalal in *Pym* can be explained in the light of contemporary accounts of the mineral waters found in Virginia.

C83   ——. "The Two Narratives of Arthur Gordon Pym." *TSLL,* V (Summer 1963), 232–41.

Critic argues that the *Grampus* story and the *Jane Guy* story are entirely distinct narratives.

C84   Chadwick, Rev. John W. *Edgar Allan Poe: English Literature.* Philadelphia: J. B. Lippincott, 1903.
  Stresses Poe's fame as poet; dismisses his criticism, but argues that Poe's tales compare favorably with Hawthorne's.

C85   Chapman, Edward Mortimer. *English Literature in Account with Religion, 1800–1900.* Boston: Houghton, Mifflin, 1910.
  "Poe's best work is a telling reminder of man's powerlessness and misery in the realm where faith is denied to him." See pp. 260–67.

C86   Chari, V. K. "Poe and Whitman's Short-Poem Style." *Walt Whitman Rev,* XIII (Sept. 1967), 95–97.
  Poe could have influenced Whitman's "short-poem" style.

C87   Charlton, Jay. "Bohemians in America." *Record of the Year,* I, No. 5 (May 1876), 511–16.
  Poe's peculiarities and Bohemianism; see pp. 514–16.

C88   Charvat, William. *American Critical Thought, 1810–1835.* Philadelphia: University of Pennsylvania Press, 1936.
  A discussion of American criticism before Poe; see *passim.*

C89   ———. *Literary Publishing in America: 1790–1850.* Philadelphia: University of Pennsylvania Press, 1959.
  Considers Poe and the publishing business.

C90   ———. "A Note on [the Publication of] Poe's 'Tales of the Grotesque and Arabesque.' " *PW,* CL (Nov. 23, 1946), 2957–58.
  Only 750 copies appeared in the first edition of Poe's stories.

C91   ———. "Poe: Journalism and The Theory of Poetry." *Aspects of American Poetry.* Ed. Richard M. Ludwig. Columbus: Ohio State University Press, 1963, pp. 61–78.
  Eureka, having a literary form of broader scope than the lyric and the tale, was Poe's attempt to compose a work having audience appeal and at the same time allowing free play to both imagination and erudition.

C92   Chase, Lewis [Nathaniel]. "John Bransby, Poe's Schoolmaster." *Athenaeum,* No. 4605 (May 1916), pp. 221–22.

C93   ———. "More Notes on Poe's First School in London." *Dial,* LX (May 25, 1916), 499.
  A note on the Misses Dubourg's school at 146 Sloane St., Chelsea, which Poe attended in 1816.

C94   ———. "A New Poe Letter." *AL,* VI (March 1934), 66–69.
  Letter dated Philadelphia, Oct. 27, 1841, addressed to F. W. Thomas, referring to the authorship of *The Partisan Leader* and disclosing the fact that Poe had visited several phrenologists.

C95 ——. *Poe and His Poetry*. London: G. G. Harrap, 1913.
Largely biographical and some discussion of the development of Poe's skill in composing poetry.

C96 ——. "Poe's First London School." *Dial,* LX (May 11, 1916), 458–59.
Presents a bill substantiating that Poe attended the Misses Dubourg's school before "Dr." Bransby's school.

C97 ——. "Poe's Playmates in Kilmarnock." *Dial,* LXI (Oct. 19, 1916), 303.
Reprints a letter from a John Haggo declaring that one James Anderson of Kilmarnock knew Poe. Also appears in *Athenaeum,* No. 4611 (Nov. 1916), p. 554.

C98 ——. "Poe's School in Chelsea." *TLS,* April 27, 1916, pp. 201–2.
The Dubourg school on Sloane Square is located.

C99 ——. "Poe's School in Stoke Newington." *Athenaeum,* No. 4606 (June 1916), p. 294.

C100 ——. "Why Was 'The Raven' Published Anonymously?" *Nation,* CII (Feb. 10, 1916), sec. 2, 15–16.

C101 Cherry, Fannye N. "The Source of Poe's 'Three Sundays in a Week.'" *AL,* II (Nov. 1930), 232–35.
The immediate source is "Three Thursdays in One Week," published in the Philadelphia *Public Ledger* of Oct. 29, 1841.

C102 Chiari, Joseph. *Symbolisme from Poe to Mallarmé: The Growth of a Myth*. London: Rockliff, 1956.
Mallarmé's critical theory and practice owe very little to Poe's writings.

C103 Chinol, Elio. "Poe's Essays on Poetry." Trans. B. M. Arnett. *SR,* LXVIII (Summer 1960), 390–97.
Poe's insistence upon a definable subject, definite order and harmony, and the reader's sympathy for the feelings expressed in poetry separate Poe from the "pale of decadentism." Article first published in Italian in 1946.

C104 Chivers, Thomas Holley. "Caelicola." *Peterson's Mag,* XVII (Feb. 1850), 102.
An elegy on the death of Poe.

C105 ——. *The Complete Works of Thomas Holley Chivers*. Ed. S. Foster Damon and Charles H. Watts. Vol. I. Providence, R.I.: Brown University Press, 1957.
Contains Chivers's correspondence to and from Poe.

C106 ———. *Life of Poe.* Ed. and introd. Richard B. Davis. New York: E. P. Dutton, 1952.

> A contemporary of Poe and close friend recognizes Poe's genius in art as largely distinct from the moral character of the artist.
> Reviewed:
> A. H. Quinn, *AL,* XXIV, 417.
> Joseph Wood Krutch, *New York Herald-Tribune Books* (Sept. 7, 1952), p. 4.
> L. F. Parks and E. Chase, *JSH,* XVIII, 549–51.
> S. Bradley, *SatR* (May 13, 1952), p. 15.
> A. C. Gordon, Jr. *NYTBR* (June 22, 1952), p. 4.
> Jay B. Hubbell, *SAQ,* LII, 307–9.

C107 Chubb, Edwin Watts. "Last Days of Edgar Allan Poe." *Stories of Authors, British and American.* New York: Sturgis and Walton, 1910.

> An essay which quotes from Weiss and challenges Griswold's picture of Poe; see pp. 303–12.

C108 Church, Henry Ward. "Hervey Allen, Poe and Nature." *SatRL,* XI (April 6, 1935), 598.

> At the University of Virginia, Poe read *Nature Displayed,* a French grammar and reader.

C109 Church, Randolph W. "*Al Aaraaf* and the Unknown Critic." *Virginia Cavalcade* (Richmond), V (Summer 1955), 4–7.

> Extracts from a review in an unidentified Baltimore newspaper that discerningly comments on Poe's early poetry.

C110 Church, Richard. "Edgar Allan Poe Today." *Muse Anthology of Modern Poetry.* Ed. Dorothy Kissling and Arthur H. Nethercot. Poe Memorial Edition. New York: Carlyle Straub, 1938, p. 170.

> Emphasis on Poe's uniqueness.

C111 Clark, David Lee. "The Sources of Poe's 'The Pit and the Pendulum.'" *MLN,* XLIV (June 1929), 349–56.

> Poe's tale resembles two narratives in *Blackwood's* but more closely a chapter in Brockden Brown's *Edgar Huntly.*

C112 [Clark, Lewis Gaylord.] "Editor's Table." *Knickerbocker,* XV (April 1840), 359.

> Alludes to Poe as author of *Journal of Julius Rodman.*

C113 [———.] "Editor's Table." *Knickerbocker,* XVI (July 1840), 88.

> Announces that the *Gentleman's Magazine* is for sale and that Poe is retiring from the magazine.

C114 [———.] "Editor's Table." *Knickerbocker,* XXVI (May 1846), 461.

C115   [———.] [Review of *Arthur Gordon Pym*.] *Knickerbocker*, XII (Aug. 1838), 167.

Raises objections to the style and to the narrative filled with "horrid circumstance of blood and battle."

C116   [———.] [Review of the Griswold edition.] *Knickerbocker*, XXXV (Feb. 1850), 163–64.

Praises Poe's creative energy, but declares that Poe was destitute of moral principle, a plagiarist, and wrote worthless criticism.

C117   [———.] [Review of the Griswold edition.] *Knickerbocker*, XXXVI (Oct. 1850), 370–72.

Commentary on Poe's "unhappy" life and says little about his works.

C118   [———.] [Review of *The Raven and Other Poems*.] *Knickerbocker*, XXVII (Jan. 1846), 69–72.

Unfavorable criticism of Poe's literary criticism and poetry.

C119   Clark, Thomas A. "Edgar Allan Poe, 1809–1849." *Edgar Allan Poe*. Biographies of Great American Authors, No. 8. Taylorsville, Ill.: C. M. Parker, 1901, pp. 251–71.

Biographical essay.

C120   Clarke, George Herbert. "To Edgar Poe." *The Hasting Day*. Toronto: Ryerson Press, 1933.

Verse, p. 93.

C121   Clarke, T. Cottrell. "The Late N. P. Willis, and Literary Men Forty Years Ago." *Northern Monthly Mag* [Newark?], II, No. 3 (Jan. 1868), 234–42.

Eulogizes Willis and quotes from Willis's writings that reveal his working relationship with Poe and his respect for Poe's work.

C122   "Clear, Claudius." "Edgar Allan Poe and Dickens: A Mystification." *British Weekly*, LII (Aug. 1, 1912), 441.

Asks for information about the Poe review of *Barnaby Rudge*.

C123   ———. "Poe and Dickens: A Mystery Cleared Up." *British Weekly*, LIV (June 26, 1913), 325.

Points to errors Poe made in forecasting plot of Dickens's *Barnaby Rudge*.

C124   Clemens, Will M. "The Tragedy of Mary Rogers." *Era Mag*, XVI (Nov. 1904), 450–63.

C125   Cleveland, Stanley Matthews. "A Brief Discussion of Poe's Literary Genius." *UVaMag*, LXIX (Jan. 1909), 236–39.

Poe's genius "was essentially that of the artist."

C126   Clough, Wilson O. "Poe's 'The City in the Sea' Revisited." *Essays on American Literature in Honor of Jay B. Hubbell*. Ed. Clar-

ence Gohdes. Durham, N.C.: Duke University Press, 1967, pp. 77–89.
Poe's "The City in the Sea" is a masterpiece of inner consistency.

C127   ——. "The Use of Color Words by Edgar Allen [*sic*] Poe."
PMLA, XLV (June 1930), 598–613.
A systematized study of the use of color words in the tales and poetry.

C128   Clutton-Brock, Arthur. "Edgar Allan Poe." *More Essays on Books*. London: Methuen, 1921, pp. 109–19.
Emphasizes Poe's influence and admires a few poems and "The Power of Words."
Reviewed:
Boston *Times,* Oct. 12, 1921, p. 7.
Edward L. Pearson, *Independent*, CVII (Oct. 8, 1921), 38.
Literary Rev, Oct. 22, 1921, p. 106.
"J. W. M." *TLS*, Dec. 29, 1921, p. 872.

C129   Coad, Oral S. "Introduction." *Edgar Poe and His Critics*, by Sarah Helen Whitman. New Brunswick, N.J.: Rutgers University Press, 1949, pp. 7–25.
Discusses the various circumstances leading to the composition of Sarah Helen Whitman's biography.

C130   ——. "The Meaning of Poe's 'Eldorado.'" *MLN,* LIX (Jan. 1944), 59–61.
The conclusion of the poem suggests that "Eldorado" symbolizes death rather than unconquerable idealism.

C131   Cobb, Palmer. "Edgar Allan Poe and Frederick Spielhagen: Their Theory of the Short Story." *MLN*, XXV (March 1910), 67–72.
Concerned with the ideas Spielhagen obtained from Poe and transplanted to German soil.

C132   ——. *The Influence of E. T. A. Hoffmann on the Tales of Edgar Allan Poe*. Chapel Hill: University of North Carolina Press, 1908.
Hoffmann's influence "was solely a borrowing and adaptation of motive."

C133   ——. "The Influence of E. T. A. Hoffmann on the Tales of Edgar Allan Poe." Diss., Columbia University, 1908.

C134   ——. "Poe and Hoffman." *SAQ*, VIII (Jan. 1909), 68–81.
A concise statement of the author's book, *The Influence of E. T. A. Hoffmann on the Tales of Edgar Allan Poe* (1908).

C135   Coburn, Frederick W. "Lowell's [Mass.] Association with Edgar Allen [*sic*] Poe in 1840." Lowell, Mass., *Courier-Citizen,* Jan. 20, 1941, p. 11.

The first of a four-part article touching on Poe's relationships with his friends at Lowell and Westford in 1848—not in 1840 as the initial title indicates. The other installments appear in the *Courier-Citizen* on Jan. 27, 1941, p. 11; Feb. 3, 1941, p. 11; and Feb. 10, 1941, p. 11.

C136 ——. "Poe as Seen by the Brother of 'Annie.'" *NEQ*, XVI (Sept. 1943), 468–76.
A new Englander records his impressions of Poe.

C137 Cocke, C. P. "To Edgar Allen [*sic*] Poe." *UVaMag*, LI (March 1891), 346.
Verse with the subtitle, "Sometime a student at the University of Virginia."

C138 Cody, Sherwin. "Biographical Study; Chronology of Poe's Life." *Poe—Man, Poet, and Creative Thinker.* New York: Boni and Liveright, 1924, pp. 1–58.
Some emphasis given to Poe's journalistic activities and ambitions.

C139 ——. "Edgar Allan Poe." *Four Famous American Writers.* New York: Werner School Book, 1899, pp. 72–132.
An essay to be read by young teenagers.

C140 ——. "General Introduction." *The Best Tales of Edgar Allan Poe.* New York: Modern Library, 1924, pp. xiii–xix.
Poe "stood for clear scientific thinking in literature." See also Cody's essay "Poe, Creator of the Short Story," pp. vii–xii, for critical commentary.

C141 ——. "Poe as a Critic." *Putnam's Monthly and The Reader,* V (Jan. 1909), 438–40.
A discussion of Poe's criticism of fiction.

C142 ——. "Poe in the Twentieth Century." *Poe—Man, Poet, and Creative Thinker.* New York: Boni and Liveright, 1924, pp. v–xi.
Poe is now recognized as a great creative thinker.

C143 ——. "Poe, the Creative Thinker." *Poe—Man, Poet, and Creative Thinker.* New York: Boni and Liveright, 1924, pp. 105–21.
"As an analyst of the principles of literary art he [Poe] is supreme."

C144 ——. "Poe the Poet." *Poe—Man, Poet, and Creative Thinker.* New York: Boni and Liveright, 1924, pp. 59–62.
Poe recognizes the lyric as the highest form of poetry.

C145 ——. "Poe's Contribution to American Literary History." *Dial,* XXXV (Sept. 16, 1903), 161–62.

C146 ——. *The Story of Edgar Allan Poe for Young Readers.* New York: Werner School Book, 1899.

Poe was an unfortunate and unhappy artist, and at the same time a brilliant poetic genius.

C147 ——, ed. *The Best Poems and Essays of Edgar Allan Poe.* Chicago: A. C. McClurg, 1903.

See "Biographical Study," pp. 1–55; "Poe's Best Poems," pp. 59–62; and "Poe's Literary Creed," pp. 105–21—all by Cody.

C148 Coe, H. C. "Poe and Hawthorne." *Yale Literary Mag,* XLII (Oct. 1876), 16–19.

Hawthorne wrote to present an earnest lesson; Poe wrote simply to entertain.

C149 Coeuroy, André. "Poe and Music." *Sackbut,* II, No. 10 (April–May 1922), 6–10.

C150 Cohen, B. Bernard, and Lucien A. "Poe and Griswold Once More." *AL,* XXXIV (March 1962), 97–101.

Examination of a Griswold review in the *Nation* and Poe's comment on Griswold in *The Autography* reveals how the hostility between Poe and Griswold began.

C151 Cohen, Hennig. "Roderick Usher's Tragic Struggle." *NCF,* XIV (Dec. 1959), 270–72.

Tragic elements are "present in a struggle which occurs within Usher himself, a struggle between his will to live and the price he must pay in order to remain alive."

C152 Cohen, J. M. "The Dream World of Edgar Allan Poe." *Listener,* XLII (Sept. 29, 1949), 540–41.

"Poe's attitude to the unconscious rather than his positive achievement 'stimulated' a development in literature which was to reach its conclusion only with surrealism."

C153 Colby, Robert A. "Poe's Philosophy of Composition." *UKCR,* XX (Spring 1954), 211–14.

"The Philosophy of Composition" in its general theoretical discussion of the function of poetry—particularly of the effects of beauty—suggests hints as to the construction of "To Helen."

C154 Cole, Samuel V. "Stedman and Poe Again." *Critic,* VII (Nov. 28, 1885), 257.

C155 Collins, John C. *Studies in Poetry and Criticism.* London: George Bell and Sons, 1905.

Praises Poe's artistry and his transporting poetry "into a world of imagination and fantasy"; see pp. 42–45.

C156 Colton, Cullen B. "George Hooker Colton and the Publication of 'The Raven.'" *AL,* X (Nov. 1938), 319–30.

Evidence is presented that the Poe-Colton relationship was cordial.

C157   Colum, Mary M. "The Outside Literatures in English: The Irish and the American." *From These Roots: The Ideas That Have Made Modern Literature.* New York: Scribner's, 1937, pp. 260–311.
     Poe, Walt Whitman, and Henry James left behind the most "penetrating" influences on literature; see pp. 289–311.
     Reviewed:
     F. B. Millett, *AL,* X, 366–68.

C158   Colum, Pádraic. "Introduction." *Edgar Allan Poe's Tales of Mystery and Imagination.* London: J. M. Dent and Sons, 1912, pp. vii–xv.
     Poe's work gives us experience "not out of the mainway of life, but out of the border of existence."

C159   Colvin, Ann. "Quest." *Muse Anthology of Modern Poetry.* Ed. Dorothy Kissling and Arthur H. Nethercot. Poe Memorial Edition. New York: Carlyle Straub, 1938, p. 191.
     Verse.

C160   Comstock, Sarah. "More about Poe." *Our World Weekly,* III (Nov. 16, 1925), 117.

C161   Conklin, Groff. "Introduction." *Ten Great Mysteries,* by Edgar Allan Poe. Ed. Conklin. New York: Scholastic Book Services, 1960, pp. v–vii.

C162   Connely, Willard. *Adventures in Biography: A Chronicle of Encounters and Findings.* London: W. Laurie, 1956.
     Discusses Poe as a schoolboy in England and his subsequent relationships with English citizens and writers, pp. 162–83.

C163   Conner, Frederick William. "Poe and John Nichol: Notes on a Source of *Eureka." All These to Teach: Essays in Honor of C. A. Robertson.* Ed. Robert A. Bryan *et al.* Gainesville: University of Florida Press, 1965, pp. 190–208.
     On Poe's use of J. P. Nichol's *Architecture of the Heavens* (1837).

C164   ——. "Poe's *Eureka:* The Problem of Mechanism." *Cosmic Optimism: A Study of the Interpretation of Evolution by American Poets from Emerson to Robinson.* Gainesville: University of Florida Press, 1949, pp. 67–91.
     Poe conceived a "thoroughly mechanistic theory of evolution to which only in the end he attached a 'transcendental' interpretation."

C165   Connolly, Thomas E. "Poe's 'Ulalume.'" *Expl,* XXII (Sept. 1963), item 4.
     An interpretation and analysis of the imagery.

C166   Conway, Moncure D. [Review of Ingram's *Life* . . . .] *Academy,* NS XVIII (July 24, 1880), 55–56.

Commends Poe's ability to "invest an illusion with intensity" and the "aeolian quality" of his poetry.

C167   Cook, Harry T. *The Borough of the Bronx, 1639–1913: Its Marvelous Development and Historical Surroundings.* New York: Privately printed, 1913.
See especially Chap. 18 entitled "Fordham Manor," pp. 150–57.

C168   Cooke, Alice L. "The Popular Conception of Edgar Allan Poe from 1850 to 1890." *UTSE,* No. 22 (1942), pp. 144–70.
Between 1850 and 1890 critics were not primarily concerned with recognizing Poe's genius, but rather to clear "his name from the slanders which caused it to be anathema for the world in general."

C169   Cooke, Arthur L. "Edgar Allan Poe—Critic." *Cornhill Mag,* CL (Nov. 1934), 588–97.
Reviews Poe's chief principles of criticism.

C170   Cooke, John Esten. *Poe as a Literary Critic.* Ed. and introd. and notes N. Bryllion Fagin. Baltimore: Johns Hopkins Press, 1946.
A Poe contemporary argues that Poe as a critic descended into "petty spites and rivalries of the hour."
Reviewed:
D. J. Gordon, *RES,* XXV, 184–85.

C171   Cooke, P. Pendleton. "Edgar Allan Poe." *SLM,* XIV (Jan. 1848), 34–38.
Praises Poe's poetic imagination and comments that his analytic and narrative powers are unequaled by any living writer. Reprinted in Eric Carlson, ed., *The Recognition of Edgar Allan Poe* (Ann Arbor: University of Michigan Press, 1966), pp. 21–28.

C172   Cooper, C. B. "Tintinnabulation." *MLN,* XLI (May 1926), 318.
The word perhaps comes from John Hookham Frere's *Monks and Giants* (1817).

C173   Cooper, Lettice. *The Young Edgar Allan Poe.* New York: Roy Publishers, 1964.
Fiction account of Poe's life through March 18, 1827.

C174   Costello, Robin V. "Poe and Marie Rogêt." New York *Evening Post,* Jan. 10, 1920, sec. III, p. 11.
On the identity of the murderers of Mary Rogers.

C175   Courson, Della. "Poe and The Raven." *Education* (Boston), XX (May 1900), 566–70.
"Whether Poe intended it or not, the Raven is emblematic of his life."

C176　Coventry, R. G. T. "Edgar Allan Poe." *Academy*, LXIX (Nov. 4, 1905), 1234.
Attacks Poe as critic of poetry.

C177　——. "Edgar Allan Poe and His Commentators." *Academy*, LXIX (Dec. 16, 1905), 1291.
Declares Ingram, in defending Poe, is determined "to pick a quarrel."

C178　——. "What Makes the Perfect Lyric." *Academy*, LXIX (Nov. 4, 1905), 1149–51.
He thinks Poe's conception of "a perfect lyric" was decidedly faulty.

C179　Cowardin, S. P. "In Memory of Poe's Mother." *UVaAB*, 3rd ser., V (Oct. 1912), 563–64.
A reporting of Cowardin's efforts to locate the grave of Elizabeth Arnold Poe.

C180　——. "The Treasure of Old St. John's." *UVaMag*, NS LIV (Feb. 1912), 266–69.
Concerned with the grave of Elizabeth Poe.

C181　Cowie, Alexander. "Edgar Allan Poe." *The Rise of the American Novel*. New York: American Book Co., 1948, pp. 300–306.
Except for the controversial *The Narrative of Arthur Gordon Pym*, "Poe is now associated with the history of the novel principally as a reviewer and a critic."

C182　Cowley, Malcolm. "Aidgarpo." *New Republic*, CXIII (Nov. 5, 1945), 607–10.
Emphasizes Poe's foreign influence.

C183　——. "The Edgar Allan Poe Tradition." *Outlook*, CXLIX (July 23, 1928), 497–99, 511.
Poe is an important man of American letters who has been subjected to prejudicial criticism.

C184　Cox, John L. "Poe as a Critic." *EJ* (College Edition), XXI (Nov. 1932), 757–63.
Poe is assigned an important place in the evolution of American criticism.

C185　Craig, Hardin. "The Truth about Poe." *VQR*, XVIII (April 1942), 285–90.
Review of Quinn's critical biography of Poe (1941).

C186　Crandall, Charles H., ed. *Representative Sonnets by American Poets*. Boston: Houghton, Mifflin, 1890.
Contains Poe's "To Science" (p. 255); see p. 340 for brief comment on Poe as poet.

C187   Crane, Hart. *"The Bridge* from 'The Tunnel' section." *The Recognition of Edgar Allan Poe.* Ed. Eric Carlson. Ann Arbor: University of Michigan Press, 1966, pp. 159–60.
Passage on Poe.

C188   Crane, Nathalia. "The Agate Lamp." *Muse Anthology of Modern Poetry.* Ed. Dorothy Kissling and Arthur H. Nethercot. Poe Memorial Edition. New York: Carlyle Straub, 1938, p. 168.
An appreciative essay on Poe. See also author's "Poe's Critic," p. 185.

C189   Crawford, Nelson A. "The Life of Edgar Allan Poe." *Poems of Edgar Allan Poe.* Ed. Crawford. Girard, Kans.: Haldeman-Julius, 1924, pp. 7–20.
Largely factual; see also "The Poems of Edgar Allan Poe," pp. 14–20, for brief description of Poe's theory of poetry.

C190   Crawford, Polly Pearl. "Lewis and Clark's *Expedition* as a Source for Poe's 'Journal of Julius Rodman.'" *UTSE,* No. 12 (1932), pp. 158–70.
Points out similarity of many passages in Poe's story with many portions of *The History of the Expedition under the Commands of Captains Lewis and Clark* (Philadelphia, 1814).

C191   Cronin, James E. "Poe's Vaults." *N&Q,* CXCVIII (Sept. 1953), 395–96.
Some details in "The Fall of the House of Usher" do not contribute to the ultimate effect of the story.

C192   Crouse, Russell. *Murder Won't Out.* Garden City, N.Y.: Doubleday, Doran, 1932.
Concerns Mary Rogers, pp. 52–74.

*C193   Culhane, Mary J. "Thoreau, Melville, Poe, and the Romantic Quest." Diss., University of Minnesota, 1945.

*C194   Culver, Francis B. "Lineage of Edgar Allan Poe and the Complex Pattern of the Family Genealogy." *Maryland Historical Mag,* XXXVII (Dec. 1942), 420–22.
"Includes genealogical chart." *AL.*

C195   Cumston, C. G. "The Medical History of Edgar Allan Poe." *St. Paul Medical Jour* (St. Paul, Minn.), XI (March 1909), 129–46.
Poe suffered from dipsomania, a form of alcoholic indulgence.

C196   Curtis, George William. "Easy Chair." *Harper's Monthly,* VIII (Feb. 1854), 418.
Praises Poe's "The Bells."

C197   ———. "Easy Chair." *Harper's Monthly,* LXI (Oct. 1880), 787–88.

A discussion of Poe and Willis, primarily an informal reminiscence with a slight mention of the critics Minto and Ingram on Poe.

C198   Curtis, John, ed. *Selected Tales* [by Edgar Allan Poe]. With intro. Hammondsworth, Middlesex: Penguin Books, 1956.

Poe's best stories are those in which the author "lays bare the mysterious and irrational processes of the subconscious." See "Introduction," pp. 9–15.

C199   Curtis, William O'Leary. "Edgar Allan Poe." *American Catholic Quarterly,* XVI (Oct. 1891), 818–33.

A sympathetic biographical account along with some comments on Poe's poetry.

C200   Curwen, Henry. *Sorrow and Song: Studies of Literary Struggle.* 2 vols. London: H. S. King, 1875.

See II, 93–166 for an essay emphasizing Poe's misfortunes along with some critical appraisal of Poe's works.

C201   Cutler, S. P. "Poe's 'Eureka' Reconsidered." *New Eclectic Mag,* V (Nov. 1869), 533–38.

Unfavorable criticism of *Eureka.* Also appears in *Southern Mag,* V (Nov. 1869), 533–38.

D

D1   D., E. L. [Didier, Eugene L.]. "An Early Poem by Edgar Allan Poe." *Scribner's Monthly,* X (Sept. 1875), 608.

The poem, "Alone," dated "Baltimore, March 17, 1829," is given in facsimile.

D2   D—, H. M. "The Philosophy of Composition." *Yale Literary Mag,* XXXVIII (Feb. 1873), 188–91.

A review of Poe's essay.

D3   Daggett, Windsor. *A Down-East Yankee from the District of Maine.* Portland, Maine: A. J. Huston, 1920.

See pp. 55–56 for comments on Poe's mother.

D4   Dahlberg Edward. "Chivers and Poe." *Alms for Oblivion.* Minneapolis: University of Minnesota Press, pp. 73–76.

Chivers recognized Poe's genius.

D5   Dalby, John Watson. "Edgar Allan Poe." *St. James Mag,* XXXVI (Aug. 1875), 473–87.

Poe is known for his imagination and for the "scientific attainments he pressed into its service."

D6 Daly, C. D. "The Mother Complex in Literature." *Yearbook of Psychoanalysis,* IV (1948), 172–210.

A scientist characterizes the role of the "Menstruation Complex" as source of dramatic inspiration in several of Poe's stories.

D7 Dameron, J. Lasley. "Another 'Raven' for Edgar Allan Poe." *N&Q,* CCVIII (Jan. 1963), 21–22.

Poe may have read a poem entitled "The Raven" in *Bentley's Miscellany.*

D8 ——. *Edgar Allan Poe: A Checklist of Criticism, 1942–1960.* Charlottesville: Bibliographical Society of University of Virginia, 1966.

Checklist of both English and foreign criticism with Appendix. Entries in English are annotated.

D9 ——. *Edgar Allan Poe in the Mid-Twentieth Century: His Literary Reputation in England and America 1928–1960 and a Bibliography of Poe Criticism 1942–1960.* Ann Arbor, Mich.: University Microfilms, 1962.

D10 ——. "Edgar Allan Poe in the Mid-Twentieth Century: His Literary Reputation in England and America, 1928–1960, and a Bibliography of Poe Criticism, 1942–1960." *DA,* XXIII (Nov. 1962), 1699.

Critics, both Freudian and anti-Freudian, consider Poe a versatile artist and particularly appreciate his fiction.

D11 ——. "Edgar Allan Poe in the Mid-Twentieth Century: His Literary Reputation in England and America, 1928–1960, and a Bibliography of Poe Criticism, 1942–1960." Diss., University of Tennessee, 1962.

D12 ——. "Poe and *Blackwood's* on the Art of Reviewing." *ESQ,* No. 31 (2nd quarter 1963), pp. 29–30.

Poe had opportunity to learn an analytical method of reviewing from an article published in *Blackwood's.*

D13 ——. "Poe at Mid-Century: Anglo-American Criticism, 1928–1960." *BSUF,* VIII (Winter 1967), 36–44.

Critics tend "to recognize Poe's versatile literary talents and his worldwide influence."

D14 ——. "Poe's Reading of the British Periodicals." *MissQ,* XVIII (Winter 1964–65), 19–25.

Poe read extensively in the British periodicals, and "his dependence upon them should be re-studied in the light of other influences."

D15 ———. "Schiller's 'Das Lied Von der Glocke' as a Source of Poe's 'The Bells.'" *N&Q*, CCXII (Oct. 1967), 368–69.

D16 ———, and Louis C. Stagg. *An Index to Poe's Critical Vocabulary*. Hartford: Transcendental Books, 1966.
Indexes selected terms and phrases from Poe's letters, reviews, and essays. Reprinted in *ESQ*, No. 46 (2nd quarter 1967), pp. 1–51.

D17 Damon, Samuel Foster. *Thomas Holley Chivers, Friend of Poe*. New York: Harper, 1930.
Comments that Chivers inspired Poe's poetry and traces the relationship between the two men; see *passim*.

D18 [Dana, Charles A.] [Review of the *Tales* (1845).] *The Harbinger*, I (July 12, 1845), 73–74.

D19 Dandridge, Danske. "Poe on Happiness." *Poet-Lore*, XV (Winter 1904), 108–10.
Poe, in his pronouncement concerning happiness in "Arnheim," makes little provision for "the cultivation of the spiritual nature."

D20 [Daniel, J. M.] [Account of Poe's Lecture.] Richmond *Weekly Examiner*, Aug. 24, 1849, p. 1.
Generally admires Poe's poetry but does not approve of his manner of reciting poetry.

D21 ———. "Edgar Allan Poe." *SLM*, XVI (March 1850), 172–87.
Censures Poe's editors (Willis, Lowell, and Griswold) and praises Poe's short stories and criticism.

D22 Daniel, Robert. "Poe's Detective God." *Furioso*, VI (Summer 1951), 45–54.
Poe creates a secular God in Dupin whose "supernatural exploits" are made credible through Poe's frequent use of paradox.

D23 Danner, Richard. "The Poe-Matthews Theory of the American Short Story." *BSUF*, VIII (Winter 1967), 45–50.
Poe did not originate the short story genre, but he contributed a great deal to its development.

D24 Darnall, F. M. "The Americanism of Edgar Allan Poe." *EJ*, XVI (March 1927), 185–92.
Poe has qualities that link him "with the very inner moods and attitudes most peculiar to the American mind."

D25 Daughrity, Kenneth Leroy. "The Life and Work of Nathaniel Parker Willis, 1806–1836." Diss., University of Virginia, 1935.
Poe's relationships with Willis are stressed.

D26 ———. "Notes: Poe and *Blackwood's*." *AL*, II (Nov. 1930), 289–92.
Overtones of *Blackwood's* stories are indicated in "Bon-Bon," "How

to Write a Blackwood Article," "Von Kempelen and His Discovery," and "Maezel's Chess-Player."

D27 ———. "Poe's Quiz on Willis." *AL,* V (March 1933), 55–62.
The early career of N. P. Willis is satirized in "The Duc De L'Ome-lette."

D28 ———. "A Source for a Line of Poe's 'Ulalume.' " *N&Q,* CLXI (July 11, 1931), 27.
Finds a similarity between a line of "Ulalume" and a line from Willis's "My Birth-Place."

D29 Davidson, Edward H. *Poe: A Critical Study.* Cambridge, Mass.: Harvard University Press, 1957.
Poe, belonging to the Romantic Age, charted deeper ranges for symbolic expression of the "dark-underside of human consciousness," but his imagination never developed beyond the stage of self-as-subject.
    Reviewed:
W. Bittner, *Nation,* CLXXXV (Dec. 28, 1957), 501–2.
Roy P. Basler, *AL,* XXX, 379–80.
Robert D. Jacobs, *MLN,* LXXIV, 75–76.
George R. Thomas, *RES,* X, 425–27.

D30 ———. "Tale as Allegory." *Interpretations of American Litera-ture.* Ed. Charles Feidelson and Paul Brodtkoeb, Jr. New York: Oxford University Press, 1959, pp. 63–82.
Reprint from author's critical study of Poe (1957).

D31 ———, ed. *Selected Writings of Edgar Allan Poe.* With introd. Boston: Houghton Mifflin, 1956.
Poe helped to found the modern short story and has been in the "forefront of aesthetic and critical debates on the nature and autonomy of art itself." See "Introduction," pp. vii–xxviii.

D32 Davidson, Frank. "A Note on Poe's 'Berenice.' " *AL,* XI (May 1939), 212–13.
Reports the discovery in *Affection's Gift* (1854) of an unlocated Bulwer's "A Manuscript Found in a Madhouse" to which Poe re-ferred in answering T. W. White's criticism of "Berenice."

D33 Davidson, James Wood. "Edgar A. Poe." *Russell's Mag,* II (Nov. 1857), 161–73.
Declares that Poe is defamed because of the "wholesome truths" he "dared to tell."

D34 ———. "Poe's Guardian Angel." *Home Jour,* March 20, 1871.
Concerning Mrs. Clemm.

D35 ———. "To Mrs. M. C." *SLM,* XXXI (Nov. 1860), 394.
A verse tribute to Maria Clemm, "the 'more than mother' to Edgar

Poe." Reprint in Ingram Collection dated "Columbia, S.C., 27 September, 1860."

D36 Davis, H. C. "Poe's Stormy Voyage in 1827 Is Described." Charleston, S.C., *News and Courier,* Jan. 5, 1941, sec. II, p. 3.

D37 Davis, Harriet Eager. *Elmira: The Girl Who Loved Edgar Allan Poe.* Boston: Houghton Mifflin, 1966.
Mingles fact with fiction "to give readers an understanding of Edgar Allan Poe through the eyes of his first love, Elmira Royster."

*D38 Davis, Jeff. "The Lady Madeleine as Symbol." *The Annotator* (Purdue), No. 2 (April 1954), pp. 8–11.
"Roderick Usher's sister symbolizes his insanity." *AL.*

D39 Davis, Malcolm W. "Poets at Midnight." *Yale Literary Mag,* LXXV (Dec. 1909), 144–48.
A whimsical article in which the author offers verse parodies on the style of Poe, Kipling, Stevenson, and Browning.

D40 Davis, Richard B. *Intellectual Life in Jefferson's Virginia, 1790–1830.* Chapel Hill: University of North Carolina Press, 1964.
See especially chap. 8 entitled "Literature, Principally Belletristic," pp. [253]–350.

D41 ———. "Introduction." *Chivers' Life of Poe.* New York: E. P. Dutton, 1952, pp. 9–21.
Editor discusses major items of personal record that throw light on Poe's life and personality.

D42 ———. "Moncure D. Conway Looks at Edgar Poe—Through Dr. Griswold." *MissQ,* XVIII (Winter 1964–65), 12–18.
Reprints a Conway review of Poe's works and comments that Conway demonstrated a "perceptive grasp of what Poe had attempted to do."

D43 ———. "Poe and William Wirt." *AL,* XVI (Nov. 1944), 212–20.
Traces the personal and literary relations of Poe and William Wirt and suggests that a section from Wirt's *The Old Bachelor* influenced Poe's "William Wilson."

D44 Dawson, William J. *Makers of English Fiction.* 2nd ed. New York: F. H. Revell, 1905.
"With all his faults and limitations he [Poe] was a man of supreme literary ability and a great artist"; see pp. 298–301.

D45 DeCasseres, Benjamin. "The Ghost of Poe Returns to Broadway." *NYTM,* Jan. 4, 1920, p. 5.
Concerning the dramatization of certain tales with some remarks about Poe's not being truly American.

D46 ——. "Poe." *Forty Immortals.* New York: Lawren, 1926.
Poe, along with Balzac and Goethe, began modern literature; see
pp. 266–71.

D47 Dedmond, Francis B. "An Additional Source of Poe's 'The Cask
of Amontillado.' " *N&Q,* CXCVII (May 1952), 212–14.
" 'The Tun of Red Wine: An Incident That Occurred at a Town in
Spain During the Peninsular War' in the May 1838 issue of Burton's
Gentleman's Magazine is the source from which Poe adapted the
title of his tale and the source from which he got several of his
descriptive and narrative details for 'The Cask of Amontillado.' " *AL.*

D48 ——. " 'The Cask of Amontillado' and the 'War of the
Literati.' " *MLQ,* XV (June 1954), 137–46.
Relates Poe's story to the Poe-English feud.

D49 ——. "A Check-List of Edgar Allan Poe's Works in Book
Form Published in the British Isles." *BB,* XXI (May–Aug. 1953), 16–
20.

D50 ——. "Poe in Drama, Fiction, and Poetry: A Bibliography."
BB, XXI (Dec. 1954), 107–14.
Lists creative works in which Poe has appeared as a character or
which eulogize, criticize, or have been dedicated to him.

D51 ——. "Poe's Libel Suit against T. D. English." *BPLQ,* V (Jan.
1953), 31–37.
Poe, in spite of advice from friends, was determined to win his case.

D52 ——. "The War of the Literati: Documents of the Legal
Phase." *N&Q,* CXCVIII (July 1953), 303–8.
An account of Poe's legal case against Thomas Dunn English and
the *New-York Mirror.*

D53 ——. "Willis and Morris Add a Partner—and Poe." *N&Q,*
CXCVIII (June 1953), 253–54.

D54 ——. "The Word 'Tintinnabulation' and a Source for Poe's
'The Bells.' " *N&Q,* CXCVI (Nov. 1951), 520–21.
"Mirabilia Exempla, No. IV," by "A Gentleman" in Burton's
Gentleman's Magazine (April 1838), is a possible source.

D55 deFord, Miriam Allen. "Cherry-Tree Legend." *AN&Q,* I (Aug.
1941), 69.
An apocryphal legend about Virginia's having a hemorrhage after
catching cherries Poe was throwing down from a tree.

D56 De La Mare, Walter J. *Private View.* London: Faber & Faber,
1953.
Author's essay on Poe (pp. 194–200) first appeared in the *TSL*
(Jan. 14, 1909).

D57   DeMille, George E. "Poe." *Literary Criticism in America.* New York: Dial Press, 1931, pp. 86–117.

Poe "formulated, earlier than any other American critic, a consistent and comprehensible theory of criticism." Reprinted New York: Russell and Russell, 1967.

D58   ——. "Poe as a Critic." *American Mercury,* IV (April 1925), 433–40.

Poe was the first critic of the nineteenth century to formulate a consistent and comprehensible theory of criticism. Reprinted in *Readings from the American Mercury,* ed. G. C. Knight (New York: Knopf, 1926), pp. 106–24.

D59   Derby, James Cephas. *Fifty Years among Authors, Books, and Publishers.* Hartford: Winter and Hatch, 1886.

Passing references to Poe.

D60   Derleth, August W. *H. P. L.: A Memoir.* New York: B. Abramson, 1945.

H. P. Lovecraft's affinity with Poe, *passim.*

D61   Deshler, Charles D. *Afternoons with the Poets.* New York: Harper and Brothers, 1879.

None "of Poe's sonnets are specially noteworthy"; see pp. 307–8.

D62   DeTernant, Andrew. "Edgar Allan Poe and Alexandre Dumas." *N&Q,* CLVII (Dec. 28, 1929), 456.

Declares that the alleged Poe visit to France was not unknown in French literary circles.

D63   Dick, Kay. "Introduction." *Edgar Allan Poe: Bizarre and Arabesque, a New Anthology of Tales, Poems, and Prose.* London: Panther Books, 1967, pp. 13–16.

Emphasizes the variety and range of Poe's work.

D64   Didier, Eugene L. "Account from Baltimore of Monument to Be Erected over Poe's Grave." *Appleton's Jour,* XIII (May 15, 1875), 629.

D65   ——. "The Boyhood of Edgar Allan Poe." *No Name Mag,* III, No. 4 (Jan. 1892), 57–58.

A repetition of the usual details. Reprinted in Didier's *The Poe Cult, and Other Poe Papers* (1909), pp. 96–101.

D66   ——. "Edgar Allan Poe in Society." *Bookman,* XXVIII (Jan. 1909), 455–60.

Discusses Poe's movements in the social world of his time. Reprinted in Didier's *The Poe Cult and Other Poe Papers* (1909), pp. 241–51.

D67   ——. "The Grave of Poe." *Appleton's Jour,* VII (Jan. 27, 1872), 104.

Comments on Poe's grave, life, and death. Reprinted in Didier's *The Poe Cult, and Other Poe Papers* (1909), pp. 180–83.

D68 ———. "Life of Edgar Poe." *The Life and Poems of Edgar Allan Poe.* New York: W. J. Widdleton, 1877, pp. 19–129.

Factual and a very laudatory essay on Poe's life. Revised edition in 1879 has an introductory letter by Sarah Helen Whitman, pp. 1–20.
Reviewed:
Civil Service Rev, Feb. 17, 1877, pp. 161–62.
Mag of American History, I (1877), 770.

D69 ———. "The Poe Cult." *Bookman,* XVI (Dec. 1902), 336–40.
Discusses the rising interest in Poe since his death in 1849.

D70 ———. *The Poe Cult, and Other Poe Papers.* New York: Broadway Publishing, 1909.

A collection of essays on a variety of subjects relating to Poe's life. Reprinted Ann Arbor, Mich.: University Microfilms, 1967. The title paper "The Poe Cult" was first printed in *Bookman,* XVI (Dec. 1902), 336–40.
Reviewed:
Baltimore *Evening Sun,* June 27, 1902, p. 27.

D71 ———. "Poe: Real and Reputed." *Godey's Mag,* CXXVIII (April 1894), 452–55.

Defends Poe's moral and spiritual character against the implications of Griswold, "self-chosen biographer of Poe."

D72 ———. "Poe's Female Friends." *Chatauquan,* XV (Sept. 1892), 723–29.

Poe's relations with Mrs. Allan, Jane Craig Stanard, Virginia Clemm, Mrs. Osgood, Mrs. Shew, Mrs. Lewis, and Mrs. Whitman are summarily discussed. Reprinted in Didier's *The Poe Cult, and Other Poe Papers* (1909), pp. 102–16.

D73 ———. "Poe's Two Funerals." *Book-Lover,* III (Jan.–Feb. 1903), 543–44.

An account of the unveiling of the monument in Baltimore.

D74 ———. "Portraits of Poe." *Literary World,* XVI (March 7, 1885), 81–83.

A brief discussion of the various portraits. Reprinted in Didier's *The Poe Cult, and Other Poe Papers* (1909), pp. 191–202.

D75 ———. "Recent Biographies of Edgar A. Poe." *International Rev,* X (Jan. 1881), 26–36.

Some commentary on the biographies of Ingram and Gill. Reprinted in Didier's *The Poe Cult, and Other Poe Papers* (1909), pp. 150–74.

D76 ——. "The Truth about Edgar A. Poe." *Book-Lover,* IV (March–April 1903), 1–9.

Statements concerning Poe's character made by contemporaries who knew Poe. Reprinted in Didier's *The Poe Cult, and Other Poe Papers* (1909), pp. 216–40.

D77 Dietz, Frieda Meredith. "Poe's First and Final Love." *SLM,* V (March 1943), 38–47.

On Elmira Royster Shelton.

D78 ——. "Poe's 'Mysterious Year.'" *Commonwealth* (Mag. of Va.), VIII (Sept. 1941), 11–12, 23.

D79 ——. "Return of Edgar Allan Poe." *SLM,* III (Aug. 1941), 365–66.

Believes that Poe's restless spirit is guiding the mind of Mrs. Diana Pittman [Quarles] to a revelation of some of his mysteries.

D80 Dillon, John M. *Edgar Allan Poe, His Genius and Character.* New York: Knickerbocker, 1911.

An "outline of some of the events which played so conspicuous a part in an unhappy life" of a "wretched man" having "extraordinary talents."

D81 Dimmock, Thomas. "Notes on Poe." *Century Mag,* NS XXVIII (June 1895), 315–16.

Comments on the Traylor daguerrotype and quotes from a conversation with John R. Thompson about Poe's relations with the *Southern Literary Messenger.*

D82 ——. "Wizard of Poetry." Baltimore *American,* Feb. 9, 1896, p. 18.

Poe receives tardy honor.

D83 Diskin, Patrick. "Poe, Le Fanu, and the Sealed Room Mystery." *N&Q,* CCXI (Sept. 1966), 337–39.

Points out parallels between "The Murders in the Rue Morgue" and a story by Le Fanu, appearing in the *Dublin University Magazine.*

D84 Dixon, Jeannie B. "Poe: A Borrowing from Goldsmith." *N&Q,* CLXIII (Nov. 12, 1932), 350.

The situation of "The Visionary" (or "The Assignation") is from Goldsmith's *Vicar of Wakefield,* chapter 23, paragraph 2.

D85 Dobie, Armistead Mason. "Is 'The Raven' the Most Original Production in American Literature." *UVaMag,* LX (Nov. 1899), 118–25.

"By reason of its originality, 'The Raven' is probably the most widely read American lyric."

D86 Dodd, Evelyn Baker. "The Real Edgar Allan Poe." *Methodist Quarterly Rev,* LXX (July 1921), 451–57.
Blames Poe's actions on heredity, declaring, however, that his nature was chaste but that he lacked "the omnipotent Christian graces."

D87 Doherty, Edward. "The Spectacles: The Lost Short Story by Edgar Allan Poe." *Liberty,* XV (Sept. 24, 1938), 12–14.
A reprint, with an introduction, of a short story which Richard Gimbel found in an unnamed American periodical.

D88 Dole, Nathan H. "Biographical Sketch." *Poems of Edgar Allan Poe.* New York: Thomas Y. Crowell, 1892, pp. 9–29.
Tends to melodramatize Poe's life.

D89 ———. "Introduction: The Life of Edgar Allan Poe." *The Complete Works of Edgar Allan Poe.* 10 vols. Akron, Ohio: Werner Co., 1908, I, [1–38].
Poe's life was distressful, but the world has recognized his transcendent genius.

D90 Dolson, Eugene C. "A Foote [*sic*] Note on Poe." *New England Mag,* NS XXV (Sept. 1906), 79–80.
Presents the first version of "The Bells" (*Sartain's,* 1849).

*D91 Dorset, Gerald. *An Aristocrat of Intellect.* London: n.p., 1959.

D92 ———. *An Aristocrat of Intellect.* New York: Haskell House, 1966.
Points to certain works by Poe that reflect a "suffering soul" and a "unique poet and short story writer." First printed London: n.p., 1959.

D93 Doten, Elizabeth. *Poems from the Inner Life.* Boston: W. White, 1864.
Poems written by "Lizzie" Doten while under the influence of several poets' spirits, including Poe.

D94 Douglas, Norman. "Edgar Allan Poe." *Experiments.* New York: Robert M. McBride, 1925, pp. 106–19.
Argues that Poe's life and works have been often misunderstood and presents a generally favorable judgment of Poe's contribution to literature.

D95 ———. "Edgar Allan Poe." *The Spectator,* CII (Jan. 23, 1909), 122–23.
Poe's versatile accomplishments as an artist.

D96 ———. "Edgar Allan Poe from an English Point of View." *Putnam's Monthly and the Reader,* V (Jan. 1909), 433–38.
Emphasizes Poe's part in the making of American literature and comments on Poe's style and "intellectual strivings."

*D97   Douglas-Lithgow, Robert Alexander. *The Individuality of Edgar Allan Poe.* Boston: Everett Publishing, 1911.

D98   ——. "Poe's Place in American Literary History." *Massachusetts Mag,* IV (April 1911), 75–81.
Claims that Poe is "the supremest genius which has shown over American fields" and is entitled to the "highest praise in the Literary History of his country."

D99   Dow, Dorothy. *Dark Glory.* New York: Farrar and Rinehart, 1931.
A romanticized biography which is designed to be read rather as fiction than as scholarship.

D100   Dowdey, Clifford. "Poe's Last Visit to Richmond." *AH,* VII (April 1956), 22–25, 96–97.
"Brief summary of Poe's last days." *AL.*

D101   Doxey, William S. "Concerning Fortunato's 'Courtesy.'" *SSF,* IV (Spring 1967), 266.
On Poe's "The Cask of Amontillado."

D102   [Doyle, Sir Arthur Conan, ed.] *The Edgar Allan Poe Shrine, the Old Stone House, Richmond, Virginia.* [Richmond, Va. ?, 1923.]
Presents brief appraisals of Poe by A. C. Doyle, George Woodbury, and others. Appears also in New York *World,* Jan. 21, 1923.

D103   Dredd, Firmin. "Poe and Secret Writing." *Bookman,* XXVIII (Jan. 1909), 450–51.
An informal article on Poe's skill as a cryptographer.

D104   The Drexel Institute of Technology. *The Murders in the Rue Morgue.* Facsimile of the Ms. in the Drexel Institute. Philadelphia: G. Barrie, 1895.
Also contains an autograph letter of Poe to his publishers, Lea and Blanchard of Philadelphia, dated "August 13/41."

D105   DuBois, Arthur E. "The Jazz Bells of Poe." *CE,* II (Dec. 1940), 230–44.
In "The Bells" Poe came nearest to achieving an organic flow expressive of his meaning or mood.

D106   ——. "Poe and *Lolita.*" *CEA,* XXVI (March 1964), vi, 1, 7.
Nabokov's *Lolita* "should be added to the bibliography of reflections about Poe."

D107   Du Bos, Charles. "VI.—Poe and the French Mind." *Athenaeum,* No. 4732 (Jan. 7, 14, 1921), pp. 26–27, 54–55.
On what Poe had in common with French artists.

D108   Dudley, Fred A. "*Tintinnabulation:* And a Source of Poe's 'The Bells.'" *AL,* IV (Nov. 1932), 296–300.

Maintains that Poe "probably encountered at intervals various derivations of a sounding and not uncommon Latin word which he may well have known as a schoolboy."

D109   Duffy, Charles. "Poe's Mother-in-Law: Two Letters to Bayard Taylor." *AN&Q,* II (Jan. 1943), 148.

"Two begging letters—in the Cornell University Library—written by Maria Clemm to Bayard Taylor [in 1850 and 1859] bear out the portrait of her drawn by Arthur Hobson Quinn in his recent life of Poe." *AL.*

D110   Dugdale, Jennie Bard. "The Grave of Edgar Allan Poe." *Poet-Lore,* XI (1899), 583–88.

Some comments on Poe's artistic character.

D111   Duke, Thomas S. *Celebrated Criminal Cases of America.* San Francisco: James H. Barry, 1910.

On the murder of Mary Rogers, pp. 577–82.

D112   Dumas, A. [Account of a Visit by Poe to Paris.] *SatRL,* VI (Dec. 21, 1929), 594–95.

Describes the finding of a manuscript purported to be Dumas's with a description of Poe's visit to Paris in 1832.

D113   Dunlop, G. B. "A Poe Story." *TLS,* Jan. 15, 1944, p. 36.

On an English edition of *Pym* published by Wiley and Putnam in 1838—"the first English edition of any work by Poe."

D114   DuPont, P. F. "To the Memory of E. A. Poe." *UVaMag,* LXIX (Jan. 1909), 227.

Verse.

D115   Durham, Frank M. "A Possible Relationship between Poe's 'To Helen' and Milton's *Paradise Lost,* Book IV." *AL,* XVI (Jan. 1945), 340–43.

"Only in Milton are possible sources for all three epithets ('Nicean barks,' 'perfumed sea,' and 'hyacinth hair') found together in two passages of less than 150 lines." *AL.*

D116   Durick, Jeremiah K. "The Incorporate Silence and the Heart Divine." *American Classics Reconsidered.* Ed. H. C. Gardiner. New York: Charles Scribner's Sons, 1958, pp. 176–92.

Critic emphasizes Poe's dual role as journalist and dedicated artist and argues that much opinion about Poe is legendary.

D117   [Du Solle, J. Stephenson.] [Edgar A. Poe.] Philadelphia *Spirit of the Times,* Jan. 8, 1847, p. 2.

Comments on Poe's gall to withstand his enemies.

D118   Duyckinck, Evert A. [Review of] *Poe's Works* [Griswold's two-volume edition]. *Literary World,* VI (Jan. 26, 1850), 81.

Poe "lacks reality, imagination, every-day power, but he is remark-
ably subtle, acute, and earnest in his own way." Reprinted in Eric
Carlson, ed., *The Recognition of Edgar Allan Poe* (Ann Arbor:
University of Michigan Press, 1966), pp. 41–43.

D119   ———. [Review of *The Literati.*] *Literary World,* VII (Sept.
26, 1850), 228–29.

Comments on the Griswold memoir and asks pertinent questions
about Griswold's editorship.

D120   ———, and George A. Duyckinck. *Cyclopedia of American
Literature.* New York: Scribner, 1856.

As a critic, Poe had much perception but he lacked sincerity; in
"ingenuity of invention, musical effects, and artificial terrors for the
imagination, his poems as well as his prose sketches are remarkable";
see II, 536–45.

D121   Dyson, Arthur T. *An Appeal for the Preservation of the Edgar
Allan Poe Cottage in Fordham, New York City.* New York: The
author, 1915.

A three-page commentary with a brief commentary by Pendennis in
the New York *Times,* Aug. 20, 1905, on Poe in New York.

E

E1   E., G. W. [Eveleth, George W.]. [Note on "Marie Rogêt."]
Round Table, V (Jan. 26, 1867), 62.

On the conclusion of "The Mystery of Marie Rogêt."

E1a   E., P. A. "Stevenson and Poe." *N&Q,* CLXXXV (Dec. 1943),
367–68.

A commentary on Stevenson's review (1875) of Poe's tales.

E2   Eastman, Max F. "American Ideals of Poetry: A Preface." *Colors
of Life.* New York: Alfred A. Knopf, 1918, pp. 13–39.

An essay on Whitman and Poe as the "two strongest influences in all
modern poetry of the occident."

E3   Eaton, Margaret A. "Introduction." *The Poetical Works of Edgar
Allen* [sic] *Poe Together with His Essay on the Philosophy of Composition.* New York: Educational Publishing, 1906, pp. 5–8.

Poe possessed a poetic genius that "neither temperament nor adverse
circumstances could dim."

E4 ——. Poe's Tales: Selected for Use in Schools, with Introduction and Notes. . . . Boston: Educational Publishing, 1906.

E5 Eaves, T. C. Duncan. "Poe's Last Visit to Philadelphia." *AL,* XXVI (March 1954), 44–51.

An attempt to determine what Poe did and what happened to him during his last visit to Philadelphia in the summer of 1849.

E6 Eby, Edwin Harold. "American Romantic Criticism, 1815 to 1860." Diss., Univ. of Washington, 1927. Abstracted in the *Univ. of Washington Publication,* I (Dec. 1931), 131–34.

See chap. 4: "Richmond and Edgar Allan Poe."

E7 The Edgar Allan Poe Memorial Association. *Edgar Allan Poe: A Centenary Tribute.* Ed. Heinrich Ewald Buchholz. Baltimore: For the Association by Warwick and York, 1910.

Contains "Westminster Churchyard" (verse) by Lizette Woodworth Reese; "The Centenary of Poe" by W. P. Trent; "The Unique Genius of Poe's Poetry" by Oliver Huckel; "The Personality of Poe" by John P. Poe; and "The Life of Poe . . . from the Testimony of His Friends" by Mrs. John C. Wrenshall.

E8 Edgerton, Kathleen. "The Lecturing of Edgar Allan Poe." *Southern Speech Jour,* XXVIII (Summer 1963), 268–73.

As a lecturer, Poe generally pleased both audiences and critics.

E9 Edmunds, A. J. "German Translations of Poe's 'Raven.' " *N&Q,* CLXXIV (Feb. 5, 1938), 106.

In *Vier Americanische Gedichte* (Philadelphia, 1864), there is a German translation of "The Raven."

E10 Edward, Georg. "Poe in Germany." *UVaAB,* 3rd ser., II (April 1909), 170–83.

"Extracts from an address delivered in Madison Hall, January 19, 1909." Also printed in Charles William Kent and John S. Patton, eds., *The Book of the Poe Centenary* (Charlottesville, Va.: Michie, 1909), pp. 73–99.

E11 Eliot, Thomas Stearns. "American Literature and the American Language." *Washington University Studies,* New Series in Language and Literature, No. 23 (1953), pp. 3–24.

Poe, Whitman, and Twain are chosen as characteristic American writers of the nineteenth century.

E12 ——. "Foreword." *Symbolisme from Poe to Mallarmé: The Growth of a Myth,* by Joseph Chiari. London: Rockliff, 1956, pp. v–viii.

"If the influence of Poe upon Baudelaire, Mallarmé, and Valéry was based upon misunderstanding, it was a fecund and significant misunderstanding."

E13   ——. "From Poe to Valéry." *HudR,* II (Aug. 1949), 327–43.
Traces the development and descent of one particular theory of the
nature of poetry—an emphasis upon "introspective critical activity"—
through Baudelaire, Mallarmé, and Paul Valéry. First published New
York: Harcourt Brace, 1948. Also appears in Morton D. Zabel's
Literary Opinion in America (New York: Harpers, 1951), pp. 628–
38; in S. Ratner's *Vision and Action* (New Brunswick, N.J.: Rutgers
University Press, 1953), pp. 167–83; and in Eric Carlson, ed., *The
Recognition of Edgar Allan Poe* (Ann Arbor: University of Michigan
Press, 1966), pp. 205–19.

E14   Ellington, John James. "Edgar Allan Poe, A Monody."
UVaMag, LXIX (Jan. 1909), 240–41.
Verse.

E15   Elliot, William, Jr. "History of the Movement." *Poems and
Essays of Edgar Allan Poe.* New York: W. J. Widdleton, 1876, pp.
cxxix–cxxxi.
Comments on the actions resulting in a monument dedicated to Poe
in Baltimore.

E16   Elliott, William Young. "Virginia to Poe." *Verse Craft,* II
(Nov.–Dec. 1932), 7.
Verse.

E17   Ellis, Thomas H. "Edgar Allan Poe." Richmond *Standard,*
May 7, 1881, p. [2].
The relationship between Poe and Mrs. Louisa Allan (the second
Mrs. Allan).

E18   Elwell, T. E. "A Poe Story." *TLS,* Oct. 23, 1943, p. 516.
An English print of *Pym* in the *Novel Newspaper* (No. 145 and
Supplement) in 1841.

E19   Emerson, Joyce. "Introduction." *Edgar Allan Poe: The Murders
in the Rue Morgue; Raven.* London: Centaur, 1946, pp. 3–11.
A general appraisal.

E20   Englekirk, John E., Jr. "A Critical Study of Two Tales by
Amado Nervo." *NMQ,* II (Feb. 1932), 53–65.
The influence of Poe on Amado Nervo (1870–1919) is discussed.

E21   ——. *Edgar Allan Poe in Hispanic Literature.* New York:
Instituto de las Españas en los Estados Unidos, 1934.
Poe's "greatest influence upon Hispanic letters coincides with the
appearance of those revolutionary esthetics" of the closing decades
of the nineteenth century.
Reviewed:
C. F. Fraker, *NMQ,* IV, 248–50.

E22 ——. "Edgar Allan Poe in Hispanic Literature." Diss., Columbia University, 1934.

E23 ——. " 'My Nightmare': The Last Tale by Poe." *PMLA,* LII (June 1937), 511–27.
The author of the Mexican hoax "Mi Pesadilla" is Francisco Zárate Ruiz. Also contains Englekirk's bibliography of Mexican versions and criticisms of Poe.

E24 ——. " 'The Raven' in Spanish America." *Spanish Rev,* I (Nov. 1934), 52–56.
Nineteen translations and many critical studies of "The Raven" have appeared in Spanish America.

E25 ——. " 'The Song of Hollands,' An Unedited Tale Ascribed to Poe." *NMQ,* I (Aug. 1931), 247–69.
Evidence that the hoax was the work of Aurélian Scholl, a French journalist.

E26 English, Thomas Dunn. "He Is Tired of Trilby." *Washington Post,* March 10, 1895, p. 15.
Informal reminiscences of Poe.

E27 ——. [Letter to W. M. Griswold, Jan. 10, 1895.] *Nation,* LX (May 16, 1895), 382.
The letter declares that "in morals . . . [Poe] was an idiot."

E28 ——. "Reminiscences of Poe." *Independent,* XLVIII (Oct. 15, 22, 29, Nov. 5, 1896), 1381–82, 1415–16, 1448, 1480–81.
Poe in relation to English and other literary figures.

E29 ——. [Review of the *Tales.*] *The Aristidean,* I (Oct. 1845), 316.

E30 Engstrom, Alfred G. "Chateaubriand's *Itinéraire de Paris à Jerusalem* and Poe's 'The Assignation.' " *MLN,* LXIX (Nov. 1954), 506–07.
A Poe allusion reveals a remarkable familiarity with Chateaubriand's text.

E31 ——. "Poe, Leconte de Lisle, and Tzara's Formula for Poetry." *MLN,* LXXIII (June 1958), 434–36.
Poe and Dadaism.

E32 Erskine, John. [Poem on Poe.] *Columbia University Quarterly,* XI (March 1909), 233–34.
Printed in the *Quarterly* in connection with a reporting of the celebration of the centennial at Columbia University. Reprinted in *Muse Anthology of Modern Poetry,* ed. Dorothy Kissling and Arthur H. Nethercot, Poe Memorial Edition (New York: Carlyle Straub, 1938), pp. 176–77.

E33   Eshleman, Lloyd W. "Mr. Huxley and 'Vulgarity.'" *SatRL,* VII (Oct. 25, 1930), 276.

E34   Evans, Henry R. *Edgar Allan Poe and Baron von Kempelen's Chess-Playing Automaton.* Kenyon, Ohio: International Brotherhood of Magicians, 1939.

Presents more information about the mechanism of the chess-playing automaton. In "Introduction," pp. 9–11, Poe is credited with solving the "secret of the so-called automaton."

Reviewed:

D. K. Jackson, *AL,* XII, 395.

E35   Evans, May Garrettson. "Facts about Mistake in Marking Original Burial Place of Poe." Baltimore *Evening Sun,* Aug. 1, 1920, sec. IV, pp. 2–3.

Concerning a mistake in the marking of Poe's burial place.

E36   ——. *Music and Edgar Allan Poe: A Bibliographical Study.* Baltimore: Johns Hopkins Press, 1939.

A discussion and listing of Poe-inspired compositions.

Reviewed:

D. K. Jackson, *AL,* II, 476.

E37   ——. "Poe in Amity Street." *MHM,* XXXVI (Dec. 1941), 363–80.

The housing authority spared a house at 203 North Amity St., Baltimore, after the Poe Society had presented proof that Poe had lived there between 1832 and 1835.

E38   ——. "When Edgar Allan Poe Sold a Slave." Baltimore *Evening Sun,* April 6, 1940, p. 4.

Poe's part in assigning a slave.

E39   Evans, Oliver. "Infernal Illumination in Poe." *MLN,* LXXV (April 1960), 295–97.

Poe exploited infernal illumination "as a dramatic device to heighten the atmosphere of horror and supernaturalism."

E40   [Eveleth, George Washington.] [Editorial on E. C. Stedman's "Elements in the Art of Poetry" with a Comment on Poe.] *Old Guard* (New York), IV (Nov. 1866), 672–78.

Poe is mentioned in connection with certain poetical theories.

E41   ——. "Poe and His Biographer, Griswold." *Old Guard* (New York), IV (June 1866), 353–58.

Critics are cited to contradict Griswold.

E42   Ewers, Hanns Heinz. *Edgar Allan Poe.* Trans. from the German by Adele Lewisohn. New York: B. W. Huebsch, 1917.

Expresses a strong affinity with Poe. Originally appeared in *Die*

Dichtung (Berlin), XLII (1905).
    Reviewed:
H. B. Fuller, *Dial,* LXII (May 17, 1917), 433–34.

E43   Exman, Eugene. *The Brothers Harper: A Unique Publishing Partnership and Its Impact upon the Cultural Life of America from 1817 to 1853.* New York: Harper and Row, 1965.
    Poe is mentioned frequently.

F

F1   Fadiman, Clifton. "An Afterword." *Tales and Poems of Edgar Allan Poe.* New York: Macmillan, 1963, pp. [337–38].
    Poe "is best read at night."

F2   Fagin, N. Bryllion. "Edgar Allan Poe." *SAQ,* LI (April 1952), 276–85.
    A general commentary upon Poe's commendable qualities as poet, storyteller, and critic.

F3   ———. *The Histrionic Mr. Poe.* Baltimore: Johns Hopkins Press, 1949.
    Poe's literary work was to a remarkable extent an expression of a histrionic impulse.
    Reviewed:
M. L. William, *AL,* XXII, 198–200.
Richard Wilbur, *NEQ,* XXIII, 121–23.
T. O. Mabbott, *MLN,* LXV, 209–10.
Joseph W. Krutch, *New York Herald-Tribune Books* (July 31, 1950), p. 3.

F4   ———. "Poe—Drama Critic." *Theatre Annual* (1946), 23–28.
    Poe is modern in that he advocated "realistic drama, containing plausible plots and presenting characters that are recognizable human beings."

F5   Fairchild, Lee. "Tributes." *Open Court,* I (Dec. 22, 1887), 641.

F6   [Fairfield, Francis Gerry.] "A Mad Man of Letters." *Scribner's Monthly,* X (Oct. 1875), 690–99.
    Declares that Poe was a victim of "cerebral epilepsy."

F7   Falk, Robert P., ed. "The Decline and Fall of the House of Usher." *American Literature in Parody.* New York: Twayne, 1955, pp. 105–25.

Parodies of Poe along with quoted passages from Aldous Huxley's
"The Vulgarity of Poe."

F8   Farrar, John. "A New Poe." *Bookman,* LXII (Dec. 1925), 502.
Compliments Mrs. Stanard's edition of the Valentine letters.

F9   Faust, Bertha. *Hawthorne's Contemporaneous Reputation.* Phil-
adelphia: Privately printed, 1939.
See especially pp. 56–59 for commentary on Poe's criticism of
Hawthorne. Originally a dissertation, University of Pennsylvania.
Reviewed:
R. Stewart, *AL,* XII, 373–74.

F10   Fawcett, Edgar. "Poe as a Poet." *Literary World,* XIII (Nov. 25,
1882), 96–97.
Poe "was inflamed with the ambition to be poetic and the craze to
be eccentric."

F11   Fehrman, Carl. "The Moment of Creation." *Orbis Litterarum*
(Copenhagen), XXII (1967), 13–23.
Poe's aim in "The Philosophy of Composition" was to "de-roman-
ticise the process of poetic creation, to expose it to investigation";
see pp. 17–20.

F12   Feidelson, Charles. *Symbolism and American Literature.* Chicago: University of Chicago Press, 1957.
Traces symbolism as a point of view through the central work of
Poe, Hawthorne, Whitman, and Melville. See pp. 35–42 for a
discussion of Poe.

F13   Felheim, Marvin. "The Cask of Amontillado." *N&Q,* CXCIX
(Oct. 1954), 447–48.
"Montresor's revenge succeeds." *AL.*

F14   Ferguson, John D. "Charles Hine and His Portrait of Poe."
AL, III (Jan. 1932), 465–70.
Declares that the Hine portrait was painted from a daguerrotype lent
him by Mrs. Whitman (1852).

F15   ———. "Edgar Allan Poe['s Influence in Spain]." *American
Literature in Spain.* New York: Columbia University Press, 1916.
See pp. 55–86, 229–36. Originally a Ph.D. diss., Columbia Univer-
sity, 1916.

F16   Fiedler, Leslie A. "American Literature." *Contemporary Literary
Scholarship: A Critical View.* Ed. Lewis Leary. New York: Appleton-
Century-Crofts, 1958.
See pp. 171–73 for a brief discussion of recent Poe criticism.

F17   ———. "Blackness of Darkness: E. A. Poe and the Development
of the Gothic." *Love and Death in the American Novel.* New York:
Criterion Books, 1960, pp. 370–414.

In his longer prose compositions (*Pym* and *Julius Rodman*) Poe fails to "transform the gothic into the tragic."

F18 ———. "Edgar Allan Poe and the Invention of the American Writer." *ChiR,* XIII (Winter 1959), 80–86.
Poe as an image of failure and impotence appeals to Americans living in a world of success and power.

F19 Field, Eugene. *Some Letters of Edgar Allan Poe to E. H. N. Patterson of Oquawka, Illinois, with Comments by Eugene Field.* Chicago: The Caxton Club, 1898.
Facsimiles of six Poe manuscripts are presented along with a reprint from *America* of Eugene Field's article entitled "Poe, Patterson, and Oquawka," II (April 11 and May 16, 1889), 45–50, 208–10.

F20 Finton, Margaret. "Our Charity." *Muse Anthology of Modern Poetry.* Ed. Dorothy Kissling and Arthur H. Nethercot. Poe Memorial Edition. New York: Carlyle Straub, 1932, p. 194.
Verse.

F21 Fisher, Mary. "Edgar Allan Poe (1809–1849)," *A General Survey of American Literature.* Chicago: A. C. McClurg, 1899, pp. 231–59.
Poe has genius of a narrow range, "and within that range morbid and analytic rather than sound and creative."

F22 Fisher, R. B. "Immortality in Reverse." *Coronet,* CLXXII (Summer 1949), 165.

F23 Fitch, George Hamlin. "Art of Edgar Allan Poe." *Great Spiritual Writers of America.* San Francisco: Paul Elder, 1916, pp. 28–36.
"Poe had the greatest genius for literary form of any American writer."

F24 Flanagan, Thomas. "The Life and Early Death of the Detective Story." *Columbia University Forum,* I (Winter 1957), 7–10.
Emphasis upon sensationalism rather than the logical solution of a mystery has largely effected an end to the "classic" form of the detective story.

F25 Fletcher, J. B. "Poe, Hawthorne, and Morality." *Harvard Monthly,* III (Feb. 1887), 176–81.
Hawthorne's writings, compared with Poe's, reflect more concern with ethical principles.

F26 Fletcher, John Gould. "Edgar Allan Poe." *Selected Poems* [by Poe]. New York: Simon & Schuster, 1926, pp. [5–6].
Poe had a "keen and just" musical sense, and completely "observed the limitations of his own medium."

F27 ———. "Foreword." *Muse Anthology of Modern Poetry.* Ed.

Dorothy Kissling and Arthur H. Nethercot. Poe Memorial Edition. New York: Carlyle Straub, 1938, pp. 17–28.

Admires Poe's works of symbolism such as "Ulalume," "Silence," and "The Masque of the Red Death" and terms *Eureka* a "perfect symbolist philosophical fantasy."

F28   Flickinger, Roy C. "Poe's 'To Helen' Once More." *CJ,* XXIX (April 1934), 540.

On Poe's "Nicean barks."

F29   Flower, Gurtrude. "Edgar Allan Poe." *Poetical Works of Coleridge, Poe, and Rossetti.* Ed. Gurtrude Flower, New York: Clover Press, 1910, pp. 85–86.

Excerpts from Charles F. Richardson's essay in the Arnheim Edition of Poe.

F30   Flower, Newman. "Most Interesting Sinner in Literature." *World Rev,* V (Jan. 16, 1928), 250.

F31   ———. "Three Interesting Sinners." *Bookman,* LXIV (Oct. 1926), 148–55.

The unholy three are Poe, Wilde, and Ernest Dowson.

F32   ———. "Two Interesting Sinners." *Bookman* (London), LXXI (Oct. 1926), 16–18.

Presents part of the American *Bookman* article, LXIV (Oct. 1926), 148–55.

F33   Foerster, Norman. *American Criticism: A Study in Theory from Poe to the Present.* New York: Houghton Mifflin, 1928.

Poe as a critic is fully discussed as to philosophical background and as to his attempt to work out the implication of the movement to which he belonged; see pp. 1–51 *et passim.*

F34   ———. *The Chief American Prose Writers.* Boston: Houghton Mifflin, 1916.

Includes selections of Poe's criticism and tales, pp. 131–74. Revised edition appeared in 1931.

F35   ———. "Quantity and Quality in the Aesthetic of Poe." *SP,* XX (July 1923), 310–335.

Censures Poe's romantic doctrine of the indefinite, which encourages an aimless order, premature harmony and the illusion of unreality.

F36   ———, ed. "Introduction." *American Critical Essays, XIXth and XXth Centuries.* London: H. Milford. Oxford University Press, 1930, pp. vii–xii.

Poe was the first critic of distinction during the 1830's and 1840's. Contains Poe's "The Poetic Principle" (pp. 1–28) and W. C. Brownell's "Poe" from *American Prose Masters* (pp. 235–92).

F37   Foley, P. K. "Edgar Allan Poe." *American Authors, 1795–1895.* Boston: Printed for subscribers, 1897, pp. 230–32.
A brief bibliography of first and notable editions of Poe.

F38   Foote, Dorothy Norris. "Poe's 'The Cask of Amontillado.' " *Expl,* XX (Nov. 1961), item 27.
Montresor's revenge is unsatisfying because he did not explain to Fortunato the reasons for the grudge.

F39   Foote, Henry Wilder. "Poe's 'Silence.' " *Nation,* XC (Jan. 20, 1910), 62.
Hood is the author of a sonnet heretofore attributed to Poe.

F40   Forbes, E. A. "Poe and the University of Virginia." *Dial,* XXXIII (Aug. 16, 1902), 85–86.
Reprinted in *Book-Lover,* III (Nov.–Dec. 1902), 457.

F41   Fornelli, Guido. "Edgar Allan Poe." *Four American Writers: Longfellow, Whitman, Emerson, Poe.* Livorno: Raffaello Guisti, 1926, pp. 9–13.
Appreciative commentary followed by selections of Poe in English with notes in Italian.

F42   Forrest, William Mentzel. *Biblical Allusions in Poe.* New York: Macmillan, 1928.
Poe's compositions reveal his knowledge of the Bible, his versatility, and his technical skill.
    Reviewed:
T. O. Mabbott, *AL,* I, 104–5.

F43   ———. "Edgar Allan Poe among the Prophets." *UVaAB,* 3rd ser., XVII (April, July 1924), 163–77, 326–35.
Discusses Poe's affinity with the Hebraic prophets.

F44   Forster, John. "American Poetry." *Foreign Quarterly Rev,* XXXII (Jan. 1844), 291–324.
Poe is "a capital artist after the manner of Tennyson, and approaches the spirit of his original more closely" than any of Tennyson's followers; see pp. 321–22.

F45   Forsythe, Robert S. "Poe's 'Nevermore': A Note." *AL,* VII (Jan. 1936), 439–52.
The word is a poetic commonplace.

F46   Fortier, Alcée. "Poe in France." *UVaAB,* 3rd ser., II (April 1909), 161–70.
Concerned with the work of E. D. Forgues, Mme. Gabrielle Meunier, Baudelaire, Gautier, Arvède Barine, Lauvrière, and with the influence of Poe on French writers.

F47   Fossum, Robert H. "Poe's 'The Cask of Amontillado.' " *Expl,*
XVII (Nov. 1958), Item 16.
One element of irony is Montresor's deranged state of mind.

*F48   Foster, Edward F. *A Study of Grim Humor in the Works of Poe,
Melville, and Twain.* Ann Arbor, Mich.: University Microfilms, 1957.

F49   ———. "A Study of Grim Humor in the Works of Poe, Melville, and Twain." *DA,* XVII (Aug. 1957), 1761–62.

F50   ———. "A Study of Grim Humor in the Works of Poe, Melville,
and Twain." Diss., Vanderbilt University, 1957.
Poe's "Grim Humor"—primarily European in origin—reflects Poe's
exaggeration in the comic fashion of catastrophes found in narratives typical of contemporary plot and form.

*F51   Fox, Hugh B. *Poe and Cosmology: The God-Universe Relation-
ship in a Romantic Context.* Ann Arbor, Mich.: University Microfilms,
1958.

F52   ———. "Poe and Cosmology: The God-Universe Relationship in
a Romantic Context." *DA,* XIX (July 1958), 138.
Poe's works reflect a curiously ambivalent rebellion to Mechanism
and Deism of the seventeenth and eighteenth centuries.

*F53   ———. "Poe and Cosmology: The God-Universe Relationship
in a Romantic Context." Diss., University of Illinois, 1958.

F54   Fraiberg, Louis. "Joseph Wood Krutch: Poe's Art as an Ab-
normal Condition of the Nerves." *Psychoanalysis and American Literary
Criticism.* Detroit: Wayne State University Press, 1960, pp. 134–44.
Krutch's use of psychoanalysis is questionable.

F55   Frailey, Charles S. [Letter to F. W. Thomas on Poe's Successful
Reading of a Cryptograph.] *Graham's,* XIX (Oct. 1841), 192.

F56   Frank, Waldo David. "Poe at Last." *New Republic,* XLV (Dec.
30, 1925), 163–64.
Comments on Poe's creative genius. Reprinted in author's *In the
American Jungle* (New York: Farrar, 1937), 161–64.

F57   Franklin, Howard Bruce. *Future Perfect: American Science
Fiction of the Nineteenth Century.* New York: Oxford University Press,
1966.
See pp. 93–103 for discussion of Poe's science fiction. Poe's "A Tale
of the Ragged Mountains," "The Facts in the Case of M. Valdemar,"
and "Mellonta Tauta" are included in this collection.

*F58   Frasconi, Antonio. *The Face of Edgar Allan Poe.* With a note
on Poe by Charles Baudelaire. Woodcuts by Frasconi. [South Nor-
walk?] Conn., 1959.
"Other than the woodcuts by Frasconi, the book includes only a 3

page note on Poe by Baudelaire." (Comment by staff member of the New York Public Library.)

F59   Frayne, Anthony J. *The Rose-Covered Cottage of Edgar Allan Poe in Philadelphia.* Philadelphia: Anthony J. Frayne, 1934.
Poe's life in Philadelphia.

F60   Freeman, Fred B., Jr. "The Identity of Poe's 'Miss B.'" *AL,* XXXIX (Nov. 1967), 389–91.
"Miss B"—mentioned in Poe's letter to "Annie" Richmond, dated June 16, 1849—is Eliza J. Butterfield, an assistant in Franklin Grammar School, Lowell, Mass.

F61   Freeman, John. "Edgar Allan Poe." *London Mercury,* XVI (June 1927), 162–69.
A biographical and critical essay on the man, the husband, the innovator in verse, and the master-tale writer.

F62   French, Donald G. "The Poe Poem That Riley Wrote [The Story of the Leonainie Hoax]." *Canadian Bookman,* XIV (April 1932), 46–47.

*****F63**   French, John C. "The Day of Poe's Burial." Baltimore *Sun,* June 3, 1949, p. 14.
"On the basis of weather records, establishes October 8, not October 9, as the day of the burial."

F64   ———. "Poe and *Baltimore Saturday Visiter.*" *MLN,* XXXIII (May 1918), 257–67.
Volume III of the *Visiter* presents firsthand information about Poe's winning the *Visiter* contest and contains one new poem by Poe and two more which he may have written.

F65   ———. "Poe's Literary Baltimore." *MHM,* XXXII (June 1937), 101–12.
A scholarly reconstruction of Poe in the Baltimore of 1831–35.

F66   ———. "Poe's Revision of Marginalia." *Ex Libris, Quarterly Leaflet Issued by Friends of the Library* [at Johns Hopkins], IX (Jan. 1940), 2–3.
Lists Poe's own corrections to the first two installments of "Marginalia."

F67   French, Warren G. "T. S. Arthur: An Unexpected Champion of Poe." *TSL,* V (1960), 35–41.
A leading literary luminary of the nineteenth-century American temperance movement defended Poe.

F68   Frey, Jacob. "In the Roaring Forties." *Reminiscences of Baltimore.* Baltimore: Maryland Book Concern, 1893, pp. 80–101.
See pp. 84–88 for some critical commentary and discussion of testi-

mony with regard to Poe's swimming in the Hudson River and his relationship with his family. On p. 381, Poe's monument in "Westminster Presbyterian church-yard" is briefly mentioned.

F69   Friedman, William F. "Edgar Allan Poe, Cryptographer." *AL,* VIII (Nov. 1936), 266–80.

Poe was "only a dabbler in cryptography."

F70   ——. "Edgar Allan Poe, Cryptographer." *Signal Corps Bulletin,* No. 97 (July–Sept. 1937), pp. 41–53; No. 98 (Oct.–Dec. 1937), pp. 54–75.

A reprinting of the *American Literature* article with additional information and with actual cryptograms.

F71   Frieseke, Frances. "Poe." *Muse Anthology of Modern Poetry.* Ed. Dorothy Kissling and Arthur H. Nethercot. Poe Memorial Edition. New York: Carlyle Straub, 1938, p. 171.

An essay.

F72   Friesner, Donald Neil. "Ellis Bell and Israfel." *Brontë Society Transactions,* XIV, iv (1964), 11–18.

The poems of Poe and Emily Brontë are compared.

F73   Fruit, John Phelps. *The Mind and Art of Poe's Poetry.* New York: A. S. Barnes, 1899.

Analyzes Poe's poetic theory and practice in an appreciative vein and emphasizes artistic development. Reprinted New York: AMS Press, 1966.

   Reviewed:
Dial, XXVIII (1900), 56.

F74   ——. "The Obsession of Edgar Allan Poe." *Poet-Lore,* XII (1900), 42–58.

Defines Poe's "theory of life and destiny" which gradually possessed him to the climax of genius in *Eureka.*

F75   ——. "The Rationale of the Short Story According to Poe." *Poet-Lore,* XVI (Spring 1905), 57–65.

"The chief interest, technically considered, in Poe's stories, resides in his preserving, with the true instinct of the artist" an "equation between the inner and outer factors" of the narrated situation.

F76   Fuller, Henry B. "An Idol of the Parnassians." *Dial,* LXII (May 17, 1917), 433–34.

A review of Ewers's *Edgar Allan Poe.*

F77   ——. "The Thirteenth Goddess." *Harper's Monthly,* CXLVIII (Dec. 1923), 125–27.

The "goddess" is "Publicity" who gloats over having saved the Poe cottage in Fordham.

F78   Fulton, Chandos. "Portraits of Poe." *Home Jour,* March 12, 1873.
Lists five portraits of Poe.

F79   Funkhouser, A. P. "Meteoric Literary Career of Edgar Allan Poe." *Religious Telescope* (Dayton, Ohio), Feb. 10, 1909, pp. 6–8.
Biography.

F80   Fussell, Edwin S. "Edgar Allan Poe." *Frontier: American Literature and the American West.* Princeton, N.J.: Princeton University Press, 1965, pp. 132–74.
Analyzes Poe's attitude and treatment of the West, emphasizing his "Narratives of Exploration."

F81   ———. "Poe's 'Raven'; or, How to Concoct a Popular Poem from Almost Nothing at All." *ELN,* II (Sept. 1964), 36–39.
Poe worked up a modern poem out of hints furnished by a well-known scene in *The Duchess of Malfi.*

F82   Fyleman, Rose. "Poe." *Muse Anthology of Modern Poetry.* Ed. Dorothy Kissling and Arthur H. Nethercot. Poe Memorial Edition. New York: Carlyle Straub, 1938, p. 169.
Poe's influence on English poets.

G

G1   Deleted.

G2   G., J. B. "Poe and His 'Precursor.'" *Critic,* NS XXVII (May 8, 1897), 327–28.
On Poe and Chivers.

G3   G., W. M. "Poe's 'The Pit and the Pendulum.'" *Critic,* XVII (July 5, 1890), 7.

G4   Galloway, David. "Introduction." *Selected Writings of Edgar Allan Poe.* Baltimore: Penguin Books, 1967, pp. 9–46.
Poe breaks "through the conventional frontiers of consciousness."
Reviewed:
London *Times,* (Oct. 28, 1967), p. 20.

G5   Gambrill, J. Montgomery. "Introduction." *Selections from Poe.* New York: Ginn, 1907, pp. xi–xxix.
Commentary on Poe's life, character, and art; see bibliography, pp. xxx–xxxii.

G6   Gargano, James W. " 'The Black Cat': Perverseness Reconsidered." *TSLL*, II (Summer 1960), 172–78.

"Far from being a mere treatise on perverseness, 'The Black Cat' is
on one level an intense study of the protagonist's discovery of, and
infatuated immersion in, evil, and on another level a subtle examination of the protagonist's refusal to recognize the moral meaning of his career."

G7   ——. " 'The Cask of Amontillado': A Masquerade of Motive
and Identity." *SSF*, IV (Winter 1967), 119–26.

Poe's tale "presents an ironic vision of two men who, as surrogates
of mankind, enter upon a 'cooperative' venture that really exposes
their psychological isolation."

G8   ——. "Poe's 'Ligeia': Dream and Destruction." *CE*, XXIII
(Feb. 1962), 337–42.

The tale can best be understood as the story of a man "who, having
once inhabited the realm of the Ideal, seeks even into madness to
recreate his lost ecstasy."

G9   ——. "Poe's 'To Helen.' " *MLN*, LXXV (Dec. 1960), 652–53.
Poem contains consistent and functional imagery.

G10   ——. "The Question of Poe's Narrators." *CE*, XXV (Dec.
1963), 177–81.

Poe's depiction of his narrators reveals "deliberate craftsmanship
and penetrating sense of irony." Reprinted in Eric Carlson, ed., *The
Recognition of Edgar Allan Poe* (Ann Arbor: University of Michigan Press, 1966), pp. 308–16; and in Robert Regan, ed., *Poe: A
Collection of Critical Essays* (Englewood Cliffs, N.J.: Prentice-Hall,
1967), pp. 164–71.

G11   ——. "William Wilson: The Wildest of Sublunary Visions."
Washington and Jefferson Literary Jour, Poe Issue, I (1967), 9–15.

Argues that Poe's story depicts a problem of the modern consciousness: "to live not so much 'beyond' but outside of good and evil."

G12   Garnett, R. S. "The Mystery of Edgar Allan Poe." *Blackwood's
Mag*, CCXXVII (Feb. 1930), 235–48.

On the publication of W. Roberts's letter in *TLS* concerning the
purported Poe visit to Dumas in Paris "about 1832."

G13   Garrison, Joseph M., Jr. "The Function of Terror in the Work
of Edgar Allan Poe." *AQ*, XVIII (Summer 1966), 136–50.

Poe's tales of horror "advanced negatively the ethereal 'discoveries'
announced in 'Al Aaraaf' or *Eureka*."

G14   Gary, Lorena M. "Poet Who Dwells in 'The Valley Nis.' "
Poet-Lore, XLVII (Spring 1941), 59–63.

Poe lacked "spiritual insight."

G15 Gaston, Charles R. "Introduction." *The Raven* by Edgar Allan Poe, *The Courtship of Miles Standish* by Henry Wadsworth Longfellow, *Snow-bound* by John Greenleaf Whittier. New York: Charles E. Merrill, 1909, pp. 7–12, 28–30.
Biographical sketch followed by excerpts from several favorable criticisms.

G16 Gates, Lewis Edwards. "The Fantastic Tales of Poe." *Studies and Appreciations*. New York: Macmillan, 1900.
Discusses Poe's achievement in prose, pp. 110–28.

G17 Gates, William Bryan. "Poe's *Politian* Again." *MLN,* XLIX (Dec. 1934), 561.
Poe's source is Byron.

G18 George, Miles. "To the Editor of the State." Richmond *State,* May 22, 1880, [p. 2].
A letter concerning Poe at the University of Virginia by one who knew him there.

G19 Gerber, Gerald E. "Additional Sources for 'The Masque of the Red Death.'" *AL,* XXXVII (March 1965), 52–54.
Sources occur in an etiquette book which Poe reviewed in *Burton's Gentleman's Magazine.*

G20 ———. "Science vs. Poetry: The Beginnings of the Ideological Significance of a Modern Literary Idea." *DA,* XXV (Dec. 1964), 3553.
Poe emphasized the "epistemological significance of the opposition between poetic and scientific ways of thinking."

G21 Ghiselin, Brewster. "Reading Sprung Rhythms." *Poetry,* LXX (May 1947), 86–93.
Discusses Gerard Manley Hopkins's commentaries on Poe's "The Raven."

G22 Gibson, T. H. "Poe at West Point." *Harper's Monthly,* XXXV (Nov. 1867), 754–56.
An informal reminiscence of Poe at the academy. Reprinted in Ingram's biography, I, 82–87, and in Harrison's *Life,* pp. 85–94.

G23 Gildemeister, Theda. "A Biographical Sketch." *The Gold Bug,* by Edgar Allan Poe. New York: Rand, McNally, 1902, pp. 75–84.
Offers some critical appraisal of Poe followed by "Suggestions to Teachers" in presenting Poe's story.

G24 [Gilfillan, George.] "Edgar Allan Poe." *Littell's Living Age,* XLI (April 22, 1854), 166–71.
Pays tribute to Poe's power of analysis, his invention, and his imagination, but finds him a "wicked" person. Reprinted (with biographical deletions) in *SLM,* XX (April 1854), 249–53, and

appears in the author's *Third Gallery of Portraits* (New York: Sheldon, Lamport, and Blakeman, 1855), pp. 325–38. Also, first appeared in *Critic* (London), XIII (March 1, 1854), 119–21, under title "Edgar Poe," signed "Apollorus."

G25   Gill, William Fearing. "The Author of 'The Raven.' " *Baldwin's Monthly,* XIV (Aug. 1877), 5.

Poe's career in letters was "purely accidental and enforced."

G26   ——. "Edgar A. Poe and His Biographer." *The Poetical Works of Edgar Allan Poe.* New York: W. J. Widdleton, 1876.

"A vindication of Poe from the aspersions of Rufus W. Griswold"; see also "Biographical Sketch of Edgar A. Poe," pp. 3–7.

G27   ——. "Edgar Allan Poe—After Fifty Years." *Arena,* XXII (Oct. 1899), 526–29.

A brief and unimportant résumé of the Griswold-Willis controversy over Poe's character.

G28   ——. *The Life of Edgar Allan Poe.* New York: Dillingham, 1877.

Attempts to plead the cause of a genius who has been unjustly condemned and to include "everything of importance that has been written or related of Poe." Third edition, rev. and enl., London: Chatto and Windus, 1878.

Reviewed:

ATL, XL, 373–74.
Mag of American History, I, 775.
Nation, XXVI (April 11, 1878), 248.
J. Vila Blake, *Radical Rev,* I, 790–93.
John A. Ingram, *Athenaeum,* No. 2606, (Oct. 6, 1877), pp. 426–27.

G29   ——. "The Rationale of the Raven." *Papyrus Leaves: Poems, Stories, and Essays.* Ed. Gill. New York: Belford, Clarke, 1888, pp. 394–403.

Attempts to determine the origin and artistic inspiration of "The Raven."

G30   ——. "Some New Facts about Edgar A. Poe." *Laurel Leaves: Original Poems, Short Stories, and Essays.* Ed. Gill. Boston: William F. Gill, 1876, pp. 359–88.

Discusses various aspects of Poe's life, including his life at West Point, his work as journalist, and the cause of his death.

G31   Gimbel, Richard. " 'Quoth the Raven': A Catalogue of the Exhibition." *YULG,* XXXIII (April 1959), 139–89.

"Annotated and illus. catalogue of works from the collections of H. Bradley Martin and Colonel Richard Gimbel." *PMLA.*

G32　　Gingerich, Solomon F. "The Conception of Beauty in the Works of Shelley, Keats, and Poe." *Essays and Studies in English and Comparative Literature,* by Members of the English Department of the University of Michigan. Ann Arbor: University of Michigan Press, 1932, pp. 169–94.
　　The "unconsciously stored richness and beauty becoming active in the conscious act of creation lifts Poe's best poems into a place of permanency and immortality in literary art."

G33　　Glaenzer, R. B. "The Husk." *Bookman,* XXXVII (June 1913), 380–81.

G34　　Gobeille, Jos. Léon. "Introduction." *The Raven by Quarles.* Cleveland: Robert H. Perdue, 1901, pp. xi–xiii.
　　Discusses Poe's genius as poet, and record as a soldier.

G35　　Gohdes, Clarence. *American Literature in Nineteenth-Century England.* New York: Columbia University Press, 1944.
　　Commentaries on British publications of Poe and his reputation in England, *passim.*

G36　　Gold, Joseph. "Reconstructing the 'House of Usher.'" *ESQ,* No. 37 (4th quarter 1964), pp. 74–76.
　　Usher is victim to the "destructive phobia of premature burial."

G37　　Goldberg, Isaac. "Foreword." *Critical Excerpts from Poe.* Girard, Kans.: Haldeman-Julius, 1925, pp. 5–6.
　　Excerpts "reveal aspects of the greater and the lesser Poe."

G38　　———. "Foreword." *Poe's Marginalia.* Girard, Kans.: Haldeman-Julius, 1924, pp. 3–5.
　　Poe's marginalia reveals the author's independent and far-ranging mind.

G39　　———. "Poe and Mencken." *Stratford Monthly,* NS I (May 1924), 137–45.
　　Compares Poe and Mencken.

G40　　———. *Poe as a Literary Critic.* Girard, Kans.: Haldeman-Julius, 1924.
　　Discusses misconceptions of Poe and then proceeds "to correlate in him the theorist, the pedant, the practising critic."

G41　　Gonzalez, Joseph F. "A Scrim for Poe's Screams." *EJ,* LIII (Oct. 1964), 531–32.
　　On the use of graphic representations of Poe's work in the classroom.

G42　　Goodspeed, Charles E. "Fortune in an Attic." *Literary Digest,* CXXIV (Nov. 27, 1937), 24, 26.
　　A reprint from his book, *Yankee Bookseller* (New York: Houghton

Mifflin, 1937), which describes a sale of *Tamerlane* for more than $15,000.

G43   Goodwin, Katherine C. "Old Documents and Their Marketing." *Daughters of the American Revolution Mag*, LXVII (Sept. 1933), 539–46.

Contains a Poe letter dealing with Mrs. Clemm's claim against the government.

G44   Goodwin, K. L. "Roderick Usher's Overrated Knowledge." *NCF*, XVI (Sept. 1961), 173–75.

Usher's struggle involves the prospect of his forthcoming death.

G45   Goodwin, Parke. *A Biography of William Cullen Bryant.* 2 vols. New York: Appleton, 1883.

See I, 370, and II, 22.

G46   Gordan, John D. "Edgar Allan Poe: An Exhibition on the Centenary of His Death, October 7, 1849; A Catalogue of the First Editions, Manuscripts, Autograph Letters from the Berg Collection." *BNYPL*, LIII (Oct. 1949), 471–91.

Contains detailed annotations.

G47   ———. *Edgar Allan Poe.* An Exhibition on the Centenary of His Death, October 7, 1849. A Catalogue of First Editions, Manuscripts, Autograph Letters from the Berg Collection. New York: New York Public Library, 1949.

G48   Gordon, Caroline, and Allen Tate. "Commentary." *The House of Fiction.* New York: Scribner's, 1950, pp. 114–17.

Poe's "The Fall of the House of Usher" illuminates "some of the later, more mature work in the naturalistic-symbolic technique of Flaubert, Joyce, and James."

G49   Gorman, Herbert S. "Poe Sits for a Final Portrait." New York *Times*, Dec. 5, 1926, sec. III, p. 1.

A review of Allen's *Israfel* and Phillips's *Edgar Allan Poe.*

G50   Gosse, Edmund. "The Centenary of Edgar Allan Poe." *Contemporary Rev* (London), XCV (Feb. 1909), Literary Supplement, Nos. 17, 1–8.

Praises Poe's poetry and declares that Poe "was the discoverer and founder of symbolism."

G51   ———. "The Centenary of Edgar Allan Poe." *Some Diversions of a Man of Letters.* London: Heinemann, 1918, pp. 101–12.

Poe, founder and discoverer of Symbolism, was "one of the most significant poetic artists of a century rich in poetic artists."

G52   ———. "Edgar Poe and His Detractors." *Books on the Table.* New York: Scribner's, 1921, pp. 95–102.

Amusing commentary on interpretations of Poe's life. Reprinted in *Selected Essays* (2 vols, London: W. Heinemann, 1928), I, 211–20.
Reviewed:
TLS, Aug. 2, 1928, p. 565.
A. W. Pollard, *Library,* IX, 226–27.

G53 ———. *Questions at Issue.* New York: D. Appleton, 1893.
Poe's lyrics are "still fresh and fragrant"; see pp. 88–90.

G54 Gostwick, Joseph. *Handbook of American Literature.* London: W. & J. Chambers, 1856.
Questions some aspects of the Griswold biography and comments favorably upon Poe's poetry; see pp. 85–94, 187–88.

*G55 Gottsschalk, Hans W. "The Imagery of Poe's Poems and Tales: A Chronological Interpretive Study." Diss., University of Iowa, 1949.

G56 Gould, Edward S. "Church Bells." *Appleton's Jour,* XV (April 8, 1876), 470.
This lyric is "an attempt to complete the poem Poe left incomplete."

*G57 Gowans, William. [Memoir of Poe.] *Catalogue of American Books for Sale,* No. 28 (1869?), p. 11.

G58 Grabo, Carl Henry. *The Art of the Short Story.* New York: Scribner's, 1913.
Reprints "The Philosophy of Composition" because it is "one of the few definite and helpful discussions of constructive method to be found in English literature"; see pp. 295–311.

G59 Graham, George R. "The Genius and Characteristics of the Late Edgar Allan Poe." *Graham's,* XLIV (Feb. 1854), 216–25.
Poe struggled against temptation and poverty and wrote good tales and superior poetry. Reprinted in part in *Book-Lover,* IV (Dec. 1903), 553–57, V (Feb. 1904), 193–98.

G60 ———. "The Late Edgar Allan Poe" [from "Editor's Table"]. *Graham's,* XXXVI (March 1850), 224–26.
A letter to N. P. Willis on Poe's life and critical powers as a writer. Reprinted as "Defense of Poe," *The Complete Works of Edgar Allan Poe,* ed. James A. Harrison (17 vols, New York: T. Y. Crowell, 1902), I, 399–410.

G61 ———. *Poems,* [by] Edgar Allan Poe. New York: H. M. Caldwell, 1850.
Contains Graham's memoir and Willis's obituary on Poe.

G62 Graham, Kenneth. "Introduction." *Edgar Allan Poe: Selected Tales.* London: Oxford University Press, 1967, pp. vii–xxii.
Finds power in Poe's symbolism, "cold frenzy" in his form, and depth in his "descent into the maelström of the mind."

G63   Grant, Douglas. "Edgar Allan Poe: The Croak of the Raven." *Purpose and Place: Essays on American Writers*. New York: St. Martin's Press, 1965, pp. 40–45.

Briefly evaluates recent biographical approaches to Poe and comments on a few of his "unforgettable stories and as many poems."

G64   Grasset, Joseph. *The Semi-Insane and the Semi-Responsible*. Trans. Smith Ely Jelliffe. New York: Funk and Wagnalls, 1907.

Poe suffered from psychoneurosis; see pp. 239–43.

G65   Gravely, William H., Jr. "Christopher North and the Genesis of 'The Raven.' " *PMLA*, LXVI (March 1951), 149–61.

The chief source of Poe's conception of the symbolic raven may be found in the pages of *Blackwood's Magazine,* more specifically in a scene from John Wilson's "Noctes Ambrosianae."

*G66   ———. *The Early Political and Literary Career of Thomas Dunn English*. Ann Arbor, Mich.: University Microfilms, 1954.

G67   ———. "The Early Political and Literary Career of Thomas Dunn English." *DA*, XIV (1954), 821.

Contains an analysis of the Poe-English feud.

*G68   ———. "The Early Political and Literary Career of Thomas Dunn English." Diss., University of Virginia, 1953.

G69   ———. "An Incipient Libel Suit Involving Poe." *MLN*, LX (May 1945), 308–11.

Poe's "The Gold Bug" and a charge of plagiarism.

G70   ———. "Thomas Dunn English's *Walter Woofe*—A Reply to 'A Minor Poe Mystery.' " *PULC*, V (April 1944), 108–14.

A brief account of the relationship between Poe and Thomas Dunn English.

G71   Graves, Charles M. "Introduction." *Selected Poems and Tales of Edgar Allan Poe*. Ed. Graves. New York: Silver, Burdett, 1906, pp. ix–xxv.

Largely biographical and complimentary of Poe's fiction.

G72   ———. "Landmarks of Poe in Richmond. Including Some Hitherto Unpublished Portraits of His Friends." *Century Mag*, NS XLV (April 1904), 909–11, 914–20.

The Richmond theater, the homes of the Allans, Ellises, Galts, Mackenzies, Joseph Clark's school, Burke's school, the Swan Tavern, and other places of interest are discussed.

G73   Gray, John W. "The Public Reading of Edgar Allan Poe." *Southern Speech Jour*, XXVIII (Winter 1962), 109–15.

Poe "displayed an interest in the dramatic and excelled in the arts of oratory and recitation."

G74 [Greeley, Horace.] "The American Review." New York *Tribune*, Feb. 3, 1845, [p. 2].
Brief comment on "The Raven."

G75 Green, A. Wigfall. "The Weekly Magazines and Poe." *English Studies in Honor of James Southall Wilson*. Richmond: William Byrd Press, 1951, pp. 53–65.
Traces Poe's contributions to the "weekly" magazine.

G76 Green, Andrew J. "Essays in Miniature: *The Raven.*" *CE*, IV (Dec. 1942), 194–95.
Poe used considerable imagination in composing "The Raven."

G77 Green, George Henry. "The Composition of 'The Raven.'" *Aberystwyth Studies,* XII (1932), 1–20.
Diffuse discussion of Poe's composition of "The Raven."

G78 ———. "'William Wilson' and the Conscience of Edgar Allan Poe." *Aberystwyth Studies,* XI (1929), 1–22.
Analyzes "William Wilson" to determine Poe's concept of "conscience."

G79 Greenlaw, Edwin. "Poe in the Light of Literary History." *Johns Hopkins Alumni Mag,* XVIII (June 1930), 273–90.
Compares Poe to the figures of the early English Renaissance.

G80 Greenough, Chester Noyes. "Edgar Allan Poe." *The Works of Edgar Allan Poe.* 10 vols. New York: Hearst's International Library, 1914, I, 1–6.
Discusses some of the facets related to the widely different appraisals of Poe's work. Volume I also has "Preface to the 1849 Edition," by Maria Clemm; "Edgar Allan Poe," by James Russell Lowell; "Death of Edgar Allan Poe," by N. P. Willis; and Griswold's "Memoir of the Author" and an eight-page "Preface" to the "Memoir" by R. W. G. Some of these texts vary a bit from their original printings.

G81 Greever, Garland. "Edgar Allan Poe." *Three American Poems.* Ed. Greever. Chicago: Scott, Foresman, 1910, pp. 9–20.
Poe achieved distinction in criticism, the short story, and in poetry.

G82 Gregory, Horace. "On Edgar Poe: A Belated Epitaph." *Shield of Achilles.* New York: Harcourt, Brace, 1944, pp. 62–75.
Critic reprints his "Within the Private View," *PR,* X (May–June 1943), 263–74.

G83 ———. "Within the Private View." *PR,* X (May–June 1943), 263–74.
Poe's poetry is best when he "freed himself from the conscious skills" he practiced in "The Raven" and depicted "a truth that illuminated

the hidden chambers of the human psyche" as in the second "To Helen" and in "The City in the Sea."

G84   Griffis, William Eliot. "Behind the Mystery of Poe's 'Raven.' " *NYTBR,* Jan. 20, 1924, p. 2.

On the tradition of the composition of "The Raven" at Yaddo in the Barhyte home.

G85   Griffith, Clark. "Caves and Cave Dwellers: The Study of a Romantic Image." *JEGP,* LXII (July 1963), 551–68.

Poe uses the image of the cave as a specifically psychological dimension, "but an experience too limited and eccentric to have much application."

G86   ———. " 'Emersonianism' and 'Poeism': Some Versions of the Romantic Sensibility." *MLQ,* XXII (June 1961), 125–34.

Emerson and Poe reflect two markedly different tendencies of romanticism.

G87   ———. "Poe's 'Ligeia' and the English Romantics." *UTQ,* XXIV (Oct. 1954), 8–25.

Critic, in examining the predecessor ("Siope") and the sequel ("Psyche Zenobia") of "Ligeia," argues that "Ligeia" is "an allegory of terror, almost perfectly co-ordinated with the subtlest of allegorized jests."

G88   Griffith, Malcolm A. "The Grotesque in American Fiction." *DA,* XXVII (March 1967), 3047A.

Poe integrated the Grotesque into fiction.

G89   Griffith, William. "To the Least American, If Not the Greatest, of All American Poets." *Bookman,* LXIV (Jan. 1927), 616.

Verse.

G90   Griggs, Earl Leslie. "Five Sources of Edgar Allan Poe's 'Pinakidia.' " *AL,* I (May 1929), 196–99.

They are Disraeli's *Curiosities of Literature,* Baron Bielfeld's *Elements of Universal Erudition,* Jacob Bryant's *Mythology,* James Montgomery's *Lectures on Literature,* and James Fenimore Cooper's *Excursions in Switzerland.*

G91   Griswold, Hattie T. *Home Life of Great Authors.* Chicago: A. C. McClurg, 1891, pp. 312–21.

Poe's domestic life was happy, but his tendency to drink brought grave misfortune.

G92   Griswold, Rufus Wilmot. "The Chief Tale Writers of America." Washington *National Intelligencer,* Aug. 30, 1845, [p. 2].

Poe's tales are the "result of consummate art."

G93 [——] "Ludwig." "Death of Edgar Allan Poe." New York *Tribune*, Oct. 9, 1849, p. [2].

The famous obituary signed "Ludwig." Poe was a "bad man" without moral susceptibility or honor, but possessed unique descriptive ability and will retain an honored rank among poets. Latest reprinting is found in Eric Carlson, ed., *The Recognition of Edgar Allan Poe* (Ann Arbor: University of Michigan Press, 1966), pp. 28–35.

G94 ——. "Edgar A. Poe." *Poets and Poetry of America*. Philadelphia: Carey and Hart, 1842, p. 387.

Biographical sketch contains many errors. Subsequent editions after 1850 have longer sketches and some complimentary criticism.

G95 ——. "Edgar A. Poe." *Tait's Mag*, NS XXII (April 1852), 231–34.

Condenses two memoirs by Griswold and briefly comments on Poe's works. Reprinted in *Littell's Living Age*, XXXIII (May 1852), 422–24, and in *Eclectic Mag*, XXVI (May 1852), 115–19.

G96 ——. "Edgar Allan Poe." *International Mag*, I (Oct. 1850), 325–44.

Published as the memoir in the third volume of Griswold's edition.

G97 ——. "Edgar Allan Poe." *Prose Writers of America*. Philadelphia: Carey and Hart, 1847, pp. 523–24.

Inaccurate biography, but complimentary of Poe's fiction.

G98 ——. "The Late Edgar Allan Poe." *Literary American*, (New York), III, No. 19 (Nov. 10, 1849), 372–73.

G99 ——. "Memoir of the Author." *Tales of Mystery, Imagination and Humour, and Poems*, by Edgar A. Poe. London: Vizetelly, 1852.

A reprinting of the essential text of Griswold's famous "Memoir."

G100 ——. "Memoir of the Author." *The Works of the Late Edgar Allan Poe*. 3 vols. New York: J. S. Redfield, 1850–53, III, vii–xxxix.

The most controversial essay on Poe, exemplifying the moralistic approach to Poe's work. See also Griswold's "Preface" to the "Memoir," III, v–vii. (A prefatory letter by Mrs. Maria Clemm appears in some of Griswold's editions, and vol. IV of the series appeared in 1956.)

Reviewed:

SLM, XVI, 128.

Littell's Living Age, XXV, 77–78.

Sartain's Mag, VI, 311–12.

Graham's, XLVII, 466.

National Era, X (Nov. 27, 1856), 190.

Westminster Rev. LVII, 162–64.

G101 ——. "Poe, Longfellow, and Peter Pindar." *Literary World,* VII (Sept. 28, 1850), 247.

An extract from Griswold's memoir which points out that Poe's "The Haunted Palace" is plagiarized from Longfellow's "Beleagured City" and Peter Pindar's "Ballad."

G102 Griswold, W. M., ed. *Passages from the Correspondence and Other Papers of Rufus W. Griswold.* Cambridge, Mass.: W. M. Griswold, 1898.

Poe is mentioned in several letters.

G103 ——. "Poe's Moral Nature." *Nation,* LX (May 16, 1895), 381–82.

Poe had "an utter lack of honor."

G104 Gross, Seymour L. "Poe's Revision of 'The Oval Portrait." *MLN,* LXXIV (Jan. 1959), 16–20.

In his revision of this story, Poe demonstrates his ability to achieve "thematic coherence and totality of impression."

G105 ——. "The Reflection of Poe in Conrad Aiken's 'Strange Moonlight.'" *MLN,* LXXII (March 1957), 185–89.

Aiken consciously alludes to Poe.

G106 Grubb, Gerald C. "The Personal and Literary Relationships of Dickens and Poe." *NCF,* V (June 1950), 1–22; (Sept. 1950), 101–20; (Dec. 1950), 209–21.

Examines in detail the relationship between Poe and Dickens and offers conclusions as to the Englishman's influence upon Poe.

G107 Gruener, Gustav. "Notes on the Influence of E. T. A. Hoffmann upon Edgar Allan Poe." *PMLA,* XIX (March 1904), 1–25.

Although Poe denied any German influence, there are many points of similarity between Hoffmann and Poe.

G108 ——. "Poe's Knowledge of German." *MP,* II (June 1904), 125–40.

Poe, having "an unusual natural capacity for languages," probably had a careful and "discriminating" knowledge of German.

G109 Guilds, John C., Jr. "Poe's 'MS. Found in a Bottle': A Possible Source." *N&Q,* CCI (Oct. 1956), 452.

"It is possible that Poe's story owed some credit to a short tale by William Gilmore Simms." *AL.*

G110 ——. "Poe's Vaults Again," *N&Q,* CCII (May 1957), 220–21.

Comments on why Madeline was buried alive.

G111 Gwathmey, E. M. *John Pendleton Kennedy.* New York: Thomas Nelson, 1931.

See chap. 7: "Kennedy the Patron of Poe."

H

H1   H., F. M. "Life of Edgar Allan Poe." *The Poetical Works of Edgar Allan Poe.* London: Ward, Lock, n.d.
Lays emphasis on the unevenness of Poe's work; the criticism is general but favorable, pp. xvii–cxi. First published in 1870.

H2   H., J. L. "The Origin and History of the Jefferson Literary Society." *UVaMag,* LIX (April–May 1899), 331–35.
Mentions Poe briefly in connection with his relations with the society.

H3   Hafley, James. "Malice in Wonderland." *ArQ,* XV (Spring 1959), 5–12.
Poe and James on the relationship between art and life.

H4   ———. "A Tour of the House of Usher." *ESQ,* No. 31 (2nd quarter 1963), pp. 18–20.
The drama of the story is revealed by what happens to the language.

H5   Hagemann, E. R. "Two 'Lost' Letters by Poe." *AL,* XXVIII (Jan. 1957), 507–10.
"The letters, dated Feb. 9, 1836, and June 8, 1836, are to S. G. Bulfinch, then living in Augusta, Ga." *AL.*

H6   Haigh, Henry A. "Colonial Village of the Dearborn Inn." *Michigan Historical Mag,* XXI (Summer–Autumn 1937), 252–55.
Concerning a reproduction of the Fordham Cottage in the Dearborn village.

H7   Hale, Edward Everett, Jr. "Edgar Allen [*sic*] Poe." *Reader,* V (March 1905), 487–90.

H8   ———. "Introduction." *The Stories and Poems,* by Edgar Allan Poe. New York: University Publishing, 1904, pp. v–xviii.
Briefly analyzes selections from Poe's tales and poems.

H9   ———. "Mr. John Burroughs on Poe." *Dial,* XV (Nov. 1893), 254.

H10   [Hale, Mrs. Sarah Josepha.] *"Al Aaraaf, Tamerlane* &c., by Edgar A. Poe." *American Ladies Mag,* III (Jan. 1830), 47.
A brief notice.

H11   Halff, M. L. "Was Poe Vulgar?" *UVaMag,* LVI (Nov. 1896), 57–61.
Griswold declares, says this writer, that Poe was vulgar, but his poems, the testimony of his friends, and Poe's actions to Mrs. Clemm and Virginia contradict Griswold.

H12   Hall, Carroll Douglas. *Bierce and the Poe Hoax.* Intro. Carey McWilliams. San Francisco: Book Club of California, 1934.

A hoax perpetrated by Bierce, Carroll Carrington, and Herman Scheffauer, in printing Scheffauer's poem, "The Sea of Serenity," in the literary supplement of the San Francisco *Examiner,* March 12, 1899, as "an unpublished poem of Poe."

H13   Hall, J. A. "Was Poe's 'Raven' Suggested by a Georgian?" Atlanta *Jour,* July 24, 1921, mag. sec., p. 9.

An inconclusive reporting of the Poe-Chivers relationship.

H14   Halliburton, David G. *The Grotesque in American Literature: Poe, Hawthorne and Melville.* Ann Arbor, Mich.: University Microfilms, 1966.

H15   ——. "The Grotesque in American Literature: Poe, Hawthorne, and Melville." *DA,* XXVII (May 1967), 3840A–41A.

Discusses Poe's theory and use of the Grotesque.

*H16   ——. "The Grotesque in American Literature: Poe, Hawthorne and Melville." Diss., University of California, Riverside, 1966.

H17   Halline, Allan G. "Moral and Religious Concepts in Poe." *Bucknell University Studies,* II (Jan. 1951), 126–50.

"Poe's *characteristic* position is not to exclude morality and religion from art, but to admit them as 'background' materials."

H18   Halsey, Francis W. *American Authors and Their Homes.* New York: James Pott, 1901.

See pp. 1–16.

H19   Hamilton, Robert. "Poe and the Imagination." *QR,* CCLXXXVIII (Oct. 1950), 514–25.

In an essay-review of *The Centenary Poe,* edited by Montague Slater, critic finds Poe a versatile artist who had the "force of imagination" but a limited emotional capacity.

H20   Hamilton, Walter, ed., "Edgar Allan Poe." *Parodies of the Works of English and American Authors.* 6 vols. London: Reeves and Turner, 1884–89, II, 25–29.

A fine compilation of parodies of Poe's poetry.

H21   Hancock, Albert E. [Edgar Allan Poe and] "The Dual Personality in Literature and Life." *Booklover's Mag,* II (Oct. 1903), 355–68.

"William Wilson" is seen as "an allegory of the dual personality."

H22   Hannay, David. "Edgar Allan Poe." *Encyclopaedia Britannica,* 1911.

Sketch is primarily biographical, including a conservative estimate of Poe's writings.

H23   Hannay, James. "Edgar Allan Poe." *The Poetical Works of Edgar Allan Poe.* London: J. and C. Brown, n.d., pp. xi–xxx.
Poe's range is narrow, but "his poetry is sheer poetry" and he "gives a certain musical air, as a soul, to each poem."
Reviewed:
Eclectic Mag, XXX (Feb. 6, 1854), 263–72.

H24   Haraszti, Zoltan. "Poe Centenary." *BPLQ,* I (Oct. 1949), 151–55.
Contains a brief biographical essay on Poe and a discussion of Poe materials in the Boston Public Library.

H25   Harbert, Earl N. "A New Poe Letter." *AL,* XXXV (March 1963), 80–81.
Poe apprises Mrs. St. Leon Loud of his intention to visit her and to issue her poems.

H26   Harper, Henry H. "Introduction and Commentary." *The Raven,* by Edgar Allan Poe. Boston: Bibliophile Society, 1927, pp. 9–27.
"Poe's *magnum opus* requires but little elucidation or analysis other than what the average reader or listener can readily supply."

H27   Harrington, H. F. "Poe Not to Be Apotheosized." *Critic,* NS IV (Oct. 3, 1885), 157–58.
Attacks the tendency to condone Poe's personal vices.

H28   Harris, David P. "Preface." *Stories,* by Edgar Allan Poe. Adapted with Notes and Exercises by Harris. Englewood Cliffs, N.J.: Prentice-Hall International, 1962, pp. v–viii.
Suggests that "the future will value Poe less for his poetry than for his short stories."

H29   Harris, Joel Chandler. "Poe and Griswold." *The Countryman,* XXI (Feb. 13, 1866), 24.

H30   Harrison, Benjamin I. "A Chronological Concordance to the *Fleurs du Mal* of Baudelaire Together with Baudelairian Studies Based on the Concordance. 2 vols. Diss., Univ. of Virginia, 1938.
Baudelaire's affinity with Poe was genuine; see pp. lxxxv–cxx of vol. I of 2 vols.

H31   [Harrison, Gabriel.] "Edgar A. Poe: Reminiscences of Gabriel Harrison, an Actor, Still Living in Brooklyn." New York *Times–Saturday Rev,* March 4, 1899, p. 144.
"A staunch defender of Poe's memory."

H32   Harrison, James A. "Bibliography of Edgar Allan Poe." *The Complete Works of Edgar Allan Poe.* Ed. Harrison. 17 vols. New York: T. Y. Crowell, 1902, XVI, 335–79.
Year by year listing of Poe's works.

H33 ———. "Edgar Allan Poe." *The Library of Southern Literature.* Ed. E. A. Alderman *et al.* 16 vols. New Orleans: Martin and Hoyt, 1907, IX, 4079–84.
  Biographical sketch.

H34 ———. "Introduction" [to Early Criticism]. *The Complete Works of Edgar Allan Poe.* Ed. Harrison. 17 vols. New York: T. Y. Crowell, 1902, VIII, v–xvii. Reprinted Ney York: AMS Press, 1965.

H35 ———. "Introduction" [to *Eureka* and *Marginalia*]. *The Complete Works of Edgar Allan Poe.* Ed. Harrison. 17 vols. New York: T. Y. Crowell, 1902, XVI, vii–viii. Reprinted New York: AMS Press, 1965.

H36 ———. "Introduction." [to the Essays and Miscellanies]. *The Complete Works of Edgar Allan Poe.* Ed. Harrison. 17 vols. New York: T. Y. Crowell, 1902, XIV, v–viii. Reprinted New York: AMS Press, 1965.

H37 ———. "Introduction" [to the Later Criticism]. *The Complete Works of Edgar Allan Poe.* Ed. Harrison. 17 vols. New York: T. Y. Crowell, 1902, XII, vii–ix. Reprinted New York: AMS Press, 1965.

H38 ———. "Introduction" [to the Letters]. *The Complete Works of Edgar Allan Poe.* Ed. Harrison. 17 vols. New York: T. Y. Crowell, 1902, XVII, v–viii. Reprinted New York: AMS Press, 1965.

H39 ———. "Introduction" [to the *Literati* and *Autography*]. *The Complete Works of Edgar Allan Poe.* Ed. Harrison. 17 vols. New York: T. Y. Crowell, 1902, XV, vii–x. Reprinted New York: AMS Press, 1965.

H40 ———. "Introduction" [to the Middle Criticism]. *The Complete Works of Edgar Allan Poe.* Ed. Harrison. 17 vols. New York: T. Y. Crowell, 1902, X, v–viii. Reprinted New York: AMS Press, 1965.

H41 ———. *The Life of Edgar Allan Poe. The Complete Works of Edgar Allan Poe.* Ed. Harrison. 17 vols. New York: T. Y. Crowell, 1902, I, 1–340.
  By inquiry and correspondence with Poe's still surviving contemporaries, the author throws "new light" on Poe's early and middle life.
    Reviewed (*Life* and/or *Works*):
  J. L. Gilder, *Critic,* XLII, 499–503.
  Outlook, LXXII (Nov. 8, 1902), 581–82.
  W. M. Payne, *Nation,* LXXV (Dec. 4, 1902), 445–47.
  W. M. Payne, *Dial,* XXXIII (Nov. 1, 1902), 277–78.
  UVaAB, NS II, 31–34.
  P. E. Moore, *Independent.* LIV (Oct. 16, 1902), 2453–60.

H42 ———. *New Glimpses of Poe.* New York: M. F. Mansfield, 1901.

Presented here are Thomas A. Ellis's recollection of Poe's childhood, William Wertenbaker's account of Poe at the University of Virginia Professor B. L. Gildersleeve's description of Poe's lecture in Richmond in 1849, and Bishop O. P. Fitzgerald's reminiscences of Poe as a lecturer.

Reviewed:

Nation, LXXIII (Dec. 12, 1901), 456.

Athenaeum, No. 3878 (Feb. 22, 1902), p. 241.

H43 ———. "A Poe Miscellany." *Independent,* LXI (Nov. 1, 1906), 1044–51.

Various letters written after Poe's death which either condemn or condone his character.

H44 ———. "Preface." *The Last Letters of Edgar Allan Poe to Sarah Helen Whitman.* Ed. Harrison, New York: G. P. Putnam's Sons, 1909, pp. v–vi.

"These glowing letters rival the 'Sonnets from the Portuguese' or the letters of Abelard and Héloise in interest and eloquence."

Reviewed:

UVaAB, 3rd ser., II, 210–11.

Baltimore *Evening Sun,* March 21, 1909.

H45 ———, and Charlotte F. Dailey. "Poe and Mrs. Whitman—New Light on a Romantic Episode." *Century Mag,* NS LV (Jan. 1909), 439–52.

Prints documents from the Poe-Whitman correspondence with much other related matter.

H46 Harrison, Stanley R. "Through a Nineteenth-Century Looking Glass: The Letters of Edgar Fawcett." *TSE,* XV (1967), pp. 107–57.

Fawcett disagrees with Poe's definition of poetry; see p. 137.

H47 Hart, John S. *A Manual of American Literature.* Philadelphia: Eldredge & Brother, 1873.

Regrets that Poe did not unite his "rarest and most wonderful" poetical gifts with "high moral principle"; see pp. 140–44.

H48 Hart, Richard H. *Poe and Baltimore.* Baltimore: Enoch Pratt Free Library, 1942, [6 pp.].

"The stormy life and tragic death of Edgar Allan Poe are inseparably linked with Baltimore."

H49 Hartley, Lodwick. "From Crazy Castle to the House of Usher: A Note toward a Source." *SSF* (Spring 1965), 256–61.

Poe might have found material for his story "in circumstances surrounding a well-known eccentric John Hall-Stevenson, the friend of Laurence Sterne."

H50   Harwell, Richard B. "A Reputation by Reflection: John Hill Hewitt and Edgar Allan Poe." *EUQ,* III (June 1947), 104–14.
Poe's innate abilities and talents partially account for his fame; whereas his friend Hewitt, largely lacking these qualities, has been largely forgotten.

H51   Hassell, J. Woodrow, Jr. "The Problem of Realism in 'The Gold Bug.'" *AL,* XXV (May 1953), 179–92.
"The Gold Bug" is a "romantic narrative, in which realism and fantasy are in general nicely blended but in which they are also sometimes in conflict."

H52   Hatvary, George E. "Horace Binney Wallace: A Study in Self-Destruction." *PULC,* XXV (Winter 1964), 137–49.
Examines the literary relationship between Poe and Wallace.

H53   ———. "Poe's Borrowings from H. B. Wallace." *AL,* XXXVIII (Nov. 1966), 365–72.
Poe borrowed from Wallace's novel *Stanley* and three articles Wallace contributed to *Burton's* magazine.

H54   Haviland, Thomas P. "How Well Did Poe Know Milton?" *PMLA,* LXIX (Sept. 1954), 841–60.
Presents evidence that Poe often used Milton as a touchstone in his criticism and was indebted to Milton, particularly in the form and structure of Poe's early poems.

H55   ———. "Readings in Poe." *ESQ,* No. 31 (2nd quarter 1963), pp. 32–34.
Emphasizes reading, explication, and student evaluation in an undergraduate course in Poe.

H56   Haweis, Rev. Hugh R. "Introduction." *Tales of Mystery and Imagination,* by Edgar Allan Poe. London: George Routledge and Sons, 1886, pp. 5–14.
Poe, "the most gifted poet that America has yet produced," has the "extraordinary genius" to raise "his strange and awful tales out of the plane of mere hysterics."

H57   Hawkins, John. "Poe's Letter about 'The Raven.'" *AN&Q,* III (Jan. 1965), item 67.
Letter to Eli Bowen of the *Columbia Spy* about the holograph copy of "The Raven" inscribed to Dr. S. A. Whitaker.

H58   ———. "Poe's 'The Murders in the Rue Morgue.'" *Expl,* XXIII (Feb. 1965), item 49.

The structure of Poe's story "corresponds to the intellectual process which it exploits."

H59   Hawthorne, Julian. "My Adventure with Edgar Allan Poe." *Lippincott's,* XLVIII (Aug. 1891), 240–46.
A fantasy describing a meeting with Poe in Baltimore.

H60   ——, and Leonard Lemmon. *American Literature: A Textbook for the Use of Schools and Colleges.* Boston: D. C. Heath, 1893.
Poe "was the victim of the disproportion between his nature and his intellect,—between his character and his genius"; see pp. 52–62.

H61   Haycraft, Howard. "Father of the Detective Story." *SatRL,* XXIV (Aug. 23, 1941), 12–15.

H62   ——. "Poe and 'The Musiad.'" *PBSA,* LIX (4th quarter 1965), 437–38.
On the authorship of *The Musiad or Ninead* by "Diabolus" (Baltimore, 1830).

H63   ——. "Poe's 'Purloined Letter.'" *PBSA,* LVI (Oct.–Dec. 1962), 486–87.
On the first publication of Poe's tale.

H64   Hayford, Harrison. "Poe in *The Confidence Man.*" *NCF,* XIV (Dec. 1959), 207–18.
One unnamed passenger in Melville's story is a characterization of Poe.

H65   Hayne, Paul H. "Poe's Method of Writing." *Appleton's Jour,* VII (May 4, 1872), 490–91.
Calls especial attention to the careful revisions that some of Poe's poems underwent after their first publication.

H66   Hazleton, George. *The Raven: The Love Story of Edgar Allan Poe.* New York: D. Appleton, 1909.
A novel.

H67   [Hearn, Lafcadio.] "Edgar Allan Poe." Cincinnati *Commercial,* July 13, 1877, p. 5.

H68   ——. "Poe's Verse." *Interpretations of Literature.* Ed. John Erskine. 2 vols. New York: Dodd, Mead, 1915, II, 150–66.
One of the reasons for Poe's influence as a poet is his "wonderful sense of the values of words, of their particular colours and sounds, of their physiognomy, so to speak, which Poe shared with the greatest masters of language that ever lived."

H69   Heartman, Charles F. "The Curse of Edgar Allan Poe." *ABC,* IV (July 1933), 45–49.
Concerning the theft of *Al Aaraaf* from the New York Public Library and its consequences.

H70   ——. "A Remarkable Addition to the Poe Census." *ABC,* III (April 1933), 246.
    Prints the Poe items acquired by Mr. Gabriel Wells.

H71   ——, and James R. Canny. *A Bibliography of First Printings of the Writings of Edgar Allan Poe.* Hattiesburg, Miss.: Book Farm, 1940.
    See Randall review for correction of errors.
        Reviewed:
    David Randall, *PW,* CXXXVIII (Nov. 30, 1940), 2033–38.
    J. S. Wilson, *AL,* XIII, 176–77.

H72   ——, and James R. Canny. *A Bibliography of First Printings of the Writings of Edgar Allan Poe.* Rev. ed. Hattiesburg, Miss.: Book Farm, 1943.
    This important contribution of Poe bibliography was first printed in 1940.

H73   ——, and Kenneth Rede. *A Census of First Editions and Source Materials by or Relating to Edgar Allan Poe in American Public and Private Collections.* 2 vols. Metuchen, N.J.: American Book Collector, 1932.
    Contains a bibliographical checklist of first editions (vol. I) and a checklist of Poe's contributions to annuals and periodicals (vol. II). Also appears in *ABC,* I (1932), 45–49, 80–84, 143–47, 207–11, 274–77, 339–43; II (1932), 28–32, 141–53, 232–34, 338–42.
        Reviewed:
    TLS, May 6, 1932, p. 391.
    T. O. Mabbott, *AL,* VI, 92–94.
    Dublin Mag, VIII, 56–57.

H74   Heinrich, Max. *The Raven: A Melodrama. Poem of Edgar Allan Poe.* Cincinnati: John Church Co., 1905.
    Music by the author.
        Reviewed:
    Balz, Albert G. *UVaMag,* LXIX, 211–15.

H75   Heintzelman, Arthur W. "Legros' Illustrations for Poe's *Tales.*" *BPLQ,* VIII (Jan. 1956), 43–48.
    Alphonse Legros (1837–1911), one of the great engravers of all time, interpreted several of Poe's stories in the form of prints which are bizarre and keenly imaginative.

*H76   Heiser, Merrill M. "Satire in Poe's Tales," in "Representative Early American Satirists." Diss., University of Wisconsin, 1947, pp. 441–91.

H77 Hemstreet, Charles. "Literary Landmarks of New York: Eighth Paper [Edgar Allan Poe]." *Critic,* XLII (March 1903), 237–43.
Poe and the literary New York of 1844–49.

H78 Hertz, Robert M. "English and American Romanticism." *Person,* XLVI (Winter 1965), 81–92.
Poe's "detachment from actual human experience is almost complete"; see pp. 84–86.

H79 Hervey, John L. "Is Poe Rejected in America?" *Dial,* XXVI (Feb. 1, 1899), 73.

H80 Hewitt, John Hill. *Recollections of Poe.* Ed. Richard Barksdale Harwell. Atlanta: Emory University Publications, 1949.
Hewitt's commentaries on Poe are collected in this single volume.

H81 ———. *Shadows on the Wall; or Glimpses of the Past, a Retrospect of the Past Fifty Years.* Baltimore: Turnbull Bros., 1877.
Comments on the *Visiter* contest and the author's impressions of Poe; see pp. 154–57.

H82 Heyward, Du Bose. "Edgar Allan Poe." *Poetry,* XX (April 1922), 2–4.
Some verses to Poe.

H83 Hibbard, Addison. "Introduction [to Poe's Criticism]." *The Book of Poe: Tales, Criticisms, Poems.* Ed. Hibbard. Garden City, N.Y.: Doubleday, Doran, 1929, pp. 3–12.
"In writing of the literary art and of humanity Poe was, like others of his time and since, a perfectionist."
Reviewed:
T. O. Mabbott, *AL,* II, 101–2.

H84 ———. "Introduction [to Poe's Poetry]." *The Book of Poe: Tales, Criticisms, Poems.* Ed. Hibbard. Garden City, N.Y.: Doubleday, Doran, 1929, pp. 159–62.
Poe is a "poet of a mood, of a manner."

H85 ———. "Introduction [to Poe's Tales]." *The Book of Poe: Tales, Criticisms, Poems.* Ed. Hibbard. Garden City, N.Y.: Doubleday, Doran, 1929, pp. 235–40.
"At a time when the tale was almost an amorphous form, Poe stood for deliberate art."

H86 Hicks, Granville. "Margaret Fuller to Sarah Helen Whitman, an Unpublished Letter." *AL,* I (Jan. 1930), 419–21.
A letter, dated "Jamaica Plain. 27th Jan'y., 1840," from one of Poe's critics to the woman he was to become engaged to.

H87   Higgins, Frances. "The Man from Oquawka." *Americana,* XX (Oct. 1926), 519–33.
A careful account of E. H. N. Patterson, who was to have published *The Stylus.*

H88   ——. " 'Sniktau,' Pioneer Journalist." *Colorado Mag,* V (June 1928), 102–08.
E. H. N. Patterson, Colorado's beloved pioneer journalist, was to have published Poe's dream magazine, *The Stylus.*

H89   Higginson, Thomas Wentworth. "Letter to Charles W. Kent: 'Cambridge, Mass., October 6th, 1899.' " *UVaMag,* LX (Dec. 1899), 181.
Declares that Poe's tales are "the most remarkable production of the imaginative genius of this nation."

H90   ——. "Poe." *Short Studies of American Authors.* Boston: Lee and Shepard; New York: Charles T. Dillingham, 1888, pp. 12–21.
Poe's place in imaginative prose writing is as secure as Hawthorne's, but Poe's critical essays lowered the tone of literary criticism in America. Essay first appeared in *Literary World* (March 15, 1879), 89–90, and in Eric Carlson, ed., *The Recognition of Edgar Allan Poe* (Ann Arbor: University of Michigan Press, 1966), pp. 67–73.

H91   ——. "Recent Works on Edgar Poe." *Nation,* XXXI (Nov. 18, 1880), 360–61.
Declares that Ingram's attitude toward Poe is incorrect, for "new evidence" proves the correctness of Griswold's attitude.

H92   ——. "Woodberry's Life of Poe." *Nation,* XL (Feb. 19, 1885), 157–58.
Expresses an evident dislike for Poe and implies a near contempt for Woodberry's efforts to write about Poe.

H93   Hill, Archibald A. "Principles Governing Semantic Parallels." *TSLL,* I (Autumn 1959), 356–65.
"Statistical analysis applied to cruxes in Frost's 'Bereft,' Poe's 'The Fall of the House of Usher,' and Harte's 'Tennessee's Partner.' " *AL.*

H94   ——. "The Sound Symbolism of Poe." *UVaMag (The Spectator),* CI (Jan. 1940), 3–5, 18–19.
Poe "seems to have wound up the subject of sound symbolism as a literary device for all time."

H95   Hill, John S. "The Dual Hallucination in 'The Fall of the House of Usher.' " *SWR,* XLVIII (Autumn 1963), 396–402.
Both the narrator and Roderick Usher go mad and envision Madeline's form after her interment.

H96 ———. "Poe's 'Fall of the House of Usher' and Frank Norris' Early Short Stories." *Huntington Library Quarterly,* XXVI (Nov. 1962), 111–12.

Similar characterization is found in Poe's "The Fall of the House of Usher" and Norris's "A Case for Lombroso" and "His Single Blessedness."

H97 Hindus, Milton. "Whitman and Poe: A Note." *WWN,* III (March 1957), 5–6.

"Some similarities in the love-death themes of the two poets." *AL.*

H98 Hinton, Richard. "Poe's Last Poem." *Southern Bivouac,* NS II (June 1886), 66.

H99 Hirsch, David H. "Another Source for Poe's 'The Duc De L'Omelette.' " *AL,* XXXVIII (Jan. 1937), 532–36.

Poe parody owes much to a review of Disraeli's novel *The Young Duke* appearing in the *Westminster Review.*

H100 Hirst, Henry B. "Edgar A. Poe." Philadelphia *Saturday Museum,* I (March 4, 1843), pp. [1–2].

Presents critical commentary from a variety of sources, nearly altogether favorable, and includes quoted passages from Poe's poems.

H101 ———. "Edgar Allan Poe." Philadelphia *M'Makin's Model American Courier,* Oct. 20, 1849, p. [2].

Personal recollections of Poe along with a brief notice of Poe's death.

H102 Hoagland, Clayton. "The Universe of Eureka: A Comparison of the Theories of Eddington and Poe." *SLM,* I (May 1939), 307–13.

Draws parallels to illustrate some points in *Eureka.*

H103 Hoare, B. George. "Poe's Reference to Tennyson." *Academy,* LXIX (Dec. 16, 1905), 1317–18.

Points out Poe's accurate judgment of Wordsworth's "great successor."

H104 Hoffman, Michael J. "The House of Usher and Negative Romanticism." *Studies in Romanticism,* IV (Spring 1965), 158–68.

Views Poe's story as an expression of the "new post-Enlightenment man" alienated from self and world around him.

H105 Hoffman, Paul Phillips, ed. *Guide to Microfilm Edition of John Henry Ingram's Poe Collection.* Charlottesville: University of Virginia Library, 1967.

General introduction to the collection along with a very useful description; see especially pp. 17–29.

H106 Hofrichter, Laura. "From Poe to Kafka." *UTQ,* XXIX (July 1960), 405–19.

Poe and Kafka depict the inner world of man.

H107   Hogan, Frank J. "First Edition of The Raven." *AN&Q,* I (April 1941), 8.
A query about the binding of the volume.

H108   Hogrefe, Pearl. "A Question of Fair Play." *EJ,* XIV (Feb. 1925), 151–55.
A defense of Poe on the basis of recent discoveries concerning his character.

H109   Hoisington, May F. "Poe Cottage." *Muse Anthology of Modern Poetry.* Ed. Dorothy Kissling and Arthur H. Nethercot. Poe Memorial Edition. New York: Carlyle Straub, 1938, pp. 116–29.
Verse.

H110   Holliday, Carl. "Edgar Allan Poe (1809–1849)." *Three Centuries of Southern Poetry.* Nashville: Publishing House of the M. E. Church, South, 1908, pp. 65–81.
The "technical and artistic phases of Poe's poetry is scarcely equaled." Six poems of Poe are included.

H111   ——. *A History of Southern Literature.* New York: Neale Publishing, 1906.
Some biography and generally a sound appraisal of the qualities and purpose of Poe's art; see especially pp. 225–39.

H112   Holman, C. Hugh, *et al.* "Rhetoric in Southern Writing." *GaR,* XII (Spring 1958), 74–86.
"Introduction and three papers: Robert D. Jacobs, 'Poe'; Floyd C. Watkins, 'Wolfe'; William Van O'Conner, 'Faulkner.'" *AL.*

H113   Holme, George. "The Poet of the People." *Munsey's Mag,* XII (Dec. 1894), 243–48.
See p. 248 for discussion on Poe.

H114   Holsapple, Cortell King. "*The Masque of the Red Death* and *I Promessi Sposi.*" *UTSE,* No. 18 (1938), pp. 137–39.
Notes parallels and comments that *I Promessi Sposi* suggested "The Masque of the Red Death."

H115   ——. "Poe and Conradus." *AL,* IV (March 1932), 62–65.
Poe may have borrowed the technique of solving cryptograms used in "The Gold Bug" from an article on cryptography by David Arnold Conradus.

H116   Holt, Palmer C. "Notes on Poe's 'To Science,' 'To Helen,' and 'Ulalume.'" *BNYPL,* LXIII (Oct. 1959), 568–70.
Discusses possible sources of several Poe phrases.

H117   ——. "Poe and H. N. Coleridge's *Greek Classic Poets:* 'Pinakidia,' 'Politian,' and 'Morella' Sources." *AL,* XXXIV (March 1962), 8–30.

H. N. Coleridge's *Greek Classic Poets* contributed directly to confirming the "classical and scholarlike" image Poe desired.

H118   Honig, Edwin. "In Defense of Allegory." *KR,* XX (Winter 1958), 1–19.

See pp. 10–11 for a discussion of Poe and the allegorical method reflected in American literature.

H119   Hoole, William Stanley. "Poe in Charleston, S.C." *AL,* VI (March 1934), 78–80.

A determination of the time Poe spent in Charleston.

H120   Hopkins, Frederick M. "Shall We Preserve the Poe Cottage at Fordham?" *Rev of Reviews,* XIII (April 1896), 458–62.

Prints letters from distinguished writers and others who urge the preservation of the Fordham Cottage.

H121   Hopkins, Tighe. "Introduction." *Edgar Allan Poe's Tales.* London: Cassell, 1904, pp. 7–16.

Poe's "quality as a writer has never been in question," and "his character, honestly laid bare, will stand the scrutiny of time."

H122   Hough, Robert L., ed. *Literary Criticism of Edgar Allan Poe.* With introd. Lincoln: University of Nebraska Press, 1965.

Poe's significance as a critic; see "Introduction," pp. ix–xxviii.

Reviewed:

Moore, *YWES,* XLVI, 347–48.

Choice, II, 1965.

H123   Howard, Leon. "The Case of the Sanded Signature." *Manuscripts,* XIII (Spring 1961), 13–17.

On Poe's dealings with Lowell.

H124   ——. "The Empirical Attitude." *Literature and the American Tradition.* New York: Doubleday, 1960, pp. 105–35.

Poe's romantic and rational approach to art can be explained as an effort "to adapt borrowed literary symbols to an inbred attitude of mind."

H125   Howard, William Lee. "Poe and Misunderstood Personality." *Arena,* XXXI (Jan. 1904), 78–83.

Finds Poe a dipsomaniac.

H126   Howe, Mark Antony de Wolfe. "American Bookmen. IV.—Edgar Allan Poe." *Bookman,* V (May 1897), 205–16.

Biography based on Woodberry.

H127   ——. *American Bookmen: Sketches, Chiefly Biographical, of Certain Writers of the Nineteenth Century.* New York: Dodd, Mead, 1898.

See chap. 4, pp. 76–98.

H128   Howells, William Dean. "Edgar Allan Poe. *Harper's Weekly,*
LIII (Jan. 16, 1909), 12–13.
  Finds Poe an old-fashioned master: his fictions do not appeal to
  modern tastes, and if he submitted his stories to any editor now he
  would receive a rejection slip.

H129   Hubbell, Jay B. "Charles Chauncey Burr: Friend of Poe."
PMLA, LXIX (Sept. 1954), 833–40.
  Burr was a journalist who defended Poe.

H130   ———. "Edgar Allan Poe." *The South in American Literature,*
1607–1900. Durham, N.C.: Duke University Press, 1954, 528–50.
  Analyzes Poe's relationships with both North and South.

*H131   ———. " 'O Tempora! O, Mores,' a Juvenile Poem by Edgar
Allan Poe." *University of Colorado Studies,* II, ser. B (Oct. 1945),
314–21.
  "Examines the authenticity and the publication of 'the earliest poem
  of any length which we have from Poe's pen.' " *AL.*

H132   ———. "Poe." *Eight American Authors.* Ed. Floyd Stovall.
New York: Modern Language Association of America, 1956, pp. 1–46.
  Students of Poe should not neglect this important essay upon the
  bibliography of Poe criticism and scholarship.

H133   ———. "Poe and the Southern Literary Tradition." *TSLL,* II
(Summer 1960), 151–71.
  Appraises Poe's significance and influence in the South and discusses
  his contribution to a tradition reflected in contemporary literature.
  Reprinted as "Edgar Allan Poe and the South" in Hubbell's *South
  and Southwest* (Durham, N.C.: Duke University Press, 1965), pp.
  100–122.

H134   ———. "Poe's Mother, with a Note on John Allan." *WMQ,*
XXI (July 1941), 250–54.
  Primarily concerning Mrs. Poe's dramatic career.

H135   Hubner, Charles W. "Poe and Some of His Critics." *Representative Southern Poets.* New York: Neale Publishing, 1906, pp.
194–201.
  Poe "will rank among the eminent poets of the nineteenth century."

H136   Hudson, Ruth L. "Edgar Allan Poe's Craftsmanship in the
Short Story." Diss., University of Virginia, 1935.
  Traces the origins of Poe's technique of fiction and includes much
  original source material.

H137   ———. "Poe and Disraeli." *AL,* VIII (Jan. 1931), 402–16.
  Poe borrowed details from Disraeli and in two stories burlesqued
  Disraeli's writings.

H138 ———. "Poe Recognizes 'Ligeia' as His Masterpiece." *English Studies in Honor of James Southall Wilson.* Richmond: William Byrd Press, 1951, pp. 33–45.
> "In writing *Ligeia* Poe gathered up the threads of his dreams—the figures of speech, the phrases, the ideals of characters and interiors, the poetic overtones—which had been taking shape in earlier stories and wove them unconsciously into its fabric."

H139 ———. "Poe's Craftsmanship in the Short Story." *Abstracts of Dissertations* (1935). Charlottesville: University of Virginia, 1935, pp. 12–14.

H140 Hughes, David. "The Influence of Poe." *Fortnightly Rev,* NS No. 964 (Nov. 1949), pp. 342–43.
> "A brief discussion of the reasons for Poe's continuing popularity in England." *AL.*

*H141 Huguenin, Charles Arthur. "Nathaniel Parker Willis: His Literary Criticism of His Contemporaries." Diss., St. John's College, 1940.

H142 Hull, William D. "A Canon of the Critical Works of Edgar Allan Poe with a Study of Edgar Allan Poe the Magazinist." Diss., University of Virginia, 1941.
> Attempts to determine what Poe wrote and discusses his relationship with contemporary critic and magazinists.

H143 Huneker, James G. "Poe and His Polish Contemporary [Chopin]." New York *Times,* April 20, 1919, Sec. 4, p. 4.
> Reprinted in *Bedouins* (New York: Scribner's, 1920), pp. 94–105, and in *Essay Backgrounds for Writing and Speaking,* ed. A. F. Blanks (New York: Scribner's, 1929), pp. 58–66.

H144 Hungerford, Edward. "Poe and Phrenology." *AL,* II (Nov. 1930), 209–31.
> Traces Poe's "interest in the science of phrenology with considerable exactness."

H145 Hunter, R. "The Grave of Edgar Allan Poe." *Bookman,* (London), LXV (March 1924), 292–93.

H146 Hunter, William B., Jr. "Poe's 'The Sleeper' and *Macbeth.*" *AL,* XX (March 1948), 55–57.
> "*Macbeth,* Act III, scene v, lines 20–24, as a source of Poe's moon vapor." *AL.*

H147 Hunter, William Elijah. "Poe and His English Schoolmaster." *Athenaeum,* No. 2660 (Oct. 19, 1878), pp. 496–97.
> Reminiscences of the Bransby family.

H148   Huntington, H. A. "Edgar Allan Poe." *Dial,* I (Dec. 1880), 155–58.
Reviews Ingram's biography and Stedman's essay on Poe.

H149   Huntress, Keith. "Another Source for Poe's 'The Narrative of Arthur Gordon Pym.' " *AL,* XVI (March 1944), 19–25.
Offers *Remarkable Events and Remarkable Shipwrecks* by R. Thomas, A.M., as one source for *Pym.*

H150   Hurd, C. O. "The Logic of Poe's 'Murders in the Rue Morgue.' " *Harvard Monthly,* I (Oct. 1885), 7–10.

H151   Hurley, Leonard B. "A New Note in the War of the Literati." *AL,* VII (Jan. 1936), 376–94.
Thomas Dunn English's "scandalous portrait" of Poe in his novel, *1884; or, The Power of the S. F.*

H152   Hutcherson, Dudley Robert. "One Hundred Years of Poe: A Study of Edgar Allan Poe in American and English Criticism, 1827–1927." *Abstracts of Dissertations* (1936). Charlottesville: University of Virginia, 1936, pp. 12–14.

H153   ———. "One Hundred Years of Poe: A Study of Edgar Allan Poe in American and English Criticism, 1827–1927." Diss., University of Virginia, 1936.
Unbiased assessment of Poe's works began after 1900.

H154   ———. "The Philadelphia *Saturday Museum* Text of Poe's Poems." *AL,* V (March 1933), 36–48.
The publication of twenty poems in the *Museum,* 1843, is the only publication approximating an edition between 1831 and 1845.

H155   ———. "Poe's Reputation in England and America, 1850–1909." *AL,* XIV (Nov. 1942), 211–33.
Poe's fame steadily grew year by year.

H156   Hutchison, Earl R. "Giftbooks and Literary Annuals: Mass Communications Ornaments." *JQ,* XLIV (Autumn 1967), 470–74.
Poe's stories were often published in giftbooks and literary annuals; see p. 471.

H157   Hutton, Edward. "Introduction." *The Poems of Edgar Allan Poe.* Ed. Hutton. London: Alexander Morning, 1906, pp. vii–xlviii.
Largely biographical; see pp. xli–xlviii for critical discussion of Poe's versification.

H158   Hutton, Richard H. "Edgar Poe." *Criticisms on Contemporary Thought and Thinkers.* 2 vols. London: Macmillan, 1894, I, 59–68.
Qualified praise of Poe's stories and poetry, but commends Poe's criticism of poetry. Reprinted from London *Spectator* as review of

Ingram's edition of Poe's tales, vol. I of *The Works of Edgar Allan Poe.*

H159   Huxley, Aldous. "Vulgarity in Literature." *SatRL,* VII (Sept. 27, 1930), 158–59.

"A taint of vulgarity spoils . . . all but two or three of his poems." Reprinted in Eric Carlson, ed., *The Recognition of Edgar Allan Poe* (Ann Arbor: University of Michigan Press, 1966), pp. 160–67, and in Robert Regan, ed., *Poe: A Collection of Critical Essays* (Englewood Cliffs, N.J.: Prentice Hall, 1967), pp. 31–37.

I

I1   I., K. P. [Boyd, Andrew Kennedy Hutchinson]. "Edgar Allan Poe." *Littell's Living Age,* LIV (July 18, 1857), 150–64.

Finds Poe's tales to be the best of Poe; commends Poe's intellect and imagination, but declares he had "an utterly evil heart, and a career of guilt, misery, and despair." First appeared in *Fraser's,* LV (June 1857), 684–700.

I2   Ichiriki, Hideo. "Thomas Holley Chivers." *Essays in English and American Literature: In Commemoration of Professor Takejiro Nakayama's Sixty-first Birthday.* Tokyo: Shohakusha, 1961, pp. 207–19.

A critique of Chivers's *Life of Poe.*

I3   Ingraham, Joseph H. *The Beautiful Cigar Vender; or, The Mysteries of Broadway.* New York: n.p., [1849?], pp. 1–48.

Some obvious reminiscences of Mary Rogers.

I4   Ingram, Henry B. "The Cottage at Fordham." *Illustrated American* (New York), XIX (1896), 663–64.

I5   Ingram, John H. [Correspondence on "Edgar Poe and His Biographers."] *Academy,* XXIV (Oct. 13, 1883), 248–49.

A critical assault upon Poe's biographers.

I6   ——. "A Disclaimer." *Athenaeum,* No. 2516 (Jan. 15, 1876), p. 89.

Declares that W. F. Gill has borrowed his material and used it as his own.

I7   ——. "Edgar Allan Poe." *International Rev,* II (March 1875), 145–72.

A reprinting of the memoir prefixed to the author's *Works of Poe,*

1874–75. Also appears in Edwin P. Whipple *et al., Men of Mark: Bryant, Longfellow, Poe* (New York: Barnes, [1877]), pp. 127–54.

I8   ——. "Edgar Allan Poe." *The Tales and Poems of Edgar Allan Poe.* 4 vols. New York: Scribner and Welford, 1885, I, xi–xxxix.
A very sympathetic biographical essay and some comparison of Poe and Hawthorne.

I9   ——. "Edgar Allan Poe and His Commentators." *Academy,* LXIX (Dec. 2, 1905), 1269.
Defends Poe as poet.

I10   ——. "Edgar Allan Poe and 'Stella.' " *Albany Rev,* I (July 1907), 417–23.
The relations of Poe and Mrs. S. A. Lewis.

I11   ——. *Edgar Allan Poe: His Life, Letters and Opinions.* 2 vols. London: John Hogg, 1880.
Effectively assimilates "new matter" and previous biographies and alludes only slightly to the Poe scandals. Later editions appear in one volume, and in 1965 were reprinted by AMS Co.
  Reviewed:
Athenaeum, No. 2752 (July 24, 1880), pp. 107–9.
New York *Times,* Oct. 24, 1880, p. 10.
New York *Herald,* Oct. 25, 1880, p. 8.
H. Zimnern, *Beilage Zur Allgemeinen Beitung,* July 17, 1880, pp. 2913–15.
Das Telephon, Aug. 15, 1882, pp. 3–4.
Allen's Indian Mail, Jan. 10, 1887, pp. 34–35.

I12   ——. "Edgar Allan Poe's Early Poems." *Every Saturday,* NS I (June 13, 1874), pp. 659–62.
Poe's early poems are a valuable index of the precocity of his genius.

I13   ——. "Edgar Allan Poe's Last Poem, 'The Beautiful Physician.' " *Bookman,* XXVIII (Jan. 1909), 452–54.
Argues that "The Beautiful Physician" was written to Mrs. Shew.

I14   ——. "Edgar Poe." *Athenaeum,* No. 2742 (May 15, 1880), p. 3.
Sharply critical of Stedman's article in *Scribner's Monthly.*

I15   ——. "Edgar Poe." *Temple Bar,* XLI (June 1874), 375.
Slashing attack on Griswold's memoir and indirectly upon those who accept it. Reprinted in *Eclectic Mag,* NS XX (Aug. 1874), 203–10.

I16   "Edgar Poe: A Sketch." *Poems of Edgar Allan Poe,* n.d., pp. 9–30.
Biographical essay and little criticism.

117 ——. "Edgar Poe and Some Commentators." *Academy,* LXIX (Nov. 18, 1905), 1205.
Argues that Poe was "up to his trade as a poet."

118 ——. "Edgar Poe and Some of His Friends." *Bookman* (London), XXXV (Jan. 1909), 167–73.
A biographical account of Poe's relations with his contemporaries.

119 ——. "Edgar Poe's 'Raven.'" *Athenaeum,* No. 2651 (Aug. 17, 1878), p. 210.
Albert Pike's poem "Isadore," published in the *New-York Mirror* for Oct. 14, 1843, is a source of "The Raven."

120 ——. "Editorial Note." *Tales,* by Edgar Allan Poe. Ed. Ingram. Leipzig: Bernhard Tauchnitz, 1884, pp. v–vi.
Explains why only eleven of Poe's tales are included in this edition.

121 ——. "Genesis." *The Raven,* by Edgar Allan Poe. London: George Redway, 1885, pp. 1–16.
Discusses sources of "The Raven" and regards Poe's "The Philosophy of Composition" as "an afterthought." (The texts of translations, fabrications, and parodies of "The Raven" are included in this volume.)
Reviewed:
Critic, VII (Dec. 26, 1885), 302.

122 ——. "History." *The Raven,* by Edgar Allan Poe. London: George Redway, 1885, pp. 24–34.
Composition, publication, and critical reception of "The Raven."

123 ——. *John Henry Ingram's Poe Collection.* Ed. Paul P. Hoffman *et al.* Charlottesville: University of Virginia Library, 1966.
Microfilm of nine reels presenting the assortment of materials composed and collected by one of Poe's most indefatigable defenders.

124 ——. [Letter to the Editor.] *Southern Mag,* XV (Oct. 1874), 428–30.
Asks for any information about Poe; see p. 429.

125 ——. "The Lunar Hoax." *Athenaeum,* No. 2547 (Aug. 19, 1876), pp. 241–42.
Discusses Poe's hoax in the light of Richard Adams Locke's "Moon Hoax."

126 ——. "Memoir of Edgar Allan Poe." *The Complete Poetical Works and Essays on Poetry of Edgar Allan Poe Together with His Narrative of Arthur Gordon Pym.* Ed. Ingram. London: Frederick Warne, 1888, pp. xi–xxxii.
Biographical and quotes contemporaries who knew Poe.

127   ——. "Memoir of Poe." *The Works of Edgar Allan Poe.* Ed.
Ingram. 4 vols. Edinburgh: Black, 1874–75, I, xvii–ci.
   An attempt "for the first time to do justice to the poet's memory."
   Vol. I also contains Lowell's sketch of Poe (reprinted from Griswold
   edition), pp. cii–cvii, and Willis's notice of Poe's death, pp. cix–cxv.
   Ingram's "Memoir" also appears in *International Rev,* II (March–
   April, 1875), 145–72.
      Reviewed:
   Harpers Mag, L, 600.
   Nation, XX (May 25, 1875), 208–9.
   Mag of American History, I, 770.

128   ——. "More New Facts about Poe." St. Louis *Mirror,* Feb. 21,
1874, pp. 248–50.
   Some biographical discoveries stated in a concise form.

129   ——. "Poe's Politian." *Southern Mag,* XVII (Nov. 1875),
588–94.
   Describes *Politian* as "unequal in execution, a fragment, and a
   mystery."

130   ——. " 'Recollections of Edgar Allan Poe.' " *Athenaeum,* No.
3248 (Jan. 25, 1890), p. 117.
   Points out errors in Howard Paul's article "Recollections of Edgar
   Allen [*sic*] Poe" appearing in *Lambert's Monthly.*

131   ——. "The Unknown Poetry of Edgar Poe." *Belgravia,* XXIX
(June 1876), 502–13.
   On the 1827 edition of Poe's poetry. Reprinted in the New York
   Graphic, June 8, 1876, pp. 804–05.

132   ——. "Unpublished Correspondence by Edgar A. Poe." *Appleton's Jour,* NS IV (May 1878), 421–29.
   Poe's letters of the last years of his life are presented with some
   editorial commentary.

133   ——. "Variations in Edgar Poe's Poetry." *The Bibliophile,* III
(May 1909), 128–36.
   Variations are listed in versions of "The Raven," "The Bells,"
   "Ulalume," "Annabel Lee," "The Coliseum," "The Conqueror
   Worm," and other poems.

134   ——, and H. Buxton Forman. "Bibliography of Edgar Allan
Poe." *Athenaeum,* Nos. 2544, 2545, 2547 (July 29, Aug. 5, Aug. 19,
1876), pp. 145–46, 177, 241.
   Printings of Poe's poetry during his lifetime are given.

135   Ingram, Susan V. C. [Poe at Norfolk—Old Point Comfort.]
New York *Herald,* Feb. 19, 1905, p. 4.
   Concerning Poe's reading of his poems.

136   Irvine, Leigh H. "Poe and Emerson." *Coming Age,* III (Feb. 1900), 172–74.

137   Isaacs, J. *The Background of Modern Poetry.* New York: E. P. Dutton, 1952.

Poe is a "phenomenon of the profoundest significance for modern European poetry"; see pp. 21–25.

J

J1   J., H. "Complexes of Genius." *Independent,* CXVI (May 15, 1926), 582.

J2   Jackdaw. "The Raven, the Parrot, and the Pidgin." *Academy,* LXII (April 19, 1902), 418–19.

Asks for information concerning "The Parrot by Penzoni" which J. A. Joyce included in his Poe biography.

J3   Jackowska, Suzanne d'Olivera. " 'The Raven.' " *Christian Science Monitor,* XXVII (Aug. 8, 1935), 12.

The author, vice-president of the International Poe Society, protests the treatment of "The Raven" and of Poe himself in the motion picture *The Raven.*

J4   Jackson, David Kelly. *The Contributions and Contributors to the Southern Literary Messenger.* Charlottesville, Va.: Historical Publishing Co., 1936.

Attempts to list the contributions and contributors to the *Messenger.*

J5   ———. "An Estimate of the Influence of 'The Southern Literary Messenger.' " *SLM,* I (Aug. 1939), 508–14.

See pp. 510–11.

J6   ———. "Four of Poe's Critiques in the Baltimore Newspapers." *MLN,* L (April 1935), 251–56.

Reprinted for the first time are four of Poe's critiques from the Baltimore *Republican and Commercial Advertiser,* May 14, June 13, and July 10, 1835, and from the Baltimore *American,* June 15, 1835.

J7   ———. "Poe and the 'Messenger.' " *SLM,* I (Jan. 1939), 5–11.
A sketch of T. W. White's founding and editorship.

J8   ———. *Poe and the Southern Literary Messenger.* Richmond: Dietz, 1934.

A study of Poe's relations with and contributions to the *Messenger.*
Reviewed:

T. O. Mabbott, *AL*, VI, 364–66.
TLS, Jan. 24, 1935, p. 44.
Killis Campbell, *MLN*, LI, 487–88.

J9   ——. "Poe Notes: 'Pinakidia' and 'Some Ancient Greek Authors.' " *AL*, V (Nov. 1933), 258–67.
Twenty-eight fillers in the *Southern Literary Messenger* are ascribed to Poe. A. W. Schlegel's *Lectures on Dramatic Art* is the source of "Pinakidia," and Charles Anthon's revised edition of J. Lamprière's *Classical Dictionary* is a source of "Some Ancient Greek Authors."

J10   ——. "Poe's Knowledge of Law during the Messenger Period: Some Comments on Chapter II of Margaret Alterton's *Origins of Poe's Critical Theory.*" *AL*, X (Nov. 1938), 331–39.
Miss Alterton's attributions of certain articles to Poe which actually are not Poe's make some of her assumptions incorrect.

J11   ——. " 'Some Ancient Greek Authors,' a Work of E. A. Poe." *N&Q*, CLXIX (May 26, 1934), 368.
Poe used his "Some Ancient Greek Authors" as a source for "Lionizing."

J12   ——. "Some Unpublished Letters of T. W. White to Lucian Minor." *Tyler's Quarterly Hist and Genealogical Mag*, XVII (April 1936), 224–43; XVIII (July 1936), 32–49.
Letters concern the *Messenger* and its contributors.

J13   Jackson, Holbrook. "Edgar Allan Poe." *All Manner of Folk.* London: Grant Richards, 1912, pp. 91–102.
Poe's strength "was the ready brilliance of a mind which gave him extraordinary versatility in the art of letters and in intellectual interests."

J14   Jackson, Joseph. "Foreword." *English Notes.* New York: Lewis M. Thompson, 1920, pp. 11–35.
Commentary and background for attributing *English Notes for Very Extensive Circulation by Quarles Quickens, Esq.* (Boston, 1842).
Reviewed:
TLS, Sept. 16, 1920, p. 595.
NYTBR, Aug. 1, 1920, p. 9.

J15   ——. "Foreword I: Poe as a Timely Writer." *The Philosophy of Animal Magneticism.* Philadelphia: n.p., 1928, pp. 5–13.
Poe as a journalist.

J16   ——. "Foreword II: The Philosophy of Animal Magnetism Identified." *The Philosophy of Animal Magneticism.* Philadelphia: n.p., 1928, pp. 14–31.

Circumstantial and internal evidences are the bases for attributing "The Philosophy of Animal Magnetism" to Poe.

J17 ———. "George Lippard: Misunderstood Man of Letters." *PMHB*, LIX (Oct. 1935), 376–91.
Poe is mentioned in this discussion of an obscure novelist.

J18 ———. "Poe's Signature to 'The Raven.'" *SR*, XXVI (July 1918), 272–75.
The signature of "Quarles" to "The Raven" was designed as a confession of the authorship of *English Notes by Quarles Quickens.*

J19 Jacobs, Robert D. "Poe among the Virginians." *VMHB*, LXVII (Jan. 1959), 30–48.
"Virginia and the South gave much honor to Poe while he was still alive."

J20 ———. "Poe and the Agrarian Critics." *Hopkins Rev*, V (Spring 1952), 43–54.
Except for Poe's emphasis upon platonic beauty and taste, he and the Agrarian critics have a great deal in common. Reprinted in *The Southern Renascence,* ed. Robert D. Jacobs and Louis D. Rubin (Baltimore: Johns Hopkins Press, 1953), pp. 35–46.

J21 ———. "Poe as a Literary Critic: A Teaching." *ESQ*, No. 31 (2nd quarter 1963), pp. 7–11.
Presents a plan for classroom study of Poe as critic.

J22 ———. "Poe in Richmond: The Double Image." *The Dilemma of the Southern Writer.* Ed. R. K. Meeker. Farmville, Va.: Longwood College, 1961, pp. 27–59.
Poe's role as competitive journalist was considered in Poe's day as beneath the dignity of a middle-class Southerner.

J23 ———. "Poe's Earthly Paradise." *AQ*, XII (Fall 1960), 404–13.
Poe's concept of art reflects a well-established aesthetic tradition which proposed the artist can give happiness by lending form and expression to the raw material of nature.

J24 ———. "Poe's Heritage from Jefferson's Virginia." Diss., Johns Hopkins University, 1953.
The regional culture of Virginia made an important contribution to Poe's attitudes and critical theory.

J25 ———. "Rhetoric in Southern Writing: Poe." *GaR*, XII (Spring 1958), 76–79.
Suggests that Poe's style of rhetorical effects to stir the reader's emotion was in part due to a Southern rhetorical tradition.

J26 James, Henry. *French Poets and Novelists.* London: Macmillan, 1878.

"It seems to me that to take him [Poe] with more than a certain degree of seriousness is to lack seriousness one's self. An enthusiasm for Poe is the mark of a decidedly primitive stage of reflection"; see p. 60. Some passages by James on Baudelaire appear in Eric Carlson, ed., *The Recognition of Edgar Allan Poe* (Ann Arbor: University of Michigan Press, 1966), pp. 65–66.

J27   ——. *Hawthorne*. New York: Harper, 1880.
In his collection of critical sketches, Poe was provincial, "pretentious, spiteful, vulgar; but they contain a great deal of sense and discrimination as well," p. 50. Reprinted Ithaca, N.Y.: Cornell University Press, 1956. Some passages pertaining to Poe appear in Eric Carlson, ed., *The Recognition of Edgar Allan Poe* (Ann Arbor: University of Michigan Press, 1966), pp. 66–67.

J28   Jameson, Edward. "Edgar A. Poe." *Golden Age,* V (Sept. 25, 1875), 12.
A four-quatrain tribute to Poe.

J29   January, Josephine Poe. "Edgar Allan Poe's 'Child Wife' with an Unpublished Acrostic by Her to Her Husband." *Century Mag,* NS LVI (Oct. 1909), 894–96.
Reproduces an acrostic by Virginia Poe.

J30   [Japp, A. H.] "Edgar Allan Poe." *British Quarterly Rev,* LXII (July 1875), 194–218.
The Britisher sees Poe as a "representative American" because of his "practicality, . . . pantheistic scepticism, and his feverish curiosity and ambition."

J31   Jenkins, Oliver L. *The Student's Handbook of British and American Literature*. Baltimore: John Murphy, 1880.
The poems and tales are "characterized by a keen sense of beauty and subtle power of analysis, and a masterly skill of forcible expression"; see pp. 433–36.

J32   Jessup, Alexander. "Poe and the Short Story." *Literary Review,* New York *Evening Post,* Oct. 23, 1920, p. 30.
Concerning the publication dates of Poe's short stories.

J33   Jillson, Willard Rouse. "The Beauchamp-Sharp Tragedy in American Literature." *KHSR,* XXXVI (Jan. 1938), 54–60.
The tragedy was a theme used by Chivers, Poe, C. F. Hoffman, Simms, and others. A bibliography of some hundred items shows the wide influence of the tragedy on American literature.

J34   Johnson, Charles Frederick. *Outline History of English and American Literature*. New York: American Book Co., 1900.
A not very enthusiastic account of Poe's accomplishment; see pp. 483–85.

J35 Johnson, Reginald Brimley. "Memoir." *The Complete Poetical Works of Edgar Allan Poe with Three Essays on Poetry*. Ed. Johnson. London: Henry Frowde, 1909, pp. xi–xliv.

"The man [Poe] eludes analysis." Some descriptive bibliography of the texts of Poe's poem is found in the editor's "Bibliography," pp. xlvii–lx.

J36 ———. "Preface to the Poems." *The Works of Edgar Allan Poe*. Ed. Johnson. London: Oxford University Press, Humphrey Milford, 1927, pp. 1–2.

An introduction to the notes of Poe's poetry that is followed by the texts of *Pym* and three of Poe's critical essays on poetry.

J37 Johnston, Marjorie C. "Rubén Darío's Acquaintance with Poe." *Hispania*, XVII (Oct. 1934), 271–78.

An estimate of Poe's influence on Darío's poetry.

J38 Jones, Howard M. "Introduction." *Poems of Edgar Allan Poe*. New York: Spiral Press, 1929, pp. iii–vi.

Emphasizes Poe's "active idealism" having its roots in romanticism.
Reviewed:
Hubbell, *AL,* I, 226–27.

J39 ———. "Poe, 'The Raven,' and the Anonymous Young Man." *WHR,* IX (Spring 1955), 127–38.

Poe's characters are successfully humanized, and "The Raven" combines successfully the thematic and prosodic interests.

J40 Jones, Joe J. "Poe's 'Nicean Barks.'" *AL,* II (Jan. 1931), 433–38.

Poe may have derived his phrase from Catullus.

J41 Jones, Joseph. "'The Raven' and 'The Raven': Another Source of Poe's Poem." *AL,* XXX (May 1958), 185–93.

The ancestor to Poe's raven is found in a poem entitled "The Raven; or, The Power of Conscience" published in *Fraser's* magazine (March 1839).

J42 ———, et al. *American Literary Manuscripts: A Checklist of Holdings in Academic, Historical, and Public Libraries in the United States*. Austin: University of Texas Press, 1960.

See pp. 298–99 for locations of Poe depositories.

J43 Jones, Lucy Thweatt. *The Use of the Episodic Story in the English Novel*. Diss., University of Virginia, 1929.

See pp. 4–17.

J44 Jones, P. Mansell. "Poe and Baudelaire: The 'Affinity.'" *MLR,* XL (Oct. 1945), 279–83.

Critic emphasizes the affinity rather than any possible influence.

Article later reprinted in the author's *Modern French Poetry* (Cambridge: University Press, 1951), pp. 38–68.

J45   ———. "Poe, Baudelaire and Mallarmé: A Problem of Literary Judgment." *MLR*, XXXIX (July 1944), 236–46.

Poe's "theoretic persistence in emphasizing the autonomy of Beauty and his perception of the untrammelled realization of the Poetic Sentiment in music and in poetry conceived as music" appealed to the French poets. Article later reprinted in the author's *Modern French Poetry* (Cambridge: University Press, 1951), pp. 38–68.

J46   Jones, Rhys S. "The Influence of Edgar Allan Poe on Paul Valéry prior to 1900." *Comparative Literature Studies*, XXI–XXII (1946), 10–15.

"In addition to 'pure poetry' and music, Valéry was indirectly indebted to Poe (again *via* Baudelaire) for his philosophic and psychological approach to creation."

J47   [Jones, Timothy Pickering.] "At West Point with Poe." New York *Sun*, May 10, 1903, sec. II, p. 6.

J48   Jordan, Hoover H. "Poe's Debt to Thomas Moore." *PMLA*, LXIII (June 1948), 753–57.

Close parallels suggest that "Moore had fully as great an influence as any poet upon the verse of Poe."

J49   Joyce, John A. *Edgar Allan Poe.* New York: F. T. Neely, 1901.

Analyzes Poe and his poetry as reflecting the qualities that constitute the genuine poet: truth, pride and lunacy.

J50   "Justitia, Fiat" [Thomas H. Chivers]. "Origin of Poe's 'Raven.'" *Waverley Mag. and Literary Repository*, VII (July 30, 1853), 73.

Argues that Poe's "The Raven" has its origin in "To Allegra Florence in Heaven" by T. H. Chivers, M. D. Succeeding issues (Aug. 13, 20, Sept. 10, 24, Oct. 1 and 8) take up the controversy.

K

K1   Kahn, David. *The Codebreakers.* New York: Macmillan, 1967.
Poe as a code-breaker; see pp. 783–93.

K2   Kane, Margaret. "Edgar Allan Poe and Architecture." *SR*, XL (April–June 1932), 149–60.

Poe's architecture is derived from the haunted castle of the Gothic romance.

K3 Kaplan, Sidney, ed. *The Narrative of Arthur Gordon Pym*. With introd. New York: Hill and Wang, 1960.

Surveys critical opinion of Poe's novel and concludes that the black and white symbolism suggests a religious allegory. See "Introduction," pp. vii–xxv; reprinted in Robert Regan, ed., *Poe: A Collection of Critical Essays* (Englewood Cliffs, N.J.: Prentice-Hall, 1967), pp. 145–63.

K4 Kaun, Alexander. "Poe and Gogol: A Comparison." *Slavonic Rev* (London), XV (Jan. 1937), 389–99.

Both Poe and Gogol "manifested their over-valuation of the opposite sex."

K5 Kayser, Wolfgang J. "The Grotesque in the Age of Romanticism." *The Grotesque in Art and Literature*. Trans. Ulrich Weisstein. Gloucester, Mass.: Peter Smith, 1963, pp. 48–99.

Poe's use of the "grotesque"; see pp. 76–81.

K6 Keefer, Lubov Breit. "Poe in Russia." *Poe in Foreign Lands and Tongues*. A Symposium of the Edgar Allan Poe Society of Baltimore, January 19, 1941. Ed. John C. French. Baltimore: Johns Hopkins, 1941, pp. 11–21.

Poe's reputation was high at the turn of the century.

K7 Keefer, T. Frederick. " 'The City in the Sea': A Reexamination." *CE*, XXV (March 1964), 436–39.

Poe's poem is a word picture of a dead city.

K8 Keiley, Jarvis. *Edgar Allan Poe: A Probe*. New York: Prometheus Press, 1927.

Attempts to find a key to Poe's personality and ends inconclusively by quoting "Silence" as a key.

K9 Kelley, Abner Wellington. "Literary Theories about Program Music." *PMLA*, LII (June 1937), 581–95.

Includes comments on program music by J. K. Paulding, C. P. Cranch, Thoreau, Emerson, Lanier, and Poe. For Poe's remarks, see pp. 592–93.

*K10 Kelly, George E. *The Aesthetic Theories of Edgar Allan Poe: An Analytical Study of His Literary Criticism*. Ann Arbor, Mich.: University Microfilms, 1953.

K11 ———. "The Aesthetic Theories of Edgar Allan Poe: An Analytical Study of His Literary Criticism." *DA*, XIII (1953), 1184–85.

K12 ———. "The Aesthetic Theories of Edgar Allan Poe: An Analytical Study of His Literary Criticism." Diss., University of Iowa, 1953.

Poe's concepts of unity and of Beauty are the bases of his clearly conceived aesthetic theory.

K13   ———. "Poe's Theory of Beauty." *AL,* XXVII (Jan. 1956),
521–36.
Critic examines Poe's theory of beauty and finds that "the funda-
mental construct in Poe's theory is his hypostatization of beauty as a
transempirical and ideal entity" (primarily Platonic) and that Poe's
comprehensive theory is curiously original and remarkably consistent.

K14   ———. "Poe's Theory of Unity." *PQ,* XXXVII (Jan. 1958),
34–44.
Traces the growth of Poe's theory of unity of effect that posits both
structural and psychological unity and emphasizes Poe's concern for
the single response created in the mind of the reader and for the
denouement as a structural concept.

K15   Kendall, Lyle H., Jr. "The Vampire Motif in 'The Fall of
the House of Usher.'" *CE,* XXIV (March 1963), 450–53.
"Madeline is a vampire—a succubus."

K16   Kennedy, Ralph Clarence, Jr. *The Poems and Short Stories of
Edgar Allan Poe: Their Composition, Publication, and Reception.* Ann
Arbor, Mich.: University Microfilms, 1961.

K17   ———. "The Poems and Short Stories of Edgar Allan Poe: Their
Composition, Publication, and Reception." *DA* (Oct. 1961), 1158.
Collects information of what is known about the composition, pub-
lication, and contemporary reception of Poe's poems and stories.

*K18   ———. "The Poems and Short Stories of Edgar Allan Poe:
Their Composition, Publication, and Reception." Diss., University of
Arkansas, 1961.

K19   Kent, Charles William. "A Biographical Sketch." *Poems,* by
Edgar Allan Poe. Ed. Kent. New York: Macmillan, 1903, pp. xiii–xxv.
Biographical details taken from Virginia edition of Poe's works
edited by James A. Harrison, New York: Thomas Crowell, 1902.

K20   ———. A Critical Introduction." *Poems,* by Edgar Allan Poe. Ed.
Kent. New York: Macmillan, 1903, pp. xxvii–xxxvii.
Divides the poems into: "Poems of Personal Address," "Poems of
Aspiration and Regret," "Poems of Death," "Poems of Meditation,"
"Poems of Fancy," and "An Unpublished Drama" (*Politian*).

K21   ———. "An Episode in the Early Life of Poe." *Century Mag.* NS
XL (Oct. 1901), 955–56.
Finds evidence in a letter from William Galt to Allen Fowlds that
Poe made a visit to the continent during his early visit in England.

K22   ———. "Introduction." *The Complete Poetical Works of Edgar
Allan Poe.* Vol. VII of *The Complete Works of Edgar Allan Poe.* Ed.

James A. Harrison. 17 vols. New York: T. Y. Crowell, 1902, pp. ix–xxxiii.

Poe's genius is "not of mental power but of melody." Reprinted New York: AMS Press, 1965.

K23   ———. "Poe's Student Days at the University of Virginia." *Bookman,* XIII (July 1901), 430–40.

Largely based on Wertenbaker's account of Poe's stay at the University. Reprinted in *Bookman* XLIV (Jan. 1917), 517–25.

K24   ———. *The Unveiling of the Bust of Edgar Allan Poe in the Library of the University of Virginia, October the Seventh, 1899.* Lynchburg, Va.: J. P. Bell Co., 1901.

Concerns "Poe's connection with the University of Virginia, the Origin and History of the Poe Memorial Association, and the Exercises attending the Unveiling of Zolnay's Bust of Poe."

K25   ———, and John S. Patton, eds. *The Book of the Poe Centenary.* Charlottesville, Va.: Michie, 1909.

A record of the exercises at the University of Virginia, January 16–19, 1909, in commemoration of Poe's one hundredth birthday.

K26   Kent, Mariner J. "Poe's Last Poem." *Southern Bivouac,* NS II (Oct. 1886), 298–300.

K27   Kerlin, Robert T. *"Wieland* and *The Raven." MLN,* XXXI (Dec. 1916), 503–5.

K28   Kern, Alfred Allan. "News for Bibliophiles." *Nation,* XCVII (Oct. 22, 1913), 381–82.

On the accuracy of Poe's cryptograph in "The Gold Bug."

K29   ———. "Poe's Theory of Poetry." *Bulletin of Randolph-Macon Woman's College,* XIX (Oct.–Dec. 1932), 10–13.

K30   Kettell, Samuel. *Specimens of American Poetry.* 3 vols. Boston: S. G. Goodrich, 1829.

In a twenty-five page "Catalogue of American Poetry" there is a mere listing of Poe's *Tamerlane . . . by a Bostonian.* See III, 405.

K31   Kiehl, James M. "The Valley of Unrest: A Major Metaphor in the Poetry of Edgar Allan Poe." *Thoth,* V (Winter 1964), 45–52.

Poe's valley-of-unrest metaphor "provides ingress to the misty regions of his private symbolism."

K32   Kiely, Robert. "The Comic Masks of Edgar Allan Poe." *Umanesimo,* I (Sept. 1967), pp. 31–41.

Poe's comic mode suggests his laughing "at what in his life he appears to have taken most seriously."

K33   King, Albion Roy. "Edgar Allan Poe: A Study in the Motives

to Drink." *International Student,* XXXIX (Nov. 1941), 35–38, 52–56.
Poe's inspiration sprang from scholarship and not from drink.

K34   King, Clement. "Poe's Raven, A Note on the Meaning of the
Poem." *Mentor* (New York), X (Sept. 1922), 9.
The raven is "an emblem of the Irreparable, the guardian of pitiless
memories."

K35   King, Lucile. "Notes on Poe's Sources." *UTSE,* No. 10 (1930),
pp. 128–34.
Sources for "Premature Burial," "Metzengerstein," and "Some Words
with a Mummy."

K36   Kinsolving, Wythe Leigh. "Does Poe Resemble Hawthorne in
Work?" *UVaMag,* LX (Dec. 1899), 198–205.
"Poe differs from Hawthorne in the nature, the extent, and the
purpose of his productions."

K37   Kipling, Rudyard. "A Letter Concerning a Proposal to Buy the
Cottage in Which Edgar Allan Poe Wrote Ulalume." Chicago: n.p.,
1924.
Facsimile of unpublished original letter in the collection of William
Carpenter.

K38   Kirby, John P. "Poe's *Ulalume." Expl,* I (Oct. 1942), item 8.
Analyzes the rhythm of Poe's poem.

K39   Knapp, George L. "Poe." *Lippincott's,* LXXXIII (Jan. 1909),
74–81.
Poe's "morbid" genius arises from his loneliness and isolation, not
from liquor and opium.

K40   Knox, Robert B. " 'La mariposa negra' and 'The Raven.' "
Symposium, XI (Spring, 1957), 111–16.
Finds a noteworthy resemblance between Poe's "The Raven" and
"La mariposa negra" of Nicomedes Pastor Díaz.

K41   Kogan, Bernard. "Poe, the 'Penn,' and the 'Stylus.' " *SLM,* II
(Aug. 1940), 442–45.
Of the lifelong dreams of Poe and the nonfulfillment of national
literary journals.

K42   Koopman, Harry Lyman. "Poe in Providence." *Brown Alumni
Monthly,* IX (Jan. 1909), 137–39.
Poe's relations with Mrs. Whitman and Brown University Library's
acceptance of the Whitman papers.

K43   ——. "Poe's Hundredth Birthday." *Brown Alumni Monthly,*
IX (Feb. 1909), 168.
Verse.

K44   Korponay, Béla. "Edgar Allan Poe in Hungary." *Hungarian
Studies in English,* I (1963), 43–62.

Traces Poe's reputation in Hungary. Reprinted Budapest: Tankön-yvkiadó, 1963.

K45 Kramer, Aaron. "The Prophetic Tradition in American Poetry: 1835–1900 (Volumes One and Two)." *DA*, XXVII (April 1967), 3461A.
Poe's "pertinence to this investigation is slight."

K46 Krappe, Edith S. "A Possible Source for Poe's 'The Tell-Tale Heart' and 'The Black Cat.' " *AL*, XII (March 1940), 84–88.
Points out "striking" parallels with Dickens's "The Clock-Case: A Confession Found in a Prison in the Time of Charles the Second," published in *Master Humphrey's Clock.*

*K47 Kremenliev, Elva Baer. *The Literary Uses of Astronomy in the Writings of Edgar Allan Poe.* Ann Arbor, Mich.: University Micro-films, 1963.

K48 ———. "The Literary Uses of Astronomy in the Writings of Edgar Allan Poe." *DA*, XXIV (April 1964), 4176.
Poe "incorporated ideas and data from astronomical science into every type of work he produced."

*K49 ———. "The Literary Uses of Astronomy in the Writings of Edgar Allan Poe." Diss., University of California at Los Angeles, 1963.

K50 Kreymborg, Alfred. "Edgar Allan Poe." *Our Singing Strength.* New York: Coward-McCann, 1929.
Poe's influence "has been profounder than his performance as a poet"; to magazine work Poe "brought a constructive genius of the first order"; see pp. 53–66.

K51 [Kroeger, A. E.] "Edgar A. Poe: His Life and Literary Labors." St. Louis *Republican,* Nov. 2, 1875, p. 2.
Praises Poe's prose and style, but has little liking for his subject matter.

K52 Kronegger, M. E. "Joyce's Debt to Poe and the French Symbolists." *RLC,* XXXIX (April–June 1965), 243–54.
Some of Joyce's most important artistic devices were derived from Poe.

K53 ———. "The Theory of Unity and Effect in the Works of E. A. Poe and James Joyce." *RLC,* XL (April–June 1966), 226–34.
"Poe and Joyce, like all impressionists, do not state essentials; instead they describe the detail."

K54 Krutch, Joseph W. "Correspondence: Mr. Krutch Stands His Ground." New York *Herald-Tribune,* May 2, 1926, sec. 7, p. 19.
On James S. Wilson's criticism of Krutch's *Edgar Allan Poe.*

K55 ———. *Edgar Allan Poe: A Study in Genius.* New York: A. A. Knopf, 1926.

Attempts to analyze Poe's works as a projection of the writer's personality affected by heredity and environment. Reprinted New York: Russell & Russell, 1965. Krutch's section "The Philosophy of Composition" appears in Robert Regan, ed., *Poe: A Collection of Critical Essays* (Englewood Cliffs, N.J.: Prentice-Hall, 1967), pp. 15–30.
    Reviewed:
TLS, Aug. 5, 1926, p. 523.
Edward Shanks, *SatR,* CXLII (Sept. 18, 1926), 314.
H. L. Mencken, *Nation,* CXXII (March 17, 1926), 289–90.
P. H. Boynton, *New Republic,* XLVII (June 9, 1926), 92–93.
T. M. Parrott, *YR,* XVI, 172–74.
N. Foerster, *SatRL,* II (June 5, 1926), 834–35.
B. Matthews, *Literary Digest International Book Rev,* IV (July 1926), 478–80.
Pruette, Lorine, *Bookman,* LXIII, 483–84.
Mary Austin, *Forum,* LXXVI, 474–75.
Ernest Boyd, *Independent,* CXVI (March 20, 1926), 333.
H.J., *Independent,* CXVI (May 15, 1926), 582.
J. A. Coblentz, *Literary Digest International Book Rev,* IV (April 1926), 326.
J. S. Wilson, *NYHTBR,* April 18, 1926, p. 22.

K56 ———. "His Nightmares Go on Forevermore." *NYTBR,* Jan. 18, 1959, pp. 1, 22.
Krutch qualifies his earlier observations based on psychological theory.

K57 ———. "Introduction." *The Narrative of Arthur Gordon Pym,* by Edgar Allan Poe. New York: Heritage, 1930, pp. vii–xvi.
Pym reflects Poe's imaginative mind and depicts a "purely fantastic world."

K58 ———. "Poe's Idea of Beauty." *Nation,* CXXII (March 17, 1926), 285–87.
Traces Poe's "art to an abnormal condition of the nerves and his critical ideas to a rationalized defense of the limitations of his own taste."

K59 ———. "Poe's Wife and Art." *Modern American Prose.* Ed. Carl Van Doren. New York: Harcourt, Brace, 1934, pp. 550–72.
Many of Poe's stories reflect an "attempt to adjust himself to actuality" and an "attempt to create, after the manner of neurotics, an imaginary world to fit the needs of his mind."

K60 ———. "The Strange Case of Poe." *American Mercury,* VI (Nov. 1925), 349–56.

Poe clung to his logic as a proof of his sanity: he "invented the detective story in order that he might not go mad."

K61 ———. "Young Poe." *Nation,* CXXI (Nov. 4, 1925), 518–19.
A review of the Valentine letters.

K62 Kummer, George. "Another Poe-Coleridge Parallel?" *AL,* VIII (March 1936), 72.
A suggestion of parallelism between Poe's "the weary, way worn wanderer" and Coleridge's "minister refreshment to the tired way-wanderer," a passage from vol. II of "The Destiny of Nations."

L

L1 L., E. E. " 'Pallid Bust' Is the Subject [of] Controversy." Baltimore *Sun,* Jan. 15, 1922, sec. VI, p. 3.
Was "the pallid bust" in "The Raven" one of Pallas or of Dante?

L2 Labree, Lawrence. " 'Old Kit' and James Russell Lowell." *Illustrated Mag of Literature and Art* (New York), I (Oct. 11, 1845), 64.
Approves Poe's defensive position in regard to James Russell Lowell.

L3 [———.] [Review of Poe's Tales.] *The Rover,* V (June 28, 1845), 240.

L4 ———. [Review of *The Raven and Other Poems.*] *Illustrated Mag of Literature and Art* (New York), I (Dec. 6, 1845), 192.
Mildly praises Poe's poetry, especially "The Raven."

L5 Lafleur, Laurence. "Edgar Allan Poe as a Philosopher." *Person,* XXII (Oct. 1941), 401–5.
Poe's *Eureka,* although lacking in several respects, is to be admired and touches upon an original suggestion: "the identification of the repulsive principle with mind."

L6 Lamb, M. J. "Poe's House at Fordham." *Appleton's Jour,* XII (July 18, 1874), 75–77.
A description of the Fordham Cottage with an illustration of it captioned "The House in which Poe Wrote 'The Raven.' "

L7 Lane, Winthrop D. "The Mystery of Mary Rogers." *Collier's* LXXXV (March 8, 1930), 19, 50, 52.

L8 Lang, Andrew. "Edgar Allan Poe." *Independent,* LI (Nov. 1899), 3132–34.
Reflections on Poe's life, his work, and literary reputation.

L9   ———. *Letters to Dead Authors.* New York: C. Scribner's Sons, 1886.

"Best known in your own day as a critic, it is as a poet and a writer of short tales that you must live"; see pp. 140–51 for letter to Poe.

L10   ———. "The Poetry of Edgar Allan Poe." *The Poems of Edgar Allan Poe.* Ed. Lang. London: Kegan Paul, Trench, 1881, pp. xiii–xxvi.

L11   Lanier, Sidney. *The Science of English Verse.* New York: Charles Scribner's Sons, 1880.

Briefly discusses Poe's "The Rationale of Verse," *The Raven,* and *Eureka, passim.*

L12   Laser, Marvin. "The Growth and Structure of Poe's Concept of Beauty." *ELH,* XV (March 1948), 69–84.

Traces the threefold influence of Coleridge, phrenology, and Shelley's "Defence" upon "Poe's meaningful but not particularly original theory of Beauty."

L13   ———. "Poe's Critical Theories—Sense or Nonsense?" *ESQ,* No. 31 (2nd Quarter 1963), pp. 20–23.

Poe's critical theories throw light upon his own art but have little relationship to most of the world's great literature.

L14   Lathrop, George. "Poe, Irving, and Hawthorne." *Scribner's Monthly,* XI (April 1876), 799–808.

Irving "ranks higher than Poe for human sympathy, and incipient humor . . . . Neither of them had insight. . . . But Hawthorne had insight in the profoundest sense."

L15   Latimer, George D. "The Tales of Poe and Hawthorne." *New England Mag,* NS XXX (Aug. 1904), 692–703.

Poe's lack of moral emphasis is a commendable element.

L16   Latrobe, John H. B. "Reminiscences of Poe by John H. B. Latrobe." *Poems and Essays of Edgar Allan Poe.* New York: W. J. Widdleton, 1876, pp. cxlvii–clii.

"Personal Recollections" delivered during the dedicatory ceremonies of the Poe monument in Baltimore.

L17   Lauber, John. " 'Ligeia' and Its Critics: A Plea for Liberalism." *SSF,* IV (Fall 1966), 28–32.

Argues for a literal reading of Poe's story.

L18   Laughlin, Clara E. "Stories of Authors' Loves. III—Poor Poe." *Good Words,* XLIV (Sept. 1903), 664–69.

L19   Lauter, Paul. "The Narrator of 'The Blessed Damozel.' " *MLN,* LXXIII (May 1958), 344–48.

"Includes a discussion of similarities between the poem and Poe's 'The Raven.' " *AL.*

L20   Laverty, Carroll. "The Death's-Head on the Gold-Bug." *AL,*
XII (March 1940), 88–91.
One element "going into the gold-bug was the death's-head moth of
which Poe had read" and had described in "The Sphinx."

L21   ———. "A Note on Poe in 1838." *MLN,* LXIV (March 1949),
174–76.
Presents evidence as to when Poe left for Philadelphia from New
York in 1838.

L22   ———. "Poe in 1847." *AL,* XX (May 1948), 163–68.
"Reminiscences entitled 'Recollections of Edgar A. Poe' by an un-
known woman; first published in the *Home* journal, July 21, 1860."
II.

L23   ———. "Poe in His Place: In His Time." *ESQ,* No. 31 (2nd
quarter 1963), pp. 23–25.
"In his knowledge of science and pseudo-science and in his use of
both in much of his writing, Poe was in his place—in his time."

L24   ———. "Science and Pseudo-Science in the Writings of Edgar
Allan Poe." Diss., Duke University, 1951.
Treats separately the various sciences that Poe used as a literary
artist.

L25   Law, Frederick Houk. "An Estimate of the Poetry of Long-
fellow, Whittier, Poe, and Lowell." *Selections from American Poetry.*
Ed. Law. Boston: Houghton Mifflin, 1915, pp. 71–121.
Poe employed his art in the service of beauty; see pp. 119–20.

L26   ———. "Introduction. Poe's Fascinating Power." *Tales and
Poems,* by Edgar Allan Poe. Ed. Law. New York: Charles E. Merrill,
1914, pp. 7–15.
Briefly attempts to determine Poe's significance in the development
of poetry and the short story.

L27   Law, Robert Adger. "A Source for 'Annabel Lee.' " *JEGP,* XXI
(April 1922), 341–46.
The source is a poem in the Charleston, S.C., *Courier* of Dec. 4,
1807, perhaps discovered by Poe when looking for notices of his
parents' acting in Charleston.

L28   Lawrence, D. H. "Poe." *Studies in Classic American Literature.*
New York: Boni, 1923, 93–120.
Stresses Poe's emphasis upon love and upon the desire of self-destruc-
tion of the soul. Shorter version appeared in the *English Rev,*
XXVIII (April 1919), 278–91. Reprinted in Eric Carlson, ed., *The
Recognition of Edgar Allan Poe* (Ann Arbor, University of Michi-
gan Press, 1966), pp. 110–26.

*L29   ———. *The Symbolic Meaning: The Uncollected Version of Studies in Classic American Literature.* Ed. Armin Arnold. Fontwell, Arundel: Centaur Press, 1962.

"Contains Lawrence's original essay on Poe that appeared in the *English Review* for April 1919, and which the editor believes is superior to the revised essay." *PN.*

L30   Lawson, Lewis A. "Poe's Conception of the Grotesque." *MissQ,* XIX (Fall 1966), 200–205.

For Poe, the term *grotesque* characterizes the desirable elements of his art.

L31   Lea, Henry C. "Poe's Tales of the Grotesque." *Nation,* XXXI (Dec. 9, 1880), 408.

Letter to editor on the reception of Poe's *Tales.*

L32   Leary, Lewis. "Poe, Edgar Allan." *Articles on American Literature, 1900–1950.* Durham, N.C.: Duke University Press, 1954, pp. 236–49.

Most complete bibliography of articles on Poe.

L33   ———. "Poe's *Ulalume." Expl,* VI (Feb. 1948), item 25.

Poe's "misty mid regions" and the paintings of Robert Walter Weir.

L34   Lee, Agnes. "Singer of the Shadows." *North American Rev,* CLXXXIX (Jan. 1909), 127–29.

Verse. Also appeared in *Current Literature,* XLVI (March 1909), 332–33.

L35   Lee, Helen. "Possibilities of *Pym." EJ,* LV (Dec. 1966), 1149–54.

By coordinating image and structure throughout *Pym,* Poe "uses artistic order to demonstrate the disorder of human experience."

L36   Lee, Muna. "Brother of Poe." *Southwest Rev,* XI (July 1926), 305–12.

Concerning José Asunción Silva, Poe's "Spanish interpreter and occasional translator."

L37   Legler, Henry Edward. *Poe's Raven: Its Origin and Genesis, a Compilation and a Survey.* Wausau, Wis.: Philosopher Press, 1907.

An examination of the alleged sources of the poem.

*L38   Lehmner, Derrick N. "Edgar Allan Poe." *Overland Monthly,* NS LXXXVII (July 1929), 213.

L39   Leigh, Oliver. ["Geoffrey Quarles"] [*sic*]. *Edgar Allan Poe, the Man, the Master, the Martyr.* Chicago: Frank M. Morris, 1906.

Contains extended discussion of Poe portraits with some commentary on Poe's critics and theory of poetry.

L40 [———.] "Introductory Argument." *The Poets and Poetry of America: A Satire.* New York: Benjamin and Bell, 1887, pp. 5–36.

> Argues that Poe was "Levante," the author of the satiric poem entitled *The Poets and Poetry of America.*

L41 Lenhart, Charmian S. "Poe and Music." *Musical Influence on American Poetry.* Athens: University of Georgia Press, 1956, pp. 125–60.

> Poe deliberately composed poetry to musical principles and achieved perhaps incomparable "verbal melody, rhythmic flow, and a certain fascinating 'tone.' "

L42 Lesser, Maximus. " 'Annabel Lee' and 'Rosalie Lee.' " New York *Times,* May 4, 1913, p. 270.

> Denies that "Annabel Lee" had "ancestor in 'Rosalie Lee' of the eccentric Dr. Thomas Holley Chivers."

L43 Levin, Harry. *The Power of Blackness: Hawthorne, Poe, Melville.* New York: A. A. Knopf, 1958.

> Poe, by means of his analytic vigor, makes a bold attempt in his work "to face the true darkness in its most tangible manifestations."
> Reviewed:

Newt Arvin, *AL,* XXX, 379–80.

A. C. Kettle, *RES,* XI, 114–17.

L44 Levine, Stuart G. "Poe's *Julius Rodman:* Judaism, Plagiarism, and the Wild West." *MQ,* I (Spring 1960), 245–59.

> Poe's *Julius Rodman* is an inferior composition of a hard-working journalist, but it suggests Poe's possible intent to compose a sustained picaresque novel.

L45 ———. *"The Proper Spirit": A Study of the Prose Fiction of Edgar Poe.* Ann Arbor, Mich.: University Microfilms, 1958.

L46 ———. " 'The Proper Spirit': A Study of the Prose Fiction of Edgar Poe." *DA,* XIX (Jan. 1959), 1742.

L47 ———. " 'The Proper Spirit': A Study of the Prose Fiction of Edgar Poe." Diss. in American Civilization, Brown University, 1958.

> Emphasizes the variety of predominant themes in Poe's fiction, but largely overlooks Poe's satiric qualities.

L48 ———. "Scholarly Strategy: The Poe Case." *AQ,* XVII (Spring 1965), 133–44.

> Poe scholarship has not been cumulative and does not establish his worth as a writer.

L49 Lewis, Charles Lee. "Edgar Allan Poe and the Sea." *SLM,* III (Jan. 1941), 5–10.

Evidence demonstrates that "Poe felt strongly the fascination of the sea."

*L50   Ligon, John Frank, Jr. *On Desperate Seas: A Study of Poe's Imaginary Journeys.* Ann Arbor, Mich.: University Microfilms, 1961.

L51   ——. "On Desperate Seas: A Study of Poe's Imaginary Journeys." *DA,* XXII (March 1962), 3201–2.

"Poe's artistic development is marked by an increasingly organic functioning of the concept of the soul's pilgrimage."

*L52   ——. "On Desperate Seas: A Study of Poe's Imaginary Journeys." Diss., University of Washington, 1961.

L53   Lind, Sidney E. "Poe and Mesmerism." *PMLA,* LXII (Dec. 1947), 1077–94.

Poe's "A Tale of the Ragged Mountains," "Mesmeric Revelation," and "The Facts in the Case of M. Valdemar" reflect elements of contemporary mesmeric theory.

L54   Lindsay, N. Vachel. "The Wizard in the Street (Concerning Edgar Allan Poe)." *Collected Poems.* New York: Macmillan, 1923, pp. 256–58.

Sees Poe as entertaining "wizard." Reprinted in Eric Carlson, ed., *The Recognition of Edgar Allan Poe* (Ann Arbor: University of Michigan Press, 1966), pp. 101–2.

L55   Lindsay, Philip. *The Haunted Man: A Portrait of Edgar Allan Poe.* London: Hutchinson, 1953.

Poe, affected by the "fever of living" and haunted by the death of women closest to him, longed for death—a longing reflected in his works.

Reviewed:

N. B. Fagin, *SatR* (Sept. 4, 1954), pp. 16–17.

L56   Link, Samuel Albert. *Pioneers of Southern Literature.* 2 vols. Nashville: Publishing House of the Methodist Episcopal Church, South, 1903.

This is little more than a résumé of all the favorable estimates of Poe; see II, 288–331.

L57   [Linton, William James] "Abel Reid." *Pot-Pourri.* New York: S. W. Green, 1875.

Parodies of Poe's poems.

L58   Lipscomb, Herbert C. "Poe's 'Nicean Barks' Again." *CJ,* XXIX (March 1934), 454.

Allusions in "To Helen" are not particular or specific.

L59   Lisenby, Annie White. "In Memory of Edgar Allan Poe." *Christian Advocate* (Nashville), LXX (Jan. 15, 1909), 8, [72].

A verse tribute.

L60   Livingston, Luther S. "The First Books of Some American Authors. III—Irving, Poe and Whitman." *Bookman,* VIII (Nov. 1898), 230–35.

Bibliographical commentary on *Tamerlane;* see pp. 232–33.

L61   Lloyd, John Arthur Thomas. "Edgar Allan Poe." *Fortnightly Rev,* NS 123 (June 1928), pp. 828–40.

Review of *Edgar Allan Poe, the Man* by Mary E. Phillips.

L62   ———. *The Murder of Edgar Allan Poe.* London. Stanley Paul, 1931.

Poe's "life struggle reads like a veritable novel, the villain of which is his first biographer"—Rufus Griswold.

Reviewed:

TLS, Nov. 19, 1931, p. 911.

SatR, CLXII (Dec. 5, 1931), 728.

L63   ———. "Who Wrote 'English Notes'?" *Colophon,* NS I (Summer 1935), 107–18.

Argues that Poe is the author of "English Notes."

L64   Locke, Jane Ermina Starkweather. "Requiem for Edgar A. Poe." *The Recalled: In Voices of the Past, and Poems of the Ideal.* Boston: James Monroe, 1854, pp. 29–31.

A verse tribute.

L65   Lockspeiser, Edward. "Debussy and Edgar Allan Poe." *Listener,* LXVIII (Oct. 18, 1962), 609–10.

Debussy was "profoundly affected by Poe."

L66   Lograsso, Angeline H. "Poe's Piero Maroncelli." *PMLA,* LVIII (Sept. 1943), 780–89.

"In his *Literati* Edgar Allan Poe has left for students of Italian literature and history, a very precious contemporary picture of Piero Marconelli."

L67   Loisette, Prof. A. *Assimilative Memory; or, How to Attend and Never Forget.* New York: Funk & Wagnalls, 1896.

Poe's "The Bells" used as illustrative poem in the methods of memorizing poetry; see pp. 56–60.

L68   Lombroso, Cesare. *The Man of Genius.* London: Walter Scott, 1891.

See pp. 318–19.

*L69   Long, Amelia Reynolds. *Death Looks Down.* New York: Ziff-Davis, 1945.

Uses Poe's work to embellish an interesting murder yarn. See Fagin's *The Histrionic Mr. Poe,* p. 223.

L70   Longfellow, Henry Wadsworth. *Final Memorials of Henry Wadsworth Longfellow.* Boston: Ticknor, 1887.

Longfellow's remarks on Poe to William Winter are quoted; see p. 310.

L71   Loomis, C. B. "Poe's Raven in an Elevator." *Ladies Home Jour,* XX (Oct. 1903), 8.

L72   Lovecraft, Howard P. "Edgar Allan Poe." *The Supernatural Horror in Literature.* New York: B. Abramson, 1945, pp. 52–59.
To Poe "we owe the modern horror-story in its final and perfected state."

L73   Lowell, Amy. "The Saturday Club." *NYTBR,* May 14, 1919, pp. 253, 261–62 ff.
Some remarks concern Poe's relations with Longfellow.

L74   Lowell, James Russell. "Edgar A. Poe." *The Works of the Late Edgar Allan Poe,* by N. P. Willis, J. R. Lowell, and R. W. Griswold. 2 vols. New York: J. S. Redfield, 1850, I, vii–xiii.
Poe has "a faculty of vigorous and yet minute analysis, and a wonderful fecundity of imagination." Reprinted from *Graham's Mag,* XXVII (Feb. 1845), 49–53, with a few alterations and omissions. Appearing also in *Prose Tales,* by Edgar Allan Poe (London: George Routledge and Sons, 1897), pp. vii–xviii; and in Eric Carlson, ed., *The Recognition of Edgar Allan Poe* (Ann Arbor: University of Michigan Press, 1966), pp. 5–17.

L75   Lubbers, Klaus. "Poe's 'The Conqueror Worm.' " *AL,* XXXIX (Nov. 1967), 375–79.
Poe's poem depicts a "broken cosmic order."

L76   Lubell, Albert J. "Edgar Allan Poe: Critic and Reviewer." Diss., New York University, 1951.
Poe's critical theory, developed from various sources, marks an initial trend toward aestheticism.

L77   ———. "Poe and A. W. Schlegel." *JEGP,* LII (Jan. 1953), 1–12.
Argues that Poe absorbed and used the ideas in Schlegel's *Lectures.*

L78   Lucas, Frank L. *Literature and Psychology.* Ann Arbor: University of Michigan Press, 1957.
Comments on Marie Bonaparte's life of Poe, pp. 130–35.

L79   Luck, John Jennings. "Poe and the University of Virginia." *UVaMag,* LXIX (Jan. 1909), 204–9.
The traditions of Poe's nickname "Guffy" and of his broadjump of twenty-one and one-half feet are repeated.

L80   Lynch, James J. "The Devil in the Writings of Irving, Hawthorne, and Poe." *NYFQ,* VIII (Summer 1952), 111–13.
"Bon-Bon," "The Devil in the Belfry," "Never Bet the Devil Your

Head" reveal Poe's conception of his devil "in terms of the grotesque with admixture of grisly and clumsy humor, to which are added a satirical and debunking attitude."

L81 Lyne, Mrs. William. "Reminiscences of Mrs. William Lyne of Orange." *WMQ,* XIII (July 1933), 184–85.

Mentions Poe with Dickens, Thackeray, Owen Meredith, and John R. Thompson in her reminiscences.

L82 Lynn, Kenneth S., ed. *The Comic Tradition in America.* New York: Doubleday, 1958.

Contains Poe's "How to Write a Blackwood Article" and "Diddling Considered as One of the Exact Sciences" and a commentary by the editor (pp. 124–26).

L83 Lyons, Nathan. "Kafka and Poe—and Hope." *Minnesota Rev,* V (May–July 1965), 158–68.

Kafka's work was "prayer," a beginning of a whole knowledge of life, and "his similarities to Poe reveal not only a consummate growth in craft and existential engagement," but a link with a romantic and sentimental tradition.

Mc

Mc1 McAleer, John J. "Poe and Gothic Elements in *Moby-Dick.*" *ESQ,* No. 27 (2nd quarter 1962), p. 34.

Compares Poe's description of the House of Usher with Melville's first description of Captain Ahab.

Mc2 McCabe, Lida R. "A Pilgrimage to Poe's Cottage." *Book Buyer,* NS XXV (Jan. 1903), 592–98.

Mc3 MacCarthy, Sir Desmond. "Edgar Allan Poe." *Humanities.* New York: Oxford University Press, 1954, pp. 176–79.

Reprint of 1930 essay.

Mc4 McClary, Ben H. "A Poesque Lincoln: Orpheus C. Kerr's 'Baltimore.' " *Lincoln Herald,* LXIV (Winter 1962), 182–84.

Presents an adaptation of "The Raven" by Robert Henry Newell.

Mc5 McCorison, Marcus Allen. "An Unpublished Poe Letter." *AL,* XXXII (Jan. 1961), 455–56.

Poe replies to an invitation to attend the annual exercises of the literary societies of the University of Vermont in the spring of 1846.

Mc6   McCusker, Honor. "The Correspondence of R. W. Griswold." *More Books* (*Bulletin of the Boston Public Library*), XVI (March, April, May, and June 1941), 105–16, 152–56, 190–96, 286–89.

The Griswold collection includes over twelve hundred letters; in this group there are nineteen autograph letters by Poe.

Mc7   McDevitt, William. "Un Poe de Chambre." *Book Collecting* (For Love or Money), VIII (Aug. 1938), 1, 7.

Biographical commentary upon Poe's life before the 1827 publication of *Tamerlane and Other Poems*.

Mc8   [Macdonald, Dwight.] "Introduction." *Poems of Edgar Allan Poe*. Selected by Macdonald. New York: Thomas Y. Crowell, 1965, pp. 1–21.

"Poetry was Poe's natural voice" and reflected a personal "literary charisma."

Reviewed:

L. S. Seacord, *Library Jour,* XC, 4632.

R. A. Thompson, *Bookweek,* April 10, 1966, p. 10.

Booklist, LXII, 444.

R. H. Viguers, *Horn Book,* XLII, 63.

Mc9   ——. "Masscult and Midcult." *PR,* XXVII (Spring 1960), 203–33 (Fall 1960), 589–631.

"Includes discussion of Poe, Frost, Hemingway, and MacLeish." *AL.*

Mc10   McDowell, Tremaine. "Edgar Allan Poe and William Cullen Bryant." *PQ,* XVI (Jan. 1937), 83–84.

Bryant had little sympathy for Poe, while Poe frequently read Bryant's poems.

Mc11   ——, ed. *The Romantic Triumph: American Literature from 1830 to 1860*. Vol. II of *American Literature: A Period Anthology*. 4 vols. New York: Macmillan, 1933.

See pp. 899–905 for editorial commentary on Poe's life and work along with a selected bibliography of Poe scholarship.

Reviewed:

George Paine, *AL,* VI, 219.

*****Mc12**   McElderry, Bruce R., Jr. "The Edgar Allan Poe Collection." *University of Southern California Library Bulletin,* No. 4 (Jan. 1948), pp. 4–6.

Poe material at the University of Southern California. *AL.*

Mc13   ——. "Poe's Concept of the Soul." *N&Q,* CC (April 1955), 173–74.

Poe obtruded a nonrational concept of soul in "The Philosophy of Composition."

Mc14   McGaffey, Ernest. "Coronation Ode." *National Mag,* XVII (Nov. 1902), 175–76.
Verse tribute to Poe.

Mc15   MacKaye, Percy. *The Far Familiar: Fifty New Poems.* London: Richards, 1938.
Poe engages in a dialogue in "Cronklands," pp. 46–50.

Mc16   McKeithan, Daniel Morley. "Two Sources of Poe's 'Narrative of Arthur Gordon Pym.'" *USTE,* No. 13 (1933), pp. 116–37.
Sources are Archibald Duncan's *The Mariner's Chronicle* (1806) and Capt. Benjamin Morrell's *A Narrative of Four Voyages to the South Seas* (1832).

Mc17   MacKintosh, Emily J. "Homes of American Poets." *Peterson's Mag,* XCI (Jan. 1887), 33–39.

Mc18   McLean, Francis Elliott Hall. "Periodicals Published in the South before 1880." Diss., University of Virginia, 1928.
Some slight discussion of Poe in connection with the *Southern Literary Messenger.*

Mc19   McLean, Frank. "The Conditions under Which Poe Did His Imaginative Work." *SR,* XXXIV (April–June 1926), 184–85.
Poe "needed leisure to create, and a purpose more compelling than that of creation for its own sake."

Mc20   McLean, Sydney R. "Poeana: I. A Valentine." *Colophon,* NS I (Autumn 1935), 183–87.
Annotations on "A Valentine" which Poe wrote in 1846 to Miss Louisa Oliver Hunter, the prize-winning contestant in a poetry contest for the graduates of Rutgers Female Seminary.

Mc21   McLuhan, Herbert M. "Edgar Poe's Tradition." *SR,* LII (Jan. 1944), 24–33.
"Puts Poe in tradition of Byron and Baudelaire, running back to Cicero's *De Oratore.*" *BB.*

Mc22   McNeal, Thomas H. "Poe's *Zenobia:* An Early Satire on Margaret Fuller." *MLQ,* IX (June 1950), 215–26.
"Margaret Fuller is the Psyche Zenobia of Poe's satires."

Mc23   MacPherson, H. D. "Poe and Dumas Again." *SatRL,* VI (Feb. 22, 1930), 760.

Mc24   Macready, William. "The Fried-Fiend." London *Morning Star,* Sept. 1, 1864, p. 4.
Claims Poe wrote a parody of "The Raven."

Mc25   McWilliams, Carey. "Poe Criticism." *SatRL,* III (Sept. 25, 1926), 146.

M

M1   M., P. "The Raven and Its Shadow." *Academy,* LXII (May 17, 1902), 515.
Queries the locus of the lamp that could throw the raven's shadow on the floor.

M1a   M., T. O. [Mabbott, Thomas Ollive]. *"Merlin* (Baltimore, 1827)." *Bibliographical Notes and Queries* (London), I (Jan. 1935), 9.
Inquires if any librarian can locate a published copy of *Merlin,* a play by Lambert A. Wilmer, dealing with Poe.

M2   Mabbott, Thomas Ollive. "Additions to 'A List of Poe's Tales.'" *N&Q,* CLXXXIII (Sept. 1942), 163–64.
"Additions, mainly of 'unauthorized reprints,' to John Cook Wyllie's 'A List of the Texts of Poe's Tales' in *Humanistic Studies in Honour of John Calvin Metcalf." AL.*

M3   ——. *Al Aaraaf.* . . . Reproduced from the Edition of 1829, with a Bibliographical Note. . . . New York: Facsimile Text Society, 1933.
This volume is reproduced from the copy in the Aldis collection in Yale University. The poems were first published by Hatch and Dunning, Baltimore, in 1829.

M4   ——. "Allusion to a Spanish Joke in Poe's 'A Valentine.'" *N&Q,* CLXIX (Sept. 14, 1935), 189.
Elucidates an obscure reference in Poe's lines addressed to Mrs. Osgood.

M5   ——. "Another Source of Poe's Play, 'Politian.'" *N&Q,* CXCIV (June 1949), 279.
Victor Hugo's *Hernani* is one probable source.

M6   ——. "Another Spurious Poe." *ABC,* III (April 1933), 233–34.
Points out some spurious Poe items in an unnamed book-sale catalogue.

M7   ——. "Antediluvian Antiquities: A Curiosity of American Literature and a Source of Poe's." *American Collector,* IV (July 1927), 124–26.

M8   ——. "Are There Flaws in 'The Cask of Amontillado'?" *N&Q,* CICIX (April 1954), 180.
Possible explanations of three inconsistencies in Poe's story.

M9 ———. "The Astrological Symbolism of Poe's 'Ulalume.'" *N&Q*, CLXI (July 11, 1931), 26–27.
The astrological allusions seem to indicate a reference to Poe's amour with Mrs. Osgood.

M10 ———. "Dumas and Poe." *TLS*, Jan. 2, 1930, p. 12.
Dumas probably was interested in Poe and, after reading Lowell's sketch in *Graham's* of 1845, Dumas "romanticized" by putting Poe in Paris after Poe's alleged visit to St. Petersburg.

M11 ———. "Dumas on Poe's Visit to Paris." New York *Times*, Dec. 22, 1929, sec. 3, p. 5.

M12 ———. "An Early Publication of 'Ligeia.'" *N&Q*, CLX (Feb. 28, 1931), 152.
The New World for Feb. 15, 1845, carried the story and the poem before *Graham's*, the *American Museum*, or the *Broadway Journal*.

M13 ———. "Echoes of Poe in Rossetti's 'Beryl Song.'" *N&Q*, CLXVIII (Feb. 2, 1935), 77.
There are echoes from "Annabel Lee" and "To One in Paradise" in this Rossetti poem.

M14 ———. "Edgar Allan Poe: A Find." *N&Q*, CL (April 3, 1926), 241.
Two poems in *Tamerlane*, "The Happiest Day, the Happiest Hour" and "Dreams: Extracts," were reprinted a few months later in the Baltimore *American*.

M15 ———. "Edgar Allan Poe: A Source of His Tale, 'X-ing a Paragrab.'" *N&Q*, CLX (Feb. 7, 1931), 100.
The source is an "Original Translation" in the *New-York Mirror* for March 5, 1836, entitled "No O's."

*M16 ———. "An Edition of Edgar Allan Poe's *Politian*." Diss., Columbia University, 1923.

M17 ———. "English Publications of Poe's 'Valdemar Case.'" *N&Q*, CLXXXIII (Nov. 1942), 311–12.
"The story was reprinted in the London *Morning Post*, January 5, 1846; in the *Popular Record of Modern Science*, January 10, 1846; and as a pamphlet, *Mesmerism, 'in articulo mortis,'* London. 1846." *AL*.

M18 ———. "Evidence That Poe Knew Greek." *N&Q*, CLXXXV (July 1943), 39–40.
"The evidence is found in Poe's handling of some lines from Callimachus's 'Hymn to Apollo' in a criticism of Lever's *Charles O'Malley* in *Graham's Magazine* for March, 1842." *AL*.

M19 ——. "A Few Notes on Poe." *MLN,* XXXV (June 1920), 373–74.
Some bibliographical notes and interpretative suggestions.

M20 ——. "The First Publication of Poe's 'Raven.'" *BNYPL,* XLVII (Aug. 1943), 581–84.
George Vandenhoff's *A Plain System of Elocution* (1845) first published Poe's poem.

M21 ——. "George H. Derby: A Debt to Poe." *N&Q,* CLXVI (March 10, 1934), 171.
The motto of Derby's *Phoenixiana* (New York, 1856) is taken from that of Poe's "How to Write a Blackwood Article." Derby also parodies some lines from *Al Aaraaf* in this volume.

M22 ——. "German Translations of Poe's 'Raven.'" *N&Q,* CLXXIV (Jan. 29, 1938), 88.
Points out that Ingram's edition of *The Raven . . . with Literary and Historical Commentary* gives reprints of, or references to, various translations of "The Raven."

M23 ——. "Greeley's Estimate of Poe." *Autograph Album,* I (Dec. 1933), 14–16, 61.
A letter from Greeley to Hosmer.

M24 ——. "Introduction." *Doings of Gotham,* by Edgar Allan Poe. First collected by Jacob E. Spannuth. Pottsville, Pa.: Jacob E. Spannuth, 1929, pp. xv–xxi.
On editing Poe's contributions to the *Columbia Spy.*

M25 ——. "Introduction." *Selected Poems of Edgar Allan Poe.* Ed. Mabbott. New York: Macmillan, 1928, pp. xi-xv.
Poe's poetry reflects qualities associated with both the Romantic and Victorian poets.
Reviewed:
Killis Campbell, *AL,* I, 103–4.
George Saintsbury, *Dial,* LXXXVI, 421–23.

M26 ——. "Introduction." *Tamerlane and Other Poems,* by Edgar Allan Poe. Reproduced in Facsimile from the Edition of 1827. New York: Facsimile Text Society, 1941, pp. v–lxvi.
Extensive editorial and critical commentary on Poe's first published poetry.
Reviewed:
AL, XIII, 187.

M27 ——. "Joel Chandler Harris: A Debt to Poe." *N&Q,* CLXVI (March 3, 1934), 151–52.
The title of one of Harris's sketches in *The Countryman* was taken from Poe.

M28 ———. "A Letter of Poe's Sister." *N&Q*, CLXIX (Dec. 28, 1935), 457.

Rosalie asks for financial assistance. Letter first appeared in the Newark (N.J.) *Advertiser* for Feb. 6, 1873.

M29 ———. "The Letters from George W. Eveleth to Edgar Allan Poe." *BNYPL*, XXVI (March 1922), 171–95.

See p. 172 for Professor Mabbott's comment upon the importance of Eveleth letters as criticism of Poe. Reprinted separately New York: New York Public Library, 1922.

M30 ———. "Letters from Mary E. Hewitt to Poe." *A Christmas Book from the Department of English*. Hunter College of the City of New York. Brooklyn: Comet Press, 1937, pp. 116–21.

The text of six letters is presented with brief editorial comment.

M31 ———. "A List of Books from Poe's Library." *N&Q*, CC (May 1955), 222–23.

"Lists four volumes indubitably owned by Poe and six others which probably were once his." *AL*.

M32 ———. "A Lost Jingle by Poe." *N&Q*, CLXXIX (Nov. 23, 1940), 371.

M33 ———. "Madam Pilan." *AN&Q*, I (April 1941), 12.

A query concerning a character in "The Imp of the Perverse."

M34 ———. "Mrs. Kirkland's 'Essay on Fiction.'" *BNYPL*, LXIV (July 1960), 396–97.

On Poe's relationship to Caroline Matilda Stansbury Kirkland (1801–65), whose "preface to an unpublished novel" is presented.

M35 ———. "Newly Found Verses Ascribed to Poe." *N&Q*, CCI (March 1956), 122.

"Ascribes an unsigned, minor humorous poem to Poe." *AL*.

M36 ———. "Newly-Identified Reviews by Edgar Poe." *N&Q*, CLXIII (Dec. 17, 1932), 441.

M37 ———. "Newly-Identified Verses by Poe." *N&Q*, CLXXVII (July 29, 1939), 77–78.

M38 ———. "Notes on Poe." *Literary Review*, New York *Evening Post* (May 27, 1922), p. 694.

Gives the location of some Poe items.

M39 ———. "Numismatic References of Three American Writers." *Numismatist*, XLVI (Nov. 1933), 688–89.

The reference in "William Wilson" to the "exergues of the Carthaginian medals" is explained as a coinage of Gaiseric.

M40 ———. *An Old Parody on Poe's Raven*, by J. Chickering. First

Published in 1849, Now Reprinted with a Note. . . . Montreal: J. A. Hamon, 1929.

"First printed in the Oquawka *Spectator* for Oct. 3, 1849."

M41 ———. "On Poe's 'Tales of the Folio Club.'" *SR,* XXXVI (April–June 1928), 171–76.

A guess as to the tales and their tellers in the Folio club group.

M42 ———. "Origin of Poe's 'Angel of the Odd.'" *N&Q,* CLX (Jan. 3, 1931), 8.

A news story in the Philadelphia *Public Ledger* of June 5, 1844, furnished the source.

M43 ———. "Palindromes (and Edgar Poe)." *N&Q,* CXCI (Nov. 1946), 238–39.

M44 ———. "Poe and Ash Upson." *N&Q,* CLXXII (May 8, 1937), 330–31.

Poe's befriending a young printer's devil, who was probably a helper in the *Broadway Journal* office in 1845.

M45 ———. "Poe and Dr. Lardner." *AN&Q,* III (Nov. 1943), 115–17.

On Poe's "Three Sundays in a Week."

M46 ———. "Poe and Emerson." *N&Q,* CXCVII (Dec. 1952), 566.

Points to parallel phrases and briefly comments on the relationship between Poe and Emerson.

M47 ———. "Poe and the Philadelphia *Irish Citizen.*" *Jour of American-Irish Historical Society,* XXIX (1931), 121–31.

The hoax "The Ghost of a Grey Tadpole" attributed to Poe was apparently written by Thomas Dunn English.

M48 ———. "Poe Letter about 'The Raven.'" *AN&Q,* III (Jan. 1965), 67.

Letter to Eli Bowen relates to the holograph copy of "The Raven" inscribed to Dr. S. A. Whitaker.

M49 ———. "A Poe Manuscript." *BNYPL,* XXVIII (Feb. 1924), 103–5.

Three facsimiles of the MS of "Thou Art the Man," which was first printed in *Godey's Lady's Book,* November 1844. Article reprinted New York: New York Public Library, 1924.

M50 ———. "'Poe' on Intemperance." *N&Q,* CLXXXIII (July 18, 1942), 34–35.

"A doubtful item ascribed merely to 'Poe' (without first name or initials) in *The Southern First Class Book; or Exercises in Reading and Declamation* (Macon, Georgia, 1839)." *AL.*

M51 ———. "A Poem Wrongly Ascribed to Poe." *N&Q*, XIV (Oct. 1967), 367–68.

Presents the text of an eight-line poem wrongly attributed to Poe by Miss Amelia Poe.

*M52 ———. "Poe's Balloon Hoax." New York *Sun*, Jan. 23, 1943, p. 6.

"Poe commented on Charles Green's serious plan to cross the Atlantic in a balloon in 'A Chapter on Science and Art' in *Burton's Magazine*, March 1840." *AL*.

M53 ———. "Poe's 'The Cask of Amontillado.'" *Expl*, XXV (Nov. 1966), item 30.

Explains why Poe chose particular wines.

M54 ———. "Poe's *City in the Sea*." *Expl*, IV (Oct. 1945), item 1.
Poe is describing the ruins of the City of Gomorrah in this poem.

M55 ———. "Poe's Essay on the Beet-Root." *N&Q*, CLXVII (Dec. 15, 1934), 420.

An essay in *Alexander's Weekly Messenger* for Dec. 18, 1839, thought to be Poe's.

M56 ———. "Poe's 'The Fall of the House of Usher.'" *Expl*, XV (Nov. 1956), item 7.

"The story may be a clinical study of the neurotic children of Luke and Harriet Usher." *AL*.

M57 ———. "Poe's *Israfel*." *Expl*, II (June 1944), item 54.

"The metrical regularity of 'Israfel' is far greater than usual with Poe. Even in 'The Raven' regularity is more apparent than real." *AL*.

M58 ———. "Poe's 'The Man That Was Used Up.'" *Expl*, XXV (April 1967), item 70.

In Poe's story, Theodore Sinivate's name is "Cockney for *insinuate*."

M59 ———. "Poe's Obscure Contemporaries." *AN&Q*, I (Feb. 1942), 166–67.

"A call for assistance in identifying eleven men mentioned in the *Literati* and the 'Autobiography' papers." *AL*.

M60 "Poe's Original Conundrums." *N&Q*, CLXXXIV (June 1943), 328–29.

"Reprints two sets of conundrums which Poe contributed to the *Philadelphia Saturday Museum* on March 25 and April 1, 1843." *AL*.

M61 ———. "Poe's 'Raven': First Inclusion in a Book." *N&Q*, CLXXXV (Oct. 1943), 225.

"'The Raven' appeared in *A Plain System of Elocution* . . . by G. Vandenhoff (2d ed., New York, 1845), several months before Poe published *The Raven and Other Poems*." *AL*.

M62 ——. "Poe's 'Reply to English': Completion of the Text." *AN&Q*, III (April 1943), 6–7.
Poe's reply to the attacks of Thomas Dunn English.

M63 ——. "Poe's 'The Sleeper' Again." *AL*, XXI (Nov. 1949), 339–40.
"Poe's debt to Moore's *Lalla Bookh.*" *AL*.

M64 ——. "Poe's Tale, 'The Lighthouse.' " *N&Q*, CLXXXII (April 25, 1942), 226–27.
"Reprint, with comments, of a seldom printed, unfinished tale." *AL*.

M65 ——. "Poe's *To Helen.*" *Expl*, I (June 1943), item 60.
"Explanation of several crucial points in the text." *AL*.

M66 ——. "Poe's *To the River.*" *Expl*, III (June 1945), query 21.

M67 ——. "Poe's *Ulalume.*" *Expl*, I (Feb. 1943), items 6 and 25.
Interprets the symbolism and origin of Poe's poem.

M68 ——. "Poe's *Ulalume.*" *Expl*, VI (June 1948), item 57.
Discusses Poe's allusion to Weir.

M69 ——. "Poe's 'Ulalume.' " *N&Q*, CLXIV (Feb. 25, 1933), 143.
Discusses influences on Poe's poem.

M70 ——. "Poe's Vaults." *N&Q*, CXCVIII (Dec. 1953), 542–43.
"Argues that Roderick Usher knew his sister was alive." *AL*.

M71 ——. "Poe's Word 'Porphyrogene.' " *N&Q*, CLXXVII (Dec. 2, 1939), 403.
Notes that the word *porphyrogene* is found in chap. 53 of Gibbon's *Decline and Fall*.

M72 ——. "Poe's Word 'Tintinabulation.' " *N&Q*, CLXXV (Nov. 26, 1938), 387.
The word occurs in an unpublished letter of William W. Lord of June 11, 1845.

M73 ——, ed. *Politian: An Unfinished Tragedy,* by Edgar A. Poe. Richmond: The Edgar Allan Poe Shrine, 1923.
See pp. 41–83 for editorial and bibliographical commentary.
Reviewed:
K. Campbell, *Literary Review,* Dec. 29, 1923, p. 408.
TLS, Nov. 1, 1923, p. 725.
N&Q, I (Nov. 17, 1923), 399–400.

M74 ——. "Puckle and Poe." *N&Q*, CLXIV (March 25, 1933), 205–6.
Poe's knowledge of James Puckle's *The Club; or, A Gray Cap for a Green Head.*

M75 ——. "Que Tous ses Pas." *AN&Q,* I (April 1941), 11–12.
Discusses Poe's reading of Bielfeld's *L'Erudition Universelle* (Berlin,

1768) and asks for the identification of the primary source for a quotation in "Berenice."

M76 ———. "A Reply to 'A Minor Poe Mystery.' " *PULC*, V (April 1944), 106–8.
On Poe's relationships with Thomas Dunn English.

M77 ———. "A Review of Lowell's Magazine." *N&Q*, CLXXVIII (June 29, 1940), 457–58.
On Poe's praise of Lowell's *Pioneer* in the Philadelphia *Saturday Museum*.

M78 ———. "Some Classical Allusions in Poe." *Classical Weekly*, XII (Jan. 20, 1919), 94.

M79 ———. "The Source of Poe's Motto for 'The Gold-Bug.' " *N&Q*, CXCVIII (Feb. 1953), 68.
"Thinks source is Frederick Reynolds' *The Dramatist* (1789), IV, 2." *AL.*

M80 ———. "The Source of the Title of Poe's *Morella*." *N&Q*, CLXXII (Jan. 9, 1937), 26–27.
Perhaps the title was drawn from Juliana Morella, a child prodigy born in 1595 in Barcelona.

M81 ———. "The Sources of Poe's 'Eldorado.' " *MLN*, LX (May 1945), 312–14.
Mentions several sources for the idea and form of Poe's poems.

M82 ———. "The Text of Poe's Play 'Politian.' " *N&Q*, CLXXXIX (July 1945), 14.
"Corrections of the text and notes in Professor Mabbott's edition of Poe's unfinished play, first published in 1923." *AL.*

M83 ———. "Ullahanna—A Literary Ghost." *AN&Q*, I (Sept. 1941), 83.

M84 ———. "An Unfavorable Reaction to Poe, 1842." *N&Q*, CXCIV (March 1949), 122–23.
Presents a critical notice from the *Poet's Magazine* in which Poe's poetry is censured.

M85 ———. "An Unpublished Letter to Poe." *N&Q*, CLXIV (May 28, 1938), 385.
A letter from Charles West Thomson of May 1, 1841, concerning Thomson's contributions to *Graham's*.

M86 ———. "Unrecorded Texts of Two Poe Poems." *AN&Q*, VIII (Aug. 1948), 67–68.
"A version of 'To One in Paradise' in the *Saturday Evening Post*, January 9, 1841, and of 'Leonore' in the New York *Evening Mirror*, November 28, 1844." *AL.*

M87   ———. "An Unwritten Drama." *Americana Collector*, I (Nov. 1925), 64–66.

An uncollected sketch, the possible source of Poe's "William Wilson."

M88   ———. "The Writing of Poe's 'The Bells.'" *AN&Q*, II (Oct. 1942), 110.

M89   ———, ed. *The Raven, and Other Poems*. Reproduced in Facsimile from the Lorimer Graham Copy of the Edition of 1845 with Author's Corrections. With introd. New York: Facsimile Text Society, 1942.

Contains valuable introduction, see pp. v–xxii.

M90   ———, ed. *Selected Poetry and Prose of Edgar Allan Poe*. With introd. New York: Modern Library, 1951.

Notes are very valuable.

Reviewed:

Robert D. Jacobs, *MLN*, LXVIII, 65.

James S. Wilson, *AL*, XXIV, 124.

James S. Wilson, *N&Q*, CXCVII, 263–64.

M91   Mabie, Hamilton Wright. "Edgar Allan Poe." *Outlook*, LXII (May 6, 1899), 50–62.

Essay is both biographical and critical, emphasizing Poe's individuality and his magic as artist.

M92   ———. "Introduction." *Tales*, by Edgar Allan Poe. New York: Century, 1901, pp. ix–xvi.

Poe's genius was "detached from the soil of racial and national life," and he used "imaginary conditions and facts for artistic effect solely."

M93   ———. "Introduction" [to Poe's "The Pit and the Pendulum"]. *Stories New and Old, Typical American and English Tales*. New York: Macmillan, 1908, pp. 161–64.

Poe is a "magician in his ability to evoke scenes of terror and pictures of despair."

M94   ———. "Introduction to 'The Pit and the Pendulum.'" *Outlook*, LXXXIV (March 23, 1907), 708–9.

Declares that Poe stands almost without a rival in his "short stories of mystery and terror," but his characters do not live, and the stories are "unreal."

M95   ———. "Introduction to 'To Helen' and 'Israfel.'" *Outlook*, XCI (April 24, 1909), 955–58.

Praises "To Helen" and "Israfel."

M96   ———. "Mr. Mabie Tells about Edgar Allan Poe." *Ladies' Home Jour*, XXVI (Jan. 1909), 30.

Declares that the most important part of Poe's work is his tales.

M97 ——. "Poe at the End of a Century." *UVaAB*, 3rd ser., II (July 1909), 288–302.

"Poe's work holds a first place in our literature, not by reason of its mass, its reality, its range, its spiritual or ethical significance, but by reason of its complete and beautiful individuality, the distinction of its form and workmanship, the purity of its art."

M98 ——. "Poe's Place in American Literature." *Atlantic Monthly*, LXXXIV (Dec. 1899), 733–45.

Commends Poe's technique and form. Reprinted in *UVaMag*, NS XLIII (Dec. 1899), 154–80; in Harrison edition of Poe's *Works*, II, vii–xxxiii, and New York: AMS Press, 1965.

M99 ——. "To Helen and Israfel." *Introductions to Notable Poems.* New York: Dodd, Mead, 1909, pp. 81–93.

Poe "wrote a small group of poems as lovely and as far beyond the reach of analysis as the most delicate flower."

M100 Macy, John Albert. "Biographies of Poe." *The Critical Game.* New York: Boni and Liveright, 1922.

A criticism of Poe's critics including Griswold, Stoddard, Woodberry, and others; see pp. 160–67.

M101 ——. *Edgar Allan Poe.* Boston: Small, Maynard, 1907.

A biographical sketch of Poe's life; see pp. 109–12 for bibliography.

M102 ——. "Ex Libris." *Freeman*, II (March 9, 1921), 622–23.

Praises Poe's style and literary art.

M103 ——. "The Fame of Poe." *Atlantic Monthly*, CII (Dec. 1908), 835–43.

Concerns the persistent growth of Poe's fame in spite of vicissitudes.

M104 ——. "Poe." *The Spirit of American Literature.* New York: Boni and Liveright, 1918, pp. 123–54.

Poe was a creative dreamer and devoted artist.

M105 Maddison, Carol H. "Poe's *Eureka*." *TSLL*, II (Autumn 1960), 350–67.

Poe "derived his hypothesis of the perfect unity of the universe from his aesthetic theory, under the stimulation of current scientific and philosophic thought," but "the pattern in which he arranged these materials in *Eureka* was distinctively his own."

M106 Magidoff, Robert. "American Literature in Russia." *SatRL*, XXIX (Nov. 2, 1946), pp. 9–11, 45–46.

Poe's poetry has been profoundly influential in Russia.

M107 Male, Roy. "Edgar Allan Poe, 1809–1849." *American Literary Masters.* Ed. Charles R. Anderson. 2 vols. New York: Holt, Rinehart and Winston, 1965, I, [1]–18.

Poe's writings reflect contemporary techniques and attitudes.

M108   Mallarmé, Stéphane. "Letter from Stéphane Mallarmé." Ed.
R. J. Neiss. *MLN,* LXV (May 1950), 339–41.
Letter to Sarah Helen Whitman having to do with French interest in
Poe.

M109   ———. "The Tomb of Edgar Poe." *Book-Lover,* IV (March
1903), 8.
English translation of the poem is included in the text of E. L. Didier's
essay "The Truth about Edgar A. Poe." Another translation, along
with original text, is found in Eric Carlson, ed., *The Recognition of
Edgar Allan Poe* (Ann Arbor: University of Michigan Press, 1966),
pp. 64–65.

M110   Malone, Walter. "Poe's Cottage at Fordham." *Critic,* XXXVI
(Feb. 1900), 122.
Verse.

M111   Manly, Louise. *Southern Literature.* Richmond: B. F. Johnson,
1900.
A not very enthusiastic general survey; see pp. 276–79.

M112   "Manners, Motley." "A Mirror for Authors." *Dollar Mag*
(Holden's), III (Jan. 1849), 22.

M113   Marble, Annie Russell. "Willis and Poe: A Retrospect."
Critic, XLVIII (Jan. 1906), 24–26.

M114   Marchand, Ernest. "Poe as a Social Critic." *AL,* VI (March
1934), 28–43.
Poe, aware of the problems of his time, shows in his works that he
had thoughts, colored by his earlier Virginian milieu, on matters
connected with democracy, social reform, and progress.

M115   Markham, Edwin. *Our Israfel.* New York: E. R. Trott, 1925.
"Our Israfel" was winner of the Poe Poetry contest organized by the
Poetry Review in 1924. Reprinted in *Muse Anthology of Modern
Poetry,* ed. Dorothy Kissling and Arthur H. Nethercot, Poe Memorial
Edition (New York: Carlyle Straub, 1938), pp. 178–81.

M116   ———. "Poe." *American Writers on American Literature.* Ed.
John Macy. New York: Horace Liveright, 1931, pp. 135–52.
"At his [Poe's] death he was the greatest critic, the greatest poet, and
the greatest short-story writer in America."

M117   ———. "The Poetry of Poe." *Arena,* XXXII (Aug. 1904),
170–75.
Treats Poe's poetry sympathetically, but admits that there is some
artificiality in his poetry of "narrow range." Appeared originally as
"The Art and Genius of Poe" in *The Works of Edgar Allan Poe*
(10 vols., New York: Funk and Wagnalls, 1904), I, xxvi–xxxix.

M118 Marks, Alfred H. "Two Rodericks and Two Worms: 'Egotism; or, The Bosom Serpent.'" *PMLA*, LXXIV (Dec. 1959), 607–12.
Hawthorne's story is a personal satire on Edgar Allan Poe.

M119 Marks, Emerson R. "Poe as Literary Theorist: A Reappraisal." *AL*, XXXIII (Nov. 1961), 296–306.
Compared to modern criticism, "much in Poe that once seemed obscure or perverse becomes clear and compelling."

M120 Marks, Jeannette A. "Poetry of the Outcast." *Genius and Disaster: Studies in Drugs and Genius.* New York: Adelphi, 1926, pp. 33–73.
Poe's use of opium. Reprinted in *Muse Anthology of Modern Poetry*, ed. Dorothy Kissling and Arthur H. Nethercot, Poe Memorial Edition (New York: Carlyle Straub, 1938), pp. 132–52.
Reviewed:
Carty Ranck, *SatRL*, II (Dec. 5, 1925), 366–67.

M121 Marshall, Thomas F. "The Poe Seminar: Back to the Source." *ESQ*, No. 31 (2nd quarter 1963), pp. 25–28.
Prefers "to focus upon the texts, and upon the personal and social influences which operate upon the author."

M122 ——. "The Poet and the Symbol." *Three Voices of the American Tradition: Edgar Allan Poe, Herman Melville, Ernest Hemingway.* Athens [Greece]: n.p., 1955, pp. 15–30.
Poe's influence upon the form of the modern short story and his use of symbols in his poetry explain his importance in the development of modern literature.

M123 Martin, E. J. "Edgar Allan Poe." *English Rev,* XLVIII (March 1929), 322–25.
A personal sketch.

M124 Martin, Terence. "The Imagination at Play: Edgar Allan Poe." *KR*, XXVIII (March 1966), 194–209.
Poe "makes an absolute commitment to the imagination." His works abound in hoaxes, puzzles, grotesque distortions and generally repudiate the corporeal.

M125 Martin, W. A. P. "The Poetry of the Chinese." *North American Rev,* CLXXII (June 1901), 853–62.
On p. 857 critic declares that Poe's source for "The Raven" is the poem of Kai Yi, a Chinese minister of state who flourished ca. 200 B.C. The poem is quoted.

M126 Marvin, Frederic Rowland. "Maupassant and Poe." *Fireside Papers.* Boston: Sherman, French, 1915.
A comparison of the two authors; see pp. 67–73.

M127 Mary Eleanor, Mother. "The Debate of the Body and the Soul." *Renascence,* XII (Summer 1960), 192–97.

"Includes comment on Whitman, Poe and Eliot." *AL*

M128 Mason, Leo. "More about Poe and Dickens." *Dickensian,* XXXIX (Dec. 1942), 21–28.

Poe made frequent references in his criticism to the skill and craftsmanship evidenced in the novels composed by Dickens.

M129 ———. "Poe and Dickens." *Dickensian,* XLVII (Sept. 1951), 207–10.

M130 ———. "Poe-Script." *Dickensian,* XLII (March 1946), 79–81.

"Notes from Dickensians on John Neal as the 'American Dickens,' on Lowell's 'A Fable for Critics,' on reviews of Dickens's works revealed by Poe, and on Poe's correspondence with Dickens." *AL.*

M131 Matherly, Enid Putnam. "Poe and Hawthorne as Writers of the Short Story." *Education,* XL (Jan. 1920), 294–306.

"We find some points of comparison, but contrast predominates."

M132 Mathews, Frances Aymar. "The Writing of 'The Raven.'" *Bachelor of Arts,* III (Aug.–Sept. 1896), 328–37.

Cornelius Mathews relates an account of hearing Poe read the first draft—a fanciful account, however.

M133 Mathews, Joseph Chesley. "Did Poe Read Dante?" *UTSE,* No. 18 (1938), pp. 123–36.

Poe, with some knowledge of Italian, perhaps read parts of the *Inferno* in the original or in the translation.

M134 Matthews, Brander. "Edgar Allan Poe." *An Introduction to the Study of American Literature.* New York: American Book Co., 1896, pp. 155–69.

Biographical essay.

M135 ———. *The Philosophy of the Short Story.* New York: Longmans, Green, 1901.

A comparison of Poe and Hawthorne with some suggestions of Conan Doyle's indebtedness to Poe, pp. 38–48.

M136 ———. "Poe and the Detective Story." *Scribner's Mag,* XLII (Aug. 1907), 287–93.

"The detective story which Poe invented sharply differentiates itself from the earlier tales of mystery, and also from the later narrative in which actual detectives figure incidentally." Reprinted in *Inquiries and Opinions,* Essay Index Reprint Series (Freeport: Books for Libraries Press, 1968; 1st ed. 1907), pp. 113–36. Also appears in Eric Carlson, ed., *The Recognition of Edgar Allan Poe* (Ann Arbor: University of Michigan Press, 1966), pp. 82–94.

M137 ———. "Poe's Cosmopolitan Fame." *Century Mag,* NS LIX (Dec. 1910), 271–75.

Offers no real argument to explain why Poe is esteemed more in Europe than in America and concludes his commentary by praising Poe. Reprinted in *Gateways to Literature* (New York: Scribner's, 1912), pp. 225–39.

M138 Matthiessen, Francis O. "Edgar Allan Poe." *The Literary History of the United States.* 3 vols. Ed. Robert E. Spiller *et al.* New York: Macmillan, 1948, I, 321–42. First rev. ed. in 1953.

Essay was published earlier in *SR,* LIV (Sept. 1946), 175–205.

M139 ———. "Poe." *SR,* LIV (Sept. 1946), 175–205.

Competently criticizes the scope of Poe's works and emphasizes his strengths as well as his weaknesses and analyzes his international significance.

M140 ———. "Poe's Influence." *Literature in America.* Ed. Philip Rahv. New York: Meridian Books, 1957, pp. 115–17.

Editor reprints selected passages from Matthiessen's "Edgar Allan Poe" in *SR,* LIV (Sept. 1946), 175–205.

M141 Maudsley, Henry. "Edgar Allan Poe." *American Jour of Insanity* (Oct. 1860), 152–98.

Poe inherited infirmities of mind from his father David Poe and was "destitute of that faculty of reasonable insight, by which a man sees in human life something more than what is weak, sinful and contemptible."

M142 ———. "Edgar Allan Poe." *Jour of Mental Science* (London), VI (1859/60), 328–69.

Poe's strengths and weaknesses of character were inherited from his father.

M143 Mauly, John Matthews. "Poe and the Cipher." *Literary Rev* (Sept. 9, 1922), 18.

M144 Maurice, Arthur B. "Poe the Man: How He Looked and How He Lived." *Mentor,* X (Sept. 1922), 10–12, 29–30.

Discusses Poe's financial affairs, the controversy about his drinking, his personal appearance, and his relations with women.

M145 Maxwell, Desmond E. S. "Poe and the Romantic Experiment." *American Fiction: The Intellectual Background.* New York: Columbia University Press, 1963, pp. 53–96.

Poe "very largely settled the path of American fiction in the Romantic, not, as in England, the Augustan, tradition."

M146 Mayersberg, Paul. "The Corridors of the Mind." *Listener,* LXXIV (Dec. 9, 1965), 959–60.

Poe's use of the external world in terms of an interior state of mind.

M147   Mays, Richard, Jr. "Did You Know?" *Richmond Mag,* XVIII (Aug. 1931), 13.
Sketches of Richmond buildings associated with Poe.

M148   Meekins, Lynn Roby. "Poe's Grave in Baltimore." *Critic,* XXXIII (July–Aug. 1898), 39–45.
A description of Poe's burial.

M149   Melchiori, Barbara. "The Tapestry Horse: 'Childe Roland' and 'Metzengerstein.' " *English Miscellany,* XIV (1963), 185–93.
Browning in "Childe Roland" took from Poe the atmosphere associated with the supernatural and especially "the visual impact of the tapestry horse" related in Poe's story.

M150   Mellor, Mildred F. "A Virginia Poe Tradition." *AN&Q,* I (June 1941), 36–37.
A tradition handed down by Fordham neighbors that Virginia skipped rope.

M151   Melton, Wrightman F. "Poe's Mechanical Poem." *Texas Rev,* III (Jan. 1918), 133–38.
The onomatopoeia of Poe's "The Bells" was carefully contrived.

M152   ———. "Some Autobiographical References in Poe's Poetry." *SAQ,* XI (April 1912), 175–79.
Some quotations from the poetry are considered in the light of Poe's relationship to Virginia Clemm.

M153   Melville, Lewis. "The Centenary of Edgar Allan Poe (Born January 19, 1809)." *Nineteenth Century and After,* LXV (Jan. 1909), 140–52.
Discusses Poe's life, his "originality," and comments favorably on Poe's poetry.

M154   "Menander" [Charles Longbridge Morgan]. "The Aesthetic of Poe." *TLS,* June 17, 1944), p. 291.
"Detailed analysis of certain poems (particularly 'To Helen') and a discussion of the 'pure aestheticism' revealed in 'The Philosophy of Composition.' " *AL.*

M155   Mencken, H. L. "Edgar Allan Poe." *Prejudices: First Series.* New York: Knopf, 1919.
Something of Poe's Baltimore grave, his burial, and Griswold; see pp. 247–49. Reprinted in *Selected Prejudices* (New York: Knopf, 1927), pp. 55–56.

M156   ———. "The Mystery of Poe." *Nation,* CXXII (March 17, 1926), 289–90.
Declares that Krutch's biography is the first book on Poe that offers anything approaching a rational and convincing account of him."

M157 ———. "Poe." *A Mencken Chrestomathy*. New York: A. A. Knopf, 1949, pp. 479–81.

Selection is from *The National Letters, Prejudices: Second Series* (1920), pp. 59–63.

M158 Mengeling, Marvin and Frances. "From Fancy to Failure: A Study of the Narrators in the Tales of Edgar Allan Poe." *UR* (Kansas City, Mo.), XXXIII (Summer 1967), 293–98, and XXIV (Autumn 1967), 31–37.

Poe's narrators who relied on "fancy" failed to solve their problems.

M159 Metcalf, John Calvin. "Authors, Books and Imprints." *Richmond, Capital of Virginia: Approaches to Its History, by Various Hands*. Richmond: Whittet and Shepperson, 1938.

See chap. 7, pp. 149–51, for an account of Poe and the *Southern Literary Messenger*.

M160 ———. "The Southern Writers." *American Literature*. Richmond: Johnson Publishing, 1914, pp. 255–344.

Poe's attributes as artist reflected in his fiction, poetry, and criticism; see pp. 260–73.

M161 Meynell, Laurence. "Introduction." *Tales, Poems and Essays*, [by] Edgar Allan Poe. New Collins Classics. New York: W. W. Norton, 1953, pp. 13–17.

Briefly acknowledges Poe's ability in poetry and prose.

*M162 Michael, Mary Kyle. "Stevenson and Poe." *Exercise Exchange*, XIV (1966–67), 21.

Stevenson's essay "El Dorado" and Poe's poem "Eldorado" demonstrate the difference between prose and poetry. *PN.*

M163 Mierow, Herbert E. "A Classical Allusion in Poe." *MLN*, XXXI (March 1916), 184–85.

On Poe's allusion "Nicean" in "To Helen."

M164 ———. "Stephen Phillips and Edgar Allan Poe." *MLN*, XXXII (Dec. 1917), 499–501.

A comparison of Phillips's *Cities of Hell* and Poe's "The Power of Words."

M165 Miller, Arthur M. "The Influence of Edgar Allan Poe on Ambrose Bierce." *AL*, IV (May 1932), 130–50.

"To Bierce there was only one 'right' kind of fiction form, and Poe had invented it."

M166 Miller, F. DeWolfe. "The Basis for Poe's 'The Island of the Fay.' " *AL*, XIV (May 1942), 135–40.

"This prose-fantasy was 'written under pressure' as letterpress for a mezzotint of the same title by John Sartain." *AL.*

M167   Miller, Harold P. "Hawthorne Surveys His Contemporaries."
AL, XII (May 1940), 228–35.
     For Hawthorne's attitude toward Poe, see pp. 232–33. Hawthorne
admired Poe "rather as a writer of tales than as a critic upon them."

M168   Miller, James E., Jr. " 'Ulalume' Resurrected." *PQ,* XXXIV
(April 1955), 197–205.
     Defends "Ulalume" as a poem which depicts an incoherent ex-
perience.

M169   ———. "Uncharted Interiors: The American Romantics Revisited." *Quests Surd and Absurd.* Chicago: University of Chicago Press,
1967, pp. 249–59.
     The role of symbolism in Poe, Melville, Whitman, Thoreau, Haw-
thorne, and Emerson.

*M170   ———, and Bernice Slote. *Notes for Teaching.* New York:
Dodd, Mead, 1964.
     Poe's "The Man of the Crowd," pp. 9–10. *ESQ.*

M171   Miller, John C. *John Henry Ingram's Poe Collection at the
University of Virginia.* Charlottesville: University of Virginia Press,
1960.
     See especially Miller's "John Henry Ingram: Editor, Biographer, and
Collector of Poe Materials," pp. xv–xlix.
     Reviewed:
Jacobs, *SAQ,* LX, 515–16.

M172   ———. "A Poe Letter Re-Presented." *AL,* XXXV (Nov.
1963), 359–61.
     Poe requests Thomas G. Mackenzie's help in purchasing the sub-
scription list of the *Southern Literary Messenger.*

*M173   ———. *Poe's English Biographer, John Henry Ingram: A
Biographical Account and a Study of His Contributions to Poe Scholarship.* Ann Arbor, Mich.: University Microfilms, 1954.

M174   ———. "Poe's English Biographer, John Henry Ingram: A
Biographical Account and a Study of His Contributions to Poe Scholarship." *DA,* XIV (1954), 2070–71.

*M175   ———. "Poe's English Biographer, John Henry Ingram: A
Biographical Account and a Study of His Contributions to Poe Scholarship." Diss., University of Virginia, 1954.

M176   ———. "Poe's Sister Rosalie." *TSL,* VIII (1963), 107–17.
     A biographical sketch of Rosalie M. Poe, Poe's "unfortunate" sister.

M177   ———. "An Unpublished Poe Letter." *AL,* XXVI (Jan. 1955),
560–61.
     "The letter, dated June 3, 1844, is addressed to Lewis Jacob Cist,
editor, publisher, and minor literary figure of Cincinnati." *AL.*

M178   Miller, Perry. "Europe's Faith in American Fiction." *Atlantic Monthly,* CLXXXVII (Dec. 1951), 52–56.
Comments on a reading of a Frisian translation of Poe's "The Raven" to citizens of Leeuwarden, Friesland; see pp. 53–54.

M179   ———. "Introduction." *The Golden Age of American Literature.* New York: George Braziller, 1959, pp. 1–28.
In his introduction to this anthology of "Our greatest Romantic authors," critic names Poe the "romantic artificer" and the most thoroughly conscious artist of the Romantic movement.

M180   ———. *The Raven and the Whale: The War of Words and Wits in the Era of Poe and Melville.* New York: Harcourt Brace, 1956.
Poe and the world of "Yankee" journalism.
    Reviewed:
Gay Wilson Allen, *SatR,* (June 23, 1956), 23–24.
Leon Edel, *New Republic,* CXXXIV, 22.
Blake R. Nevius, *NCF,* XI, 232–35.
Willard Thorp, *AL,* XXIX, 97–98.

M181   Milligan, J. Lewis. "Edgar Allan Poe." *Nineteenth Century and After,* XCIII (April 1923), 550–56.
In his poetry, Poe creates "an ethereal paradise of love and beauty."

M182   Mills, Nicolaus C. "Romance and Society: A Re-examination of Nineteenth Century American and British Fiction." *DA,* XXVIII (Aug. 1967), 687A–88A.
Author of this abstract does not allude to Poe; however, novels by several of Poe's contemporaries are closely analyzed.

M183   Mims, Edwin, and Bruce R. Payne. "Introduction." *Southern Prose and Poetry for Schools.* New York: Charles Scribner's, 1910, pp. 3–20.
Poe has a "pre-eminent position among the short story writers of the South, and indeed of America."

M184   Minnigerode, Patricia. "Poe and the Mad King's Castle." *NYTM,* Dec. 10, 1922, pp. 2, 14.
Ludwig II, the Mad King of Bavaria, expressed affinity with Poe.

M185   Minor, Benjamin Blake. *The Southern Literary Messenger, 1834–1864.* New York: Neale Publishing, 1905.
A history of the *Messenger.*

M186   ———. "Who Wrote 'The Raven'—Poe or Hirst?" Richmond *Times,* Feb. 17, 1895.
Poe's claim is, he believes, undisturbed.

M187   Minto, William. "Edgar Allan Poe." *Fortnightly Rev,* NS XXVIII (July 1, 1880), 69–82.
Poe's "mental habits and methods of work" led to his failure as a

journalist. Reprinted in *Littell's Living Age,* CXLVI (Sept. 11, 1880), 690–99, and in *Eclectic Mag,* NS XXXII (Sept. 1880), 270–79.

M188   Mitchell, Donald G. *American Lands and Letters.* 2 vols. New York: Charles Scribner's, 1899.
Sketchy essay on Poe's life; see II, 373–400.

M189   Mitchell, Robert McBurney. "Poe and Spielhagen: Novelle and Short Story." *MLN,* XXIX (Feb. 1914), 36–41.
A reply to Palmer Cobb's "Edgar Allan Poe and . . . Spielhagen." Declares that the relationship is not so close as Cobb has made it.

M190   Moffatt, W. D. "Open Letter." *Mentor* (New York), X (Sept. 1922), 44.
Concerning the restoration of the Fordham Cottage.

M191   Moffett, Harold Young. "Applied Tactics in Teaching Literature—The Fall of the House of Usher." *EJ* (College edition), XVII (Sept. 1928), 556–59.
Recommends studying the design and intended effect of Poe's story.

M192   ———. "Edgar Allan Poe." *Tales,* [by] Edgar Allan Poe. Revised by Moffett. New York: Macmillan, 1930, pp. xi–xlvii.
Asserts that Poe's reputation must rest on his poetry.

M193   Mohr, Frank K. "The Influence of Eichendorff's 'Ahnung und Gegenwart' on Poe's 'Masque of the Red Death.' " *MLQ,* X (March 1949), 3–15.
Poe was indebted to the account of a "Maskenball" in the eleventh chapter of Eichendorff's novel.

M194   Monahan, Michael. "Foreword." *Poems,* by Edgar Allan Poe. East Aurora, N.Y.: Roycrafters, 1901.
Discusses a visit to Poe's Fordham Cottage, pp. i–v.

M195   ———. "Poe Legend." *Attic Dreamer.* New York: Mitchell Kennerly, 1922, pp. 22–56.
Reexamines questionable generalizations about Poe's life.

M196   Monroe, Harriet. "Poe and Longfellow." *Poetry,* XXIX (1927), 266–74.
Contrasts the two men biographically and temperamentally.

M197   ———. "Poe and Whistler." *Poet-Lore,* XXI (Sept.–Oct. 1910), 391–96.
A brief comparison between the poet and the artist with high praise for Poe's genius.

M198   Moon, Sam. "The Cask of Amontillado." *N&Q,* CXCIX (Oct. 1954), 448.

M199 Mooney, Stephen LeRoy. "The Comic in Poe's Fiction." *AL,* XXXIII (Jan. 1962), 433–41.

Poe's humor can be understood "in the light of Bergson's treatment of the comic."

M200 ———. "Comic Intent in Poe's Tales: Five Criteria." *MLN,* LXXVI (Jan. 1961), 432–34.

M201 ———. "Poe's Gothic Waste Land." *SR,* LXX (Spring 1962), 261–83.

Poe adapted the dehumanizing forces of his day in terms of the Gothic mode. Reprinted in Eric Carlson, ed., *The Recognition of Edgar Allan Poe* (Ann Arbor: University of Michigan Press, 1966), pp. 278–97.

M202 ———. *Poe's Grand Design: A Study of Theme and Unity in the Tales.* Ann Arbor, Mich.: University Microfilms, 1960.

M203 ———. "Poe's Grand Design: A Study of Theme and Unity in the Tales." *DA,* XXI (June 1961), 3788–89.

Poe's "Grand Design" "may be construed as the Folio Club scheme magnified, to include extensions and developments of the early tales, and unified by the repetition of motifs and by a steady thematic continuity that runs throughout the fiction."

M204 ———. "Poe's Grand Design: A Study of Theme and Unity in the Tales." Diss., University of Tennessee, 1960.

M205 Moore, Charles Leonard. "The American Rejection of Poe." *Dial,* XXVI (Jan. 16, 1899), 40–42.

Points out Poe's limitations and weaknesses as an artist and critic.

M206 ———. "The Case of Poe and His Critics." *Dial,* XLVII (Nov. 16, 1909), 367–70.

"The strange misshapen stone rejected by the builders has become the top of the temple."

M207 ———. "Edgar Allan Poe Again." *Dial,* XXVI (April 1, 1899), 236–37.

Poe's writings, "unprevailingly tragic," are "controlled by too strong a sense of beauty to be unpleasant."

M208 ———. "Poe's Place as a Critic." *Dial,* XXXIV (Feb. 16, 1903), 111–12.

Poe, although he had an "unerring instinct" for separating the good from the bad, "had not the breadth of view or the knowledge necessary for a great critic." Reprinted in *Book-Lover,* IV (March–April 1903), 86–88.

M209 Moore, George. *Conversations in Ebury Street.* London: W. Heinemann, 1930.

See pp. 201–4 for critical commentary on Poe's poetry. Also printed in *An Anthology of Pure Poetry,* ed. George Moore (New York: Boni and Liveright, 1924), pp. 37–40.

M210   Moore, John B. "Introduction." *Selections from Poe's Literary Criticism.* Ed. Brooks. New York: F. S. Crofts, 1926, pp. vii–xix.

Discusses Poe's relationship with his times and compares Poe and Lowell.

M211   Moore, John Robert. "Poe, Scott, and 'The Murders in the Rue Morgue.'" *AL,* VIII (March 1936), 52–58.

An important element in the story, the strange murder without human agency, is borrowed from Scott's *Count Robert of Paris* (1831).

M212   ———. "Poe's Reading of *Anne of Geierstein.*" *AL,* XXII (Jan. 1951), 493–96.

"Poe's use of Scott's novel in 'The Raven' and 'The Domain of Arnheim.'"

M213   Moore, Merrill. "Edgar Allan Poe: The Butcher." *SR,* XXXVII (Jan. 1929), 72.

Verse.

M214   Moore, Rayburn S. "A Note on Poe and the Sons of Temperance." *AL,* XXX (Nov. 1958), 359–61.

Poe joined a Richmond temperance society on August 27, 1849.

M215   Moorefield, Robert. "Salt for These Wounds." *Muse Anthology of Modern Poetry.* Ed. Dorothy Kissling and Arthur H. Nethercot. Poe Memorial Edition. New York: Carlyle Straub, 1938, p. 190.

Verse.

M216   Moran, John J. *A Defense of Edgar Allan Poe.* Washington, D.C.: W. F. Boogher, 1885.

Commentary on Poe's life and character along with an account of his death.

M217   ———. "Official Memoranda of the Death of Edgar A. Poe." *Poems and Essays of Edgar Allan Poe.* New York: W. J. Widdleton, 1876, pp. cxvii–cxxiv.

Vivid description of Poe's death followed by two editorial articles from the *Herald* on Poe's life and character; see pp. cxxiv–cxxvii.

M218   Mordell, Albert. "Psychoanalytic Study of Edgar Allan Poe." *The Erotic Motive in Literature.* New, rev. ed. New York: Collier Books, 1962, pp. 166–81.

On the origins of Poe's women, his depiction of characters suffering from anxiety, and on his preoccupation with the dream motif. First appeared in 1919 published by Boni and Liveright.

M219   More, Paul Elmer. "A Note on Poe's Method." *SP*, XX (July 1923), 302–9.

In accordance with "his own canon of art, Poe must rank high," but at the same time he "remains chiefly the poet of unripe boys and unsound men." Reprinted in More's *The Demon of the Absolute*, vol. I of New Shelburne Essays (Princeton, N.J.: University Press, 1928), pp. 77–87.

M220   Morgan, Appleton. "The Personality of Poe." *Munsey's Mag,* XVII (July 1897), 522–30.

He accepts Poe as merely human and is willing to condone his errors.

M221   Morgan, Mrs. Edmund Nash. "The Poe Revival: Mr. Robert Hartley Perdue's 'The Raven.'" *Book-Lover,* IV (March–April 1903), 53–56.

A bibliographical appreciation of Robert Hartley Perdue's edition of "The Raven," which has an introduction by Jos. Léon Gobeille.

M222   Morgan, Horace Hills. *English and American Literature for Schools and Colleges.* Boston: Leach, Shewell and Sanborn, 1889.

Emphasizes Poe's imagination, pp. 185–87.

M223   Moriarty, Joseph F. *A Literary Tomahawking: The Libel Action of Edgar Allan Poe vs. Thomas Dunn English—A Complete Report of the Documents of the Case and Materials about Poe Published for the First Time.* Privately printed, 1963.

A narrative of Poe's lawsuit.

M224   Morley, Christopher. "The Allergy of Roderick Usher." *TLS,* April 9, 1949, p. 233.

"Usher's symptoms are those thought to be the classic symptoms of allergy." *AL.*

M225   ———. "Catterina of Spring Garden Street." *Essays.* New York: Doubleday, Doran, 1928, pp. 415–21.

On Poe's home in Philadelphia.

M226   Morris, George D. "American Traits as Seen by the French." *Mid-West Quarterly* (Univ. of Nebraska), II (Jan. 1915), 169–83.

Frequent allusions to Poe.

M227   ———. "French Criticism of Poe." *SAQ,* XIV (Oct. 1915), 324–29.

He shows that not all French criticism of Poe is extravagantly complimentary.

M228   [Morris, George P.] [Review of *Poems*, by Edgar Poe.] *New York Mirror,* VIII (May 7, 1831), 349–50.

M229 Morris, Lineta Belle Caples. "Poe." *Verse Craft,* II (Jan.–Feb. 1932), 21.

Verse.

M230 Morris, O. "To the Memory of Edgar Allan Poe." *London Mercury,* XIX (April 1929), 574–76.

Verse in the meter of "The Raven."

M231 Morrison, Claudia C. "Poe's 'Ligeia': An Analysis." *SSF,* IV (Spring 1967), 234–44.

The unconscious germ of "Ligeia" originated in Poe's feelings concerning the loss of his mother.

M232 Morrison, Robert. "Poe's *The Lake: To* ———." *Expl,* VII (Dec. 1948), item 22.

Suggests that Poe's lake is Lake Drummond located in the center of the Great Dismal Swamp.

M233 Morrow, L. C. "The American Appreciation of Poe." *UVaMag,* LXIX (Jan. 1909), 242–47.

Traces rather superficially the growing appreciation of Poe in America.

M234 Morse, James Herbert. "Edgar Allan Poe." *Critic,* V (Nov. 15, 1884), 229–30.

Poe had a powerful imagination but overemphasized artistic effect.

M235 Morton, Maxwell V. Z. W. *A Builder of the Beautiful: Some Unsuspected Aspects of Poe—Literary and Emotional Alike.* Boston: R. G. Badger, 1928.

Tries to unfathom Poe's private traits by analyzing his literary style.

M236 Moskowitz, Samuel. "The Prophetic Edgar Allan Poe." *Explorers of the Infinite: Shapers of Science Fiction.* Cleveland: World Publishing, 1963, pp. 46–61.

Poe's greatest contribution to science fiction was "the precept that every departure from norm must be logically explained *scientifically."*

M237 Moss, Sidney P. *"Arthur Gordon Pym,* or the Fallacy of Thematic Interpretation." *UR* (Kansas City, Mo.), XXXIII (Summer 1967), 299–306.

Pym "does consist of two separate tales."

M238 ———. "A Conjecture concerning the Writing of 'Arthur Gordon Pym.'" *SSF,* IV (Fall 1966), 83–85.

The two-part division in *Pym* is largely due to Poe's rendering of the serial version into a book version.

M239 ———. "Poe and His Nemesis—Lewis Gaylord Clark." *AL,* XXVIII (March 1956), 30–49.

An examination of the quarrel between Poe and Clark strongly suggests that Poe "became one of the most maligned persons in literary history."

M240 ——. "Poe and the Literary Cliques." *ABC,* VII (May 1957), 13–19.
Poe, dissatisfied with current journalistic practices, fought to raise the standards of literary performance.

M241 ——. "Poe and the *Norman Leslie* Incident." *AL,* XXV (Nov. 1953), 293–306.
Poe's review of T. S. Fay's novel *Norman Leslie* was the beginning of "one of the first real battles of American periodicals": Poe drew the ire of four Northern journals and made enemies of three Southern periodicals.

M242 ——. "Poe, Hiram Fuller, and the Duyckinck Circle." *ABC,* XVIII, No. 2 (Oct. 1967), 8–18.
Traces Fuller's editorial attacks upon Poe.

M243 ——. "Poe's Infamous Reputation: A Crux in the Biography." *ABC,* IX (Nov. 1958), 3–10.
Poe's literary battles were in part responsible for the tradition of his infamous reputation.

*M244 ——. *Poe's Literary Battles.* Ann Arbor, Mich.: University Microfilms, 1954.

M245 ——. "Poe's Literary Battles." *DA,* XV (1955), 125.
Poe was a literary reformer, "a lone figure who waged uncompromising war against the evils that were besetting American letters."

*M246 ——. "Poe's Literary Battles." Diss., University of Illinois, 1954.

M247 ——. *Poe's Literary Battles: The Critic in the Context of His Literary Milieu.* Durham, N.C.: Duke University Press, 1963.
Specific presentation of Poe's journalistic activities which reflect his militant efforts to establish high standards for American literature.
Reviewed:
Bogart, *JEGP,* LXIII, 832–34.
Davis, *ABC,* XIII, 3.
Hook, *MLR,* LIX, 649–50.
Howard, *NCF,* XVIII, 99.
Levine, *AQ,* XVII, 133–44.
UQR, XL, cliv.
Moore, *YWES,* XLV, 364.
Parks, *GaR,* XVII, 479–81.
Prichard, *Books Abroad,* XXXVII, 449.
Levine, *MASJ,* IV, 78.

Stovall, *AL,* XXXV, 374–75.

Tanselle, *AN&Q,* I, 161–62.

Willingham, *Library Jour,* LXXXVIII, 1015.

M248   Mossop, D. J. "Poe's Theory of Pure Poetry," *DUJ,* XVII (March 1956), 60–67.

Poe identifies the value of poetry with expression of certain emotions.

M249   Mott, Frank Luther. "A Brief History of *Graham's Magazine,*" *SP,* XXV (July 1928), 362–74.

Poe's connection with the magazine is discussed, pp. 368–70.

M250   ———. *A History of American Magazines, 1741-1850.* New York: D. Appleton, 1930.

See *passim* for Poe's relations with various magazines.

M251   Mott, Hopper Striker. "Poe's 'Raven.' " New York *Times,* May 25, 1919, sec. 3, p. 2.

Points out that the poem was not written at the Fordham Cottage but at the home of the Brennans in Bloomingdale.

M252   Moyne, Ernest John. "Did Edgar Allan Poe Lecture at Newark Academy?" *Delaware Notes,* 26th ser. (1953), 1–9.

Various accounts strongly suggest that Poe did lecture at the Newark Academy.

M253   Muchnic, Helen. *The Unhappy Consciousness: Gogol, Poe, Baudelaire.* Northampton, Mass.: Smith College, 1967.

Gogol, Poe, and Baudelaire were alienated poets whose philosophic desires encompassed "a yearning for the unattainable."

M254   Mühlenfels, Astrid A. von. "A Bibliography of German Scholarship on Early American Literature, 1850—." *Early American Literature Newsletter,* II (Fall 1967), 32–35.

Some entries touch upon Poe.

M255   Mumford, Lewis. *The Golden Day.* New York: Boni and Liveright, 1926.

Relates Poe to pioneering and industrialism in America, pp. 76–78.

M256   ———. "Poe and an American Myth." *Literary Rev,* IV (April 5, 1924), 641–42.

Poe, primarily an artist, "encountered the paralyzing enmity of the pioneer tradition."

M257   Murch, Alma E. *The Development of the Detective Novel.* New York: Philosophical Library, 1958.

Poe is an important figure in the evolution of the detective novel, *passim.*

M258   Murphy, George D. "A Source for Ballistics in Poe." *AN&Q,* IV (March 1966), 99.

Ballistic evidence in "Thou Art the Man" closely parallels evidence used in solving an actual English murder in 1835.

M259   Murrell, John D. "Poe in Virginia." *Taylor-Trotwood Mag,* May 1908, 125–29.

M260   Murry, John Middleton. "Poe's Poetry." *Discoveries.* London: Jonathan Cape, 1930, pp. 231–39.

Poe is the successor of the English Romantics.

M261   ———. "Problem of Size." *Pencillings.* New York: Boni and Thomas Seltzer, 1925, pp. 81–89.

Poe is discussed as to his influence upon literary art in his dictum of a short poem.

M262   Myers, Frederic W. H. "Edgar Allan Poe." *Library of the World's Best Literature.* 30 vols. Ed. Charles O. Warner *et al.* New York: R. S. Peale and J. A. Hill, 1897, XX, 11651–54.

Poe's tales are historically significant, and some of his verse has strange beauty.

M263   Myers, W. T. "To Poe." *UVaMag,* LXIX (Jan. 1909), 210.
A sonnet to Poe.

N

N1   N., H. E. "Man Who Knew Edgar Allen [*sic*] Poe Well Tells Incidents of His Life." *Sunday World-Herald* (Omaha), July 13, 1902, p. 24.

Reminiscences of an office boy, Alexander T. Crane, who worked in the office of the *Broadway Journal* and whom Poe befriended. Digest of article appears in *Book-Lover,* III (Nov.–Dec. 1902), 441.

N2   Deleted.

N3   Nakamura, Junichi. *Edgar Allan Poe's Relations with New England.* Tokyo: Hokuseido Press, 1957.

Consists mainly of summaries of what Poe wrote about the New England writers of his time and of what the latter wrote about the former.

N4   Nash, Herbert N. "Reminiscences of Poe." *UVaAB,* 3rd ser., II (April 1909), 193–95.

Tells of his meeting with Poe in 1849 at the time of the Norfolk lecture.

N5   Neal, John. "Edgar A. Poe." Portland (Maine) *Daily Adver-*
tiser, April 26, 1850, p. 2.
      Poe "was by nature, of a just and generous temper, thwarted, baffled,
      and self-harnessed by his own wilfulness to the most unbecoming
      drudgery." Passages from this review quoted in *The Life of Edgar
      Allan Poe* by George E. Woodberry (2 vols., Boston: Houghton
      Mifflin, 1909), I, 451–52.

*N6   ——. *John Neal to Edgar A. Poe.* Ysleta, Tex.: E. B. Hill, 1942.
      "Includes two letters, the first from John Neal to Poe, dated Portland,
      June 8, '40; the second from Edmund C. Stedman to Edwin B. Hill,
      dated New York, July 1st, 1888." *LCC.*

N7   ——. "Unpublished Poetry." *Yankee and Boston Literary
Gazette,* NS II (Dec. 1829), 295–98.
      Early praise of Poe's poetry. See also September issue (1829), p. 168,
      for Neal's brief comment on Poe's poetic style. Extracts reprinted in
      Eric Carlson, ed., *The Recognition of Edgar Allan Poe* (Ann Arbor:
      University of Michigan Press, 1966), pp. 3–4.

N8   Neale, Walter G. "The Source of Poe's 'Morella.' " *AL,* IX
(May 1937), 237–39.
      Henry G. Bell's "The Dead Daughter" published in Edinburgh
      Literary Jour, Jan. 1, 1831, is the source of Poe's story.

N9   Nelson, Charles Alex. "Edgar Allan Poe Raven Mantel." *Columbia University Quarterly,* X (March 1908), 193–94.
      The mantel from the Brennan house "in which he [Poe] wrote 'The
      Raven' " is reported to be preserved at Columbia University.

N10   Neu, Jacob L. "Rufus Wilmot Griswold." *UTSE,* No. 5
(1925), pp. 101–65.
      Discusses Griswold's relations with Poe.

N11   Nevi, Charles N. "Irony and 'The Cask of Amontillado.' " *EJ,*
LVI (March 1967), 461–63.
      Poe's story presents an opportunity to teach irony.

N12   New York University Libraries. *Index to Early American Periodical Literature, 1728–1870.* Part 2. *Edgar Allan Poe.* New York:
Pamphlet Distributing Co., 1941.
      A listing (sometimes inaccurate) of Poe's works and literary activi-
      ties as represented in early American periodicals. See Thomas O.
      Mabbott's "Introduction," pp. 3–4.
         Reviewed:
      AL, XIII, 195–96.

N13   Newcomer, Alphonso Gerald. *American Literature.* Chicago:
Scott, Foresman, 1901.
      See chap. 5, pp. 112–27.

N14 ——. "Editing of Poe." *Dial,* XXX (March 16, 1901), 183.

N15 ——. "Introduction." *Poems and Tales of Edgar Allan Poe.*
Ed. Newcomer. Chicago: Scott, Foresman, 1902, pp. 9–27.
Evaluates and categorizes some of Poe's poems and tales.

N16 ——. "Mr. Sartain and Poe." *Dial,* XXVII (Dec. 16, 1899),
482.

N17 ——. "The Poe-Chivers Tradition Re-examined." *SR,* XII
(Jan. 1904), 20–35.
Points out that Chivers perhaps came under the Poe influence.

N18 Newmann, Joshua H. "Poe's Contributions to English." *AS,*
XVIII (Feb. 1943), 73–74.
Evidence that Poe was not a coiner of "simple, common words."

N19 Nichol, John. *American Literature: An Historical Sketch,*
1620–1880. Edinburgh: Adam and Charles Black, 1882.
See pp. 163–70, 217–19.

N20 Nicholls, Norah. "The French Association with Edgar Allan
Poe." *Bookseller and Collector,* V (Nov. 13, 1930), 135–38.
Reviews W. Roberts's article on the Dumas MS.

N21 Nichols, Mary Gove. *Reminiscences of Edgar Allan Poe.* New
York: Union Square Book Shop, 1931.
A reprint from the *Six Penny Magazine* (Feb. 1863) with a biblio-
graphical note by T. O. Mabbott.

N22 Nicolson, Marjorie H. *Voyages to the Moon.* New York: Macmillan, 1948.
In "Hans Pfaall" Poe added very little to the tradition he inherited;
see pp. 238–41.

N23 Nisbet, Ada B. "New Light on the Poe-Dickens Relationship."
NCF, V (March 1951), 295–302.
The review of Dickens's *American Notes in Blackwood's Magazine*
(Dec. 1842) signed "Q. Q. Q." was not written by Poe but by
Samuel Warren, author of *Ten Thousand a Year.*

N24 Noble, James Ashcroft. "Edgar Allan Poe." *New Quarterly*
Mag, VIII (July 1877), 410–27.
Biographical.

N25 Nolan, J. Bennett. *Israfel in Berkshire.* Reading, Pa.: Pennsylvania Optical Co., 1948.
An account of Poe's lecture in Reading in March 1844.

N26 Nordstedt, George. "Poe and Einstein." *Open Court,* XLIV
(March 1930), 173–80.
Poe's "intuitive glimpses" in *Eureka* are found to be similar to certain
theories of the "new physics."

N27 ——. "Prototype of 'The Raven.'" *North American Rev,* CCXXIV (Dec. 1927), 692–701.

Traces "The Raven" to two anonymous poems and discusses other influences upon Poe's poem.

N28 Norman, Emma Katherine. "Poe's Knowledge of Latin." *AL,* VI (March 1934), 72–77.

Poe had a "good working knowledge" of Latin for his critical purposes.

N29 Norman, H. L. "A Possible Source for E. A. Butti's *Castello del Sogno.*" *MLN,* LII (April 1937), 256–58.

The source is Poe's "The Fall of the House of Usher."

N30 Norris, Walter B. "Poe's Balloon Hoax." *Nation,* XLI (Oct. 27, 1910), 389–90.

Poe's "balloon hoax" was based "chiefly on the account of Monck Mason of an actual balloon trip made by Mason, Charles Green, and Robert Holland in November, 1836."

N31 "Novalis." "The Works of Edgar A. Poe." *UVaMag,* XI (March 1873), 311–16.

On Poe's style—diction, expression, and imagery.

N32 Noyes, Alfred. "Edgar Allan Poe." *Bookman* (London), LXXII (June 1927), 157–60.

Compares Poe, among other things, to the Gothic writers.

N33 ——. "Revaluation of Poe." *Opalescent Parrot.* London: Sheed, 1929, pp. 31–50.

Admires Poe's imaginative power, but finds forced ingenuity in much of Poe's writings.

O

O1 O., E. V. "Edinburgh Version of the Purloined Letter." *AN&Q,* I (April 1941), 8–9.

A query as to the whereabouts of the MS of the "Edinburgh" or short version of this Poe tale.

O2 Oakes-Smith, Mrs. E. "Autobiographic Notes: Edgar A. Poe." *Beadle's Monthly,* III (Feb. 1867), 147–56.

Gives personal reaction to Poe's personality and claims that Poe was murdered.

O3   Obear, Emily H. "To Edgar Allan Poe." *EJ* (College edition), XVII (Jan. 1928), 49.
   Verse. Also appears in *EJ* (High School edition), XVII (Feb. 1928), 155.

O4   [O'Beirne, James R.] "Poe and 'The Raven.' " New York *Mail and Express* (April 21, 1900), p. [15].

O5   Ober, Warren U., *et al.*, eds. *The Enigma of Poe.* Boston: D. C. Heath, 1960.
   "The materials here presented fall into three general sections: 1. Imaginative and critical works by Poe. 2. Selected letters of Poe and his circle. 3. Biographical and critical evaluations of Poe." *LCC.*

O6   O'Brien, Edward J. "Poe." *The Advance of the American Short Story.* New York: Dodd, Mead, 1923, pp. 65–87.
   Discusses Poe's "consummate craftsmanship, great logical lucidity," and his gift of "imaginative revery."

O7   O'Donnell, Charles. "From Earth to Ether: Poe's Flight into Space." *PMLA,* LXXVII (March 1962), 85–91.
   From *Pym* to *Eureka* Poe dramatizes "the tension between the self and the universe as it operates in men."

O8   O'Donnell, William Francis. "Did Pike Influence Poe?" *Book News Monthly,* XXVII (Jan. 1909), 329–30.
   Albert Pike had no influence on Poe.

O9   Oliver, Wade. "For Edgar Allan Poe." *Muse Anthology of Modern Poetry.* Ed. Dorothy Kissling and Arthur H. Nethercot. Poe Memorial Edition. New York: Carlyle Straub, 1938, p. 189.
   Verse.

O10   Olivero, Federico. "Symbolism in Poe's Poetry." *Westminster Rev,* CLXXX (Aug. 1913), 201–7.
   Poe uses landscape imagery to express personal emotions.

O11   Olney, Clarke. "Edgar Allan Poe—Science Fiction Pioneer." *GaR,* XII (Winter 1958), 416–21.
   Poe was the "first writer of science-centered fiction to base his stories firmly on a rational kind of extrapolation, avoiding the supernatural."

O12   Olson, Bruce. "Poe's Strategy in 'The Fall of the House of Usher.' " *MLN,* LXXIX (Nov. 1960), 556–59.
   Poe, through his arrangement of incidents and motifs in this story, contrives to prove that the "Pure Intellect cannot rationally understand the process of creating Beauty."

O13   "Olybrius" [Thomas O. Mabbott]. "A Cento by Poe." *N&Q,* CLXI (Nov. 28, 1931), 388.
   An early production of Poe's found in an autograph album.

O14 ———. "An Early Discussion of Poe." *N&Q,* CXCI (Sept. 1946), 102.

"Discussion of Poe in the introduction to L. A. Norton's *The Restoration, A Metrical Romance of Canada* (Chicago, 1851) is 'interesting as evidence of widespread admiration of Poe in the West.'" *AL.*

O15 ———. "Poe and the Artist John P. Frankenstein." *N&Q,* CLXXXII (Jan. 17, 1942), 31–32.

"A reprint of a passage in Frankenstein's *American Art* (Cincinnati, Ohio, 1864) attacking Poe." *AL.*

O16 Onderdonk, James L. "Edgar Allan Poe." *Mid-Continent,* VI (June 1895), 166–73.

O17 ———. "The Lyric Poet of America." *Mid-Continent Mag,* VI (1895), 166–73.

Poe "was unquestionably our greatest lyric poet."

O18 ———. "Poe and the Brownings." *Dial,* XIV (June 16, 1893), 353–55.

O19 O'Neill, Edward H. "The Poe-Griswold-Harrison Texts of the 'Marginalia.'" *AL,* XV (Nov. 1943), 238–50.

Griswold did not print the various installments of the "Marginalia" as they originally appeared, but "made a new text, dropping and adding for no apparent reason."

*O20 Oppel, Ilse. "Edgar Allan Poe and Charles Baudelaire." Diss., Vienna, 1950.

O21 Orcutt, William D. "Mr. Poe Turns Thumbs Down on Boston." *From My Library Walls: A Kaleidoscope of Memories.* Toronto: Longmans, Green, 1945, pp. 184–87.

Poe's attitude toward Boston was a curious paradox.

O22 Orgain, Kate Alma. *Southern Authors in Poetry and Prose.* New York: Neale Publishing, 1908.

See pp. 194–213 for a compilation of critical quotations on Poe.

O23 Orians, George H. *A Short History of American Literature.* New York: Crofts & Co., 1940.

Briefly summarizes Poe's achievement in fiction and poetry; see pp. 136–37, 139–40.

O24 Osborne, William S. "John Pendleton Kennedy: A Study of His Literary Career." *DA,* XXI (July 1960), 190.

Discusses Kennedy's relationship with Poe.

*O25 ———. "John Pendleton Kennedy: A Study of His Literary Career." Diss., Columbia University, 1960.

O26 ———. "Kennedy on Poe: An Unpublished Letter." *MLN,* LXXV (Jan. 1960), 17–18.

Commentary on Kennedy's letter (1869) to G. W. Fahnestock of Philadelphia.

O27   Osgoode, Joseph A. "Poe, the Artist." *Tell It in Gath.* Sewanee, Tenn.: University Press, 1918, pp. 140–82.
Poe "triumphed gloriously as a representative of his country in the world of art."

O28   ———. "Poe, the Humorist." *Libertarian,* I (Aug. 1923), 43–51.
Points out evidences of humor in Poe's criticism.

O29   Ossoli, Margaret Fuller. "Poe's Poems." *The Writings of Margaret Fuller.* Selected and ed. Mason Wade. New York: Viking Press, 1941, pp. 398–403.
Poe "needs a sustained flight and far range to show what his powers really are." Reprinted from the New York *Daily Tribune,* Nov. 26, 1845.

O30   ———. "Poe's Tales." *The Writings of Margaret Fuller.* Selected and ed. Mason Wade. New York: Viking Press, 1941, pp. 396–97.
Praises Poe's tales, especially "The Murders in the Rue Morgue," and wishes that Poe would compose a "metaphysical novel." First appeared in the New York *Daily Tribune,* July 11, 1845, and appears in Eric Carlson, ed., *The Recognition of Edgar Allan Poe* (Ann Arbor: University of Michigan Press, 1966), pp. 17–18.

O31   Ostrom, John Ward. "Another Griswold Forgery in a Poe Letter." *MLN,* LVIII (May 1943), 394–96.
By changing a date, Griswold made it appear that Poe "had made the overtures to be included in the *Poets and Poetry of America,* without invitation from Griswold."

O32   ———. *A Check List of Letters to and from Poe.* University of Virginia Bibliographical Series, No. 4. Charlottesville, Va.: Alderman Library, 1941.
Mentions where some of Poe's letters are held.

*O33   ———. "A Critical Edition of the Letters of Edgar Allan Poe." Diss., University of Virginia, 1947.

O34   ———. "Foreword." *The Letters of Edgar Allan Poe.* 2 vols. New York: Gordian Press, 1966, I, [iii–vi].
"The present edition of *The Letters of Edgar Allan Poe* reprints the original two-volume edition (1948), page for page, and includes an extensive *Supplement* that brings the work up to date."

O35   ———. "The Letters of Edgar Allan Poe." *Abstracts of Dissertations* (1947). Charlottesville: University of Virginia, 1945–47, pp. 3–5.

O36   ———. *The Letters of Poe: Quest and Answer.* Baltimore: The Edgar Allan Poe Society, 1967.
Poe's correspondence, once established and his letters are in hand, provides "the kaleidoscope of his life." Reprinted from the *Baltimore Bulletin of Education,* XLIII, No. 1 (1967), 1–8.

O37   ———. "A Poe Correspondence Re-Edited." *Americana,* XXXIV (July 1940), 409–46.
Twelve letters of the Poe–Joseph Evans Snodgrass correspondence.

O38   ———. "Second Supplement to *The Letters of Poe.*" *AL,* XXIX (March 1957), 79–86.
"Brings up to date author's edition of Poe's letters." *AL.*

O39   ———. "Supplement to *The Letters of Poe.*" *AL,* XXIV (Nov. 1952), 358–66.
Poe's letters to Edward L. Carey, Abraham Hart, Peter S. Duponceau, Lewis Cass, J. Beauchamp Jones, Philip P. Cooke, Washington Irving, Joseph Evans Snodgrass, Lucian Minor, Frederick W. Thomas, C. P. Bronson, N. P. Willis, and John R. Thompson.

O40   ———. "Two 'Lost' Poe Letters." *AN&Q,* I (Aug. 1941), 68–69.
Presents evidence that two letters of the Poe-Eveleth correspondence are not lost.

O41   ———. "Two Unpublished Poe Letters." *Americana,* XXXVI (Jan. 1942), 67–71.
"The two letters were written to Hiram Haines, editor of the *Virginia Star,* in 1836 and 1840." *AL.*

O42   ———, ed. *The Letters of Edgar Allan Poe.* 2 vols. Cambridge, Mass.: Harvard University Press, 1948.
Represents seven years of gathering and editing Poe's letters.
    Reviewed:
UTQ, XX, 85–89.
Marcus Cunliffe, *MLR,* XLV, 249–50.
Marius Bewley, *PR,* XVI, 100–102.
C. D. Laverty, *AL,* XXI, 246–48.
J. B. Hubbell, *SAQ,* XLVIII, 297–98.
W. Thorp, *VQR,* XXV, 119.
N. A. Pearson, *YR,* XXXVIII, 568–69.
H. Rago, *Cweal,* (Jan. 21, 1949), pp. 381–82.
Joseph W. Krutch, *New York Herald-Tribune Books* (Dec. 19, 1948), p. 12.

O43   O'Sullivan, Vincent. "Edgar Allan Poe." *The Raven; The Pit and the Pendulum.* London: Leonard Smithers, 1899, pp. ix–xxix.
Generally unsympathetic in denouncing Poe's character.

O44 ———. "Edgar Allen [*sic*] Poe." *Academy*, LXII (May 31, 1902), 562.

Poe was never in Europe.

O45 O'Taylor, Quaker. "Edgar Allan Poe, A Man of Tragedy." Washington *National Republican* (weekly ed.), Jan. 19, 1924, pp. 5 and 9.

A biographical news story.

O46 Owlett, F. C. "Edgar Allen [*sic*] Poe." *Bibliophile*, II (Jan. 1909), 231–34.

Has high praise for the prose, but little for the poetry. He emphasizes Poe's *"visual intensity."*

P

P1 "P." "Edgar A. Poe." Boston *Daily Evening Transcript*, Oct. 18, 1845, p. 2.

Critical of Poe's theory of poetry, but acknowledges the fact that his theories and his poetry are *novel.*

P2 Deleted.

P3 P—, A. S. "Fugitive Poetry of America." *Southern Quarterly Rev*, XIV (July 1848), 101–31.

"The Raven" is criticized for its "wild and unbridled extravagance"; see pp. 115–19.

P4 Page, Curtis Hidden. "Edgar Allan Poe." *The Chief American Poets: Selected Poems.* Boston: Houghton, Mifflin, 1905, pp. 658–63.

Poe's character is "one rather for human pity than for harsh judgment."

P5 ———. "Poe in France." *Nation*, LXXXVIII (Jan. 14, 1909), 32–34.

Gives reasons for Poe's popularity in France: "the essence of his work is logic—logic entirely divorced from reality, and seeming to rise superior to reality." Reprinted in New York *Evening Post*, Jan. 16, 1909, p. 6.

P6 Pain, Barry, *et al.* "The Decline and Fall of the House of Usher." *American Literature in Parody.* Ed. R. P. Falk. New York: Twayne Publishers, 1955.

Parodies of Poe.

P7   Painter, Franklin Verzelius Newton. *Poets of the South: A Series of Biographical and Critical Studies with Typical Poems.* New York: American Book Co., 1903.

Poe's brilliant talents were wasted because he lacked "the moral element"; see pp. 29–47.

P8   Pancoast, Henry S. "Edgar Allan Poe (1809–1849)." *An Introduction to American Literature.* New York: Henry Holt, 1898, pp. 262–75.

"Poe claims our attention as a critic, a poet, and a story-writer."

P9   Parkes, Henry B. "Poe, Hawthorne, Melville: An Essay in Sociological Criticism." *PR,* XVI (Feb. 1949), 157–65.

Poe, as Hawthorne and Melville, treats the individual as an isolated entity, seeking its "own way of dealing with chaos."

P10   Parks, Edd W. *Edgar Allan Poe as a Literary Critic.* Athens: University of Georgia Press, 1964.

Poe's critical theories were mainly formed by his work as magazine editor and critic.

Reviewed:

Current-Garcia, *MissQ,* XVIII, 109–11.

Gerber, *SAQ,* LXIV, 428–29.

Hoag, *ELN,* III, 151–52.

Moore, *YWES,* XLV, 364.

Stovall, *AL,* 77–78.

P11   ——. "Teaching Poe to Brasilians and Danes." *ESQ,* No. 31 (2nd quarter 1963), pp. 28–29.

It is better "to teach Poe's poetry to Brasilians, and Poe's stories to the Scandinavians."

P12   ——. "Introduction." *Essays of Henry Timrod.* Ed. Parks. Athens: University of Georgia Press, 1942, pp. 3–60.

See pp. 17–18.

P13   Parrington, Vernon Louis. *The Romantic Revolution in American Literature, 1800–1860.* Vol. II of *Main Currents in American Thought.* 3 vols. New York: Harcourt, Brace, 1927.

Poe is the "first of our artists and the first of our critics," but a product of "the indolent life of the planter gentry, shot through with a pugnacious pride of locality"; see pp. 57–59.

P14   Parry, Albert. *Garrets and Pretenders: A History of Bohemianism in America.* New York: Covici, Friede, 1933.

See pp. 3–13 for Poe's position as "founder" of American bohemianism and for his bohemian influence as furthered by Baudelaire.

Reviewed:

W. H. Riback, *AL,* V, 196–98.

P15   Partridge, H. M., and D. C. Partridge. *The Most Remarkable Echo in the World.* New York: Cosmo Printing, 1933.
Twain on Poe; see pp. 19–46.

P16   Pattee, Fred L. "Critical Studies in American Literature." *Chatauquan,* XXXI (Aug. 1900), 182–86.
Poe's "Ulalume" is one of the "fine lyric poems" in American literature. Reprinted in *Side-Lights on American Literature* (New York: D. Appleton-Century, 1922).

P17   ———. "Edgar Allan Poe." *The Development of the American Short Story.* New York: Harper, 1923, pp. 115–41.
Concludes that Poe did not discover the world of the short story, but charted "the new regions" and demonstrated "how this chart might best be used."

P18   ———. *The First Century of American Literature.* New York: Appleton-Century, 1935.
Poe was first a magazinist but also a brilliant artist who is read for the "curious quality of his atmospheres"; see pp. 503–14.
Reviewed:
E. E. Leisy, *AL,* VII, 481–83.

P19   Patton, John Shelton. "Poe at the University." New York *Times,* Dec. 5, 1908, Book Number, p. 738.
Poe at the University of Virginia.

P19a   Patty, James S. "Baudelaire's View of America." *Kentucky Foreign Language Quarterly,* II (1955), 166–79.
Views America as "the telescopic image of bourgeois France."

P20   Paul, Harry Gilbert. "Introduction." *Poems and Tales,* by Edgar Allan Poe. Ed. Paul. New York: D. C. Heath, 1918, pp. v–xvi.
On Poe's achievements as critic, poet, and a writer of tales.

P21   Paul, Howard. "Recollections of Edgar Allan Poe." *Munsey's Mag,* VII (Aug. 1892), 554–58.

P22   Payne, L. W., Jr. "Poe and Emerson." *Texas Rev,* VII (Oct. 1921), 54–69.
Reviews C. Alphonso Smith's *Poe, How to Know Him* and Samuel McCord Crothers's *Emerson, How to Know Him.* Compares and contrasts talents of Poe and Emerson, pp. 64–69.

P23   Payne, Raphael S. "The Night When Poe Wrote 'The Bells.' " *Illustrated American,* XXI (Dec. 1896), 8–9.

P24   Payne, William Morton, ed. *American Literary Criticism.* Essay Index Reprint Series. Freeport, N.Y.: Books for Libraries Press, 1968.
A new era of American literary criticism begins with Edgar Allan

Poe; see pp. 14–18. First printed New York: Longmans, Green, 1904.

P25   Pearce, Charles E. *Unsolved Murder Mysteries.* London: Stanley Paul, 1924.

See pp. 225–45 for essay on Mary Rogers.

P26   Pearce, D. "The Cask of Amontillado." *N&Q,* CXCIX (Oct. 1954), 448–49.

"The tale has a strong flavor of . . . parody of archetypal events and themes in holy scripture." *AL.*

P27   Pearson, Edmund. "Mary Rogers and a Heroine of Fiction." *Vainty Fair,* XXXII (July 1929), 59, 110.

A rehashing of the contemporary accounts of the crime. Reprinted in *Instigation of the Devil* (New York: C. Scribner's Sons, 1930), pp. 177–85.

P28   Peck, George W. "Mere Music." *Literary World,* VI (March 9, 1850), 225–26.

Favorably impressed by the musical qualities of Poe's poetry.

P29   ———. "The Works of Edgar Allan Poe." *American Whig Rev,* XI (March 1850), 301–15.

Examines Poe's works and attempts to combat the Griswold attitude toward Poe.

P30   Peck, Harry Thurston. "Poe as a Story-Writer." *Studies in Several Literatures.* New York: Dodd, Mead, 1909, pp. 99–113.

Poe's tales reveal his logical and mathematical skill.

P31   Peckham, H. Houston. "Is American Literature Read and Respected in Europe?" *SAQ,* XIII (Oct. 1914), 382–88.

Mentions German and French translations of American authors, including Poe.

P32   Pellew, E. F. "Edgar Allan Poe." *Theatre,* NS VI (Sept. 1, 1882), 168–69.

Three sonnets on Poe.

P33   "Pendennis." "Where Poe Wrote 'The Raven.'" New York *Times,* Aug. 20, 1905, Part III, Mag. sec., p. 1.

On Fordham Cottage.

P34   Pendleton, T. D. "Some Memories of Poe." *Bob Taylor's Mag,* March 1906, 639–44.

An account of what Richmonders say about Poe.

P35   Perret, Jacques. "Préface." *Aventures d'Arthur Gordon Pym.* Trans. Charles Baudelaire. Paris: Le Livre de Poche, 1966, pp. i–iii.

P36   Perry, Bliss. *The American Mind.* Boston: Houghton Mifflin, 1912.

See *passim* references to Poe.

P37   ——. "Introduction." *Edgar Allan Poe.* Ed. Perry. New York: Doubleday and McClure, 1897, pp. v–xi.

Several of Poe's best short stories are included in this collection; at his best Poe demonstrates power of clear, compressed narrative and mastery of symbolism and sensuous imagery. Reprinted in *Poe,* vol. IV of the Pocket University (Garden City, N.Y.: Doubleday, Page, 1926), pp. vii–xi.

P38   ——. "Poe and Whitman." *The American Spirit in Literature.* The Chronicles of America Series, vol. 34. Ed. Allen Johnson *et al.* New Haven: Yale University Press, 1918, pp. 187–205.

Poe was a "timeless, placeless embodiment of technical artistry."

P39   Perry, Marvin B., Jr. "Keats and Poe." *English Studies in Honor of James Southall Wilson.* Richmond: William Byrd Press, 1951, pp. 45–52.

Keats exerted an influence upon Poe's poetry and aesthetics.

P40   Perry, Wilbur Dow. "Edgar Allan Poe." *Birmingham Southern College Studies in English* (Birmingham, Ala.), June 1928, pp. 29–34.

Commentary on Poe's foreign reputation and his qualified acceptance in America.

P41   Peters, H. F. "Ernest Jünger's Concern with E. A. Poe." *CL,* X (Spring 1958), 144–49.

The affinity between Poe and Jünger was rooted in their concern with one major theme—the theme of terror.

*P42   Peterson, Dewayne A. "Edgar Allan Poe's Grotesque Humor: A Study of the Grotesque Effects in His Humorous Tales." Diss., Duke University, 1962.

*P43   ——. *Poe's Grotesque Humor: A Study of the Grotesque Effects in His Humorous Tales.* Ann Arbor, Mich.: University Microfilms, 1962.

P44   ——. "Poe's Grotesque Humor: A Study of the Grotesque Effects in His Humorous Tales." *DA,* XXIII (March 1963), 3355–56.

"Close analyses of twenty-two tales reveals that appreciation of the humor depends upon recognition of the grotesque effects."

P45   Pettigrew, Richard C. "Poe's Rime." *AL,* IV (May 1932), 151–59.

Poe in his poetic practice was not a "stickler for technical precisions."

P46   ——, and Marie Morgan Pettigrew. "A Reply to Floyd Stovall's Interpretation of 'Al Aaraaf.' " *AL,* VIII (Jan. 1937), 439–45.

" 'Al Aaraaf' is not an instrument of destruction, nor is Nesace, its ruler, an agent of God's wrath."

P47   Pfennig, Hazel T. "Periodical Literary Criticism, 1800–1865: A Study of the Book Reviews from 1800 to the Close of the Civil War,

Dealing with the Successive Works of Irving, Cooper, Bryant, Poe, Hawthorne, and Thoreau, Which Appeared in American Publications within the Lifetime of the Individual Authors." Diss., New York University, 1932.

P48   Philips, Edith. "The French of Edgar Allan Poe." *American Speech,* II (March 1927), 270–74.

On Poe's use of French phrases.

*P49   Phillips, Elizabeth. *Edgar Allan Poe: The American Context.* Ann Arbor, Mich.: University Microfilms, 1957.

P50   ——. "Edgar Allan Poe: The American Context." *DA,* XVII (Nov. 1957), 2614–15.

Poe was "the supreme type of the artist isolated from his society."

*P51   ——. "Edgar Allan Poe: The American Context." Diss., University of Pennsylvania, 1957.

P52   ——. "The Hocus-Pocus of *Lolita.*" *L&P,* X (Autumn 1960), 97–101.

"Vladimir Nabokov's novel is a satire on an orthodox Freudian view of the life and writings of Edgar Allan Poe."

P53   Phillips, Elizabeth C. "The Literary Life of John Tomlin, Friend of Poe." Diss., University of Tennessee, 1954.

A biography of one of Poe's contemporaries who was active in the profession of journalism.

P54   Phillips, Mary Elizabeth. *Edgar Allan Poe, the Man.* 2 vols. Chicago: John C. Winston, 1926.

An attempt to bring a great many facts together in a somewhat romanticized version of Poe's life.

  Reviewed:

Killis Campbell, *SP,* XXIV, 474–79.

J. W. Krutch, *Nation,* CXXIV (Jan. 5, 1927), 17.

Malcolm Cowley, *Nation,* CXXIV (Jan. 29, 1927), 550.

F. Ballenspergen, *RLC,* VIII, 192–95.

J. Hoops, *Englische Studien,* LXII, 318–20.

C. Cestre, *Rev Anglo-Américaine,* IV, 385–97.

See also J. W. Krutch, *SatRL,* III (Jan. 8, 1927), 493–94.

P55   Phillips, William L. "Poe's 'The Fall of the House of Usher.' " *Expl,* IX (Feb. 1951), item 29.

Points to "parallels between the activities of Usher and his friend and the final horrible events."

P56   Pickett, La Salle Corbell. " 'The Poet of the Night': Edgar Allan Poe." *Literary Hearthstones of Dixie.* Philadelphia: Lippincott, 1912, pp. 11–38.

Biographical sketch. Reprinted from *Lippincott's*, LXXX (Sept. 1912), 326–33.

P57   Pittman, Diana. "Key to the Mystery of Edgar Allan Poe." *SLM*, III (Aug. 1941), 367–78; (Sept. 1941), 418–24; (Oct.–Nov. 1941), 499–509; (Dec. 1941), 549–56; IV (Jan. 1942), 19–24; (Feb. 1942), 81–85; (April 1942), 143–72.

An interesting but unconvincing examination of Poe's work in the light of the "political situation in England" during the early decades of the 19th century. See editorial preface to Miss Pittman's articles by F. Meredith Dietz entitled "Return of Edgar Allan Poe," *SLM*, III (Aug. 1941), 365–66. See also *SLM*, III (Aug. 1941), 417; IV (March 1942), 141–42.

P58   Pochmann, Henry August. "Germanic Materials and Motifs in the Short Story: Edgar Allan Poe." *German Culture in America*. Madison: University of Wisconsin Press, 1957, pp. 388–408.

Poe not only adapted themes and motifs from the German *Romantiker* (Hoffmann, Novalis, particularly) but drew his doctrine of effect and his theory of unity from the foremost German critic, August Wilhelm von Schlegel.

P59   ——. "The Influence of the German Tale on the Short Stories of Irving, Hawthorne, and Poe." Diss., University of North Carolina, 1928.

P60   Deleted.

*P61   ——. *Poems*. Engravings and ornaments by J. G. Daragnès. New York: Charles Breyner Art Publications, 1950.

*P62   ——. *The Raven, a Poem*, by Edgar Allan Poe. Illus. Édouard Manet. Prepared by Anne Blake Freedberg. Boston: Museum of Fine Arts, 1956.

"The illustrations and text reproduced in this picture book are from the copy of the French edition given to the Museum in 1932 by W. G. Russell Allen." *LCC*.

P63   ——. *Some Letters of Edgar Allan Poe to E. H. N. Patterson of Oquawka, Illinois, with Comments by Eugene Field*. Chicago: The Caxton Club, 1898.

Patterson, the candidate for the financial backer of the *Stylus*, corresponds with Poe.

P64   ——. *Tales of the Grotesque and Arabesque*. New York: Doubleday, n.d.

This 1960 paperback is "identical with the original in every respect except that of typography and design"; see "Preface," pp. [7]–8.

P65   Poe, Elizabeth Ellicott. "Centenary of Edgar Allan Poe, The

Greatest of American Poets." New Orleans *Daily Picayune,* Jan. 17, 1909, Third Part, p. 3.

P66 ——. "Edgar Allan Poe and Virginia Clemm." *Half-Forgotten Romances of American History.* Washington, D.C.: Stylus Publishing, 1927, pp. 103–10.
Poe's courtship and marriage.

P67 ——. "Poe and Baltimore." *Academy,* LXXVII (Jan. 30, 1909), 729–30.
Baltimore has not expressed enough appreciation of Poe.

P68 ——. "Poe, the Weird Genius." *Cosmopolitan,* XLVI (Feb. 1909), 243–52.
A biographical article with several serious mistakes.

P69 ——, and Vylla Poe Wilson. *Edgar Allan Poe: A High Priest of the Beautiful.* Washington, D.C.: Stylus Publishing, 1930.
Biographical essays with select poems by Poe.

P70 Poe, John Prentiss. "Edgar Allan Poe." *Old Maryland,* IV/V (Dec. 1908–Jan. 1909), 1–6.
Rejects the separation of the character and the work of Poe and praises both.

P71 Poitevent, Schuyler. "Some Facts about Poe's University Career." *UVaMag,* LVIII (Dec. 1897), 123–34.

P72 Pole, James T. "Note on Joseph S. Schick's 'The Origin of the Cask of Amontillado.' " *AL,* VI (March 1934), 21.
See Schick's article in this connection.

P73 Pollard, Percival. "What Literature Owes to Edgar Allan Poe." New York *Times,* Jan. 10, 1909, Part V, Mag. sec., p. 6.
Calls for more appreciation of Poe.

P74 Pollin, Burton R. "Bulwer-Lytton and 'The Tell-Tale Heart.' " *AN&Q,* IV (Sept. 1965), 7–8.
Lytton's "Monos and Daimonas" substantially contributed to "The Tell-Tale Heart."

P75 ——. "New York City in the Tales of Poe." *Bronx County Historical Society Jour,* II, No. 1 (Jan. 1965), 16–22.
Traces Poe's treatment of New York City after April, 1844.

P76 ——. "Poe and Godwin." *NCF,* XX (Dec. 1965), 237–53.
Poe admired Godwin's craftsmanship and was likely influenced by Godwin's use of "suspense, morbid psychology, and alienated heroes."

P77 ——. "Poe as 'Miserrimus': From British Epitaph to American Epithet." *Revue des Langues Vivantes* (Brussels), XXXIII (1967), 347–61.
Traces "the influence of Frederick Manselle Reynolds' novel *Miiserrimus* [sic] on Poe." *PN.*

P78 ——. "Poe's 'Von Kempelen and His Discovery': Sources and Significance." *EA,* XX (Jan.–Mar. 1967), 12–23.
Discusses the origin of "Von Kempelen and His Discovery," one of Poe's most successful hoaxes.

P79 ——. " 'The Spectacles' of Poe—Sources and Significance." *AL,* XXXVII (May 1965), 185–90.
Poe attached considerable importance to "The Spectacles," a deliberate adaptation of an anonymous tale published in the *New Monthly Belle Assemblée.*

P80 Pollock, Arthur. "A Play about Poe." *Christian Science Monitor,* XXVIII (Nov. 10, 1936), 8.

P81 Pope-Hennessy, Una. *Edgar Allan Poe, 1809–1849: A Critical Biography.* London: Macmillan, 1934.
Poe was neither understood nor valued by his compatriots.
Reviewed:
TLS, Nov. 8, 1934, p. 771.
Life and Letters, XI, 239–40.
O'Faoláin, *London Spectator,* CLIII (Nov. 23, 1934), Literary Supplement, 18.
K. Campbell, *AL,* VII, 220–24.
C. Aiken, *The Criterion,* XIV, 501–3.
Townsend-Warner, *New Statesman and Nation,* NS VIII (Nov. 17, 1934), 730.

P82 ——. "A Letter to the Editors." *AL,* VII (Nov. 1935), 334.
Refutes two errors in a review (*AL,* May 1935) of the author's *Edgar Allan Poe.*

P83 Porges, Irwin. *Edgar Allan Poe.* Philadelphia: Chilton Books, 1963.
Attempts to bring out Poe's colorful personality by emphasizing the variety of Poe's literary activities.

P84 Posey, Meredith Neill. "Notes on Poe's Hans Pfaall." *MLN,* XLV (Dec. 1930), 501–7.
There are obvious parallels between *Hans Pfaall* and J. F. W. Herschel's *Treatise on Astronomy* (Philadelphia, 1834) and Rees's *Cyclopedia.*

P85 Poulet, Georges. "Edgar Poe." *The Metamorphoses of the Circle.* Trans. Carley Dawson and Elliot Coleman. Baltimore: Johns Hopkins Press, 1966, pp. 182–202.
Poe's artistic form reveals his emphasis upon images of ever-expanding circles to convey the dimensions of knowledge and experience.

P86——. "Poe." *Studies in Human Time.* Trans. Elliot Coleman. Baltimore: Johns Hopkins Press, 1956, pp. 330–34.

Poe's dream world and the cycle of time. Original appeared in *Études sur le temps humain* (Paris: Plon, 1953); translation reprinted in Eric Carlson, ed., *The Recognition of Edgar Allan Poe* (Ann Arbor: University of Michigan Press, 1966), pp. 231–35.

P87   Pound, Louise. "On Poe's 'The City in the Sea.'" *AL,* VI (March 1934), 22–27.
Poe's city could owe something to European legends of engulfed cities.

P88 ———. "Poe's 'The City in the Sea' Again." *AL,* VIII (March 1936), 70–71.
The title may be derived from the book of Ezekiel.

P89   Powell, Thomas. "Edgar Allan Poe." *The Living Authors of America.* New York: Stringer and Townsend, 1850, pp. 108–34.
Emphasizes the mechanics of Poe's art, but admires his imagination and foretells Poe's recognition as a writer of tales.

P90   Powys, John C. "Edgar Allen [*sic*] Poe." *Visions and Revisions.* New York: G. Arnold Shaw, pp. 263–77.
Poe's "sardonic, cynical humour" and philosophy of life are reflected in his poetry.

P91 ———. "Melville and Poe." *Enjoyment of Literature.* New York: Simon and Schuster, 1938, pp. 379–405.
Poe was an inspired poet whose poetic realm narrows itself down to a certain romantic and unearthly mood.

P92   Praz, Mario. "Poe and Psychoanalysis." Trans. B. M. Arnett. *SR,* LXVIII (Summer 1960), 375–89.
Article first published in Italian in 1933.

P93 ———. *The Romantic Agony.* Trans. Angus Davidson. 2nd ed. London: Oxford University Press, 1951.
Comments on Poe's critical ideas and his influence on Romantics, *passim.*

P94   Prentice, George D. [Poe's Reference to Carlyle.] *Knickerbocker,* XXII (Oct. 1843), 392.

P95   Prescott, Frederick C. "Introduction." *Selections from the Critical Writings of Edgar Allan Poe.* New York: Henry Holt, 1909, pp. ix–li.
Essay on the sources of Poe's theory of poetry.

P96 ———. "Poe's Definition of Poetry." *Nation,* LXXXVIII (Feb. 4, 1909), 110.
An enquiry into the source of "the rhythmical creation of beauty."

P97   Preston, Raymond A. [Poe and Mudford.] *Literary Review,* New York *Evening Post,* II (July 22, 1922), 830.

Discusses similarity between a story in *Blackwood's* and "The Pit and the Pendulum."

P98   Price, Lawrence M. *The Reception of English Literature in Germany.* Berkeley: University of California Press, 1932.

Poe was popular and translated into German *in toto;* see p. 422.

P99   ——. *The Reception of United States Literature in Germany.* Chapel Hill: University of North Carolina Press, 1966.

Traces critical opinion of Poe in Germany; see especially pages 124–27.

P100   Price, Vincent. "Introduction." *18 Best Stories,* by Edgar Allan Poe. Ed. Price and Chandler Brossard. Laurel Edition. New York: Dell, 1965, pp. 7–9.

Finds that Poe brilliantly transforms "his inner visions or hallucinations into universally loved fiction and poetry" and comments upon the rendering of Poe's work into film.

Reviewed:

A. Boucher, *NYTBR,* July 11, 1965, p. 20.

P101   Pritchard, John Paul. "Aristotle's Influence upon American Criticism." *Proceedings of the American Philological Association,* LXVII (1936), 341–62.

Some remarks on Poe's indebtedness to Aristotle, pp. 344–47.

P102   ——. "Aristotle's Poetics and Certain American Literary Critics." *Classical Weekly,* XXVII (Jan. 8, 1934), 81–85.

"Fragmentary and distorted as was his [Poe's] knowledge of the *Poetics,* it had a strong shaping influence upon his criticism."

P103   ——. "Edgar Allan Poe." *Criticism in America.* Norman: University of Oklahoma Press, 1956, pp. 70–86.

Presents a competent expository discussion of Poe's critical theories.

P104   "Edgar Allan Poe." *Return to the Fountains.* Durham, N.C.: Duke University Press, 1942, pp. 26–43.

Critic presents observations found in two earlier articles: "Aristotle's Poetics and Certain American Literary Critics," *Classical Weekly,* XXVII (Jan. 8, 1934), 81–85, and "Horace and Edgar Allan Poe," *Classical Weekly,* XXVI (March 6, 1933), 129–33. Poe was indirectly influenced by Aristotle's idea of "unity," but to Horace, Poe owed a considerable debt.

P105   ——. "Horace and Edgar Allan Poe." *Classical Weekly,* XXVI (March 6, 1933), 129–33.

A careful study of the possible influence of Horace on Poe.

P106   Pritchett, Victor S. "The Poe Centenary." *Books in General.* London: Chatto and Windus, 1953, pp. 185–90.

Poe's redeeming quality is his gift of generalizing morbid experience.

P107 ———. "The Poe Centenary." *Literature in America.* Ed. Philip Rahv. New York: Meridian Books, 1957, pp. 110–14.

P108 Pruette, Lorine. "A Psycho-Analytical Study of Edgar Allan Poe." *American Jour of Psychology,* XXXI (Oct. 1920), 370–402.

A study of Poe's life from a psychologist's point of view. Reprinted in Hendrick M. Ruitenbeek's *The Literary Imagination: Psychoanalysis and the Genius of the Writer* (Chicago: Quadrangle Books, 1965), pp. 391–432.

P109 "Psi." "Poe's Soliloquy." *UVaMag,* LIX (April–May 1899), 356.

Verse reprinted from the Wofford College (S.C.) *Journal.*

P110 Publishers, The. "Introduction." *Great Tales and Poems of Edgar Allan Poe.* New York: Washington Square Press, 1961, pp. ix–xii.

Poe "captured the horror that is of the soul."

P111 Pugh, Griffith T. "Poe: An Induction." *EJ,* LXV (Dec. 1956), 509–16, 552.

A review of Poe's life and accomplishments.

P112 Purdy, S. B. "Poe and Dostoyevsky." *SSF,* IV (Winter 1967), 169–71.

Dostoyevsky's use of Poe in *Uncle's Dream* (1859).

P113 Purves, James. "Edgar Allan Poe." *Dublin University Mag,* LXXXV (March 1875), 336–51.

Declares that one can feel great sympathy for Poe whose life has been perverted and falsified by some of his biographers.

P114 ———. "Edgar Allan Poe's Works." *Dublin University Mag,* LXXXVI (Sept. 1875), 296–306.

"It is as a poet that Poe will be best known."

Q

Q1 Quarles, Diana (Pittman). "Poe and International Copyright." *SLM,* III (Jan. 1941), 4.

"The Copyright Question" (*Blackwood's,* Jan. 1842) is not Poe's, but Archibald Allison's.

Q2 Quinn, Arthur H. "Beauty and the Supernatural." *The Literature of the American People.* New York: Appleton-Century-Crofts, 1951, pp. 292–307.

Quinn summarizes much of his criticisms found in his earlier biography (1941).

Q3 ———. *Edgar Allan Poe: A Critical Biography.* New York: D. Appleton-Century, 1941.

Emphasizes Poe's role as editor who excelled in criticism, fiction, and especially in poetry. Reprinted New York: Cooper Square, 1969.
Reviewed:
Frances Winwar, *NYTBR,* Nov. 30, 1941, pp. 3, 41.
George Barker, *Nation,* CLIII (Dec. 27, 1941), 673–74.

Q4 ———. "Edgar Allan Poe and the Establishment of the Short Story." *American Fiction: An Historical and Critical Survey.* New York: D. Appleton-Century, 1936, pp. 77–101.

Analyzes the categories of Poe's short stories and cites especially Poe's treatment of the supernatural.

Q5 ———. "The Foundations of American Criticism." *The Literature of the American People.* New York: Appleton-Century-Crofts, 1951, pp. 384–97.

Quinn summarizes his earlier commentaries found in his biography of Poe (1941).

Q6 ———. "The Marriage of Poe's Parents." *AL,* XI (May 1939), 209–12.

Criticism of undue haste in the marriage is unwarranted.

Q7 ———. "Some Phases of the Supernatural in American Literature." *PMLA,* XXV (1910), 114–33.

"The supernatural lyric reaches the highest point in America in the work of Poe."

Q8 ———, ed. *The Complete Poems and Stories of Edgar Allan Poe, with Selections from His Critical Writings.* Introd. Quinn; texts established, with biographical notes, by Edward H. O'Neill. 2 vols. New York: A. A. Knopf, 1946.

Poe was a hard-working man of letters who wrote literature well above the standards of his day. See "Introduction," I, 1–14.
Reviewed:
George Arms, *NMQ,* XVIII, 107–9.

Q9 ———, and Richard H. Hart, eds. *Edgar Allan Poe: Letters and Documents in the Enoch Pratt Free Library.* New York: Scholars' Facsimiles and Reprints, 1941.

Commentary on and text of letters to, from, and about Poe.

Q10 Quinn, Patrick F. "Four Views of Edgar Poe." *JA,* V (1960), 138–46.

Poe's works reflect his "participation in a great and endless debate about one of the basic issues in western thought, the relationship between the two realms of Existence ['the real world'] and Essence ['the realm of abstraction, of imagination']."

*Q11   ——. *The French Face of Edgar Poe.* Ann Arbor, Mich.: University Microfilms, 1954.

Q12   ——. *The French Face of Edgar Poe.* Carbondale: Southern Illinois University Press, 1957.

Poe, from the French point of view, created in his fiction psychological dramas that treat effectively the "darker regions of the psyche." Section entitled "The French Response to Poe" appears in Robert Regan, ed., *Poe: A Collection of Critical Essays* (Englewood Cliffs, N.J.: Prentice-Hall, 1967), pp. 64–78.

Reviewed:

Cweal, (Nov. 29, 1957), pp. 265–66.

L. LeSage, *SatR,* (Oct. 19, 1957), p. 60.

Henri Peyre, *MLR,* LIII, 572–73.

Q13   ——. "The French Face of Edgar Poe." *DA,* XIV (1954), 131–32.

*Q14   ——. "The French Face of Edgar Poe." Diss., Columbia University, 1953.

Q15   ——. "Poe's *Eureka* and Emerson's *Nature.*" *ESQ,* No. 31 (2nd quarter 1963), pp. 4–7.

Poe, unlike Emerson, emphasizes the demise of energy and life.

Q16   ——. "Poe's Imaginary Voyage." *HudR,* IV (Winter 1952), 562–87.

Critic expounds upon the reception of *Pym* in France and concludes that "what on the surface is an episodic tale of improbabilities is fundamentally a truly imaginary voyage." Article reprinted in author's *The French Face of Edgar Poe* (1957).

Q17   ——. "The Profundities of Edgar Poe." *Yale French Studies,* No. 6 (1950), pp. 3–13.

Article is reprinted as "The French Response to Poe" in the author's *The French Face of Edgar Poe.*

Q18   Quinn, Sister M. Bernetta. "A New Approach to Early American Literature." *CE,* XXV (Jan. 1964), 267–73.

Points out a parallel between Poe and the painter Albert Pinkham Ryder; see pp. 271–72.

R

R1   R—. "The Poetry of The Messenger." *SLM*, VIII (Dec. 1842), 798–99.

Criticizes the low standard of poetry appearing in the *Messenger.*

R2   R—, H. "Poe's Earliest Poems." *The Philobiblian,* I (March 1862), 86–89.

Reprints some of the poems in the 1831 edition and expresses appreciation of Poe's early verse.

R3   R., W. H. "Edgar Allen [*sic*] Poe: An Appreciation." *The Works of Edgar Allan Poe.* 10 vols. New York: Frank F. Lovell Book Co., 1902, I, i–x.

Poe was "the finest and most original genius in American letters." Also reprinted here is Lowell's "Edgar A. Poe," pp. 5–11; and N. P. Willis's "Death of Edgar A. Poe," pp. 13–19. All three essays appear in *The Gold Bug and Other Stories,* by Edgar Allen [*sic*] Poe (New York: World Publishing Co., 1940), n.p.

R4   Radó, György. "The Works of E. A. Poe in Hungary." *Babel* (Bonn, W. Ger.), XII, No. 1 (1966), 21–22.

Poe's popularity in Hungary is a "living reality."

R5   Rago, Henry. "The Sociology of Composition." *Cweal,* XLVI (July 18, 1947), 336–38.

A commentary on the modernity of Poe's theory of poetry.

R6   Railo, Eino. *The Haunted Castle: A Study of the Elements of English Romanticism.* London: Dutton, 1927.

Traces Poe's close affiliation with the romantic movement. See pp. 188–89, 257, 265, 299.

R7   Ramakrishna, D. "The Conclusion of Poe's 'Ligeia.' " *ESQ,* No. 47 (2nd quarter 1967), pp. 69–70.

The conclusion of "Ligeia," although effective, is confusing to the reader.

R8   ——. "Poe's *Eureka* and Hindu Philosophy." *ESQ,* No. 47 (2nd quarter 1967), pp. 28–32.

In *Eureka,* Poe expresses "the essence of Emersonian Transcendentalism" and Hindu philosophical thought.

R9   ——. "Poe's 'Ligeia.' " *Expl,* XXV (Oct. 1966), item 19.

Poe's characterization demonstrates that "Ligeia" is not a repudiation of the Gothic romance.

R10   Ramsey, Paul, Jr. "Poe and Modern Art." *College Art Jour,* XVIII (Spring 1959), 210–15.
"The Fall of the House of Usher" reveals "an uncanny illumination, and foreshadowing, of some of the qualities of modern painting."

R11   Ranck, Edwin Carty. "Editor of the Bookman." *Bookman,* XLV (Aug. 1917), 658–61.
Quotes section of Thomas Mayne Reid's biography of Poe.

R12   Randall, David. "First Edition of The Raven." *AN&Q,* I (May 1941), 29.
Book was first issued in paper wrappers.

R13   Randall, David A. "The J. K. Lilly Collection of Edgar Allan Poe." *Indiana University Bookman,* No. 4 (March 1960), pp. 46–58.
Contains early editions of Poe's work as well as the papers of Sarah Helen Whitman and J. H. Whitty.

R14   ———. *The J. K. Lilly Collection of Edgar Allan Poe: An Account of Its Formation.* Bloomington: Lilly Library of the University of Indiana, 1964.
Discusses content of the Lilly Collection.
    Reviewed:
Moore, *YWES,* XLV, 364.

R15   Randall, John H., III. "Poe's 'The Cask of Amontillado' and the Code of the Duello." *Studia Germanica Gandensia,* V (1963), 175–84.
Poe's story reveals "an extreme version of the gentleman's code, that ethic which finds its most intense expression in the duello."

R16   Ranking, B. Montgomerie. "Edgar Allan Poe." *Time Monthly Mag,* IX (Sept. 1883), 352–60.
Thinks Poe's poetical gifts are overestimated and that the future will judge him by his prose.

R17   Rans, Geoffrey. *Edgar Allan Poe.* Edinburgh: Oliver and Boyd, 1965.
Touches upon Poe's chief themes and attempts to assess critical opinion of Poe as artist.
    Reviewed:
Dodsworth, *New Statesman and Nation,* LXX (Aug. 20, 1965), 257.
Moore, *YWES,* XLVI, 347–48.
TLS, June 3, 1965, p. 456.

*R18   ———. "The Origin and History of the Idea of Corruption in American Writing, and Its Expression in James Fenimore Cooper, Edgar Allan Poe, and Ralph Waldo Emerson." Diss., Leeds, 1963–64.

R19 Ransome, Arthur. "Edgar Allan Poe." *Temple Bar,* CXXXIV (Dec. 1906), 481–96.

"Poe's work is remarkable for its versatile genius, but it is still more remarkable for the uniformity of its character in spite of its versatility."

R20 ———. *Edgar Allan Poe: A Critical Study.* London: Martin Secker, 1910.

Attempts "to trace Poe's thought by discussing in the most convenient order his various activities or groups of ideas."

Reviewed:

C. L. Moore, *Dial,* L (Jan. 1, 1911), 16–18.

R21 Rascoe, Burton. "Poe the Inventor." *Titans of Literature.* New York: G. P. Putnam's Sons, 1932, pp. 395–403.

Mostly biographical with some critical commentary on Poe's work and influence. Reprinted in *Muse Anthology of Modern Poetry,* ed. Dorothy Kissling and Arthur H. Nethercot, Poe Memorial Edition (New York: Carlyle Straub, 1938), pp. 104–12.

*R22 Rasor, C. L. "Possible Sources of 'The Cask of Amontillado.' " *Furman Studies,* XXXI (Winter 1949), 46–50.

"The sources discussed are Balzac's 'La Grande Bretêche,' Bulwer-Lytton's *The Last Days of Pompeii,* and J. T. Headley's 'A Man Built in a Wall.' " *AL.*

R23 Ravenel, Beatrice. "Poe's Mother." *Muse Anthology of Modern Poetry.* Ed. Dorothy Kissling and Arthur H. Nethercot. Poe Memorial Edition. New York: Carlyle Straub, 1938, pp. 32–37.

Poetic monologue.

R24 Rea, Joy. "Classicism and Romanticism in Poe's 'Ligeia.' " *BSUF,* VIII (Winter 1967), 25–29.

Poe's feminine characters of Ligeia and Rowena are associated with Classicism and Romanticism, respectively.

R25———. "In Defense of Fortunato's Courtesy." *SSF,* IV (Spring 1967), 267–68.

On Poe's "The Cask of Amontillado."

R26 ———. "Poe's 'The Cask of Amontillado.' " *SSF,* IV (Fall 1966), 57–59.

Poe's story reflects his theory of the perverse.

R27 Rede, Kenneth. "The Father of Edgar Allan Poe." Baltimore *Sun,* Jan. 22, 1933, Mag. sec., pp. 6–7.

A sketch of David Poe's life to the time of his marriage to Elizabeth Arnold.

R28 ———. "New Poe Manuscript." *American Collector,* III (Dec.
1926), 100–102.
  Concerning MSS of "The Coliseum" and "To One in Paradise" in an
autograph album.

R29 ———. "Poe Notes: From an Investigator's Notebook." *AL,* V
(March 1933), 49–54.
  On the publication of *Pym,* "The Raven," and an extract from *Al
Aaraaf.* Poe-Lane agreement *in re* the *Broadway Journal* is presented.

R30 ———. "A Poe Society." *SatRL,* III (April 2, 1927), 706.

R31 ———. "Poe's 'Annie': Leaves from the Lonesome Latter Years."
American Collector, IV (April 1927), 21–28.
  Poe's letters to Annie Richmond are vital in understanding Poe
during the luckless last phase of his life.

R32 ———. "An Unnoted Poe Poem?" *ABC,* IV (Aug. 1933),
106–07.
  Some verse entitled "Home" from an unknown journal may be, the
author believes, an early Poe poem.

R33 ———, and Chas. F. Heartman. "Autographs of Poe." *TLS,*
March 24, 1932, p. 217.
  Asking for information as to Poe letters and MSS.

R34 Redman, Catherine. "Edgar Allan Poe—Soldier." *Quarter-
master Rev,* XVI (Jan.–Feb. 1937), 18–21, 73–74.
  Events leading to Poe's enlistment and his brief career at West Point.

R35 Reece, James B. "New Light on Poe's 'The Masque of the Red
Death.'" *MLN,* LXVIII (Feb. 1953), 114–15.
  Poe appears to have got some ideas for his "Masque" from Thomas
Campbell's *Life of Petrarch.*

*R36 ———. "Poe and the Literati." Diss., Duke University, 1954.

R37 Reed, Myrtle. "The Love Affairs of Edgar Allan Poe." *Putnam's
Monthly,* II (Aug. 1907), 574–79.
  Poe's love affairs evidence a very sensitive personality.

R38 Rees, J. Rogers. *With Friend and Book and In the Study and
the Fields.* London: W. W. Gibbings, 1892.
  See pp. 46–56 of *In the Study and the Fields* for discussion of the
composition of "The Raven."

R39 Regan, Robert. "Introduction." *Poe: A Collection of Critical
Essays.* Ed. Regan. Englewood Cliffs, N.J.: Prentice-Hall, 1967, pp.
1–13.
  Traces critical opinion of Poe and focuses attention on the com-
plexities of evaluating Poe's stature as a writer.
  Reviewed:

R. L. H., *PrS*, XLI, 356–57.

Wilbur, *NYRB*, IX (July 13, 1967), 16, 25–28.

R40   [Reid, Thomas Mayne.] "A Dead Man Defended." *Onward*, I (April 1869), 305–8.

Attacks the Griswoldian approach to Poe's character.

R41   ———. *Edgar Allan Poe*. Ysleta, Tex.: Edwin B. Hill, 1933.

A defense of Poe's character by an Irish soldier of fortune who was acquainted with Poe.

R42   Reid, Whitelaw. "The Poe Centenary." *London Commemorations: Winter of 1908–09*. London: Harrison and Sons, 1909, pp. 3–14.

Especially commends Poe's fiction in an address to the Author's Club, March 1, 1909, at Hotel Métropole, London.

*R43   Reilly, John Edward. *Poe in Imaginative Literature: A Study of American Drama, Fiction, and Poetry Devoted to Edgar Allan Poe or His Works*. Ann Arbor, Mich.: University Microfilms, 1965.

R44   ———. "Poe in Imaginative Literature: A Study of American Drama, Fiction, and Poetry Devoted to Edgar Allan Poe or His Works." *DA*, XXVI (April 1966), 6050.

Up to 1940, Poe is treated romantically and becomes a legendary image.

R45   ———. "Poe in Imaginative Literature: A Study of American Drama, Fiction, and Poetry Devoted to Edgar Allan Poe or His Works." Diss., University of Virginia, 1965.

R46   Rein, David M. *Edgar A. Poe: The Inner Pattern*. New York: Philosophical Library, 1960.

Attempts to reveal the deep feelings reflected in Poe's stories and poetry.

Reviewed:

Malin, *L&P*, X, 86–87.

Stovall, *AL*, XXXII, 83–84.

Fagin, *SAQ*, LX, 113–14.

Levine, *AQ*, XVII, 133–44.

R47   ———. "Poe and Mrs. Shelton." *AL*, XXVIII (May 1956), 225–27.

Poe was pessimistic about his hopes to marry Mrs. Shelton.

R48   ———. "Poe and Virginia Clemm." *BuR*, VII (May 1958), 207–16.

"Autobiographical interpretations of six tales." *AL*.

R49   ———. "Poe's Dreams." *AQ*, X (Fall 1958), 367–71.

Points out that Poe's "The Oval Portrait" and "Metzengerstein" reveal new glimpses into Poe's turbulent inner life. Article is reprinted in the author's *Edgar A. Poe: The Inner Pattern*, pp. 1–24.

R50 ——. "Poe's 'Introduction, XXXI–XXXIV.'" *Expl*, XX (Sept. 1961), item 8.

Interprets lines by Poe, first published in *Poems* (1831), having biographical overtones.

R51 Reiss, Edmund. "The Comic Setting of 'Hans Pfaall.'" *AL*, XXIX (Nov. 1957), 306–09.

The plot appears in sharp contrast to the actual adventures related in Hans's letter.

R52 Rendall, V. "Dumas and Poe." *TLS*, Nov. 28, 1929, p. 1001.

On the suggested affinity between Poe and Dumas.

R53 Reynolds, George F., and Garland Greever. *The Facts and Backgrounds of Literature, English and American*. New York: Century, 1920.

See especially pp. 287–89.

R54 Rhea, Robert Lee. "Some Observation on Poe's Origins." *UTSE*, No. 10 (1930), pp. 135–46.

Discusses the sources of *Pym* and one possible source of "Some Words with a Mummy."

R55 Rhodes, Charles Elbert. "Edgar Allan Poe (1809–1849)." *Poe's* Raven, *Longfellow's* Courtship of Miles Standish, *Whittier's* Snowbound. Ed. Rhodes. New York: A. S. Barnes, 1913, pp. 10–21.

Primarily biography.

R56 Rhodes, S. A. "The Influence of Poe on Baudelaire." *RR*, XVIII (Oct.–Dec. 1927), 329–33.

Emphasizes affinity and denies influence.

R57 Rhys, Ernest. "Introduction." *The Fall of the House of Usher, and Other Tales and Other Prose Writings of Edgar Poe*. London: Walter Scott, 1889, pp. vii–xxv.

In both prose and poetry, Poe was faithful to his critical theory.

R58 Rice, Diana. "The Enchanted Garden of Poe." *NYTM*, March 16, 1924, p. 13.

Concerning the Poe Shrine in Richmond, Va.

R59 Rice, Sara Sigourney. *Edgar Allan Poe: A Memorial Volume*. Baltimore: Turnbull, 1877.

Contains essays, letters, and poetic tributes on Poe by several distinguished writers.

Reviewed:

Civil Service Rev, Feb. 17, 1877, 161–62.

S. E. Gabbett, *Sunny South* (Atlanta, Ga.), Jan. 20, 1877.

R60 Richards, Irving T. "Mary Gove Nichols and John Neal." *NEQ*, VII (June 1934), 335–55.

See pp. 338, 339 for Neal's opinion of Poe.

R61 ——. "A New Poe Poem: The Three Meetings." *MLN*, XLII (March 1927), 158–62.

A reprint of a poem published in John Neal's *Yankee and Boston Literary Gazette*, Feb. 26, 1828.

R62 Richards, Seth. "Foreword to New Edition." *Philosophy of Style*, by Herbert Spencer; *The Philosophy of Composition*, by Edgar Allan Poe. New York: Pageant Press, 1959, pp. 5–7.

Considers "The Philosophy of Composition" as "one of the greatest critical essays in the English language."

R63 Richardson, Charles F. *The Development of American Thought*. Vol. I of *American Literature, 1607–1885*. 2 vols. New York: G. P. Putnam's Sons, 1889.

See pp. 402–8 for discussion of Poe's critical writings.

R64 ——. "Edgar Allan Poe." *American Poetry and Fiction*. Vol. II of *American Literature, 1607–1885*. 2 vols. New York: G. P. Putnam's Sons, 1891, pp. 97–136.

Poe lacked humanity and his range of creation is narrow, but he had a fine mind.

R65 ——. "Edgar Allan Poe, World Author." *Critic*, XLI (Aug. 1902), 139–47.

Poe's rank and influence is shown to be great.

R66 ——. "Edgar Allan Poe, World Author." *The Complete Works of Edgar Allan Poe*. 10 vols. New York: G. P. Putnam's Sons, 1902, I, ix–liii.

"As the twentieth century proceeds, it becomes increasingly evident that Poe is the American world-author."

Reviewed:

W. M. Payne, *Nation*, LXXV (Dec. 4, 1902), 445–47.

Outlook, LXXII (Dec. 20, 1902), 947–48.

P. E. Moore, *Independent*, LIV (Oct. 16, 1902), 2453–60.

R67 Richardson, George F. "Poe's Doctrine of Effect." *UCPMP*, XI (1922), 179–86.

Poe formulated a law of unity of effect for a genre (the tale of effect) and then applied it universally.

R68 Richardson, Lyon N. "Edgar Allan Poe (1809–1849)." Ed. Richardson *et al. The Heritage of American Literature*. 2 vols. Boston: Ginn and Co., 1951, I, 480–82.

Poe "continues to share with Whitman a leading position of influence among European writers and critics."

R69   Ridgely, Joseph V., and Iola S. Haverstick. "Chartless Voyage: The Many Narratives of Arthur Gordon Pym." *TSLL,* VII (Spring 1966), 63–80.
Presents the evidence for Poe's composition of *Pym* in several distinct stages.

R70   Riding, Laura. "The Facts in the Case of Monsieur Poe." *Contemporaries and Snobs.* London: Jonathan Cape, 1928, pp. 201–55.
Poe's egotism as reflected in his life and work.

R71   Riedel, Ernest. "A Possible Classical Source of Poe's Poem, 'The Raven.' " *Classical Weekly,* XX (Feb. 14, 1927), 118.

R72   Riley, James Whitcomb. *Letters of James Whitcomb Riley.* Ed. William Lyon Phelps. Indianapolis: Bobbs, Merrill, 1930.
In several letters Riley discusses his part in a "Poe-poem fraud," *passim.*
Reviewed:
Louise Pound, *AL,* III, 350–51.

R73   Robbins, J. Albert. "An Addition to Poe's 'Steamboat Letter.' " *N&Q,* X (Jan. 1963), 20–21.
A revealing addition of a Poe letter to Mrs. Whitman.

R74   ——. "Edgar Poe and His Friends: A Sampler of Letters Written to Sarah Helen Whitman." *Indiana University Bookman,* No. 4 (March 1960), pp. 5–45.
Examines a portion of Mrs. Sarah H. Whitman's correspondence concerning Poe.

R75   ——. "11. Nineteenth-Century Poetry." *American Literary Scholarship: An Annual/1963.* Ed. James Woodress. Durham, N.C.: Duke University Press, 1965, pp. 118–31.
See pp. 118–23 for an essay on literary scholarship on Poe published during 1963.

R76   ——. "11. Nineteenth-Century Poetry." *American Literary Scholarship: An Annual/1964.* Ed. James Woodress. Durham, N.C.: Duke University Press, 1966, pp. 120–39.
See pp. 120–26 for an essay on literary scholarship on Poe published during 1964.

R77   ——. "11. Nineteenth-Century Poetry." *American Literary Scholarship: An Annual/1965.* Ed. James Woodress. Durham, N.C.: Duke University Press, 1967, pp. 142–61.
See pp. 142–49 for an essay on literary scholarship on Poe published during 1965.

R78   ——. "11. Nineteenth-Century Poetry." *American Literary Scholarship: An Annual/1966.* Ed. James Woodress. Durham, N.C.: Duke University Press, 1968, pp. 129–46.

See pp. 129–36 for an essay on literary scholarship on Poe published during 1966.

R79 ——. "11. Poe and Nineteenth-Century Poetry." *American Literary Scholarship: An Annual /1967.* Ed. James Woodress. Durham, N.C.: Duke University Press, 1969, pp. 149–65.

See pp. 149–59 for an essay on literary scholarship on Poe published during 1967.

R80 Roberts, John P. "Introduction." *Eight Tales of Terror.* New York: Scholastic Magazines, 1961, pp. iv–ix.

Primarily biographical.

R81 Roberts, W. "A Dumas Manuscript. Did Edgar Allan Poe Visit Paris?" *TLS,* Nov. 21, 1929, p. 978.

Reporting the discovery of a Dumas MS which describes a visit of Poe's to Paris.

R82 Robertson, John M. "Poe." *New Essays toward a Critical Method.* London: John Lane, 1897, pp. 55–130.

General assessment of Poe's life and work. See also pp. 354–78 for a discussion of Poe's metrical theories. Essay first appeared in magazine entitled *Our Corner* (1885) and was reprinted in William Tenney Brewster's edition of *Specimens of Modern Literary Criticism* (New York: Macmillan, 1907), pp. 126–80.

R83 Robertson, John W. *A Bibliography of the Writings of Edgar A. Poe.* 2 vols. San Francisco: Russian Hill Private Press, Edwin and Robert Grabhorn, 1934.

Volume II, entitled *Commentary on the Bibliography of Edgar A. Poe,* is primarily a psychoanalytical interpretation of Poe's life and work.

Reviewed:

D. Randall, *PW,* CXX (April 21, 1934), 1540–43.

R84 ——. *Edgar A. Poe: A Psychopathic Study.* New York: G. P. Putnam's Sons, 1923.

Analyzes Poe's works that aid "in explaining certain ill-understood phases of his life."

Reviewed:

T. O. Mabbott, *SP,* XX, 370–71.

J. Collins, *Literary Digest International Book Rev,* I, 12–13, 62–63.

John Macy, *Nation,* CXVI (Feb. 14, 1923), 190–94.

Katherine Anthony, *New Republic,* XXXV (June 6, 1923), 50.

Augusta Shuford, New York *Times,* Jan. 21, 1923, Book Reviews, p. 7.

TLS, June 14, 1923, p. 397.

Spectator, CXXXI (Aug. 4, 1923), 164.

R85   ——. *Edgar A. Poe: A Study.* San Francisco: Bruce Brough, 1921.

Part I dwells upon Poe's "morbid heredity"; Part II is a bibliographic study of Poe's works.

Reviewed:
George Douglas, *Bookman* (London), LV, 423–25.
Edmund Blunden, *London Mercury,* V, 320–22.

R86   Robins, Sally Nelson. "Oldest House in Richmond, Va., Now Called the Edgar Allan Poe Shrine." *House Beautiful,* LIV (Nov. 1923), 488.

R87   Robinson, E. Arthur. "Order and Sentience in 'The Fall of the House of Usher.' " *PMLA,* LXXVI (March 1961), 68–81.

Interprets the story in terms of structure, dwelling upon sentience and the overpowering forces of decay and disorder.

R88   ——. "Poe's 'The Tell-Tale Heart.' " *NCF,* XIX (March 1965), 369–78.

Poe's story "illustrates the elaboration of design which Poe customarily sought" and "contains two of the major psychological themes dramatized in his longer works."

R89   Robinson, Edwin Arlington. "For a Copy of Poe's Poems." *The Recognition of Edgar Allan Poe: Selected Criticism since 1829.* Ed. Eric Carlson. Ann Arbor: University of Michigan Press, 1966, p. 81.

Sonnet on Poe. First appeared in *Lippincott's* (Aug. 1906).

R90   Rogers, David M. *The Major Poems and Tales of Edgar Allan Poe.* New York: Monarch Press, 1955.

A study guide to selected writings of Poe.

R91   Rogers, Edward R. *Four Southern Magazines.* University of Virginia Studies in Southern Literature. Ed. Charles W. Kent. Richard: Williams Printing, 1902.

See chap. 4 on the *Southern Literary Messenger,* pp. 92–114.

R92   Roppolo, Joseph Patrick. "Meaning and 'The Masque of the Red Death.' " *TSE,* XIII (1963), 59–69.

Poe creates a mythic parable "of the human condition, of man's fate, and of the fate of the universe." Reprinted in Robert Regan, ed., *Poe: A Collection of Critical Essays* (Englewood Cliffs, N.J.: Prentice-Hall, 1967), pp. 134–44.

R93   Rose, Marilyn Gaddis. " 'Emmanuèle'—'Morella': Gide's Poe Affinities." *TSLL,* V (Spring 1963), 127–37.

Gide identified "himself and his cousin with Poe characters" and exteriorized "his experience in Poesque conventions."

R94   Rosenbach, A. W. S. "Trail of Scarlet." *Saturday Evening Post,* CCV (Oct. 1, 1932), 8–9, 32, 34, 36.
Poe and the realm of detective fiction.

R95   Rosenbach, Hyman P. "Reminiscences of Edgar A. Poe." *American,* XIII (Feb. 26, 1887), 296.

R96   Rosenfeld, Alvin. "Description in Poe's 'Landor's Cottage.' " *SSF,* IV (Spring 1967), 264–66.

R97   ———. "Wilkins Updike to Sarah Helen Whitman: Two New Letters." *Rhode Island History,* XXV (Oct. 1966), 97–109.
Letters throw light upon the Poe-Whitman romance.

R98   Rosenthal, Lewis. "Poe in Paris." *Manhattan Illustrated Monthly Mag,* IV (Aug. 1884), 174–79.
Poe's popularity in France is due to Baudelaire's excellent translations.

R99   Rosselet, Jeanne. "Poe in France." *Poe in Foreign Lands and Tongues.* A Symposium of the Edgar Allan Poe Society of Baltimore, January 19, 1941. Ed. John C. French. Baltimore: Johns Hopkins, 1941, pp. 5–10.
Emphasizes Poe's significance for Baudelaire, Mallarmé, and Valéry.

R100   Rossetti, Christina. *Family Letters.* . . . New York: Scribner, 1908.
Alludes to *Pym,* p. 7.

R101   Rossetti, William M. *Rossetti Papers.* Comp. William M. Rossetti. New York: Charles Scribner's Sons, 1903.
In his diary, William Rossetti mentions that Swinburne cited Poe as example of an American poet with distinctive originating powers; see p. 303.

R102   Rothwell, Kenneth S. "A Source for the Motto to Poe's 'William Wilson.' " *MLN,* LXXIV (April 1959), 297–98.
Poe's motto came from his reading of William Chamberlayne's *Pharonnida* and a play entitled *Love's Victory.*

R103   Rourke, Constance. *American Humor: A Study of the National Character.* Garden City, N.Y.: Doubleday, 1953.
Poe's humor is characterized (*passim*) in this reprint of the 1931 edition. Excerpt appears in Eric Carlson, ed., *The Recognition of Edgar Allan Poe* (Ann Arbor: University of Michigan Press, 1966), pp. 167–72.

R104   Routh, James. "Notes on the Sources of Poe's Poetry: Coleridge, Keats, Shelley." *MLN,* XXIX (March 1914), 72–75.
Discusses Poe's debt to particular poems.

R105   Rubin, Joseph Jay. "John Neal's Poetics as an Influence on Whitman and Poe." *NEQ*, XIV (June 1941), 359–62.
Neal's essay "What Is Poetry?" may have had some influence upon Poe.

R106   Rubin, Louis D., Jr. "Edgar Allan Poe: A Study in Heroism." *The Curious Death of the Novel: Essays in American Literature.* Baton Rouge: Louisiana State University Press, 1967, pp. 47–66.
Considers Poe "a hero, both in his career, in what he stands for in American literary history, and in the courage of his vision."

R107   Runden, John P. "Rossetti and a Poe Image." *N&Q*, CCIII (June 1958), 257–58.
The parallels between Rossetti's "The Portrait" and Poe's 1831 "To Helen" suggest Poe's influence upon Rossetti.

R108   Russell, F. A. [pseud.]. "Edgar Allan Poe." *American Pilgrimage.* New York: Dodd, Mead, 1942, pp. 216–33.
A sentimental sketch of Poe's life.

R109   Rutherford, Mildred L. "Edgar Allan Poe." *American Authors.* Atlanta: Franklin Printing and Publishing, 1894, pp. 264–73.
Poe brought a revolution in American criticism, but his fame will rest on poetry. Reprinted in *The South in History and Literature* (Atlanta: Franklin-Turner, 1907), pp. 133–44.

R110   Ryan, Sylvester. "A Poe Oversight." *CE*, XI (April 1950), 408.
Poe failed to record the presence of blood in the room in his story "The Murders in the Rue Morgue."

S

S1   "S." [Perry, W. S.]. "An Analytical Exposition of Poe's 'Raven.'" *UVaMag*, XIV (May 1876), 391–400.
Poe's tendency to analytical refinement is evident in design, structure, and effect of "The Raven."

S1a   S., G. B. [Shaw, George Bernard]. "Edgar Allan Poe." *Nation* (London), IV (Jan. 16, 1909), 601–2.
Praises Poe's versatility and finds him to be "the most classical of modern writers." Reprinted in Eric Carlson, ed., *The Recognition of Edgar Allan Poe* (Ann Arbor: University of Michigan Press, 1966), pp. 95–100.

S2 S., M. E. "Introduction." *The Great Tales and Poems of Edgar Allan Poe.* New York: Pocket Books, 1940, pp. vii–xii.
Poe is the greatest representative of the romantic movement in America.

S3 St. Quentin. "Three Friends of Mine: De Quincey, Coleridge, and Poe." *Canadian Monthly,* XIII (April 1878), 359–65.
Despite weaknesses for drugs or alcohol, Poe, like De Quincey and Coleridge, produced melodic poems of dreamlike imagery.

S4 Saintsbury, George. "Edgar Allan Poe." *Dial,* LXXXIII (Dec. 1927), 451–63.
A favorable essay on Poe's poetry which reviews, in passing, biographies of Poe by Krutch, Phillips, and Allen. A shortened version of this essay appears in Saintsbury's *Preface and Essays* (London: Macmillan, 1933), pp. 314–23, and in Eric Carlson, ed., *The Recognition of Edgar Allan Poe* (Ann Arbor: University of Michigan Press, 1966), pp. 152–59.

S5 ——. *History of Criticism and Literary Taste in Europe.* 3 vols. Edinburgh: William Blackwood, 1900–1904, III, 634–36.
Brief appraisal of Poe's critical abilities.

S6 ——. *A History of English Prosody.* 3 vols. New York: Macmillan, 1906–10, III, 483–87.
As a prosodist, Poe ranks very high.

S7 Sale, Marian M. "Poe." *Commonwealth* (Mag. of Va.), XXXIII (April 1966), 28–37.
Poe's life in Richmond and photographs of landmarks he knew.

S8 Salinas, Pedro. "Poe in Spain and Spanish America." *Poe in Foreign Lands and Tongues.* A Symposium of the Edgar Allan Poe Society of Baltimore, January 19, 1941. Ed. John C. French. Baltimore: Johns Hopkins, 1941, pp. 25–31.
Spain prefers Poe's fiction; Spanish America his poetry.

*S9 Salzberg, Joel. *The Grotesque as Moral Aesthetic: A Study of the Tales of Edgar Allan Poe.* Ann Arbor, Mich.: University Microfilms, 1967.

S10 ——. "The Grotesque as Moral Aesthetic: A Study of the Tales of Edgar Allan Poe." *DA,* XXVIII (Jan. 1968), 2695A.
"Poe, in the evocation of the grotesque, creates what might be called a moral aesthetic: that is, the use of horror and humor for the purpose of evaluating man and society."

*S11 ——. "The Grotesque as Moral Aesthetic: A Study of the Tales of Edgar Allan Poe." Diss., University of Oklahoma, 1967.

S12   Sampson, George. "The Misfortunes of Poe." *Bookman* (London), LXIX (Jan. 1926), 199–200.
A review of M. N. Stanard's *The Dreamer* and the Valentine letters.

S13   Samuel, Dorothy J. "Poe and Baudelaire: Parallels in Form and Symbol." *CLAJ*, III (Dec. 1959), 88–105.
Baudelaire and Poe shared the same poetic principles, but were more alike in the use of symbols than in the adoption of form.

S14   Samuels, Charles Thomas. "Usher's Fall; Poe's Rise." *GaR*, XVIII (Summer 1964), 208–16.
Poe's "amoral identification with the quest for the ideal" touches upon a dominant American theme.

S15   San Juan, E., Jr. "The Form of Experience in the Poems of Edgar Allan Poe." *GaR,* XXI (Spring 1967), 65–80.
Poe's poems "preserve an intrinsic vitality in the poise, the synthesis and dialectic, between being and death."

S16   Sanderlin, W. Stephen, Jr. "Poe's 'Eldorado' Again." *MLN,* LXXI (March 1956), 189–92.
"Poe's poem, rather than being the simple and optimistic expression of a searcher for the ideal, is marked by ambiguity and pessimism." *AL.*

S17   Sandler, S. Gerald. "Poe's Indebtedness to Locke's *An Essay concerning Human Understanding.*" *BUSE*, V (Summer 1961), 107–21.
Poe incorporated Lockean ideas in many of his tales.

S18   Sanford, Charles L. "Edgar Allan Poe." *The Recognition of Edgar Poe: Selected Criticism since 1829.* Ed. Eric W. Carlson. Ann Arbor: University of Michigan Press, 1966, pp. 297–307.
Poe in the light of American Adamic individualism. First appeared in *Rives,* No. 18 (Spring 1962), pp. 1–19.

S19   "Sans Souci." "Edgar Allan Poe." *UVaMag,* XLIV (Feb. 1885), 241–51.
"An address delivered to the Jefferson Society [University of Virginia], Jan. 24, 1885."

S20   Sansom, William, ed. *The Tell-Tale Heart, and Other Stories.* With introd. Toronto: Longmans, Green, 1948.
Poe's analyses of mental processes were in many instances advanced for his time. See "Introduction," pp. v–xvii.

S21   [Sartain, John?] "Edgar A. Poe." [Editorial.] *Sartain's Mag,* V (Dec. 1849), 386–87.
A brief description of the gradual development of Poe's "The Bells."

S22   ———. "Poe's Last Poem." *Sartain's Mag,* VI (Jan. 1850), 99–100.

Sartain's Magazine purchases "Annabel Lee" and presents its authorized version.

S23 ———. "Reminiscences of Edgar Allan Poe." *Lippincott's,* XLIII (March 1889), 411–15.
An intimate glimpse of the character of the poet, editor, and friend. Reprinted in enlarged form in *The Reminiscences of a Very Old Man* (New York: D. Appleton, 1899), pp. 196–217.

S24 Sartain, William. "Edgar Allan Poe—Some Facts Recalled." *Art World,* II (July 1917), 321–23.

S25 [Savage, John.] "Edgar Allan Poe." *Democratic Rev,* XXVII (Dec. 1850), 542–44; XXVIII (Jan., Feb. 1851), 66–69, 162–72.
Primarily reviews Griswold's edition with a halfhearted defense of Poe.

S26 Scharf, John T. *The Chronicles of Baltimore.* Baltimore: Turnbull Brothers, 1874.
Discusses Poe family, *passim.*

S27 Schaumann, Herbert. "Poe in Germany." *Poe in Foreign Lands and Tongues.* A Symposium of the Edgar Allan Poe Society of Baltimore, January 19, 1941. Ed. John C. French. Baltimore: Johns Hopkins, 1941, pp. 22–24.
Poe is an "integral part" of German education and civilization.

S28 Scheffauer, Herman. "Baiting of Poe." *Overland,* NS LIII (June 1909), 491–94.
Attacks those critics, especially Bliss Carmen, who assume a patronizing attitude toward Poe.

S29 Schell, Stanley. "Authors of the Nineteenth Century. No. 5—Edgar Allan Poe." *Werner's Mag* (N.Y.), XXV (March 1900), 151–66.
An article, designed to be used as an outline for a "study club," is a collection of criticism on Poe.

S30 Scherman, David E., and Rosemarie Redlick. *Literary America: A Chronicle of American Writers from 1607–1952 with 173 Photographs of the American Scene That Inspired Them.* New York: Dodd, Mead, 1952.
See p. 44 for brief commentary on American appreciation of Poe.

S31 Schick, Joseph S. "The Origin of 'The Cask of Amontillado.' " *AL,* VI (March 1934), 18–21.
The source lies in J. T. Headley's *Letters from Italy* (1845) and in Bulwer's *The Last Days of Pompeii.*

S32 ———. "Poe and Jefferson." *VMHB,* LIV (Oct. 1946), 316–20.
"Suggests that Poe was a student of Jefferson's literary methods before December, 1835." *AL.*

S33   Schlichter, Norman C. "The Rhythm of Poe." *Poetry Rev,*
XXXVIII (July 1937), 269–73.
An appreciative and informal essay.

S34   Schmitt, G. L. "The Raven's First Flight: A One-Act Play for
Radio Broadcasting." *Scholastic,* XXVI (Feb. 2, 1935), 7–8.

S35   Schneider, Joseph. "French Appreciation of Edgar Allan Poe."
Catholic Educational Rev (Washington, D.C.), XXV (Sept. 1927),
427–37.
French criticism of Poe has been both favorable and unfavorable.

S36   Schoettle, Elmer. "A Musician's Commentary on Poe's 'The
Philosophy of Composition.' " *Forum* (Houston), Spring and Summer
1964, 14–15.
Argues that musicians "practice the kind of analytical reasoning
which Poe enunciated as his doctrine."

S37   Schorer, Mark. "Introduction." *Criticism.* Ed. Schorer *et al.* New
York: Harcourt, Brace, 1948, pp. vi–xi.
Poe is mentioned in this essay dealing with the foundations of mod-
ern criticism.

S38   Schreiber, Carl. "A Close-Up of Poe." *SatRL,* III (Oct. 9,
1926), 165–67.
Poe's relations with Thomas Dunn English are discussed.

S39   ——. "The Donkey and the Elephant." *YULG,* XIX (July
1944), 17–19.
"On some slanderous remarks by Thomas Dunn English about
Poe." *PMLA.*

S40   ——. "Mr. Poe at His Conjurations Again." *Colophon,* part 2
(May 1930), 1–11.
Argues that Poe knew very little German.

S41   Schroeter, James. "A Misreading of Poe's 'Ligeia.' " *PMLA,*
LXXVI (Sept. 1961), 397–406.
An analysis of Roy Basler's interpretation.

S42   ——. "Poe's 'Ligeia.' " *PMLA,* LXXVII (Dec. 1962), 675.

S43   Schubert, Leland. "James William Carling: Expressionist Il-
lustrator of 'The Raven.' " *SLM,* IV (April 1942), 173–81.
Contains a discussion of the famous illustrators of Poe's "Raven"
along with an appraisal of Carling's work.

S44   Schulte, Amanda Pogue. *Facts about Poe: Portraits and
Daguerrotypes of Edgar Allan Poe.* Charlottesville: University of Virginia, 1926.
Excellent discussion of Poe portraits and accurate biography of Poe's
life along with a selected bibliography of Poe's writings.

Reviewed:
A. C. Gordon, Jr., *Literary Digest International Book Rev,* IV, 480.

S45   Schuman, A. T. "Poe." *Dial,* XXI (Oct. 1896), 179.
Verse.

S46   Schwartz, Jacob, "Justification." *The Purloined Letter,* by Edgar
Allan Poe. London: Ulysses Bookshop, 1931, n.p.
The 1844 Edinburgh version of the story is reprinted here for the
first time.

S47   ――. [Essay on Poe and *Tamerlane.*] *Tamerlane and Other
Poems by a Bostonian.* London: Ulysses Bookshop, [1931].
Facsimile is accompanied by a six-page pamphlet of notes on Poe
and *Tamerlane* signed "J. Schwartz."

S48   Schwartz, William Leonard. "The Influence of E. A. Poe on
Judith Gautier," *MLN,* XLII (March 1927), 171–73.

S49   Schwartzstein, Leonard. "Poe's Criticism of William W. Lord."
N&Q, CC (July 1955), 312.
"In one instance, at least, Poe charged plagiarism as a pretext for
displaying his pretended learning." *AL.*

S50   Scollard, Clinton. "Ballad of Baltimore." *Literary Digest,* CXV
(March 11, 1933), 32.
The poet expresses admiration for Poe. Reprinted from the opening
pages of the Jan.–Feb. *Versecraft* (1933), Emory University, Ga.

S51   ――. "Ballade to Edgar Poe." *SR,* XXXIX (Oct. 1931), 484.

S52   Scott, Mary Wingfield. "Old Richmond Houses." *Richmond
News-Leader,* Jan. 23, 1941, p. 20.

S53   Scott, Rev. W. J. "Edgar Allan Poe." *Lectures and Essays.*
Atlanta: Constitution Publishing, 1889, pp. 31–71.
An appreciative essay commending Poe's stature as critic, poet, and
short-story writer.

S54   Scudder, Harold H. "Poe's 'Balloon Hoax.'" *AL,* XXI (May
1949), 179–90.
Relates how closely Poe followed the feats of aeronautical accomplishments just previous to the composition of "The Balloon Hoax."

S55   Scudder, Horace E. *James Russell Lowell, A Biography.* 2 vols.
Boston: Houghton, Mifflin, 1901.
See I, 162, for a statement of Poe's popularity in 1845.

S56   Sears, Lorenzo. "Edgar Allan Poe." *American Literature in the
Colonial and National Periods.* Boston: Little, Brown, 1902, pp. 251–
64.
Attempts to analyze Poe's writings with emphasis upon the distinct
character of his art.

S57   Seccombe, Thomas. "Reflections on the Poe Centenary." *Cornhill Mag,* XCIX (March 1909), 337–50.
Posits four reasons why Poe has gained a world-wide reputation.

S58   Seelye, John. "Introduction." *Arthur Gordon Pym, Benito Cereno, and Related Writings.* New York: J. B. Lippincott, 1967, pp. 1–13.
Examines Poe's narrative technique of "intensity of effect achieved by an economy of means."

S59   Seitz, Don C. "Foreword." *A Chapter on Autography,* by Edgar Allan Poe. Ed. Seitz. New York: Lincoln MacVeach at the Dial Press, 1926, pp. 5–7.
Poe and his interest in the subject of autography.

S60   Seronsy, Cecil C. "Poe and 'Kubla Khan.'" *N&Q,* CCII (May 1957), 219–20.
"The Fall of the House of Usher" and "Eleonora" suggest Poe's familiarity with Coleridge's "Kubla Khan."

S61   Shands, H. A. "To Poe." *Bob Taylor's Mag,* IX (March 1906), 644.
Verse.

S62   Shanks, Edward. *Edgar Allan Poe.* New York: Macmillan, 1937.
Dwells primarily upon the merits of Poe's work and his significance as a writer.
    Reviewed:
TLS, Feb. 20, 1937, p. 126.
A. C. Boyd, *London Mercury,* XXXV, 527.
G. W. Stonier, *New Statesman and Nation,* XIII (Feb. 13, 1937), 250.
D. K. Jackson, *SAQ,* XXV, 486–87.
J. G. Fletcher, *Poetry,* L, 353–56.
D. K. Jackson, *AL,* IX, 393–94.
S. Bradley, *SatRL,* XVI (Sept. 4, 1937), 15.
Francis Winwar, *NYTBR,* June 13, 1937, p. 2.
School and Society, XV (May 1, 1937), 623–24.
Cweal, XXVI (July 30, 1937), 350.

S63   Shaver, J. "Did Poe Write 'The Raven'?" New York *Tribune,* July 29, 1870, p. 6.
A reprint of a letter to the New Orleans *Times,* dated July 22, 1870, which claims that Poe, while intoxicated, signed the poem of another man.

S64   Sheldon, Caroline. "Some Causes of 'The American Rejection of Poe.' " *Dial,* XXVI (Feb. 16, 1899), 110.
Poe does not "voice in some effective manner the feelings and thoughts common to humanity."

S65   Shepherd, Henry E. "Address of Prof. Henry E. Shepherd." *Poems and Essays of Edgar Allan Poe.* New York: W. J. Widdleton, 1876, pp. cxli–cxlvii.
Commentary on Poe "as poet and man" delivered during ceremonies dedicating a monument to Poe at Baltimore.

S66   ———. "Southern Poets—Edgar Allan Poe: A Special Study." *Confederate Veteran,* XXVI (Aug. 1918), 355–57.
Links Poe and Robert E. Lee, who was in Baltimore in 1849.

S67   ———. "A Study of Edgar A. Poe." *Old Maryland* (Baltimore), II (Oct., Nov., and Dec. 1906), 131–35, 145–50, and 161–66.
Poe's poetry is original, innovative, and "a perpetual protest against the dominant materialism of our modern, and above all, our American life."

S68   Shepherd, Lilian McGregory. "A New Portrait of Edgar Allan Poe." *Century Mag,* NS LXIX (April 1916), 906–7.

S69   ———. "Some Rare Poe Pictures." Baltimore *American,* Oct. 22, 1916, Mag. sec., p. 1.
Reprinted here are some portraits including the *Century* portrait then under discussion.

S70   Shepherd, Richard Herne. "Preface." *Tamerlane and Other Poems,* by Edgar Allan Poe. Ed. Shepherd. London: George Redway, 1884, pp. 7–14.
Poe's first volume may claim to rank as a remarkable production.

S71   Sherley, Douglass. *The Valley of Unrest, a Book without a Woman; Edgar Allan Poe, an Old Oddity Paper,* Louisville, Ky.: Morton, 1883.
Adds nothing to the substantial knowledge of Poe's life.

S72   ———. *The Valley of Unrest, a Book without a Woman.* New York: White, Stokes, and Allen, 1884.
"Fictionary" glimpses of Poe's "inner life, while a student at the Virginia University."

S73   Shippen, E. "Some American Magazine Writers of Fifty Years Ago." *Godey's Lady's Book,* CXVI (April 1888), 329–31.
Discusses *The Gift* and its editors and contributors, including Poe.

S74   Shockley, Martin Staples. " 'Timour the Tartar' and Poe's 'Tamerlane.' " *PMLA,* LVII (Dec. 1941), 1103–6.

M. G. Lewis's play, acted in Richmond in 1822, may be a source of Poe's "Tamerlane."

S75   Shuman, R. Baird. "Longfellow, Poe, and *The Waif.*" *PMLA,* LXXVI (March 1961), 155–56.

In a letter to Lowell, Longfellow comments on the *Waif* controversy.

S76   "Sieve." "Edgar A. Poe's Addenda to His 'Eureka,' with Comments." *Methodist Rev,* 5th ser., XII (Jan. 1896), 9–18.

"These extracts relate to, and constitute a part of, a letter written on February 29, 1848, by Edgar A. Poe to a correspondent still living in one of the States of our Union."

S77   Silver, Rollo G. "A Note about Whitman's Essay on Poe." *AL,* VI (Jan. 1935), 435–36.

A reprinting from a Washington, D.C., newspaper of Whitman's remarks made in 1875 at the unveiling of the monument of Poe in Baltimore shows variation from the version included in *Specimen Days.*

S78   Simmons, Joseph P. "Introduction." *Poems and Tales,* by Edgar Allan Poe. Lincoln, Nebr.: University Publishing, 1924, pp. vii–xx.

Sketchy biography and criticism of Poe.

S79   Simonds, Arthur B. "Edgar Allan Poe." *American Song: A Collection of Representative American Poems.* New York: G. P. Putnam's Sons, 1894, pp. 47–55.

Recognizes Poe's accomplishments in poetry, fiction, and criticism.

S80   Simonds, William E. *A Student's History of American Literature.* Boston: Houghton Mifflin, 1909.

Poe was an eccentric genius who achieved some merit in fiction, poetry, and criticism; see pp. 200–216.

S81   Simpson, Lewis P. "Poe and the Literary Vocation in America." *ESQ,* No. 31 (2nd quarter 1963), pp. 11–14.

Poe's career is a moment in the crisis of the literary order, and he may be viewed as a forefather of "the men of solitude" in modern letters.

S82   ———. " 'Touchin 'The Stylus' ' ": Notes on Poe's Vision of Literary Order." *Studies in American Literature,* Louisiana State University Studies, No. 8 (1960), pp. 33–48.

The *Stylus* "was Poe's chief attempt to realize a vision of establishing literary order in the United States," but American culture was perhaps indifferent to the type of magazine Poe conceived.

*S83   Skaggs, Calvin L. *Narrative Point of View in Edgar Allan Poe's Criticism and Fiction.* Ann Arbor, Mich.: University Microfilms, 1966.

S84 ———. "Narrative Point of View in Edgar Allan Poe's Criticism and Fiction." *DA,* XXVII (May 1967), 3880A–81A.

Poe used whatever point of view he chose with "precision and appropriateness."

*S85 ———. "Narrative Point of View in Edgar Allan Poe's Criticism and Fiction." Diss., Duke University, 1966.

S86 Skilton, Charles S. "Musical Possibilities of Poems of Poe." *Music,* No. 3 (Jan. 1895), pp. 236–39.

S87 Skipsey, Joseph. "Prefatory Notice." *The Poetical Works of Edgar Allan Poe.* Ed. Skipsey. London: Walter Scott Publishing, 1903, pp. 9–41.

Like Tennyson and Shelley, Poe's genius was essentially lyrical and of fine quality.

S88 Slater, Montagu, ed. *The Centenary Poe; Tales, Poems, Criticism, Marginalia, and* Eureka. With introd. London: Bodley Head, 1949.

Poe's theory of Unity of Effect has resulted in the concept of Art for Art's sake—a concept that dominates the literature of Western Europe and the U.S.A. See "Introduction," pp. 11–42.

Reviewed:

David Hughes, *Fortnightly Rev,* No. 166 (Nov. 1949), pp. 342–43.

Robert Hamilton, *QR,* CCLXXXVIII, 514–25.

S89 Slicer, Thomas Roberts. *From Poet to Premier, the Centennial Cycle, 1809–1909: Poe, Lincoln, Holmes, Darwin, Tennyson, Gladstone. . . .* London: Grolier Society, 1909.

The criticism is restrained, and the author is often in error as to the facts of Poe's life. See pp. 1–40 for "Edgar Allan Poe, the Pioneer of Romantic Literature in America."

S90 Smart, Charles A. "On the Road to Page One." *YR,* XXXVII (Dec. 1947), 242–56.

Touches briefly upon Poe's theory of the short story.

S91 Smiles, Samuel. "Edgar Allan Poe." *Brief Biographies.* Boston: Ticknor and Fields, 1861, pp. 334–45.

Poe's "biography unfolds a tale of mingled admiration and horror."

S92 Smith, Alexander. "Poe and Poetry." *Dublin University Mag,* XLII (July 1853), 89–96.

A review of Hannay's edition of the poems.

S93 Smith, Bernard. "Quest of Beauty." *Forces in American Criticism: A Study in the History of American Literary Thought.* New York: Harcourt, 1939.

A discussion of Poe and Henry James in their critical quest for beauty; see pp. 185–228.

S94   Smith, Charles Alphonso. *The American Short Story.* Boston: Ginn, 1912.

Considers the famous paragraph in the Poe review of Hawthorne's tales "the most important piece of critical writing in American literature," and has only high praise for Poe's tales; see *passim.*

S95   ———. "The Americanism of Poe." *UVaAB,* 3rd ser., II (April 1909), 151–61.

Dwells upon the "constructive side of Poe's genius because it is this quality that makes him most truly American." Reprinted in Charles W. Kent and John S. Patton, eds., *The Book of the Poe Centenary* (Charlottesville, Va.: Michie, 1909), pp. 159–79.

S96   ———. "Edgar Allan Poe." *Mentor,* X (Sept. 1922), 3–8.

Discusses Poe's contribution to criticism and his role in the development of American literature.

S97   ———. "Edgar Allan Poe." *Southern Literary Studies.* Chapel Hill: University of North Carolina Press, 1927, pp. 120–27.

Poe "enriched the concept and idea of Americanism by a constructive genius still unparalleled in our literature."

S98   ———. *Edgar Allan Poe—How to Know Him.* Indianapolis: Bobbs-Merrill, 1921.

An attempt "to substitute for the travesty the real Poe, to suggest at least the diversity of his interests, his future-mindedness, his sanity, and his humanity."

Reviewed:

C. Cestre, *Rev Germanique,* No. 4 (1921), p. 439.
G. H. Clarke, *SR,* XXIX, 378–79.
Forum, LXV, 468–71.
Harold Goddard, *Nation,* CXIII (July 20, 1921), 74–75.
Killis Campbell, *Weekly Rev,* IV (March 30, 1921), 298.
J. H. Whitty, Richmond *News-Leader,* April 8, 1921, p. 6.
Brander Matthews, New York *Times,* March 13, 1921, Book Reviews, p. 3.
Bookman, LIII, 262.
E. F. Edgett, Boston *Transcript,* Feb. 19, 1921, p. 6.
Joseph Mosher, *PW,* XCIX (March 19, 1921), 964.
"W. R.," Baltimore *Evening Sun,* March 26, 1921, p. 6.

S99   ———. "Memorial Will Honor the Mother of Edgar Allan Poe." Philadelphia *Public-Ledger,* May 25, 1913, Mag. sec., p. [6].

S100   ———. "Poe and the Bible." *Biblical Rev,* V (July 1920), 354–65.

Poe's work, especially *Eureka,* reflects his belief in the Bible.

S101   ———. "Poe as a Constructive Force in World Literature." *UVaMag,* LXXII (Dec. 1911), 116–21.

Poe was "a discoverer in the realm of meter and rhythm . . . a pioneer in the short story . . . the exponent of the self-conscious in literature . . . the revealer of a distinctive Americanism." Also appeared in *Old Maryland,* VII (Nov. 1911), 145–47, and in *Kit-Kat,* V (April 1916), 13–19.

S102   ———. "Poe's Constructive Force in World Literature." Columbia, S.C., *State,* June 6, 1913, p. 12.

A newspaper report of Smith's lecture on "Poe as a Constructive Force in World Literature."

S103   ———. *Repetition and Parallelism in English Verse.* New York: University Publishing, 1894.

Poe continued the ballad revival begun with *The Ancient Mariner* and used repetition as a controlling element of his poetic style and versification; see pp. 44–56.

S104   [Smith, Mrs. E. V.?] "Edgar Allan Poe." *North American Rev,* LXXXIV (Oct. 1856), 427–55.

In commenting upon the Redfield edition of Poe (1856), this reviewer finds that Poe's accomplishments are slight.

S105   Smith, G. Barnett. "Poe: His Life and Work." *Tinsley's Mag,* XXVIII (Jan. 1881), pp. 15–32.

Poe possessed a unique genius but lacked a "commanding moral energy."

S106   Smith, Grace P. "Poe's Metzengerstein." *MLN,* XLVIII (June 1933), 356–59.

Calls attention to a possible debt to Hoffman's *Die Elixiere des Teufels.*

S107   Smith, Herbert F. "Usher's Madness and Poe's Organicism: A Source." *AL,* XXXIX (Nov. 1967), 379–89.

The source for Usher's belief that plants have the "capacity to organize themselves in the non-organic materials around them" is Richard Watson's *Chemical Essays,* V.

S108   Smith, Horatio E. "Poe's Extension of His Theory of the Tale." *MP,* XVI (Aug. 1918), 195–203.

In his reviews, Poe applied his theory of plot—totality of effect—to novels as well as to tales.

S109   Smith, John H., and Edd W. Parks. "Edgar Allan Poe." *The Great Critics*. Eds. Smith and Parks. New York: Norton, 1951, pp. 584–86.
  Contains selected passages from Poe's "The Poetic Principle," pp. 586–91.

S110   Smith, Julia Moore. "A New Light on Poe." *SLM,* I (Sept. 1939), 575–81.
  On the relationship between Mrs. Estelle Anna Lewis ("Stella") and Poe.

S111   "Smith, Mr." "Poe and Kipling." *Literary Digest International Book Rev,* IV (Sept. 1926), 623.
  A notice of a sale where literary remains of the two men brought high prices.

S112   Smith, Reed. "History of the Detective Story, Its Development and Present Status—Voltaire, Poe, and Its Other Makers." *North Carolina Rev,* Literature and History sec., Raleigh *News and Observer,* Oct. 6, 1912, pp. 3 and 10.

S113   Smithline, Arnold. *"Eureka:* Poe as Transcendentalist." *ESQ,* No. 39 (2nd quarter 1965), pp. 25–28.
  Some of Poe's ideas in *Eureka* "are very close indeed to Transcendentalism."

S114   Smyth, Albert Henry. *The Philadelphia Magazines and Their Contributors, 1741–1850.* Philadelphia: R. M. Lindsay, 1892.
  For *Graham's Magazine* and Poe's connection with it, see pp. 215–23 *et passim.*

S115   Smyth, Ellison, A., Jr. "Poe's 'Gold Bug' from the Standpoint of an Entomologist." *SR,* XVIII (Jan. 1910), 67–72.
  Poe gives an accurate picture of Sullivan's Island, and his beetle is a composite blend of several species of beetles.

S116   Snell, George D. "First of the New Critics." *QRL,* II (Summer 1945), 333–40.
  Poe is the most versatile genius in American literature and the first "textual critic."

S117   ———. "Poe." *The Shapers of American Fiction, 1798–1948.* New York: E. P. Dutton, 1947, pp. 45–60.
  Poe was a master of psychological allegory.

S118   ———. "Poe Redivivus." *ArQ,* I (Summer 1945), 49–57.
  Ambrose Bierce and Lafcadio Hearn wrote fiction in the Poe tradition.

*S119   Snider, Harry Clark. *An Edition of the Poems in Poe's Last Collection Based Largely on His Own Critical Principles.* Ann Arbor, Mich.: University Microfilms, 1963.

S120   ———. "An Edition of the Poems in Poe's Last Collection Based Largely on His Own Critical Principles." *DA,* XXIV (Feb. 1964), 3344.
Poe's critical writing furnishes a "practical, workable body of editorial principles for the editing of his poetry."

*S121   ———. "An Edition of the Poems in Edgar Allan Poe's Last Collection Based Largely on His Own Critical Principles." Diss., University of Michigan, 1963.

S122   Snodgrass, J. E. "American Biography: Edgar Allan Poe." Baltimore *Saturday Visiter,* July 29, 1843, p. 1.
Emphasizes Poe's accomplishments as reviewer and critic.

S123   ———. "The Facts of Poe's Death and Burial." *Beadle's Monthly,* III (March 1867), 283–87.
Takes issue with Mrs. Oakes-Smith's comments on Poe's death appearing in an earlier issue of *Beadle's Monthly.*

S124   ———. [Notice of the *Broadway Journal.*] Baltimore *Saturday Visiter,* April 26, 1845, p. 2.

S125   ———. "Poe as a Critic." Baltimore *Saturday Visiter,* April 2, 1842, p. 2.

S126   Snow, Edward Rowe. *Mysteries and Adventures along the Atlantic Coast.* New York: Dodd, Mead, 1950.
Discusses the murder of Mary Rogers, pp. 264–65.

*S127   ———. "The Roving Skeleton of Boston Bay." *Yankee* (Dublin, N.H.), XXV (April 1961), 52–55, 109–10.
"On a possible source for 'The Cask of Amontillado.' "

S128   Snow, Sinclair. "The Similarity of Poe's 'Eleonora' to Bernardin de Saint-Pierre's *Paul et Virginie.*" *Romance Notes,* V (Autumn 1963), 40–44.
A portion of Poe's story may be "considered a brief digest" of St. Pierre's novel.

S129   Snyder, Edward D. "Bowra on Poe: Corrections." *MLN,* XLVII (June 1952), 422–23.
Corrects Bowra's commentary on Poe's "To Helen."

S130   ———. "Poe and Amy Lowell." *MLN,* XLIII (March 1928), 152–53.
Both poets agree on the use of rhyme at unexpected intervals within the context of a poem.

S131   ——. "Poe's Nicean Barks." *CJ,* XLVIII (Feb. 1953), 159–69.
Critical commentary upon the numerous interpretations of the imagery in Poe's "To Helen."

S132   Sohn, David. "Introduction." *Great Tales of Horror.* New York: Bantam Books, 1964, pp. 1–12.
Poe's life was "harrowing and tragic," and his writing strikes a note of "recognition of something dark and foreboding in our own selves."

S133   Solomont, Susan, and Ritchie Darling. *Four Stories by Poe.* Norwich, Vt.: Green Knight Press, 1964.
Poe's literary craftsmanship reflected in "The Pit and the Pendulum," "The Masque of the Red Death," "The Cask of Amontillado," and "The Tell-Tale Heart."
Reviewed:
Moore and Willett, *YWES,* XLVI, 347–48.

S134   Somerville, J. A. "The 'Ifs' in Poe's Life." *SLM,* I (Dec. 1939), 860.
Speculates on what Poe would have accomplished if his life had been "easier."

S135   Spannuth, Jacob E. "Foreword." *Doings of Gotham,* by Edgar Allan Poe. First collected by Spannuth. Pottsville, Pa.: Jacob E. Spannuth, 1929, pp. xi–xiv.
Background on Poe's contributions to the *Columbia Spy.*
Reviewed:
L. N. Chase, *AL,* II, 200–201.

S136   Sparke, Archibald. "Edgar Allan Poe: Bibliography." *N&Q,* CLIX (Dec. 27, 1930), 465.
A list of a few works to be consulted for the bibliography of Poe.

S137   Spaulding, Kenneth A. "Poe's 'The Fall of the House of Usher.'" *Expl,* X (June 1952), item 52.
An attempt to explain why Roderick Usher does not exhume his sister Madeline.

S138   "Spectator, The." "Visit to Poe's Grave." *Outlook,* LXIII (April 13, 1907), 837–38.
Describes "quaint disorder" of Westminster Church and its churchyard.

S139   Spencer, Benjamin T. " 'Beautiful Blood and Beautiful Brain': Whitman and Poe." *ESQ,* No. 35, Part II (2nd quarter 1964), pp. 45–49.
Romanticism in Poe and Whitman.

S140 ——. "Doctor Williams' American Grain." *TSL*, VIII (1963), 1–16.

Comments on William Carlos Williams's opinion of Poe; *passim.*

S141 Sperling, Grace D. "The Minstrel Poe." *Muse Anthology of Modern Poetry.* Ed. Dorothy Kissling and Arthur H. Nethercot. Poe Memorial Edition. New York: Carlyle Straub, 1938, p. 182.

Verse.

S142 Spiller, Robert E. "The American Literary Dilemma and Edgar Allan Poe." *The Great Experiment in American Literature.* Ed. Carl Bode. New York: Praeger, 1961, pp. 3–25.

Poe was one of the first American writers to create an aesthetic tradition in a time when America was largely a transplanted culture.

S143 ——. "The Artist in America: Poe, Hawthorne." *The Cycle of American Literature.* New York: Macmillan, 1955, pp. 61–75.

Poe, very much a part of the American tradition, was one of our first introspective and conscious artists.

S144 ——, et al. *Bibliography.* Vol. III of *Literary History of the United States.* Ed. Thomas H. Johnson. 3 vols. New York: Macmillan, 1946–48.

Presents a well-selected and a standard introductory bibliography to the life and works of Poe; see pp. 686–96. (Printed as volume II in 1963.)

S145 ——, et al. *Bibliography Supplement.* Ed. Richard M. Ludwig. Supplement to *Literary History of the United States.* 3 vols. New York: Macmillan, 1946–59.

See pp. 178–80 and *Bibliography Supplement II* (1972), pp. 237–39.

S146 Spitzer, Leo. "A Reinterpretation of 'The Fall of the House of Usher.' " *CL*, IV (Fall 1952), 351–63.

Poe's story appears as a poetic expression of sociological deterministic ideals of the time and should be judged on the basis that Poe's descriptions create an effective atmosphere. Reprinted in *Essays on English and American Literature,* ed. Anna Hatcher (Princeton, N.J.: Princeton University Press, 1962), pp. 51–66.

S147 Spivey, Herman E. "Poe and Lewis Gaylord Clark." *PMLA*, LIV (Dec. 1939), 1124–32.

Gives "the facts in the background for the bitter enmity between Poe and Lewis Gaylord Clark," and offers proof of Poe's authorship of the anonymous article on "Our Magazine Literature" published in the *New World,* VI (March 11, 1843), 302–3.

S148 Sprague, Harriet. "Whitman and Poe." *AN&Q,* V (Aug. 1945), 75.

Whitman published an article entitled "Art-Singing and Heart-Singing" in Poe's *Broadway Journal.*

S149   Sprague, Jennie E., and [edited by] Elizabeth H. Bonford. "The Real Annabel Lee." *Kit-Kat,* V (Sept. 1916), 101–15.
On Virginia Poe.

S150   Sprout, Monique. "The Influence of Poe on Jules Verne." *RLC,* XLI (Jan.–March 1967), 37–53.
Traces Verne's acquaintance with Poe's works and presents evidences of Verne's debt to Poe.

S151   Stanard, Mary Newton. *The Dreamer: A Romantic Rendering of the Life-Story of Edgar Allan Poe.* Richmond: Bell Book and Stationery, 1909.
An "attempt to make something like a finished picture of the shadowy sketch the biographers, hampered by the limitations of proved fact, must, at best, give us."
    Reviewed:
VMHB, XXXIV, 96.
TLS, Dec. 3, 1925, p. 828.
C. W. Thompson, *Literary Digest International Book Rev,* IV, 14–16.

S152   ———. "Introduction." *Edgar Allan Poe Letters Till Now Unpublished in the Valentine Museum Richmond, Virginia.* Philadelphia: J. B. Lippincott, 1925, 3–21.
"The Letters a Tragic Tale unfold."
    Reviewed:
Killis Campbell, *SP,* XXIV, 474–79.
TLS, Dec. 3, 1925, p. 828.
T. O. Mabbott, *YR,* XV, 603–5.
Bookman's Jour, XIII, 124–27.
Norman Foerster, *SatRL,* II (March 6, 1926), 607.
VMHB, XXXIV, 95–96.
C. W. Thompson, *Literary Digest International Book Rev,* IV, 14–16.

S153   ———. "Poe and 'The Southern Literary Messenger.' " *Richmond, Its People and Its Story.* Philadelphia: Lippincott's, 1923.
Concerning Poe's connection with the magazine and of the *Messenger* after Poe's day; see pp. 135–40.

S154   ———. "Was Poe Never Ethical?" *Nation,* XCII (May 25, 1911), 527.
"Poe sometimes deliberately takes a text and preaches a sermon."

S155   Stanard, William G., and Mrs. Archer Jones. *A Walk around the Edgar Allan Poe Shrine.* Richmond: n.p., 1930.

The shrine, an old stone house, and the adjacent building comprise an unusual memorial, "housing some of the rarest treasures and manuscripts in the world."

S156   Stanton, Theodore. "Edgar Poe in France." *Literary Rev,* New York *Evening Post,* July 22, 1922, p. 830.
Some examples of "the high favor which Poe enjoys in the French literary world."

S157   Stark, Burwell. "Reminiscences." *UVaAB,* 1st ser., I (May 1894), 2.
Recollections of Poe's student days.

S158   Starke, Aubrey. "Poe's Friend Reynolds." *AL,* XI (1939), 152–59.
A supplement to the facts about J. N. Reynolds found in Robert Almy's "J. N. Reynolds: A Brief Biography with Particular Reference to Poe and Symmes," *The Colophon,* NS II (Winter 1937), 227–45.

S159   Starrett, Vincent. "Have You a Tamerlane in Your Attic?" *Saturday Evening Post,* CXCVII (June 27, 1925), 72.
Describes Poe's first volume of poetry.

S160   ———. "Introduction." *Tales of Mystery and Imagination,* by Edgar Allan Poe. Baltimore: Limited Editions Club [at the Garamond Press], 1941, pp. viii–xx.
Largely biographical, and stresses Poe's significant contribution to the development of the short story and to world literature. Reprinted in 1958 by the Garamond Press and New York: Heritage Press, 1958.

S161   ———. "One Who Knew Poe." *Bookman,* LXVI (Oct. 1927), 196–201.
An essay on John Hill Hewitt and his largely unhappy relationship with Poe.

S162   ———. "A Poe Mystery Uncovered: The Lost *Minerva* Review of *Al Aaraaf.*" *SatR,* XXVI (May 1, 1943), 4–5, 25.
John Hill Hewitt's review of "Al Aaraaf" discovered in papers left by Hewitt.

*S163   Stauffer, Donald Barlow. *Prose Style in the Fiction of Edgar A. Poe.* Ann Arbor, Mich.: University Microfilms, 1963.

S164   ———. "Prose Style in the Fiction of Edgar A. Poe." *DA,* XXIV (Jan. 1964), 2912.
A principal element of Poe's style is variety.

*S165   ———. "Prose Style in the Fiction of Edgar A. Poe." Diss., University of Indiana, 1963.

S167   ——. "Style and Meaning in 'Ligeia' and 'William Wilson.'"
SSF, II (Summer 1965), 316–30.
 "Ligeia" and "William Wilson" demonstrate a conscious and skilled
stylist who achieved "unity of effect."

S167   ——. "The Two Styles of Poe's 'MS Found in a Bottle.'"
Style, I (Spring 1967), 107–20.
 Poe interwove verisimilitude and the "arabesque" style to achieve a
texture of "mixed fact and fantasy."

S168   Stearns, Bertha-Monica. "Southern Magazines for Ladies
(1819–1860)." *SAQ,* XXXI (Jan. 1932), 70–87.
 Of "the lady-magazine" background in Poe's time.

S169   Stearns, Theodore Pease. "A Prohibitionist Shakes Dice with
Poe." *Outlook,* CXXVI (Sept. 1, 1920), 25–26.
 An account of Poe's supposed meetings at the University, in Boston,
and elsewhere with a certain Peter Pindar Pease.

S170   Stebbing, William. "Edgar Allan Poe." *The Poets: Geoffrey
Chaucer to Alfred Tennyson.* 2 vols. London: Henry Frowde, 1907, II,
198–206.
 Commends the grace and melody of Poe's poetry.

S171   Stedman, Edmund Clarence. "Comment on the Poem." *The
Raven,* by Edgar Allan Poe. Illus. Gustave Doré. New York: Harper,
1884, pp. 9–14.
 Concludes that Poe's "The Raven" has "consistent qualities which
even an expert must admire."
      Reviewed:
SatR, LVI (Nov. 3, 1883), 578–79.
Academy, NS XXIV (Nov. 3, 1883), 296.
Critic, III (Nov. 3, 1883), 440.

S172   ——. *Edgar Allan Poe.* Boston: Houghton, Mifflin, 1881.
 General estimation of Poe's writings with emphasis upon Poe's
"unique" genius and "neurotic" personality.
      Reviewed:
New York *Tribune,* Oct. 19, 1880, p. 6.

S173   ——. "Edgar Allan Poe." *Life and Letters of E. C. Stedman,*
by Laura Stedman and George M. Gould. 2 vols. New York: Moffat,
Yard, 1910, II, 209–39.
 In addition to letters about Poe, the biographers discuss Stedman as
critic and editor of Poe.

S174   ——. "Elements of the Art of Poetry." *The Galaxy,* I (July 1,
1866), pp. 408–15.
 See page 409 for comment on Poe's concept of poetry.

S175   ——. "Introduction." *An American Anthology.* Ed. Stedman. Boston: Houghton, Mifflin, 1901, pp. xv–xxxiv.

   Stresses Poe's influence upon aesthetics throughout the world; see p. xxiv. See also "Notes" on Poe by B. D. L. for a biographical sketch, pp. 815–16.

S176   ——. "Introduction to Literary Criticism." *The Works of Edgar Allan Poe.* Ed. Stedman and George Edward Woodberry. 10 vols. Chicago: Stone and Kimball, 1894–95, VI, xi–xxvi.

   Poe's temperament and qualities as a critic.

S177   ——. "Introduction to the 'Poems.'" *The Works of Edgar Allan Poe.* Ed. Stedman and George Edward Woodberry. 10 vols. Chicago: Stone and Kimball, 1894–95, X, xiii–xxxv.

   Comments on Poe's theory and practice of poetry and emphasizes his musical expression.

S178   ——. "Introduction to the Tales." *The Works of Edgar Allan Poe.* Ed. Stedman and George Edward Woodberry. 10 vols. Chicago: Stone and Kimball, 1894–95, I, 91–121.

   "Poe is often, and correctly enough, termed a romancer."
   Reviewed:
   Critic, XXVI (May 4, 1895), 323–24.
   Nation, LX (May 2, 1895), 349.
   Athenaeum, No. 3556 (Dec. 21, 1895), pp. 865–66.
   Richmond *Dispatch,* Feb. 10, 1885.
   Athenaeum, No. 3570 (March 28, 1896), pp. 406–7.
   Poet-Lore, VI, 519.
   D. L. Maulsby, *Dial,* XVIII (March 1, 1895), 138–41.

S179   ——. "Letter to Charles W. Kent." *UVaMag,* XL (Dec. 1899), 181–82.

   He regrets that he could not attend the unveiling of the Poe bust.

S180   ——. "On the Portraits in This Edition." *The Works of Edgar Allan Poe.* Ed. Stedman and George Edward Woodberry. 10 vols. Chicago: Stone and Kimball, 1894–95, X, 257–66.

   Commentary on the origin and printing of ten portraits of Poe.

S181   ——. "Poe, Cooper, and the Hall of Fame." *North American Rev,* CLXXXV (Aug. 16, 1907), 801–12.

   Concerning the election then recently held when Poe, Cooper, and Bryant failed to be elected to the Hall.

S182   ——. "Poe's Cottage at Fordham." *Century Mag,* NS LI (March 1907), 770–73.

S183   Steele, Charles W. "Poe's 'The Cask of Amontillado.'" *Expl,* XVIII (April 1960), item 43.

   A discussion of the "hidden" meaning of the word *Amontillado.*

S184   Stein, William B. "The Twin Motif in 'The Fall of the House of Usher.'" *MLN,* LXXV (Feb. 1960), 109–11.
The "Gothic convention of the common fate of twins is the chief vehicle both of Poe's effect of terror and of his psychological rationalization of the terror."

S185   Stephens, Mrs. H. M. "The Lost Pleiad—E. A. Poe." *Godey's Lady's Book,* XL (Feb. 1850), 143.
Verse.

S186   Sterling, George. "Poe's Gravestone." *Nation,* CXIII (Sept. 7, 1921), 259.
Verse commemorating the refusal of Lowell, Bryant, Whittier, and Longfellow to attend the services for Poe in Baltimore.

S187   ———. "To Edgar Allan Poe." *Current Literature,* XXXVIII (Feb. 1905), 141.
Verse.

S188   Stern, Madeline B. "The House of the Expanding Doors: Ann Lynch's Soirées, 1846." *NYHSQB,* XXIII (Jan. 1942), 42–51.
An account of Poe's relationship to the New York literary society who frequently gathered in Miss Lynch's fashionable home.

S189   Stern, Philip Van Doren. "The Case of the Corpse in the Blind Alley." *VQR,* XVII (Spring 1941), 227–36.
An essay on the detective story genre occasioned by the one hundredth anniversary of the publication of "The Murders in the Rue Morgue."

S190   ———. "Strange Death of Edgar Allan Poe." *SatR,* XXXII (Oct. 15, 1949), 8–9, 28–30.

S191   ———, ed. *Edgar Allan Poe, Selected and Edited.* With introd. and notes. Stern. New York: Viking Press, 1945.
Mostly biographical and praises Poe's fiction. See "Introduction," pp. xv–xxxviii.
    Reviewed:
Malcolm Cowley, *New Republic,* CXIII (Nov. 5, 1945), pp. 607–10.

S192   Stevens, H. A. "Poe's Tamerlane." *NYTM,* June 22, 1941, p. 23.

S193   Stevens, H. B., Jr. "Poe's Estimate of Longfellow." *UVaMag,* LIX (June 1899), 358–63.
Poe's estimate of Longfellow is tinged with prejudice.

S194   Stevenson, Robert Louis. "*The Works of Edgar Allan Poe.* Edited by John H. Ingram." *Academy,* VII (Jan. 2, 1875), 1–2.
In this review of vols. I and II of Ingram's edition, Stevenson praises Poe's craftsmanship and power of analysis found in the tales. Reprinted *The Works of Robert Louis Stevenson,* ed. C. C. Bigelow and

Temple Scott (10 vols., New York: Greenock Press, 1906), IX, 255–62.

S195   Stewart, Charles D. "A Pilfering by Poe." *Atlantic Monthly,* CCII (Dec. 1958), 67–68.

Poe's "The Raven" owes a great deal to Dickens's *Barnaby Rudge,* and Poe's "The Philosophy of Composition" is an attempt by the artist to keep "the public mind as far as possible from Barnaby Rudge's raven."

S196   Stewart, Robert Armistead. *The Case of Edgar Allan Poe: Pathological Study Based on the Investigations of Lauvrière.* Richmond: Whittet and Shepperson, 1910.

"Properly speaking Poe was not a drunkard, but a dipsomaniac."

S197   ——. "Edgar Allan Poe." *The Gold Bug and Other Selections from the Works of Edgar Allan Poe.* Ed. Stewart. Richmond: B. F. Johnson, 1912, pp. 5–7.

A brief biographical sketch of Poe.

S198   ——. "Introduction." *Poems and Tales of Edgar Allan Poe.* Ed. Stewart. Richmond: B. F. Johnson Publishing, 1911, pp. 7–28.

Stresses Poe's accomplishments in poetry, criticism, and fiction.

S199   ——. "Notes" [on the *Tales*]. *The Complete Works of Edgar Allan Poe.* Ed. James A. Harrison. 17 vols. New York: T. Y. Crowell, 1902, II, 297–399, III, 327–48, IV, 273–323, V, 311–33, VI, 273–301. Vols. II and IV reprinted New York: AMS Press 1965.

Textual notes to Poe's tales.

S200   ——. "The Prose Text of Edgar Allan Poe's Writings." Diss., University of Virginia, 1901.

Published as University of Virginia School of Teutonic Language Monograph no. 4.

S201   ——. *The Prose Text of Edgar Allan Poe's Writings.* University of Virginia School of Teutonic Language Monograph no. 4. Charlottesville, 1901.

Originally a dissertation at the University of Virginia, this study comprises the textual notes to Poe's tales in the Harrison or Virginia edition of Poe's works (1902).

S202   Stillman, W. J. "Edgar Allan Poe." *Nation,* XX (March 25, 1875), 208–9.

Declares that Ingram's biography is an extreme "whitewash."

S203   Stockett, Letitia. "Poe Backgrounds." *Johns Hopkins Alumni Mag,* XX (Jan. 1932), 123–32.

Poe's romanticism has "been curiously transmitted into the fabric of our own age."

S204   Stockhard, Henry Jerome. "Poe at Fordham." *Chautauquan,*
XXIV (Nov. 1896), 185.
Verse.

S205   Stockton, Eric W. "Celestial Inferno: Poe's 'The City in the
Sea.'" *TSL,* VIII (1963), 99–106.
The "poem superbly synthesizes sound, meter, diction, a complex of
overt and non-literal statement, and profound psychological revelation—in a work which meets all Poe's criteria for excellence."

S206   Stoddard, Richard Henry. "A Box of Autographs." *Scribner's
Mag,* IX (Feb. 1891), 213–27.
Reproduces parts of MS "To Zante" and comments that Poe's tales
"are remarkable for darkly imaginative powers" and his poems "for
their excess of verbal melody."

S207   ——. "Edgar Allan Poe." *Harper's Monthly,* XLV (Sept.
1872), 557–68.
Primarily biographical.

S208   ——. "Edgar Allan Poe." *Lippincott's,* XLIII (Jan. 1889),
107–15.
Retells the incident of his clash with Poe.

S209   ——. "Edgar Allan Poe." *National Mag,* II (March 1853),
193–200.
Depends upon Griswold for biography and stresses Poe's limited and
narrow accomplishments in literature.

S210   ——. "The Genius of Poe." *The Works of Edgar Allan Poe.*
6 vols. London: Kegan Paul, Trench, 1884, I, iii–xiv.
Commends Poe's tales and has only compromising praise for his
poetry and criticism.

S211   ——. "Life of Edgar Allan Poe." *Select Works of Edgar A.
Poe.* New York: W. J. Widdleton, 1880, pp. xv–clxx.
Offers some criticisms but generally concerned with Poe's "brief,
brilliant, but unhappy life."
Reviewed:
New York *Times,* Oct. 24, 1880, p. 10.

S212   ——. "Meetings with Poe." *Recollections, Personal and Literary.* New York: A. S. Barnes, 1903, pp. 145–60.
Relates his "first and last acquaintance with this highly gifted but
ill-balanced man of genius."

S213   ——. "Memoir of Edgar Allan Poe." *Poems,* by Edgar Allan
Poe. New York: W. J. Widdleton, 1875, pp. 15–99.
Largely biographical and tends to be gossipy.
Reviewed:

New York *Tribune,* Dec. 8, 1874, p. 8.
Harper's Monthly, L (March 1875), 600.
Nation, XX (May 25, 1875), 208–9.

S214   ——. "Poe's Last Residence." *Harper's Weekly,* XXVII (Dec. 15, 1883), 799.
Poe's living habits and circumstances during his second residence in New York.

S215   ——. "Reminiscences of Hawthorne and Poe." *Independent,* LIV (Nov. 20, 1902), 2756–58. Reprinted in *Book-Lover,* IV (Sept.– Oct. 1903), 352.

S216   ——. "Some Myths of the Life of Poe." *Independent,* XXXII (June 24, 1880), 1–2.

S217   Stone, Edward. "The Paving Stones of Paris: Psychometry from Poe to Proust." *AQ,* V (Summer 1953), 121–31.
Poe offers the first fictional demonstration of "the measurement and association of ideas in the human mind."

S218   ——. "Poe in and out of His Time." *ESQ,* No. 31 (2nd quarter 1963), pp. 14–17.
Poe's modernity touches upon the cynicism and despair characteristic of our time.

S219   ——. "Usher, Poquelin, and Miss Emily: The Progress of Southern Gothic." *GaR,* XIV (Winter 1960), 433–43.
Faulkner through characterization and detail achieves the effect of horror more successfully than did Poe or Cable.

S220   ——. *Voices of Despair: Four Motives in American Literature.* Columbus: Ohio University Press, 1966.
Concentrates on Poe's use of imagery, *passim.*

S221   Stonier, G. W. "Books in General." *New Statesman & Nation,* XXIV (Aug. 29, 1942), 143.
On Poe's reputation.

S222   Storey, Hedley Vicars. "The Raven and the Parrot." *Academy,* LXII (May 10, 1902), 490–91.
On a conjectural source.

S223   Stott, Roscoe Gilmore. "Introduction." *Selected Poems and Tales of Edgar Allan Poe.* New York: American Book, 1914, pp. 5–12.
Praises Poe's style and craftsmanship, for Poe is "symbolic, mystical, and fascinating."

S224   Stovall, Floyd. "The Conscious Art of Edgar Allan Poe." *CE,* XXIV (March 1963), 417–21.
Poe's works are a product of conscious effort and can be logically interpreted. Reprinted in Robert Regan, ed., *Poe: A Collection of*

Critical Essays (Englewood Cliffs, N.J.: Prentice-Hall, 1967), pp. 172–78.

S225 ——. "Edgar Poe and the University of Virginia." *VQR*, XLIII (Spring 1967), 297–317.
Examines all facets of Poe's relationship to the University of Virginia.

S226 ——. "An Interpretation of Poe's 'Al Aaraaf.'" *UTSE*, No. 9 (1929), pp. 106–33.
Sees the poem largely as an allegory of Poe's theory of poetry.

S227 ——. "Poe as a Poet of Ideas." *UTSE*, No. 11 (1931), pp. 56–62.
Traces "the idea of beauty through the body of Poe's poetry" and shows "how through it he reaches out to draw in such other ideas as may be made to harmonize with it."

S228 ——. "Poe's Debt to Coleridge." *UTSE*, No. 10 (1930), pp. 70–127.
"Poe was more deeply indebted to Coleridge in criticism and in speculative thought than has generally been supposed."
Reviewed:
M. Alterton, *MLN*, XLVII, 329–31.

S229 ——. "An Unpublished Poe Letter." *AL*, XXXVI (Jan. 1965), 514–15.
Poe writes E. L. Fancher authorizing Mrs. Maria Clemm to receive the amount of damages awarded him in his suit against the *Evening Mirror*.

S230 ——. "The Women of Poe's Poems and Tales." *UTSE*, No. 5 (1925), pp. 197–209.
Poe is consistent in his use of women as the subject of poetry.

S231 ——, ed. *The Poems of Edgar Allan Poe*. Charlottesville: University Press of Virginia, 1965.
Definitive edition of Poe's poems with an informative introduction (pp. xv–xxxii).
Reviewed:
Simpson, *ELN*, IV, 149–51.
H. A. Pochmann, *AL*, XXXVIII, 247.
Choice, II, 861.
S. P. Moss, *JEGP*, LXV, 623.
A. Turner, *SAQ*, LV, 292.
R. S. Moore, *GaR*, XX, 475.
D. Weeks, *Jour of Aesthetics and Art Criticism*, XV, 471.
J. Schroeter, *MP*, LXV, 84.
Moore and Willet, *YWES*, XLVI, 347–48.

S232   Strauch, Carl F., comp. "Symposium of Poe." *ESQ*, No. 31, Part I (2nd quarter 1963), pp. 4–34.

A collection of brief essays on Poe.

S233   ———, ed. "Critical Symposium on American Romanticism." *ESQ*, No. 35 (2nd quarter 1964).

Poe is mentioned frequently.

S234   Strickland, W. W. *The Great Divide*. New York: B. Westermann, 1931.

See Part I for a discussion of the "numerical mysticism" of twelve poems by Poe, pp. 11–95.

S235   Strong, Augustus Hopkins. "Edgar Allan Poe." *American Poets and Their Theology*. Philadelphia: Griffith and Rowland Press, 1916.

Gives outmoded biography and routine evaluations of Poe's works; see pp. 159–206.

S236   Stroupe, John H. "Poe's Imaginary Voyage: Pym as Hero." *SSF*, IV (Summer 1967), 315–21.

Pym "becomes a hero by taking part in unusual and marvelous adventures that bestow on him the attributes of hero."

S237   Stuart, Esmé. "Charles Baudelaire and Edgar Poe: A Literary Affinity." *Nineteenth Century*, XXXIV (July 1893), 65–80.

A comparison of personalities and literary writing. Reprinted in Littell's *Living Age*, CXCVIII (Sept. 16, 1893), 692–703.

S238   Suckling, Norman. "The Adaptation of Edgar Poe." *Paul Valéry and the Civilized Mind*. London: Oxford University Press, 1954, pp. 58–95.

Poe's essays aided Valéry in crystallizing aesthetic theory.

S239   Sutton, Walter. "Contextualist Theory and Criticism as a Social Act." *Jour of Aesthetics and Art Criticism*, XIX (Spring 1961), 317–25.

See pp. 318–19.

S240   Swanson, Donald R. "Poe's 'The Conqueror Worm.'" *Expl*, XIX (April 1961), item 52.

Imagery suggests the depiction of a dramatic performance.

S241   Swiggett, Glenn L. "A Plea for Poe." *Poet-Lore*, XIII (July, Aug., Sept. 1901), 379–86.

Americans should abandon the leadership of the New England school and accept Poe (following the European lead) for the intrinsic merit of his work.

S242   ———, "Poe and Recent Poetics." *SR*, VI (April 1898), 150–66.

Finds a similarity between Poe and many poets demonstrating "modern" tendencies in poetry.

S243   Swinburne, Algernon Charles. *Letters*. London: Heinemann, New York: John Lane, 1918.

See letters of March 6, March 10, April 21, 1874, to J. H. Ingram; of Jan. 9 and July 22, 1875, to Paul H. Hayne; of Nov. 9, 1875, to Mrs. S. S. Rice; of July 4, 1884, to Hayne. Letter to Mrs. Rice appears in Eric Carlson, ed., *The Recognition of Edgar Allan Poe* (Ann Arbor: University of Michigan Press, 1966), pp. 62–64.

S244   ———. *Letters Chiefly concerning Edgar Allan Poe from Algernon Charles Swinburne to John H. Ingram*. London: Printed for private circulation, 1910.

Nine letters concerning Swinburne's admiration for Poe.

S245   ———. *Under the Microscope*. Portland, Maine: Thomas B. Mosher, 1899.

Poe achieved a "pure note of original song"; see pp. 53. First printed London: D. White, 1872.

S246   Symons, Arthur. "Edgar Allan Poe." *Figures of Several Centuries*. New York: Dutton, 1906.

See pp. 115–21.

S247   ———. "Edgar Allan Poe." *Life and Letters*, II (March 1929), 163–78.

Poe "was a man haunted all his days by ghosts . . . as they stand behind the thin but not transparent curtain of his works."

S248   ———. "Introduction." *The Fall of the House of Usher*, by Edgar Poe. Illus. Alastair. Paris: Editions Narcisse, 1928, pp. i–xix.

Poe's tales reveal his genius in achieving "incredible horror" and "unsurpassable beauty."

S249   ———. "Introduction." *The Lyrical Poems of Edgar Allan Poe*. New York: E. P. Dutton, 1906, pp. v–ix.

On Poe's theory of "absolute" poetry.

T

T1   Deleted.

T2   Tabb, John B. "Edgar Allan Poe and His Critics." *Academy*, LXIX (Dec. 16, 1905), 1318.

Points out that Poe's attitude toward Wordsworth was shared by Browning.

T3 ———. "Mr. Stedman's Estimate of Poe." *Critic,* VII (Nov. 31, 1885), 247.

T4 ———. "Poe." *Poems.* n.p., and n.d. [1882?], p. 92.
A sonnet.

T5 ———. "Poe-Chopin." *Chap-Book,* V (May 15, 1896), 17.
Verse.

T6 ———. "Poe's Cottage at Fordham." *Bookman,* V (May 1897), 216; reprinted, *ibid.,* XXVIII (Jan. 1909), 428.
Verse.

T7 ———. "Poe's Purgatory." *Independent,* LVI (March 3, 1904), 494.
Verse.

T8 ———. "To Edgar Allan Poe." *UVaMag,* LX (Dec. 1899), 141.
Verse.

T9 Taft, Kendall B. "The Identity of Poe's Martin Van Buren Mavis." *AL,* XXVI (Jan. 1955), 562–63.
"The alleged translator of 'Mellonta Tauta' was probably Andrew Jackson Davis of Poughkeepsie, 'clairvoyant, spiritualist, lecturer and writer on esoteric subjects during the mid-forties.' " *AL.*

T10 Tanasoca, Donald. "Poe and Whitman." *Walt Whitman Birthplace Bulletin,* II (April 1959), 3–7 and (July 1959), 6–11.
"All in all Poe's influence on Whitman was not inconsiderable."

*T11 ———. "A Twentieth Century 'Stylus.' " *Bibliographical Society, University of Virginia, Secretary News Sheet,* No. 29 (Oct. 1953), pp. 1–2.
"The brief history of an attempt to incarnate Poe's projected magazine in New York in 1901." *AL.*

T12 Tannenbaum, Earl. "Poe's Nicean Barks: 'Small Latin, and Less Greek.' " *N&Q,* V (Aug. 1958), 353–55.
Suggests that too much emphasis has been placed upon the classical sources of Poe's "To Helen."

T13 Tannenbaum, Libby. "The Raven Abroad: Some European Illustrations of the Work of Edgar Allan Poe." *Mag of Art,* XXXVII (April 1944), 122–27.
Poe's illustrators abroad include many of the more important artists of the last century, and analysis and comparison of their illustrations tend to shed some light on our understanding of modern art.

T14   Tanselle, G. Thomas. "Poe and Vandenhoff Once More." *AN&Q,* I (Sept. 1962), 101–2.
On the early appearance of "The Raven" in an anthology.

T15   ———. "Two More Appearances of 'The Raven.' " *PBSA,* LVII (2nd quarter 1963), 229–30.

T16   ———. "An Unknown Early Appearance of 'The Raven.' " *SB,* XVI (1963), 220–23.
An early republication of Poe's poem appeared in the New York *Weekly News,* Feb. 8, 1845.

T17   ———. "Unrecorded Early Reprintings of Two Poe Tales." *PBSA,* LVI (April–June 1962), 252.
Publications of "The Purloined Letter" and "The Oval Portrait."

T18   Tappan, Eva March. *A Short History of England's and America's Literature.* Boston: Houghton, Mifflin, 1906.
Poe has "marvellous ability to make a story 'real' " and to create mood and feeling in his poetry "by the mere sound of words"; see pp. 356–59.

T19   Tarbox, Raymond. "Blank Hallucinations in the Fiction of Poe and Hemingway." *AI,* XXIV (Winter 1967), 312–43.
Poe's treatment of anxiety and hallucinations in some of his fiction.

T20   Targ, William, ed. *Selected Short Stories* [of Edgar Allan Poe]. With introd. Cleveland: Fine Editions Press, 1952.
Poe's supreme accomplishment in the short story is unquestioned. See "Introduction," pp. vii–x.

T21   [Tasistro, L. F.] [Notice of *Tales of the Grotesque and Arabesque.*] *New-York Mirror,* XVII (Dec. 28, 1839), 215.
Praises Poe's intellectual capacity, imagination, power of description, and "fecundity of invention." Passages reprinted in Eric Carlson, ed., *The Recognition of Edgar Allan Poe* (Ann Arbor: University of Michigan Press, 1966), p. 4.

T22   Tassin, Algernon. "The Grub Street Problem: Being a Consideration of the Scribe and the Cost of Living in Various Periods. Part VI.—The Time of Poe." *Bookman,* XXXVII (Aug. 1913), 646–58.
Discusses the economics of Poe's day.

T23   ———. "The Magazine in America. Part III—Philadelphia, The Valley of Self-Sufficientness." *Bookman,* XLI (May 1915), 284–96.
Commentary on the relations of Poe, Graham, and Griswold; see pp. 286–90.

T24   ———. "The Willowy Willis and the Piratical Poe in New

York." *The Magazine in America.* New York: Dodd, Mead, 1916, pp. 131–53.

Poe and Nathaniel Parker Willis as New York journalists.

T25   Tate, Allen. "The Angelic Imagination." *The Man of Letters in the Modern World: Selected Essays, 1928–1955.* New York: Meridian Books, 1955, pp. 113–31.

Reprint of article in *KR,* XIV (Summer 1952), 455–75.

T26   ———. "The Angelic Imagination: Poe and the Power of Words." *KR,* XIV (Summer 1952), 455–75.

"Poe is the transitional figure in modern literature because he discovered our great subject, the disintegration of a personality, but kept it in a language that developed in a tradition of unity and order." Reprinted in Eric Carlson, ed., *The Recognition of Edgar Allan Poe* (Ann Arbor: University of Michigan Press, 1966), pp. 236–54.

T27   ———. "Angelic Imagination: Poe as God." *Collected Essays.* Denver: A. Swallow, 1959, pp. 432–54.

Reprint of article in *KR,* XIV (Summer 1952), 455–75.

T28   ———. "Our Cousin, Mr. Poe." *PR,* XVI (Dec. 1949), 1207–19.

Tate finds Poe a writer whose prose style is competent but at times subject to bathos, whose characters are possessed by a strange fire and cast a "mysterious exaltation of spirit" although they are dehumanized, and whose descriptions directed toward the creation of sensation set a mood that is distinctly modern. Reprinted in Tate's *The Man of Letters in the Modern World* (1955); in Irving Howe, ed., *Modern Literary Criticism* (Boston: Beacon Press, 1958), pp. 255–66; in Tate's *Collected Essays* (Denver: A. Swallow, 1959), pp. 455–71; and in Robert Regan, ed., *Poe: A Collection of Critical Essays* (Englewood Cliffs, N.J.: Prentice-Hall, 1967), pp. 38–50.

T29   ———. "Three Commentaries: Poe, James, and Joyce." *SR,* LVIII (Winter 1950), 1–15.

Poe's "The Fall of the House of Usher" has significant features which help to "illuminate some of the later, more mature work in the naturalistic-symbolic technique of Flaubert, Joyce, and James."

T30   Taylor, Archer. "Poe, Dr. Lardner, and 'Three Sundays in a Week.'" *AN&Q,* III (Jan. 1944), 153–55.

"An attempt to prove that the title of Poe's story is an old locution for *never.*" *AL.*

T31   Taylor, Bayard. "Diversions of the Echo Club." *Atlantic Monthly,* XXIX (Jan. 1872), 76–84.

An excellent parody of Poe.

T32   ———. "Poe's Last Manuscript." *American Clipper* (Ridley Park, Pa.), I (Nov. 1934), 64.

Bayard Taylor's letter to Mr. Graham of *Graham's Magazine,* July 29, 1850, concerning "an unpublished article by Poe on 'The Poetic Principle.' "

T33   Taylor, George E. "Poe and Dumas." *SatRL,* VI (Feb. 8, 1930), 718.

T34   Taylor, Walter Fuller. "Israfel in Motley: A Study of Poe's Humor." *SR,* XLII (July 1934), 330–40.

Poe mocks the heavy moralizers of the age, satirizes the sentimental romance, indulges in farce, and burlesques short prose fiction.

T35   ———. *The Story of American Letters.* Rev. ed. Chicago: Henry Regnery, 1956.

Author's essay on Poe (pp. 110–19) first appeared in his *A History of American Letters* (1936).

T36   Teall, Gardner. "Poe's Venture in Conchology." *NYTBR,* Dec. 3, 1922, p. 7.

An account of Poe's book on conchology.

T37   Teiser, S. S. "Is Doyle a Plagiarist?" *UVaMag,* LXI (May–June 1901), 468–76.

Doyle has imitated Poe, if he has not plagiarized him.

T38   Temple, Ruth Z. *The Critic's Alchemy: A Study of the Introduction of French Symbolism into England.* New York: Twayne, 1953.

See especially pp. 144–45.

T39   Thal, H. Van. "Introduction." *Tales of Mystery and Imagination,* by Edgar Allan Poe. Ed. Thal. London: Folio Society, 1957, pp. i–xiii.

A general appraisal of Poe's fiction.

T40   Thomas, Edith M. "Few Words on a Master-Mechanician." *Harper's Weekly,* LIII (Jan. 16, 1909), 14.

Poe is essentially the "Master Mechanician—plus, here, Imagination; plus, there, the disordered outgivings of *cauchemar.*"

T41   Thomas, Henry, and Dana Lee Thomas. "Edgar Allan Poe 1809–1849." *Living Biographies of the Great Poets.* Garden City, N.Y.: Doubleday, Doran, 1941, pp. 233–45.

A biographical sketch with very little criticism.

T42   Thomas, J. David. "The Composition of Wilde's 'The Harlot House.' " *MLN,* LXV (Nov. 1950), 485–88.

"The Haunted Palace" and "The Masque of the Red Death" as sources for Wilde's poem.

T43 Thomas, W. Moy. "Edgar Allan Poe." *The Train: A First-Class Magazine,* III (April 1857), 193–98.

Censures Griswold and the Griswoldian interpretation of Poe.

T44 Thomas, W. M. M. "Poe and the University of Virginia Magazine." *UVaMag,* LXIII (April 1903), 380–89.

Notes and discusses the articles that have appeared in the *University of Virginia Magazine* concerning Poe.

T45 Thompson, Francis. "Dreamer of Things Impossible." *Literary Criticisms.* Newly discovered and collected by Terence L. Connolly. New York: E. P. Dutton, 1948, pp. 317–22.

A British poet, writing in 1901, emphasizes Poe as creator of detective stories and of fantastic fiction.

*T46 Thompson, Gary Richard. *Poe's Romantic Irony: A Study of the Gothic Tales in a Romantic Context.* Ann Arbor, Mich.: University Microfilms, 1967.

T47 ———. "Poe's Romantic Irony: A Study of the Gothic Tales in a Romantic Context." *DA,* XXVII (Feb. 1968), 3201A.

Poe is a "preëminent follower of the European 'Romantic Ironists.' "

*T48 ———. "Poe's Romantic Irony: A Study of the Gothic Tales in a Romantic Context." Diss., University of Southern California, 1967.

T49 Thompson, John R. "Editorial Note." *SLM,* XXVI (March 1850), 192.

Expresses regret over criticism directed against two of the editors of the Griswold edition.

T50 ———. *The Genius and Character of Edgar Allan Poe.* Ed. and arranged by James H. Whitty and James H. Rindfleisch. Richmond: Garrett & Massie, 1929.

Opinions and impressions of Poe by one of his contemporaries.

T51 ———. "The Late Edgar A. Poe." *SLM,* XV (Nov. 1849), 694–97.

A tribute by a former employer.

T52 ———. "The Editor's Table." *SLM,* XXIII (Nov. 1856), 395.

Some remarks acknowledging receipt of an excellent daguerrotype of Poe, together with intelligence concerning a movement under way to erect a monument upon his grave.

T53 ———. "The Editor's Table." *SLM,* XIX (March 1853), 184–85.

Some remarks relative to a charge of plagiarism against Poe whose poem "To One in Paradise" is alleged to have been stolen from Tennyson.

T54   Thompson, Maurice. *Genius and Morality*. Ridley Park, Pa.:
American Autograph Shop, 1934.
   This letter, dated "Crawfordsville, Indiana, 21, March, 1887," was
written to a "Mr. Hoyt" and says very little in defense of Poe.

T55   Thompson, Ralph. *American Literary Annuals and Gift Books,
1825–1865*. New York: H. W. Wilson, 1936.
   Lists the appearance and date of Poe's works published in literary
annuals and gift books.

T56   Thorner, Horace Edward. "Hawthorne, Poe, and a Literary
Ghost." *NEQ*, VII (March 1934), 146–54.
   The relation of Hawthorne's "Howe's Masquerade" and Poe's
"William Wilson" to the legend of Luis Enius, especially told by
Irving in "An Unwritten Drama of Lord Byron."

T57   Thorp, Willard. "A Minor Poe Mystery." *PULC*, V (Nov.
1943), 30–31.
   On Poe's relationships with Thomas Dunn English.

T58   ———. "Two Poe Letters at Princeton." *PULC*, X (Feb. 1949),
91–94.
   Two Poe letters not included in Ostrom collection published in
1948.

T59   Ticknor, Caroline. "Ingram—Discourager of Poe Biographies."
Bookman, XLIV (Sept. 1916), 8–14.
   Ingram was the supreme figure in the field of Poe biography.

T60   ———. *Poe's Helen*. New York: Charles Scribner's Sons, 1916.
   Life of Sarah Helen Whitman, to whom Poe was engaged.
      Reviewed:
   Killis Campbell, *Dial*, LXI (Nov. 16, 1916), 395.
   J. H. Whitty, Richmond *Times-Dispatch*, Oct. 22, 1916, sec. 6, pp.
1 and 2.
   Current Opinion, LXI (Dec. 1916), 416.

T61   Timpe, Eugene P. *American Literature in Germany, 1861–
1872*. Chapel Hill: University of North Carolina Press, 1964.
   "Edgar Allan Poe is one of several important American authors who
was long neglected in Germany." See pp. 53–56.

T62   Timrod, Henry. "A Theory of Poetry, a Rationale of Poetry."
Independent, LIII (March 28, April 4, 11, 1901), 712–16, 760–64,
830–33.
   Timrod disagrees with Poe on matters of poetic theory. Reprinted
in *Best American Essays*, ed. J. R. Howard (New York: Crowell,
1910), pp. 311–24.

T63   Tinker, Chauncey Brewster. "The Secret Impulse: The Psychological Interpretation of Poetry." *The Good Estate of Poetry*. Boston: Little, Brown, 1929.

> Points out weaknesses in the psychological interpretation of Poe's art; see pp. 35–54.

T64   Tinnon, J. A. "Poe's 'Ulalume.'" *Graham's*, XXXVIII (Feb. 1851), 120–22.

> An analysis of the poem with excerpts.

T65   Todd, William B. "The Early Issues of Poe's *Tales* (1845)." *LCUT*, VII (Fall 1961), 13–18.

> Descriptive bibliography of early issues of Poe's *Tales* in the University of Texas Library.

T66   Tolman, Albert H. "Was Poe Accurate?" *The Views about Hamlet and Other Essays*. Boston: Houghton, Mifflin, 1904, pp. 399–403.

> Questions some mathematical statements in "The Gold Bug." First appeared in *Dial*, XXVI (March 16, 1899), 189–90.

T67   Toomey, Noxon. "The Philosophy of Edgar Allan Poe." *Medical Pickwick*, IX (April 1923), 129–43.

> Critically examines various elements of "Technical" philosophy (logic and metaphysics) found in Poe's writings.

T68   Towne, C. H. "Where Poe Once Lived and Loved." *Delineator*, C (June 1922), 18–19, 68.

> On Poe's cottage in New York. Reprinted in *Muse Anthology of Modern Poetry*, ed. Dorothy Kissling and Arthur H. Nethercot, Poe Memorial Edition (New York: Carlyle Straub, 1938), pp. 60–64.

T69   Toyoda, Minoru. "Edgar Allan Poe and Akutagawa Ryunosuke: Lecture on a Comparison of Them as Short-Story Writers." *Essays in English and American Literature: In Commemoration of Professor Takejiro Nakayama's Sixty-first Birthday*. Tokyo: Shohakusha, 1961, pp. 1–12.

> Poe and Akutagawa are alike in their attention to a strong psychological effect upon the reader.

T70   Traylor, Mary Gavin. "The Richmond of Edgar Allan Poe." *Richmond Mag*, XVIII (Aug. 1931), 12, 30–32.

T71   ——. "'To Keep It in Beauty': The Poe Shrine." *SLM*, I (April 1939), 265–68.

> A description of the Richmond shrine and its holdings.

T72   Trent, William P. "The Centenary of Poe." *Longfellow and Other Essays*. New York: T. Y. Crowell, 1910, pp. 21–44.

> The rising interest in Poe is one of the best proofs "of Poe's possession of a true and unique genius." Essay also appears in *Edgar Allan*

Poe: A Centenary Tribute, ed. Heinrich Ewald Buchholz (Baltimore: Warwick and York, 1910), pp. 19–43.

T73 ———. "Edgar Allan Poe." *The Library of Southern Literature.* 16 vols. Ed. E. A. Alderman *et al.* New Orleans: Martin and Hoyt, 1908–13, IX, 4085–89.

Proclaims Poe's greatness and discusses his appeal on the European continent.

T74 ———. *A History of American Literature, 1607–1865.* New York: D. Appleton, 1903.

Dwells upon Poe's influence, originality and range, "intense power and his mastery of the forms of art he attempts."

T75 ———. "Introduction." *The Raven, The Fall of the House of Usher, and Other Poems and Tales,* by Edgar Allan Poe. Ed. Trent. Boston: Houghton, Mifflin, 1898, pp. v–xvi.

Poe was an original poet and "save only with regard to style," an accomplished writer of prose fiction.

T76 ———. "The Need of Further Study of Poe's Life." *UVaAB,* 3rd ser., II (April 1909), 185–89.

Expresses the need of reexamining the essential facts of Poe's life.

T77 ———. "Poe's Rank as a Writer." *East and West,* I (Aug. 1900), 305–13.

Poe's fame as a writer will likely increase.

T78 ———. *William Gilmore Simms.* Boston: Houghton, Mifflin, 1892.

Complimentary comments on Poe, *passim.*

T79 ———, and John Erskine. "Edgar Allan Poe." *Great American Writers.* New York: Holt, 1912, pp. 85–105.

Considers the relationship between Poe's theory of art and his practice and devotes some attention to the morality of Poe's life and behavior.

T80 Trilling, Lionel. "The Complete Tales and Poems of Edgar Allan Poe." *American Panorama.* Ed. Eric Larrabee. New York: New York University Press, 1957, p. 267.

Poe holds uncertain place in American literature, but his stories are commendable in that they deal with the extravagancies of the soul.

T81 Tripplett, Edna. "A Note on Poe's 'The Raven.' " *AL,* X (Nov. 1938), 339–41.

A possible source is "The Dervish" by William Falconer, in *Graham's* for July 1841.

T82 Trumble, Alfred. "The Beautiful Cigar Girl." *Great Crimes and Criminals of America.* New York: R. K. Fox, 1881, pp. 7–10.

Concerning Mary Rogers. First appeared in *National Police Gazette,*
May 1881, p. 3.

T83   Tucker, Beverley Randolph. *The Lost Lenore, A One Act Play.*
Richmond: Liberty Press, 1929.

T84   ———. "Poe—A Psychoanalytical View." *The Reviewer,* III
(April 1923), 829–33.
Leans heavily on Robertson's psychopathic studies of Poe and finds
that Poe had a "split personality."

T85   Tuckerman, Henry Theodore. *The Life of John Pendleton
Kennedy.* New York: G. P. Putnam, 1871.
See especially pp. 373–77 for Kennedy's associations with Poe.

T86   ———. "A Sketch of American Literature." *Outlines of English
Literature,* by Thomas B. Shaw. Philadelphia: Henry C. Lea, 1865,
p. 467.
A word on Poe's genius reflected in his tales. First printed New
York: Sheldon and Co., 1852.

T87   [Tupper, Martin Farquhar.] "American Romance." *Littell's
Living Age,* IX (May 23, 1846), 381–84.
A favorable review of Poe's *Tales* (1845) first appearing in the
London *Literary Gazette,* Jan. 1846. Passages reprinted in Eric Carl-
son, ed., *The Recognition of Edgar Allan Poe* (Ann Arbor: Uni-
versity of Michigan Press, 1966), pp. 18–21.

T88   Turnbull, Mrs. Francese H. "New Statue of Edgar Allan Poe by
Sir Moses Ezekiel." *Art and Archaeology,* V (May 1917), 307–8.

T89   Turner, H. Arlin. "Another Source of Poe's *Julius Rodman.*"
AL, VIII (March 1936), 69–70.
Alexander MacKenzie's *Voyages* (1801) is one likely source.

T90   ———. "A Note on Poe's 'Julius Rodman.'" *UTSE,* No. 10
(1930), pp. 146–51.
Poe drew details and language from Irving's *The Adventures of
Captain Bonneville* (1837).

T91   ———. "Sources of Poe's 'A Descent into the Maëlstrom.'"
JEGP, XLVI (July 1947), 298–301.
Discusses the significance of a story in *Le Magasin Universel* (1836)
as a source.

T92   ———. "Writing of Poe's 'The Bells.'" *AN&Q,* II (Aug.
1942), 73.

T93   ———, and Thomas O. Mabbott. "Two Poe Hoaxes by the Same
Hand?" *AN&Q,* II (Jan. 1943), 147–48.
"Details of the New Orleans 'Raven' hoax in 1870 bear unexpected
likeness in method to the Giles story of 'The Bells.'" *AL.*

T94   Turpin, Edna H. "Introduction." *The Gold Bug,* by Edgar
Allan Poe. Maynard's English Classic Series, No. 204. New York:
Maynard, Merrill, 1898, pp. 3–6.
   Biographical.

T95   Turquet-Milnes, G. "Predecessors. I. Edgar Poe." *The Influence
of Baudelaire in France and England.* London: Constable and Co.,
1913, pp. 63–72.
   Poe's bringing to the supernatural a psychological and artistic interest
attracted Baudelaire.

T96   Tuttleton, James W. "The Presence of Poe in *This Side of
Paradise.*" *ELN,* III (June 1966), 284–89.
   Fitzgerald uses references to Poe and his work "to define the sense
in which beauty" is associated with evil (in the mind of Amory
Blaine).

T97   Tyrrel, Henry. "In the Ragged Mountains (near Charlottesville, Va.)," *UVaMag,* LX (Dec. 1899), 152–53.
   Verse.

U

U1   Ulmann, Albert. "Edgar Allan Poe." *New Yorkers, from
Stuyvesant to Roosevelt.* New York: Chaucer Head Bookshop, 1928,
pp. 213–31.
   Poe's life in New York along with a brief account of Poe memorials
erected in the New York area.

U2   Untermeyer, Louis. "Foreword." *Selected Stories of Edgar Allan
Poe.* New York: Armed Services Editions, 1944, pp. [1–2].
   Poe "balanced his wild fantasies with studies of cool analysis."

U3   ——. " 'Weary, Way-worn Wanderer.' " *Paths of Poetry:
Twenty-five Poets and Their Poetry.* New York: Delacorte Press, 1966,
pp. 180–87.
   Emphasizes Poe's inventive craftsmanship in fiction and the biographical features of his poetry.

U4   ——, ed. *The Complete Poems of Edgar Allan Poe.* With com-
mentary. New York: Heritage Press, 1943.
   "The necessary note of suggestion" is Poe's chief contribution to
American poetry. See "Introduction," pp. ix–xviii.

V

V1   Valéry, Paul. "On Poe's 'Eureka.'" *Variety.* Trans. Malcolm Cowley. New York: Harcourt, Brace, 1927, pp. 123–46.

Poe builds in *Eureka* an abstract poem, a total explanation of the material and spiritual universe, a *cosmogony.* (A good text of the original essay has been published by the Libraire Gallimard of Paris.) Translation also appears in Eric Carlson, ed., *The Recognition of Edgar Allan Poe* (Ann Arbor: University of Michigan Press, 1966), pp. 103–10.

V2   Van Cleef, Augustus. "Poe's Mary." *Harper's Monthly,* LXXVIII (March 1889), 634–40.

Discusses Poe's relationship with Mary Devereaux.

V3   Van Doren, Carl. "Introduction." *Tales,* by Edgar Allan Poe. New York: Literary Guild of America, 1933, pp. i–iv.

For one particular form of short fiction, "Poe is still what Homer is for the epic."

V4   Van Dyke, Henry. "Edgar Allan Poe." *RdP,* XVI (March 15, 1909), 349–63.

V5   ——. "Lesser Comet." *The Man behind the Book: Essays in Understanding.* New York: Charles Scribner's Sons, 1929, pp. 29–55.

Poe is a "broken dreamer" who in America is considered only as "an incomparable carver of grotesques and arabesques in ivory and ebony."

V6   Van Every, Edward. *Sins of New York as Exposed by the Police Gazette.* New York: Frederick A. Stokes, 1930.

See pp. 95–104 for discussion of Mary Rogers.

V7   Van Nostrand, Albert D. "Introduction." *Literary Criticism in America.* Ed. Van Nostrand. New York: Liberal Arts Press, 1957, pp. vii–xviii.

Poe is mentioned in a survey of American criticism.

****V8**   Varnado, Seaborn Lowrey. *The Numinous in the Work of Edgar Allan Poe.* Ann Arbor, Mich.: University Microfilms, 1965.

V9   ——. "The Numinous in the Work of Edgar Allan Poe." *DA,* XXVI (Jan. 1966), 3364–65.

Poe's use of the preternatural can be appreciated in light of the concepts of religious experience expressed in Rudolf Otto's *The Idea of the Holy.*

*V10   ———. "The Numinous in the Work of Edgar Allan Poe."
Diss., Fordham University, 1965.

V11   Varner, Cornelia. "Notes on Poe's Use of Contemporary Materials in Certain of His Stories." *JEGP*, XXXII (Jan. 1933), 77–80.
   Poe's interest in contemporary fashions and events is clearly reflected
   in at least half of his stories.

V12   Varner, John Grier. "Introduction." *Edgar Allan Poe and the
Philadelphia* Saturday Courier. Charlottesville: University of Virginia,
Extension Division, 1933, pp. iii–ix.
   Explains the significance of the Philadelphia *Saturday Courier* ver-
   sions of Poe's stories. Facsimile reproductions of the first texts of
   Poe's earliest tales and "Raising the Wind" appear in this text.
      Reviewed:
   D. K. Jackson, *AL,* VI, 232–33.
   Vincent O'Sullivan, *DM,* IX (July–Sept. 1934), 58.
   J. Jackson, *PMHB,* LIX, 189–90.

V13   ———. "Note on a Poem Attributed to Poe." *AL,* VIII (March
1936), 66–68.
   The "Impromptu: to Kate Carol," published in the *Broadway Journal,* April 26, 1845, and attributed to Poe, was written by Mrs.
   Frances S. Osgood.

V14   ———. "Poe and Miss Barrett." *TLS,* April 11, 1935, p. 244.
   Miss Barrett's letter to John Kenyon which touches upon Poe's collected volume of works should be dated 1846 rather than 1845.

V15   ———. "Poe and Miss Barrett of Wimpole Street." *Four Arts*
(Richmond), II (Jan.–Feb. 1935), 4–5, 14–15, 17.
   An account of Poe's relation with the Brownings.

V16   ———. "Poe's *Tale of Jerusalem* and *The Talmud." ABC,* VI
(Feb. 1935), 56–57.
   Points out that the source of Poe's tale is not merely Horace Smith's
   Zillah, a Tale of Jerusalem, but that *The Talmud* furnishes the
   anecdote.

V17   ———. "Sarah Helen Whitman: Seeress of Providence." Diss.,
University of Virginia, 1941.
   See especially pp. 266–349 for a discussion of the relationship be-
   tween Poe and Mrs. Whitman.

V18   Vaughan, Joseph Lee. "The Literary Opinions of Edgar Allan
Poe." Diss., University of Virginia, 1940.
   Summarizes Poe's literary opinions.

V19   "Viater." "Byron and Poe." *UVaMag,* I (June 1857), 241–48.
   A comparison of the two poets.

V20   Victor, O. J. "Some Words of Some Authors and Critics." *Ladies' Repository,* XVII (June 1857), 334–36.
Argues that Poe emphasizes poetic method and "startling" themes.

V21   Vierra, Clifford C. "Poe's 'Oblong Box': Factual Origins." *MLN,* LXXIV (Dec. 1959), 693–95.
Events of Poe's story parallel the facts of a well-known New York murder committed in 1841.

V22   Viett, George F. "Edgar Allan Poe: A Lamentation." *Galaxy* (Norfolk, Va.), II (Jan. 1908 [*i.e.,* 1909]), 6.
Verse.

V23   Vincent, H. P. "A Sarah Helen Whitman Letter about Edgar Allan Poe." *AL,* XIII (May 1941), 162–67.
Mrs. Whitman writes to Griswold concerning her break with Poe.

V24   Vincent, Leon Henry. "Edgar Allan Poe." *American Literary Masters.* Boston: Houghton, Mifflin, 1906, pp. 189–218.
Poe had a strong and somber genius, and he relieved American literature from "any danger of uniformity" or colorlessness.

V25   Virtanen, Reino. "The Irradiations of *Eureka:* Valéry's Reflections on Poe's Cosmology." *TSL,* VII (1962), 17–25.
Valéry viewed *Eureka* "as a demonstration of the inherent naïveté of cosmologies, which only artistic form can redeem."

V26   Vivanti, Giorgina. "Edgar Allan Poe (1809–1849)." Turin: G. B. Paravia, 1955, pp. v–xi.
"Poe's existence was one long obscure tragedy."

V27   Voigt, G. P. "Timrod's Essays in Literary Criticism." *AL,* VI (May 1934), 163–67.
Timrod argued that Poe's definition of poetry was too narrow; see pp. 164–65.

W

W1   W., C. "Edgar Allan Poe." Bristol, Eng., *Times and Mirror,* Feb. 1, 1909, p. 4.

W2   W., C. E. "Poeana." *ABC,* II (Dec. 1932), 348–52.
Some corrections to Part II of the Heartman-Rede checklist.

W3   W., D. *"Tales of Mystery, and Poems.* By Edgar Allan Poe." *Canadian Jour,* NS II (Jan. 1857), 103–9.

Reviewer analyzes passages from "Lenore," "The Bells," and "The Raven."

W4   W., G. E. [Woodberry, George E.]. "Memoir." *The Works of Edgar Allan Poe.* Ed. Edmund Clarence Stedman and Woodberry. 10 vols. Chicago: Stone and Kimball, 1894–95, I, 3–87.
  Concentrates on fact and testimony of Poe's contemporaries.
  Reviewed:
  Critic, XXVI (May 4, 1895), 323–24.
  Richmond *Dispatch,* Feb. 10, 1895, p. 2.
  Nation, LX (May 2, 1895), 349.
  Athenaeum, No. 3556 (Dec. 21, 1895), pp. 865–66.
  Athenaeum, No. 3570 (March 28, 1896), pp. 406–7.
  Poet-Lore, VII, 519.

W5   W., J. T. "A Friend of Poe." *SatRL,* X (Sept. 23, 1933), 138.
  Commentary on Mayne Reid's memoir on Poe.

W5a   W., N. P. [Willis, Nathaniel Parker]. "Letter about Poe." *Home Jour,* No. 664 (Oct. 30, 1858), p. [2].
  Commends Poe's character.

W6   W., S. H. [Whitman, Sarah Helen.] "Poe, Critic, and Hobby: A Reply to Mr. Fairfield." New York *Tribune,* Oct. 13, 1875, p. 2.
  Concerns Mr. Fairfield's pronouncement that Poe had an epileptic type of personality.

W7   Wagenknecht, Edward Charles. *Edgar Allan Poe: The Man behind the Legend.* New York: Oxford University Press, 1963.
  Poe's character and personality are analyzed in terms of ascertainable evidence.
  Reviewed:
  VQR, XL (1964), xxvi.
  Mooney, *SSF,* I, 237–40.
  Moss, *ABC,* XIV, 3.
  Spiller, *SatR,* XLVI (Nov. 9, 1963), 50–51.
  Economist, CCIX (Nov. 30, 1963), 930.
  London *Times,* Feb. 20, 1964, p. 17.
  Asselineau, *EA,* XVIII, 97–98.
  Falk, *NCF,* XIX, 97–99.
  Ferguson, *NYTBR,* Oct. 6, 1963, p. 26.
  Fuson, *Lib Jour,* LXXXVIII (Oct. 15, 1963), 3847.
  Harding, Chicago *Sunday Tribune Mag of Books,* Oct. 6, 1963, p. 2.
  Hook, *MLR,* LIX, 649–50.
  Howe, *America,* CX (Jan. 25, 1964), 145–46.
  Jacobs, *ELN,* II, 69–71.

W8   ——. *Longfellow: A Full-Length Portrait*. New York: Longmans, Green, 1955.
   Comments on Poe's criticism of Longfellow, *passim*.

W9   Walcutt, Charles Child. "The Logic of Poe." *CE,* II (Feb.
1941), 438–44.
   Criticism about Poe has gone too far in "establishing him as a
   normal, sensitive *highly rational* man of his time."

W10   Walker, I. M. "The 'Legitimate Sources' of Terror in 'The
Fall of the House of Usher.' " *MLR,* LXI (Oct. 1966), 585–92.
   Poe explores "mental derangement" rather than presenting an "elab-
   orate Gothic horror story."

*W11   ——. "A Study of Edgar Allan Poe." Diss., University of
Nottingham, 1962–63.

W12   Walker, Warren S. "Poe's 'To Helen.' " *MLN,* LXXII (Nov.
1957), 491–92.
   A discussion of the classical symbols in Poe's poem.

W13   Wallace, Alfred Russel. *Edgar Allan Poe: A Series of Seven-
teen Letters concerning Poe's Scientific Erudition in Eureka and His
Authorship of Leonainie*. New York: Union Square Bookshop, 1930.
   Some letters addressed to Ernest Marriott, Esq., dealing chiefly with
   "Leonainie," James Whitcomb Riley's poem written in imitation of
   Poe.

W14   ——. "The 'Leonainie' Problem." *Fortnightly Rev,* NS No.
75 (April 1904), pp. 706–11.
   Discusses "Leonainie" as a hoax.

W15   ——. "An Unpublished Poem by Edgar Allan Poe." *Fortnightly Rev,* NS 75 (Feb. 1904), pp. 329–32.
   The text "Leonainie" is presented.

W16   Wallace, Horace Binney. *Literary Criticism and Other Papers*.
Philadelphia: Parry and McMillan, 1856.
   Poe has talent in poetry, fiction, and criticism, but is weak in literary
   content; see pp. 37–38.

W17   Wallace, Irving. "The Real Marie Roget." *The Fabulous
Originals*. New York: A. A. Knopf, 1956, pp. 172–215.
   Assumes Poe knew Mary Rogers personally.

W18   Wallace, R. W. "Edgar Allan Poe, Poet, Romancer, Critic."
Jour of Education, LXVIII (Dec. 1908), 680–81.

W19   Waller, R. D. "The Blessed Damozel." *MLR,* XXVI (April
1931), 129–41.
   See p. 130 for Poe's influence on Rossetti.

W20   Waller, W. F. "Poe's 'Murders in the Rue Morgue.' " *N&Q*, LXXXIX (May 12, 1894), 366.

Finds a parallel use of an ourang-outang for robbery or murder in a report in the "Annual Register" of the *Shrewsberry Chronicle* for 1834.

W21   Walling, George W. *Recollections of a New Chief of Police.* New York: Caxton Book Concern, 1887.

Commentary on the murder of Mary Rogers, pp. 26–29.

W22   Wallis, J. B. "Poe, Tennyson, Wordsworth." *Academy*, LXIX (Nov. 25, 1905), 1181.

W23   ——. [A Reply to Ingram.] *Academy*, LXIX (Nov. 25, 1905), 1234–35.

Upholds attack on Poe's concept of poetry.

W24   Walsh, John. *Poe the Detective: The Circumstances behind the Mystery of Marie Rogêt.* New Brunswick, N.J.: Rutgers University Press, 1967.

According to Professor Thomas O. Mabbott in his "Introduction" (pp. 1–3), "this [book] is a detective story about a detective story."

W25   Walsh, Thomas. "Julio Herrera y Ressig, A Disciple of Edgar Allan Poe." *Poet-Lore*, XXXIII (Dec. 1922), 601–7.

Julio Herrera y Ressig "not only strives to embody Poe's phrasing and tonalities, but also quotes whole passages from his imaginative poems as some Holy Scripture."

W26   [Walsh, William S.] "Edgar Allan Poe." *Pen Pictures of Victorian Authors.* Ed. William Shepard [pseud.]. New York: G. P. Putnam's Sons, 1884, pp. 240–78.

Reprints T. W. Gibson's "Poe at West Point" from *Harper's Mag* and Mrs. Susan A. T. Weiss's "Reminiscences of the Last Days of Poe" originally appearing in *Scribner's Monthly.*

W27   [Walter, Cornelia.] [Criticism on Poe as Lecturer.] Boston *Daily Evening Transcript*, Oct. 28, 1845, p. 2.

Brief comments on Poe's lecture in Boston.

W28   Walters, J. Cuming. "Dickens's Own Story." *British Weekly*, LXXV (Dec. 13, 1923), p. 274.

Touches briefly on Poe's critique on *Barnaby Rudge.*

W29   Ward, Alfred C. "Edgar Allan Poe: 'Tales of Mystery and Imagination.' " *Aspects of the Modern Short Story: English and American.* London: University of London Press, 1924, pp. 32–44.

Poe as a pioneer in the development of modern short story.

W30   Warfel, Harry R. "The Mathematics of Poe's Poetry." *CEA*, XXI (May 1959), 1, 5–6.

Poe's application of acoustical and mathematical principles to the art of poetry reflects his deep scholarship and explains his ability to compose poems that will endure.

W31 ———. "Poe's Dr. Percival: A Note on *The Fall of the House of Usher.*" *MLN,* LIV (Feb. 1939), 129–31.

Identifies Poe's "Dr. Percival" as Dr. Thomas Percival (1740–1804), English physician and author.

*W32 Wasserstrom, William. "The Spirit of Myrrha." *AI,* XIII (Winter 1956), 455–72.

"On father-daughter relationships in literature, with reference chiefly by Poe, Hawthorne, and authors of the genteel tradition." *AL.*

W33 Waterman, Arthur E. "Point of View in Poe." *CEA,* XXVII, No. 4 (Jan. 1965), 5.

Poe directs irony against Montresor in "The Cask of Amontillado."

W34 Watkins, Mildred Cabell. *American Literature.* New York: American Book Co., 1894.

Finds "no lesson in anything he gave us" for alas! "his own sad story is a moral lesson"; see pp. 56–61.

W35 Watkins, Walter K. "Letters to the Editor: The Birthplace of Edgar A. Poe." Boston *Evening Transcript,* Jan. 30, 1924, Part II, p. 3.

W36 ———. "Where Poe Was Born." *UVaAB,* 3rd ser., II (April 1909), 189–93.

Poe was born in a house on Carver Street, Boston, Mass. First appeared in Boston *Times,* Jan. 13, 1909.

W37 Watts, Charles H., Jr. "Poe, Irving, and the *Southern Literary Messenger.*" *AL,* XXVII (May 1955), 249–51.

Relates circumstances surrounding the writing of an unpublished letter from Poe to Irving.

W38 ———. *Thomas Holly Chivers: His Literary Career and His Poetry.* Athens: University of Georgia Press, 1956.

Chapter 3, "Poe and Chivers," pp. 138–68, deals with the literary affinity between Poe and Chivers, and the investigation concludes that Poe made use of Chivers's poetry and "adapted the material to his own genius."

*W39 ———. "Washington Irving and E. A. Poe." *BBr.* XVIII (May 1956), 10–13.

W40 Watts[-Dunton], Theodore. "Edgar Poe." *Athenaeum,* No. 2549 (Sept. 2, 1876), p. 306.

Believes "The Iron Shroud" by "Mr. Mudford" in *Blackwood's* suggested material to Poe for "The Pit and the Pendulum." A Scottish story "Allan Gordon," Coleridge's "Ancient Mariner," and "The

Lonely Man of the Ocean" from the *Monthly Mag* gave source material for *Pym*.

W41   Waylen, Hector. "Was It Edgar Allen [*sic*] Poe?" *Light: A Jour of Spiritualism*, LV (Dec. 26, 1935), 827, 830–31.

A resurrection of Lizzie Doten's poems from obscurity.

W42   Wayne, John L. "Journalistic Adventures of Edgar Allan Poe." *Hobbies*, XLV (Sept. 1940), 116–17.

W43   Webb, Howard W., Jr. "Contributions to Poe's 'Penn Magazine.'" *N&Q*, CCIII (Oct. 1958), 447–48.

Poe failed in his initial intention to secure the best contributions.

W44   ——. "A Further Note on the Dickens-Poe Relationship." *NCF*, XV (June 1960), 80–82.

W45   Weber, Jean-Paul. "Edgar Poe or the Theme of the Clock." *Poe: A Collection of Critical Essays*. Ed. Robert Regan. Englewood Cliffs, N.J.: Prentice-Hall, 1967, pp. 79–97.

Poe's use of the "clock" image. Translated by Claude Richard and Robert Regan from *Nouvelle Rev Française*, LXVIII and LXIX (Aug., Sept. 1958), 301–11, 498–508.

W46   Wegelin, Oscar. "Poe's First Printer [Calvin F. S. Thomas]." *American Collector*, III (Oct. 1926), 31.

W47   ——. "The Printer of Poe's *Tamerlane*." *NYHSQB*, XXIV (Jan. 1940), 23–25.

A biographical sketch of Calvin F. S. Thomas.

W48   Weidemeyer, William. "Edgar A. Poe and His Poetry." *Phrenological Jour*, NS XXII (Sept. 1880), 132–40.

"Poe represents more of the wizard than seer; has more of manner than matter; is more ingenuous than emotional; more mystic than philosophic; more amatory than heroic."

W49   Weiss, Miriam. "Poe's Catterina." *MissQ*, XIX (Winter 1965–66), 29–33.

Poe's cats are "generally cats, not sex symbols, love objects, mother figures, or anything else."

W50   Weiss, Mrs. Susan Archer. "Edgar A. Poe." New York *Herald*, April 26, 1876, p. 4.

On the circumstances of Poe's death.

W51   ——. *The Home Life of Poe*. New York: Broadway Publishing, 1907.

Poe's "private home-life, domestic and social."

W52   ——. "Last Days of Edgar A. Poe." *Scribner's Monthly*, XV (March 1878), 707–16.

Finds Poe "pre-eminently a gentleman."

W53 ———. "Reminiscences of Poe." *Independent,* LVI and LVII (May 5 and Aug. 25, 1904), 1010–14, 443–48.

Comments on Harrison's biography.

W54 ———. "The Sister of Edgar Allan Poe." *Continent,* III (June 27, 1883), 816–19.

Concerning Rosalie Poe.

W55 Weissbuch, Ted N. "Edgar Allan Poe: Hoaxer in the American Tradition." *NYHSQ,* XLV (July 1961), 291–309.

Discusses the backgrounds of Poe's hoaxes such as Negro legends and tales of explorations.

W56 Wellek, René, and Austin Warren. *Theory of Literature.* New York: Harcourt Brace, 1956.

Poe is mentioned frequently.

W57 Wells, Gabriel. "Poe as a Mystic." *ABC,* V (Feb. 1934), 54–55.

"Poe was a profound thinker, as well as a consummate artist."

W58 Wells, Henry W. "Discoveries in Imagination." *The American Way of Poetry.* New York: Columbia University Press, 1943, pp. 19–28.

Along with Whitman, Dickinson, Poe is one of America's best poets of the nineteenth century, a poet who achieved artistry by exploring new avenues of verse cadence and symbolism.

W59 Wells, Ross. "College 'Lit' First to Recognize Poe." Richmond *Times-Dispatch,* Oct. 6, 1935, sec. V., p. 3.

On Sept. 9, 1836, Poe, aged 27, was elected an honorary member of the Franklin Literary Society of Washington and Jefferson College.

W60 Wendell, Barrett. *A Literary History of America.* New York: Scribner's, 1901.

Has only praise for the man who now seems "quite as important as any" of his contemporaries; see pp. 204–18.

W61 ———. "The Nationalism of Poe." *The Book of the Poe Centenary.* Ed. Charles W. Kent and John S. Patton. Charlottesville, Va.: Michie, 1909, pp. 117–58.

"Among the enduring writers of Nineteenth Century America Poe stands unique." Reprinted as "Edgar Allan Poe" in Wendell's *The Mystery of Education* (New York: Charles Scribner's Sons, 1909), pp. 197–254. Extracts from this address were printed in the *UVaAB,* 3rd ser., II (April 1909), 140–51.

W62 ———. *Stelligeri and Other Essays concerning Americans.* New York: Scribner's, 1893.

Compares Hawthorne and Poe; see pp. 138–40.

W63   Werner, William L. "Poe's *Israfel.*" *Expl,* II (April 1944), item 44.

"'Israfel' follows Poe's usual theory and practice with respect to stanzaic irregularities. After the age of twenty, Poe wrote only one poem in regular stanzas, 'The Raven.'" *AL.*

W64   ———. "Poe's Theories and Practice in Poetic Technique." *AL,* II (May 1930), 157–65.

Discusses Poe's use of sounds, meter, vocabulary, and stanza forms.

W65   Wertenbaker, William. "Edgar A. Poe." *UVaMag,* VII (Nov.–Dec. 1868), 114–17; XLIX (Jan. 1887), 226–29.

Of Poe and his year at the University.

W66   West, Muriel. "Poe's 'Ligeia.'" *Expl,* XXII (Sept. 1963), item 15.

Tale is a metaphorical representation of Poe's efforts to compose something more than a Gothic horror story.

W67   ———. "Poe's 'Ligeia' and Isaac D'Israeli." *CL,* XVI (Winter 1964), 19–28.

Poe's character of Ligeia can be understood in the light of D'Israeli's novel *Mejnoun and Leila.*

W68   Weston, Arthur Harold. "The 'Nicean Barks' of Edgar Allan Poe." *CJ,* XXIX (Dec. 1933), 213–15.

Declares that "Nicean" is from Nicaea, a name which Poe probably got from Catullus.

W69   Wetherill, P. M. "Edgar Allan Poe and Madame Sabatier." *MLQ,* XX (Dec. 1959), 344–59.

"Poe's influence on Baudelaire's Sabatier cycle of poems." *AL.*

W70   Wetzel, George. "The Source of Poe's 'The Man That Was Used Up.'" *N&Q,* CXCVIII (Jan. 1953), 38.

"Suggests that the source of 'The Man That Was Used Up' is in Chapter III of LeSage's *The Devil upon Two Sticks.*" *AL.*

W71   Wharey, J. B. "Edgar Allan Poe." *Christian Advocate* (Nashville), LXX (Jan. 15, 1909), 6–7.

Poe's short stories are his grestest achievement.

W72   Whelpley, Philip B. "Reminiscences of Poe." *SatRL,* X (Dec. 9, 1933), 322.

Discusses Poe's reciting "The Raven" and his drinking habit attributed to a physical malady.

W73   Whibley, Charles. "Edgar Allan Poe." *New Rev,* XIV (Jan. 1896), 612–25.

Reviews the Stedman-Woodberry edition of the *Works* and emphasizes Poe's mastery of construction and weakness of style.

W74 ——. "Edgar Allan Poe." *Studies in Frankness*. London: Constable, 1910, pp. 161–85.
Poe was a "multiform genius" whose "posthumous fame has been a very conflict of opposites."

W75 Whipple, William. "Poe, Clark, and 'Thingum Bob.'" *AL*, XXIX (Nov. 1957), 312–16.
"In 'The Literary Life of Thingum Bob, Esq.' Poe strikes at Lewis Clark through his deceased twin brother, Willis, who is 'Thingum Bob.'" *AL*.

W76 ——. "Poe's Political Satire." *UTSE*, No. 35 (1956), pp. 81–95.
Poe was consistent in developing his satire of political foibles and ills, culminating in the burlesque "The Man That Was Used Up."

W77 ——. "Poe's Two-edged Satiric Tale." *NCF*, IX (Sept. 1954), 121–33.
Poe's "The System of Dr. Tarr and Prof. Fether" evidences two levels of satire: "The satire of the moral treatment which was a matter of contention at the time, and the more covert satire upon Dickens."

W78 ——. "A Study of Edgar Allan Poe's Satiric Patterns." Diss., Northwestern University, 1951.

W79 ——. "A Study of Edgar Allan Poe's Satiric Patterns." *Northwestern University Summaries of Doctoral Dissertations*, XIX (1951), 50–54.
Poe's genius was not suited for satire.

W80 White, Morton G., and Lucia White. "Bad Dreams of the City: Melville, Hawthorne, and Poe." *The Intellectual versus the City from Thomas Jefferson to Frank Lloyd Wright*. Cambridge, Mass.: Harvard University Press, 1962, pp. 36–53.
Poe did not share "Jefferson's optimism about the possible worth of the American city"; see especially pp. 46–53.

W81 White, William. "Edgar Allan Poe: Magazine Journalist." *Journalism Quarterly*, XXXVIII (Spring 1961), 196–202.
An account of Poe's activities as a journalist.

W82 Whiteside, Mary B. "Israfel." *Muse Anthology of Modern Poetry*. Ed. Dorothy Kissling and Arthur H. Nethercot. Poe Memorial Edition. New York: Carlyle Straub, 1938, p. 183.
Verse.

W83 ——. "Poe and Dickinson." *Person*, XV (Autumn 1934), 315–26.
Both Poe and Dickinson achieve a similar effect in their poetry. Re-

printed in *Muse Anthology of Modern Poetry,* ed. Dorothy Kissling and Arthur H. Nethercot, Poe Memorial Volume (New York: Carlyle Straub, 1938), pp. 17–28.

W84   Whiting, Mary Bradford. "The Life-Story of Edgar Allan Poe." *Bookman* (London), XXV (Jan. 1909), 173–81.

Places Poe high in influence "over most of the world's great short story writers, those of France and England and Germany in particular."

W85   Whitman, Sarah Helen. *Edgar Poe and His Critics.* New York: Rudd and Carleton, 1860.

Defends Poe's life and briefly compares him to other writers of his day.

Reviewed:

SLM, XXX, 237.

Knickerbocker, LX, 429, 450.

W86   ———. *Edgar Poe and His Critics.* Ed. and introd. Oral S. Coad. New Brunswick, N.J.: Rutgers University Press, 1949.

Editor includes a lengthy introduction (18 pages) to this late reprinting of the 1860 edition of Mrs. Whitman's defense of Poe.

W87   ———. *Was Poe Immoral?* Girard, Kans.: Haldeman-Julius Co., n.d.

Reprint of the first edition of *Edgar Poe and His Critics.*

W88   Whitman, Walt. "Edgar Poe's Significance." *American Literary Essays.* Ed. Lewis G. Leary. New York: Thomas Y. Crowell, 1960, pp. 88–90.

Contains excerpts from Poe's criticism and Whitman's critical commentary on Poe.

W89   ———. "Edgar Poe's Significance." *Specimen Days & Collect.* Philadelphia: Rees Welsh, 1882–83, pp. 156–58.

"Almost without the first sign of moral principle . . . Poe's verses illustrate an intense faculty for technical and abstract beauty." Appears also in *The Critic,* II (June 3, 1882), 147, and in *Rivulets of Prose: Critical Essays by Walt Whitman,* ed. Carolyn Wells and Alfred E. Goldsmith (New York: Greenberg, 1928), pp. 39–44; and in Eric Carlson, ed., *The Recognition of Edgar Allan Poe* (Ann Arbor: University of Michigan Press, 1966), pp. 73–76.

W90   Whitt, Celia. "Poe and *The Mysteries of Udolpho.*" *UTSE,* No. 17 (1937), pp. 124–31.

Specific borrowings are found in Poe's "The Assignation."

W91   Whitty, James Howard. "Annabel Lee and Rosalie Lee." New York *Times,* May 11, 1913, p. 287.

Answers Maximus A. Lesser's "'Annabel Lee' and 'Rosalie Lee,'" by declaring that Chivers took "Rosalie Lee," not from Poe's sister, but from a poem by P. P. Cook [*sic*].

W92 ———. "The Anonymity of the 'Raven.'" *Nation*, CII (April 27, 1916), 455.

W93 ———. "The Ballad 'Mrs. Poe.'" *ABC*, III (May–June 1933), 339.
The bibliography of this ballad is given.

W94 ———. "Book Notes and Byways." New York *Nation*, Jan. 27, 1916, n. pag.
On discoveries "of late years after several reinvestigations among the Griswold Poe collection."

W95 ———. "The Case of Poe." *TLS*, July 26, 1923, p. 397.
Comments on Robertson's *Edgar A. Poe: A Psychopathic Study* (1923).

W96 ———. "Did Poe Solve the Plot of *Barnaby Rudge?*" New York *Times*, May 11, 1913, p. 287.
Answers W. G. Wilkins's "Poe and *Barnaby Rudge*" by stating that the only known copy of the *Post* criticism, that of the Griswold collection, has been misplaced.

W97 ———. "Discoveries in the Uncollected Poems of Edgar Allan Poe." *Nation*, CII (Jan. 27, 1916), 105–6.
The "latest" MS is "Life's Vital Stream"; other poems printed here are "The Divine Right of Kings" and "Stanzas," both published originally in *Graham's*.

W98 ———. "Edgar Allan Poe in England and Scotland." *Bookman*, XLIV (Sept. 1916), 14–21.
A biographical account of the years 1815 and following.

W99 ———. "First and Last Publication of Poe's Raven." *PW*, CXXX (Oct. 17, 1936), p. 1635.

W100 ———. "Foreword." *Poe and the Southern Literary Messenger.* Richmond: Dietz, 1934, pp. v–ix.

W101 ———. "Israfel." *SatRL*, III (Feb. 26, 1927), 618.
A letter to the editor on Hervey Allen's biography *Israfel: The Life and Times of E. A. Poe.*

W102 ———. "Manuscript of Poe Found in Home of Old Publisher." Richmond *Times-Dispatch*, March 23, 1924, City Life sec., p. 10.
MS of "Thou Art the Man" found in family belongings of L. A. Godey.

W103 ———. "Memoir." *The Complete Poems of Edgar Allan Poe.* Boston: Houghton Mifflin, 1911, pp. xix–lxxxvi.

An account of Poe's life, summarizing previous scholarship. See also
"Preface," pp. vii–xi.
Reviewed:
Nation, XCII (June 22, 1911), 628–29.
Killis Campbell, *Dial*, LI (July 1, 1911), 13–14.
Robert Lynd, *New Statesman*, XVIII (March 25, 1922), 704–6.
Reprinted in Lynd's *Books and Authors* (New York: G. P. Putnam's
Sons, 1923), pp. 131–39.

W104 ——. "New Letters about Poe's Early Life." Richmond
Times-Dispatch, May 12, 1912, p. 14.
Some letters from the Ellis-Allan papers.

W105 ——. "A New Poe Letter: Hitherto Unpublished Note Deals
with Strange Cryptogram." Richmond *Times-Dispatch*, July 21, 1935,
sec. 5, p. 15.
A letter to Charles G. Percival.

W106 ——. "New Poe Poem and Manuscripts Found in Richmond
Firm's Papers." Richmond *News-Leader*, Dec. 18, 1915, p. 5.

W107 ——. "New Poe Poems and Manuscripts Found." Baltimore
American, Nov. 21, 1915, sec. C, p. 24.

W108 ——. "A Newly Discovered Portrait of Edgar Allan Poe."
Literary Digest International Book Rev, I (Oct. 1923), 47.
The Brady daguerrotype (?) discovered among John P. Kennedy's
papers.

W109 ——. "News for Bibliophiles." *Nation*, XCV (July 18,
1912), 55.
Letters touching the early life of Poe housed in the Library of Congress.

W110 ——. "A Parrot." *Colophon*, NS I (Autumn 1935), 188–90.
Comments on Poe's poem "Romance."

W111 ——. "The Passing of Poe's English Biographer." *Dial*,
LXI (June 22, 1916), 15.
Calls attention to the death of Ingram.

W112 ——. "Poe and *Barnaby Rudge*." New York *Times*, May 18,
1913, p. 302.

W113 ——. "Poe and Sources." *Literary Rev* of the New York
Evening Post, Aug. 18, 1923, p. 918.
Argues that Poe did not draw heavily from Macaulay for descriptive
detail in "A Tale of the Ragged Mountains."

W114 ——. "The Poe Mystery." *Bookman*, XXXVI (Feb. 1913),
604.
Concerning "The Mystery of Marie Rogêt."

W115 ———. "The Poe Portrait." *Century Mag,* NS LXX (Aug. 1916), 635–36.

Thinks that the portrait submitted to this magazine by L. McG. Shepherd is not of Poe but of some member of another early Richmond family.

W116 ———. "Poeana." *Step Ladder,* XIII (Oct. 1927), 225–43.

Comments on various areas of interest relating to Poe's biography, canon, and reputation as writer.

*W117 ———. Poem to Mark Tomb of Mother." Richmond *Times Dispatch,* Oct. 6, 1935, p. 3.

W118 ———. "Poe's Relationship to Boswell." *Nation,* CVII (Aug. 21, 1918), 227–28.

"Boswell's wife . . . was a cousin of Poe's great-grandmother."

W119 ———. "Poe's Schoolmaster." *Nation,* CIII (Aug. 24, 1916), 176.

W120 ———. "Poe's Writing Influenced by Richmond Gardens." Richmond *News-Leader,* April 24, 1937, p. 13.

W121 ———. "Three Poems by Edgar Allan Poe." *Nation,* CVII (Dec. 7, 1918), 699–700.

A reprinting of three poems found in the Baltimore *Saturday Visiter.*

W122 Widener, Emory. "A Tale of the Ragged Mountains." *UVaMag,* LXIX (Jan. 1909), 216–20.

A short story about Poe.

W123 Wiener, Philip P. "Poe's Logic and Metaphysic." *Person,* XIV (Oct. 1933), 268–74.

Poe is a nonconformist, and although much he thought is not entirely true, no one can "deny the essential beauty of the vision he depicted."

W124 Wigmore, John H. "Did Poe Plagiarize 'The Murders in the Rue Morgue'?" *Cornell Law Quarterly,* XIII (Feb. 1928), pp. 219–36.

Points out parallels between Poe's story and an account of a case cited by Dr. Karl Loeffler, once editor of the Berlin *Judicial News.*

W125 Wilbur, Richard. "Edgar Allan Poe, 1809–1849." *Major Writers of America.* 2 vols. Ed. Perry Miller. New York: Harcourt, Brace & World, 1962, I, 369–82.

Poe's cosmic view can be defined as an effort to achieve disengagement from the material world.

W126 ———. "The House of Poe." *Anniversary Lectures 1959.* Washington, D.C.: Reference Department of the Library of Congress, 1959, pp. 21–38.

Poe's prose fiction is deliberate and often brilliant architectural allegory. Reprinted in Eric Carlson, ed., *The Recognition of Edgar Allan Poe* (Ann Arbor: University of Michigan Press, 1966), pp. 255–77 and in Robert Regan, ed., *Poe: A Collection of Essays.* Englewood Cliffs, N.J.: Prentice-Hall, 1969, pp. 98–120.

W127 ——. "The Poe Mystery Case." *NYRB,* XIII (July 13, 1967), 16, 25–28.

Briefly surveys criticism on Poe and stresses the pattern of "the wavering and confused journey" found in Poe's tales.

W128 ——, ed. *Poe: Complete Poems.* With introd. and notes. New York: Dell Publishing, 1959.

Poe sought for spiritual effect in his poetry by negating "all he could of world and worldy self." See "Introduction," pp. 7–39.

W129 Wiley, Margaret L. *Creative Sceptics.* London: Allen and Unwin, 1966.

References to Poe's *Eureka,* pp. 209, 255.

W130 Wilkins, William Clyde. "Poe and *Barnaby Rudge*." New York *Times,* May 18, 1913, p. 302.

Believes that Poe read the fifth chapter of Dickens's novel before writing his critique.

W131 ——. [Poe and *Barnaby Rudge.*] *NYTBR,* May 4, 1913, p. 270.

Asks for information about the Poe review of Dickens's novel.

W132 Wilkinson, Ronald S. "Poe's 'Balloon-Hoax' Once More." *AL,* XXXII (Nov. 1960), 313–17.

In addition to Monck Mason's *Account of the Late Aeronautical Expedition from London to Weilburg* (1837), author argues that Poe also used an anonymous pamphlet containing a description on Monck Mason's model dirigible exhibited in 1843 at the Royal Adelaide Gallery in London.

W133 ——. "Poe's 'Hans Pfaall' Reconsidered." *N&Q,* CCXI (Sept. 1966), 333–37.

"Pfaall" should be reexamined as parody with a lesson to teach authors in the "moon-voyage" genre.

W134 Williams, Blanche Colton. "Introduction." *Tales,* by Edgar Allan Poe. New York: Macmillan, 1928, pp. ix–xvii.

Categorizes and evaluates Poe's tales.

Reviewed:

AL, I, 462.

W135 Williams, H. Noel. "Introduction." *The Poems of Edgar Allan Poe.* London: G. Bell and Sons, 1901, pp. xv–xxxii.

Poe achieved technical artistry and confined himself to simple ballad forms. Reprint of 1900 edition.

W136 Williams, Henry L. "Memoir of Edgar Allan Poe." *Poems of Edgar Allan Poe.* New York: Hurst, 1882, pp. 11–51.

Primarily biographical with several errors.

W137 Williams, Marshall G. "Poe's Son: An Appreciation of Charles Baudelaire." *Virginia Spectator,* CII (May 1941), 6, 9.

Baudelaire's debt to Poe.

W138 Williams, Stanley T. "New Letters about Poe." *YR,* NS XIV (July 1925), 755–73.

Mrs. Whitman defends Poe in her letters to Mrs. Hewitt.

W139 ———. *The Spanish Background of American Literature.* 2 vols. New Haven: Yale University Press, 1955.

Poe is briefly discussed throughout the study.

W140 Williams, Valentine. "The Detective in Fiction." *Fortnightly Rev,* No. 128 (Sept. 1930), pp. 380–92.

All modern detective fiction "leads ultimately back to Poe."

W141 Williams, Willam Carlos. "Edgar Allan Poe." *In the American Grain.* New York: New Directions, 1956, pp. 216–33.

Attempts to explain the intent and originality of Poe's stories and verse. First appeared in 1925 and later reprinted in Eric Carlson, ed., *The Recognition of Edgar Allan Poe* (Ann Arbor: University of Michigan Press, 1966), 142–51.

W142 Willis, Eola. "The Dramatic Careers of Poe's Parents." *Bookman,* LXIV (Nov. 1926), 288–91.

An account of the dramatic appearances of Elizabeth and David Poe.

W143 Willis, Nathaniel Parker. "Death of Edgar A. Poe." *The Works of the Late Edgar Allan Poe,* by N. P. Willis, J. R. Lowell, and R. W. Griswold. 2 vols. New York: J. S. Redfield, 1850, I, xiv–xx.

Personal impressions of Poe's personality and character. Previously appeared in the *Home Journal,* Oct. 20, 1849. Often reprinted in collections of Poe's works. Also appears in Eric Carlson, ed., *The Recognition of Edgar Allan Poe* (Ann Arbor: University of Michigan Press, 1966), pp. 36–41.

W144 ———. "Edgar Poe." *Hurry-Graphs; or, Sketches of Scenery, Celebrities and Society, Taken from Life.* New York: Charles Scribner, 1851.

See pp. 240–50 for a reprinting of his article on the "Death of Edgar A. Poe."

W145 ———. [Editorial Note to the Printing of "For Annie."] *Home Jour,* No. 168 (April 28, 1849), p. [2].

Poe is a possessor of "that gift of nature, which an abstract man should be most proud of—a type of mind different from all others without being less truthful in its perceptions for that difference."

W146   ——. "Estimates of Poe." *Home Jour*, No. 216 (March 30, 1850), p. [2].
A reply to Daniel's article on Poe which is described as "a frightful caricature." Concerning that article Willis declares that "the indictment . . . is not true."

W147   ——. "Pen and I—At Idlewood." *Home Jour*, Feb. 4, 1865.
Quotes Mrs. F. S. Osgood's opinion of Poe.

W148   ——. [Preface to the Reprinting of "Ulalume."] *Home Jour*, No. 99 (Jan. 1, 1848), p. [4].
"Ulalume" is an "exquisitely piquant and skillful exercise of variety and niceness in language."

W149   [Rejection of "Fairyland" with Editorial Comment.] *American Monthly Mag*, I (Nov. 1829), 586–87.

W150   ——. [Remarks on "The Raven."] *Broadway Jour*, I (Feb. 8, 1845), 90.
Brief commentary; see also *New-York Mirror*, I (Feb. 8, 1845), 276.

W151   ——. "Tribute to Poe." *Home Jour*, Oct. 8, 1864.
Defends Poe's character and expresses an affection for him.

W152   [Wilmer, Lambert A.?] [Comment on Poe's Tales.] Baltimore *Saturday Visiter*, Aug. 4, 1832, p. 3.

W153   ——. *Merlin; Baltimore, 1827; Together with Recollections of Edgar A. Poe by Lambert Wilmer.* Ed. with an Introd. by Thomas Ollive Mabbott. New York: Scholars' Facsimiles and Reprints, 1941.
Merlin is reprinted from photostats of the original which appeared in three installments in the Baltimore *North American*, Aug. 18, 25, and Sept. 1, 1827, and the "Recollections" from a photostat of the original in the Baltimore *Daily Commercial*, I, No. 200 (May 23, 1866) p. 1, and from *Our Press Gang* (1860).

W154   ——. *Our Press Gang; or, A Complete Exposition of the Corruptions and the Crimes of the American Newspapers.* Philadelphia: J. T. Lloyd, 1860.
Denounces Griswold's "Ludwig" article; see p. 385.

W155   ——. "Recollections of Edgar A. Poe." Baltimore Daily *Commercial*, May 23, 1866, p. 1.

W156   Wilmer, Margaret E. "Another View of Edgar A. Poe." *Bealle's Monthly*, III (April 1867), 385–86.
Defends Poe's character.

W157 Wilson, Edmund. "Poe as a Literary Critic." *Nation,* CLV (Oct. 31, 1942), 452–53.

Critic argues that Poe's critical works have been largely underestimated.

W158 ——. "Poe at Home and Abroad." *New Republic,* XLIX (Dec. 8, 1926), 77–80.

Sees Poe as a "typical romantic" and believes that Poe's poetry is significant in the development of the symbolic movement. Reprinted in *The Shores of Light* (New York: Farrar, Straus and Young, 1952), pp. 179–90 and in Eric Carlson, ed., *The Recognition of Edgar Allan Poe* (Ann Arbor: University of Michigan Press, 1966), pp. 142–51.

W159 ——, ed. *The Shock of Recognition.* New York: Doubleday, Doran, 1943.

Contains essays on Poe by James Russell Lowell, D. H. Lawrence, and Walt Whitman. See pp. 5–20 for Lowell's famous essay published in *Graham's Magazine* in Feb. 1945.

W160 Wilson, James Grant. "Edgar A. Poe." *Bryant and His Friends.* New York: Fords, Howard and Hulbert, 1886, pp. 334–46.

Poe and his literary counterpart in the New York environs.

W161 ——. "Memorials of Edgar Allan Poe." *Independent,* LIII (April 25, 1901), 940–42.

A chopped-up article which lists some new Poe items which have come to light.

W162 Wilson, James Southall. "An Appreciation." *Tamerlane and Other Poems,* by Edgar Allan Poe. San Francisco: John Henry Nash, 1923, pp. xix–xxiv.

Poe is "the most undisputed master of pure poetry that America has produced."

W163 ——. "The Devil Was in It." *American Mercury,* XXIV (Oct. 1931), 215–20.

Finds that Poe's tales satirize authors popular in Poe's day, Bulwer, Scott, Lady Morgan, Horace Smith, and others, by a deliberate burlesque of their style.

W164 ——. "Dr. Wilson Reviews 'Politian.'" *Corks and Curls* (Univ. of Virginia), XLVI (1933), 351.

Concerning the University of Virginia Players' presentation of *Politian.*

W165 ——. "Edgar Allan Poe." *Virginia Historical Portraiture.* Richmond: William Byrd Press, 1930.

A sketch of Poe's life and of his relation to the state of Virginia; see pp. 403–40.

W166 ——. "Facts about Poe." *Facts about Poe: Portraits and Daguerrotypes of Edgar Allan Poe,* by Amada Pogue Schulte. Charlottesville: University of Virginia, 1926, pp. 7–22.

Gives "in small compass a statement of the chief authentic facts of Poe's life."

W167 ——. "Famous Picture of Poe Is Placed on Exhibition." New York *Times,* Oct. 8, 1933, sec. 10, p. 12x.

Portrait is purchased for the Poe Shrine in Richmond.

W168 ——. "Introduction." *Tales of Edgar Allan Poe.* Ed. Wilson. New York: Charles Scribner's Sons, 1927, pp. v–xxi.

Evaluates Poe's burlesques, emphasizes his appeal to the reader's emotions, and classifies the tales in four distinct groups.

W169 ——. "The Letters of Edgar A. Poe to George W. Eveleth." *UVaAB,* 3rd ser., XVII (Jan. 1924), 34–59.

Professor edits fourteen letters with introductory commentary.

W170 ——. "The Personality of Poe." *VMHB,* LXVII (April 1959), 131–42.

An analysis of Poe's personality reveals "more character and as much morality . . . as may be found in the quiet peace of many good men."

W171 ——. "Poe and the Biographers." *VQR,* III (April 1927), 313–20.

Reviews Allen's *Israfel* and comments on the efforts of other Poe biographers.

W172 ——. "Poe and the University of Virginia." *Corks and Curls* (Univ. of Virginia), XLII (1929), 213–16.

W173 ——. "Poe at the University of Virgina: Unpublished Letters from the Ingram Collection." *UVaAB,* 3rd ser., XVI (April 1923), 163–67.

Three letters containing reminiscences of Poe at the University.

W174 ——. "Poe's Only Play Wins Premiere at Age of 100." Richmond *Times-Dispatch,* Jan. 15, 1933, sec. 1, p. 7.

W175 ——. "Poe's Philosophy of Composition." *North American Rev,* CCXXIII (Dec. 1926), 675–84.

Discusses Poe's "totality of effect" and its origin from Schlegel.

W176 ——. "Unpublished Letters of Edgar Allan Poe." *Century Mag,* NS LXXXV (March 1924), 652–56.

Letters to Nathaniel Beverley Tucker.

W177 ——. "The Young Man Poe." *VQR,* II (April 1926), 238–53.

An examination of Poe's relations with John Allan, based largely on the Valentine letters.

W178   Wilson, Robert Burns. "Edgar Allan Poe." *UVaMag,* LX (Dec. 1899), 149–50.

The "memorial ode . . . read on the occasion of the unveiling of the bust of Edgar Allan Poe" in the University of Virginia Library, 1899.

W179   Wilson, Rufus Rockwell, *et al. New York in Literature. The Story Told in the Landmarks of Town and Country.* Elmira, N.Y.: Primavera Press, 1947.

Poe's relationship with the state of New York, *passim.*

W180   Wilt, Napier. "Poe's Attitude toward His Tales: A New Document." *MP,* XXV (Aug. 1927), 101–5.

In a letter to T. W. White, Poe admits his models have been magazine tales by Maginn, DeQuincey, and Bulwer.

W181   Wimsatt, William K., Jr. "A Further Note on Poe's 'Balloon Hoax.' " *AL,* XXII (Jan. 1951), 491–92.

"A Reproduction of the 'Postscript' inserted in the New York *Sun* of April 13, 1844, announcing the 'Extra' containing the original publication of the 'Balloon Hoax.' "

W182   ——. "Mary Rogers, John Anderson and Others." *AL,* XXI (Jan. 1950), 482–84.

Summary observations on the mysterious death of Mary Rogers.

W183   ——. "Poe and the Chess Automaton." *AL,* XI (May 1939), 138–51.

An assessment of Poe's essay "Maelzel's Chess-Player."

W184   ——. "Poe and the Mystery of Mary Rogers." *PMLA.* LVI (March 1941), 230–48.

Discusses newspaper accounts and other details associated with Poe's acquaintance with and use of the Mary Rogers episode.

W185   ——. "What Poe Knew about Cryptography." *PMLA,* LVIII (Sept. 1943), 754–79.

Poe's work on ciphers demonstrates that he had no "wide knowledge and intricate method of procedure, but rather a kind of untrained wit, an intuition which more quickly than accurately grasped the outlines of cryptic principle and immediately with confident imagination proclaimed the whole."

W186   ——, and Cleanth Brooks. *Literary Criticism: A Short History.* New York: A. Knopf, 1957.

See chap. 22 entitled "Art for Art's Sake" for Poe's role in the development of criticism.

W187   Winslow, Harriet B. "To the Author of 'The Raven.' " *Graham's,* XXXII (April 1848), 203.

Verse. Reprinted in Washington *Post,* Jan. 17, 1909, p. 6.

W188   Winter, William. *Old Friends: Being Literary Recollections of Other Days.* New York: Moffat, Yard, 1909.

On Longfellow and Poe; see pp. 33–38.

W189   ——. *The Poems of William Winter.* New York: Moffat, Yard and Co., 1909.

Poem composed for the dedication of the Westminster cemetery monument in Baltimore; see pp. 100–101.

W190   Winterich, John T. [A Note on Poe's Parents.] *PW,* CXVIII (June 21, 1930), 3041–42.

The Emerald (printed in Boston) comments on the acting of Poe's parents.

W191   ——. "Poe and His *Tales.*" *Books and the Man.* New York: Greenberg, 1929.

Some collector's anecdotes concerning Poe items; see pp. 251–65.

W192   Winters, A. Yvor. "Edgar Allan Poe: A Crisis in the History of American Obscurantism." *AL,* VIII (Jan. 1937), 379–401.

Views Poe as a poor artist whose exaggerated reputation is deluding scholars. Reprinted in Winters's *Maule's Curse: Seven Studies in the History of American Obscurantism.* (Norfolk: New Directions, 1938), pp. 93–122; in his *In Defense of Reason* (New York: Swallow Press and W. Morrow, 1947), pp. 234–61; and in Eric Carlson, ed., *The Recognition of Edgar Allan Poe* (Ann Arbor: University of Michigan Press, 1966), pp. 176–202.

W193   ——. "T. S. Eliot: The Illusion of Reaction." *KR,* III (Winter 1941), 7–30.

Included, pp. 10–11, are some comments on Poe's influence on Eliot.

W194   Winwar, Frances [pseud.]. *The Haunted Palace: A Life of Edgar Allan Poe.* New York: Harpers, 1959.

Contains very little criticism, but qualifies as a sentimentalized but interesting biography for the general reader.

Reviewed:

Newsweek, LIII (Jan. 19, 1959), 90–91.

Richard Beale Davis, *AL,* XXXI, 347–49.

W195   Wittlin, Joseph. "Poe in the Bronx." *Polish Rev,* IV (Winter–Spring 1959), 3–14.

Discusses the hardships of life in the Bronx in relationship to the hardships Poe suffered during the last years of his life.

W196   Wolf, Edwin, 2nd. "Horace Wemys Smith's Recollections of Poe." *LCUP,* XVII (Summer 1951), 90–103.

Hints about Poe's life in Philadelphia.

W197   Wolfe, Theodore F. "Homes and Haunts of Poe." *Literary*

Haunts and Homes. Philadelphia: J. B. Lippincott, 1898, pp. 104–28.
Describes Poe's dwellings, including his grave.

W198   Wood, Clement. "Edgar Allan Poe: Kubla in Hell." *Southern Mag,* I (March 1924), 47–50, 87–96.
Praises Poe's poetry and argues that Poe possessed a strong mother fixation. Appears in Wood's *Poets of America* (New York: Dutton, 1925), pp. 13–34.

W199   ———. "The Influence of Poe and Lanier on Modern Literature." *SLM,* I (April 1939), 237–42.
Emphasizes Poe and Lanier as "realists" and practitioners "in the main channel of literature."

W200   ———. "The Striken Eagle." *Muse Anthology of Modern Poetry.* Ed. Dorothy Kissling and Arthur H. Nethercot. Poe Memorial Edition. New York: Carlyle Straub, 1938, pp. 68–102.
Poe's works reflect his personal experiences and relationships.

W201   Wood, Playsted. [Biographical Sketch of Poe.] *One Hundred Years Ago.* New York: Funk and Wagnalls, 1947, pp. 395–98.

W202   Woodberry, George Edward. *America in Literature.* New York: Harper and Brothers, 1903.
Sees in Poe "a great expression of the Southern temperament in letters"; pp. 142–49. Reprinted in Woodberry's *Appreciation of Literature and America in Literature* (New York: Harcourt, Brace, 1921), pp. 198–201.

W203   ———. "E. A. P. (On the Fly-Leaf of Whitty's 'Poe')." *North American Rev,* CXLVIII (Sept. 1913), 352–53.
Verse. Reprinted in *Literary Digest,* XLVII (Sept. 20, 1913), 500–501 and in Woodberry's *The Flight and Other Poems* (New York: Macmillan, 1914), pp. 136–38.

W204   ———. *Edgar Allan Poe.* American Men of Letters Series. Boston: Houghton, Mifflin, 1885.
A fine documentary biography of Poe. Reprinted New York: AMS, 1968.
   Reviewed:
Critic, VI (Jan. 31, 1885), 50–51.
American Mag, IX (Feb. 14, 1885), 296.
Dial, V (March 1805), 303.
Atlantic Monthly, LV, 705–7.

W205   ———. *The Life of Edgar Allan Poe, Personal and Literary.* 2 vols. Boston: Houghton Mifflin, 1909.
An excellent literary biography touching upon contemporaneous literary history. Reprinted New York: Biblo and Tannen, 1965.

Reviewed:

Nation, LXXXIX (July 29, 1909), 100–101.

W206 ———. "Lowell's Letters to Poe." *Scribner's Mag*, XVI (Aug. 1894), 170–76.

Edits Lowell's letters to Poe and comments briefly on the significance of these letters.

W207 ———. "Notes." *The Works of Edgar Allan Poe*. Ed. Edmund Clarence Stedman and Woodberry. 10 vols. Chicago: Stone and Kimball, 1894–95, IV, 281–97.

Notes on the publication of Poe's tales, along with notes on Poe's quotations, book titles, footnotes, and sources.

W208 ———. "Notes." *The Works of Edgar Allan Poe*. Ed. Edmund Clarence Stedman and Woodberry. 10 vols. Chicago: Stone and Kimball, 1894–95, V, 355–60.

Notes on *Narrative of A. Gordon Pym* and *The Journal of Julius Rodman*.

W209 ———. "Notes." *The Works of Edgar Allan Poe*. Ed. Edmund Clarence Stedman and Woodberry. 10 vols. Chicago: Stone and Kimball, 1894–95, VII, 353–55.

Notes on Poe's novels, essays, and travels.

W210 ———. "Notes." *The Works of Edgar Allan Poe*. Ed. Edmund Clarence Stedman and Woodberry. 10 vols. Chicago: Stone and Kimball, 1894–95, IX, 293–317.

Notes on *Eureka* and some miscellaneous essays.

W211 ———. "Notes." *The Works of Edgar Allan Poe*. Ed. Edmund Clarence Stedman and Woodberry. 10 vols. Chicago: Stone and Kimball, 1894–95, X, 141–237.

Notes on Poe's poems. See also "Bibliography," pp. 267–81, signed "G. E. W."

W212 ———. "The Poe Centenary." *The Torch and Other Lectures and Addresses*. New York: Harcourt, Brace, and Howe, 1920, pp. 323–26.

An address before the Bronx Society of Arts and Sciences, New York, Jan. 19, 1909.

W213 ———. "The Poe-Chivers Papers." *Century Mag*, NS XLIII (Jan. and Feb. 1903), 435–47, 545–58.

Discusses the relations of the two poets and concludes that Chivers had little influence on Poe.

W214 ———. "Poe in New York: Selections from the Correspondence of Edgar Allan Poe." *Century Mag*, NS XXVI (Oct. 1894), 854–66.

Letters reveal Poe's friendship with several women.

W215 ——. "Poe in Philadelphia: Selections from the Correspondence of Edgar Allan Poe." *Century Mag,* NS XXVI (Sept. 1894), 725–37.
Letters reveal Poe's journalistic activities and ambitions.

W216 ——. "Poe in the South: Selections from the Correspondence of Edgar Allan Poe." *Century Mag,* NS XXVI (Aug. 1894), 572–83.
Evaluates Griswold as editor of Poe's works and presents the texts of correspondence once sent to Griswold.

W217 ——. "Poe's Legendary Years." *Atlantic Monthly,* LIV (Dec. 1884), 814–28.
Examines Poe's life 1827–34 and comments that Poe was his own myth-making biographer.

W218 Woodbridge, Bernard Mather. "The Supernatural in Hawthorne and Poe." *Colorado College Publications,* Language Series, II (Nov. 1911), 135–54.
Poe concentrates upon "color and passion and maddened horror."

W219 Woodress, James, ed. *American Literary Scholarship: An Annual, 1965.* Durham, N.C.: Duke University Press, 1967.
See pp. 142–49.

W220 Woods, William Hervey. "At the Grave of Poe." *Current Literature,* XLV (Dec. 1908), 690–91.

W221 Worthen, Samuel C. "Poe and the Beautiful Cigar Girl." *AL,* XX (Nov. 1948), 305–12.
On the backgrounds of Poe's "Mystery of Marie Rogêt."

W222 ——. "A Strange Aftermath of the Mystery of 'Marie Rogêt' (Mary Rogers)." *NJHSP,* LX (April 1942), 116–23.
More facts relevant to the murder of Mary Rogers.

W223 Wright, Henrietta C. "Edgar Allan Poe." *Children's Stories in American Literature, 1660–1860.* New York: Charles Scribner's Sons, 1895, pp. 137–48.
Sketches Poe's life and commends his fiction, poetry, and literary criticism.

W224 Wright, John Charles. "Introduction." *Some Poems of Edgar Allan Poe.* Shorne, Kent, Eng.: Pear Tree Press, 1901, pp. 1–4.
A slight biographical essay with several mistakes.

W225 Wroth, Lawrence C. "Poe's Baltimore." *Johns Hopkins Alumni Mag,* XVII (June 1929), 299–312.
Attempts to reconstruct Baltimore in Poe's day.

*W226 Wuletich, Sybil. "Edgar Allan Poe: The Rationale of the Uncanny." Ann Arbor, Mich.: University Microfilms, 1961.

W227 ——. "Edgar Allan Poe: The Rationale of the Uncanny." *DA,* XXII (April 1962), 3675–76.

What unity Poe achieved in his tales and poems "arises only because he demanded that the exigencies of art yield inexorably to the demands of the 'scientific' principles which he formulated as a kind of credo early in his career."

*W228 ———. "Edgar Allan Poe: The Rationale of the Uncanny." Diss., Ohio State University, 1961.

W229 Wyatt, Edith Franklin. "The Adventures of a Poetry Reader, III–IV." *North American Rev,* CCIX (March 1919), 407–11.

Opposes Amy Lowell's view that Imagists are descended from Poe and Whitman.

W230 Wyld, Lionel D. "The Enigma of Poe: Reality vs. l'art pour l'art." *Lock Haven Bulletin,* No. 2 (1960), pp. 34–38.

Poe's poetry reflects both personal experience and a concern to demonstrate critical theory.

W231 Wylie, Clarence, Jr. "Mathematical Allusions in Poe." *Science Monthly,* LXIII (Sept. 1946), 227–35.

Poe was not a mathematician but was rooted in a reasonable appreciation of the subject.

W232 Wyllie, John Cook. "Harper Records." *Bibliographical Society, University of Virginia, Secretary News Sheet,* No. 37 (Sept. 1957), p. 6.

"Publisher's records of books by Melville, Poe, Lew Wallace, and Cooper." *AL.*

W233 ———. "A List of the Texts of Poe's Tales." *Humanistic Studies in Honor of John Calvin Metcalf.* Charlottesville: University of Virginia, 1941.

This list "records all authoritative texts of Poe's tales of which the compiler has any knowledge." Appears in *University of Virginia Humanistic Studies,* I, 322–38.

W234 Wyman, Lillie Buffum Chace. "The Strange Case of Edgar Allan Poe." Boston *Transcript,* Feb. 24, 1923, Book sec., p. 2.

The relations of Poe and Mrs. Whitman are retold in a journalistic idiom.

W235 Wyman, Mary Alice. *Selections from the Autobiography of Elizabeth Oakes Smith.* Lewiston, Maine: Lewiston Journal, 1924.

See pp. 116–26 *et passim* for recollections and discussions relative to Poe.

X

X1 "XER." "Edgar Allan Poe, A Sketch." *Literary Light,* I (March 1890), 35–38.

X2 "Xix" [W. B. Tabb?]. "E. A. Poe—The Raven and Eureka." *UVaMag,* IV (April 1860), 383–88.

An appreciative essay of "The Raven" and *Eureka* as representative works of Poe.

Y

Y1 Yarmolinsky, A. "The Russian View of American Literature." *Bookman.* XLIV (Sept. 1916), 44–48.

"Poe's influence on modern Russian literature is well established"; see pp. 44–45.

Y2 Yeats, William Butler. "To W. T. Horton." *The Letters of W. B. Yeats.* Ed. Allan Wade. London: Rupert Hart-Davis, 1954, pp. 325–26.

Qualified praise of Poe's work. Extract reprinted in Eric Carlson, ed., *The Recognition of Edgar Allan Poe* (Ann Arbor: University of Michigan Press, 1966), pp. 76–77.

Y3 Yewdale, Merton S. "Edgar Allan Poe, Pathologically." *North American Rev,* CCXII (Nov. 1920), 686–96.

Tries to analyze the causes of aberrations attributed to Poe.

Y4 Yorke, Dane. "Yankee Neal." *American Mercury,* XIX (March 1930), 361–68.

Briefly discusses Neal's opinion of Poe and Poe's opinion of Neal.

Y5 Young, Philip. "The Early Psychologists and Poe." *AL,* XXII (Jan. 1951), 442–54.

Poe criticism is predominantly psychological before the impact of modern psychology in the twentieth century.

Z

Z1   Zimmerman, Melvin. "Baudelaire, Poe and Hawthorne." *RLC,*
XXXIX (July–Sept. 1965), 448–51.
> Baudelaire in some portions of his second study of Poe translated—
> without any attribution—portions of Poe's criticism of Hawthorne's
> *Twice-Told Tales.*

Z2   Zolnay, C. Z. [Letter to Charles W Kent.] *UVaMag,* LX (Dec.
1899), 151.
> On conveying through sculpture the essence of Poe's genius.

Z3   Zu. LuLu-Mo.Zal [Douglas Sherley]. "Edgar Allan Poe While a
Student at the University of Virginia." *UVaMag,* XIX (March 1880),
376–81; (April 1880), 426–45.
> The first sketch is a study of Poe's university life, and the second is
> a repetition of the legend of Poe's love affair in college.

Z4   Zulli, Floyd. "Introduction. Edgar Allan Poe—The Man and His
World." *Edgar Allan Poe: Selected Stories and Poems.* New York:
Franklin Watts, 1967, pp. vii–xvii.
> Poe, who constructs a "harrowing yet strangely beautiful world" in
> his poetry and tales, has many literary kin among British and Euro-
> pean authors.

*Z5   Zylstra, Henry. "E. T. A. Hoffmann in England and America."
Diss., Harvard University, 1940.

Checklist of Poe Criticism in Foreign Languages

1827–1967

FA

FA1 Abe, Tomoji. "Poe and the History of the United States." *Kokoro,* Dec. 1949.

FA2 Abreu, Manual de. "Atitude oposta de Edgar Allan Poe e Walt Whitman em face do Não Ser." *Lanterna Verde,* 7 (Aug. 1943), pp. 79–96.

FA3 Acosta, Leonardo. "Edgar Allan Poe." *Nueva Revista Cubana,* I (July–Sept. 1959), 50–65.

FA4 Acosta, Osvaldo C. *Edgar Allan Poe.* Montevideo: Organización Medina, [1963?].

FA5 Adriaenssens, Ferd. "Edgar Allan Poe's 'Shadow.'" *Arsenaal,* II (1946), 69–71.

FA6 Ady, Endre. "A hazug Poe." *Budapesti Napló,* Nov. 21, 1905.

FA7 Aikhenval'd, Iu. "Edgar Po. Pamiatka" [Edgar Poe. A memorial]. *Otdel'nyo stranitsy* [Separate pages]. St. Petersburg, 1910, pp. 75–81.

FA8 Akitsune, Nomura. *Biography of Edgar Allan Poe, and Criticism of His Works.* Fuku [?]: Village Book Shop, 1959.

FA9 Aksakov, N. "Psikhologiia Edgara Poe" [The psychology of Edgar Poe]. *Vsemirnaia illiustratsiia,* Nos. 10–12 (1886), pp. 191–94, 210–11, 234–38.

FA10 Aksenov, I. A. [Review of] "Poe, E. A. Polnoe sobranie poem i stikhotvorenii" [Complete collection of poems and verse]. *Pechat' i revoliutsiia,* No. 1 (1925), pp. 178–288.

FA11 Alarcón, Pedro Antonio de. "Edgar Poe." *La Época* (Madrid), X (Sept. 1, 1858). Reprinted in *Juicios literarios y artísticos* (Madrid, 1883), pp. 107–19.

FA12 Alcalá, Manuel. "Del supuesto materialismo de Poe." *Filosofía y Letras,* No. 16 (1944), pp. 171–84.

FA13 Alegría, J. M. *Historias extraordinarias de Edgard Poe.* 1st. ser. Madrid: Imprenta de El Atalaya, 1859.

FA14 Alexander, Jean. "Poe's *For Annie* and Mallarmé's *Nuit d' Idumée.*" *MLN,* LXXVII (Dec. 1962), 534–36.

FA15   Algarra, Vicente, trans. *Doble asesinato en la Calle Morgue.* Buenos Aires: Editorial de grandes autores, 1943.

FA16   Allen, Hervey. *Israfel, vida e época de Edgar Allan Poe.* Trans. Oscar Mendes. Rio de Janeiro: Livraria do Globo, 1945.

FA17   Alonso Chávez, Josefina. *Estudio psicológico de la expresión literaria y en particular en Edgar Allan Poe.* Mexico, 1965.

FA18   Alvarez R. "Edgard Poe y las falsas leyendas." *América* (Quito), II (1927), 110–11.

FA19   Alvarez Q., Eva Maria. "Papel y aspectos de la subjetividad en la obra de Edgar Allan Poe." *Armas y Letras,* VI, No. 4 (Dec. 1963), 7–14.

FA20   Anceschi, Luciano. *Autonomia ed eteronomia dell' arte; saggio di fenomenologia delle poetiche.* 2nd ed., rev. Florence: Vallecchi, 1959.

FA21   ——. "E. A. Poe e la fondazione della poesia pura." *Autonomia ed eteronomia dell' arte: sviluppo e teoria di un problema estetico.* Florence: Sansoni, 1936, pp. 83–104.

FA22   Andô, Ichiro. "Select Poems by Poe." With notes. *Youth's Companion* (Tokyo), July 1948.

FA23   ——, trans. "To Helen," "Annabel Lee." *British and American Poetry.* Ed. Ichiro Andô. Tokyo: The Japan Society of English Study, 1951, pp. 60–69.

FA24   Andral, August. "Zu Edgar Allan Poes Geschichten." *Englische Studien,* XLVIII (1915), 479.

FA25   Angioletti, Giovanni Battista. "Rabelais e Poe rivoluzionari." *Mondo,* VI (Jan. 12, 1954), 9.

FA26   Anichkov, E. "Bodler i Edgar Po" [Baudelaire and Edgar Poe]. *Sovremennyi mir,* No. 2 (1909), pp. 75–100. Also enlarged in *Predtechi i sovremenniki* [Forerunners and contemporaries], I (St. Petersburg, 1910), 213–71.

FA27   Anon. *A Petőfi Társaság Lapja.* 1877, I, 61–62.

FA28   ——. "La casa de Edgard Allan Poe." *Revista de Revistas,* No. 648 (Dec. 17, 1922), pp. 38–39.

FA29   ——. "La casa del corvo." *Mattino,* Feb. 21, 1953, p. 3.

FA30   ——. "Centenário de Edgar Allan Poe, 1849–1949." Programa de Difusão Cultural organisado pela diretoria da União Cultural Brasil—Estados Unidos em homenagem à memória do poeta e escritor Norte-Americano. São Paulo: Casa Roosevelt, [1949?].

FA31   ——. "El centenario de Edgar Allen [*sic*] Poe. Conmovedores detalles íntimos de su vida. América y sus grandes hombres." *Repertorio Americano,* I (Dec. 1919).

FA32 ——. "Centenario de la muerte de Edgard Allan Poe y Federico Chopin." *Letras del Ecuador,* Nos. 50–52 (1949), p. 1.

FA33 ——. " 'Il corvo.' " *Radio corriere,* NS VIII (Dec. 14–20, 1952), 14.

FA34 ——. "De la dramática niñez de Edgardo Allan Poe." *Caras y Caretas,* No. 1693 (14 March 1931).

FA35 ——. "Delirium." *Radio corriere,* NS IX (Sept. 27–Oct. 3, 1953), 7.

FA36 ——. "Due poesie di Poe." *Ausonia,* V (April–May 1950), 36.

FA37 ——. "E. A. Poe, 'Die neue Polizei.' " *Monatliche Fach und Lehrschrift* (Munich), III, No. 10 (1949).

FA38 ——. "Edgar A. Poe." *Letture per tutti,* V (Apr. 1953), 24.

FA39 ——. "Edgar Allan Po. (Biograficheskii ocherk)" [Edgar Allan Poe. (Biographical sketch)]. Poe, *Sobranie sochinenii* [Collected works]. Vol. I. St. Petersburg, 1913, pp. iii–xiv.

FA40 ——. "Edgar Allan Poe." *Bluszcz,* No. 41 (1899), pp. 321–22; No. 43 (1899), pp. 338–40.

FA41 ——. "Edgar Allan Poe: El extraño matrimonio del poeta con una impúber." *Digesto Latinoamericano, Bilingual Rev,* Jan. 1, 1936, pp. 17, 24–26.

FA42 ——. "Edgar Allan Poe [Life and Works]." *Biesiada Literacka,* No. 9 (1909), pp. 173–74.

FA43 ——. "Edgar Allen Po." *Istoricheskii vestnik,* No. 10 (1907), pp. 325–28.

FA44 ——. "Edgar Po. (Biograficheskii ocherk); Primechaniia" [Edgar Po. (Biographical essay); notes]. *Edgar Po v luchshikh russkikh perovodakh* [Edgar Poe in the Best Russian translations]. St. Petersburg, 1911, pp. 3–8, 65–91.

FA45 ——. "Edgar Po." *Istoricheskii vestnik,* No. 10 (1897), pp. 369–70.

FA46 ——. "Edgar Po i ego vliianie no sovremennuiu literaturu" [Edgar Poe and his influence on contemporary literature]. *Vestnik inostrannoi literatury,* No. 12 (1910), pp. 41–45.

FA47 ——. "Edgar Poe. (Biographicheskii ockerk)" [Edgar Poe. (Biographical sketch)]. Poe, *Izbrannye sochineniia* [Selected works]. St. Petersburg, 1895, pp. iii–vii.

FA48 ——. "Edgar Poe." *Plutarkh XIX veka* [Plutarch of the 19th century]. Vol. I. St. Petersburg, 1902, p. 166.

FA49 ——. "Edgar Poe." *Zagranichnyi vestnik,* Nos. 1–2 (1866), pp. 67–78, 348–67.

FA50 ———. "Edgar Poe." *Nuova antologia* (Rome), Feb. 1, 1909.

FA51 ———. "Edgar Poe. (Po povodu 100-letiia so dnia rozhdeniia)" [Edgar Poe. (On the centenary of his birth)]. *Priroda i liudi,* No. 14 (1909), p. 213.

FA52 ———. "Edgar Poe s patologicheskoi tochki zreniia" [Edgar Poe from the pathological point of view]. *Knizhki nedeli,* No. 10 (1897), pp. 262–65.

FA53 ———. "Edgar Poe, sovremennyi severo-amerikanskii pisatel'. Ego zhizn' i sochineniia" [Edgar Poe, a contemporary North American writer. His life and works]. *Syn otechestva,* No. 14 (1856), pp. 33–36.

FA54 ———. "Edgardo Poe." *El Mundo Ilustrado,* June 29, 1902.

FA55 ———. "Los escritos de Poe, a 50 centavos por página." *Caras y Caretas,* No. 1488 (April 9, 1927).

FA56 ———. "Los Estados Unidos resuelven a honrar la memoria de la madre de Edgar Poe." *El Universal Ilustrado,* April 23, 1925, p. 44.

FA57 ———. "Evropeiskie i amerikanskie iubilei. (100-letie so dnia rozhdeniia Edgara Po)" [European and American jubilees. (100th anniversary of the birth of Edgar Poe)]. *Istoricheskii vestnik,* No. 5 (1909), pp. 746–48.

FA58 ———. " 'Il gatto nero.' " *Annali,* II (March–April 1953), iii.

FA59 ———. "Un giallo dell' ottocento." *Epoca,* V (Aug. 29, 1954), 73.

FA60 ———. "Letteratura." *Illustrazione italiana,* NS X (March 1954), 67.

FA61 ———. "La leyenda de 'La ingratitud' de Poe, destruida." *El Universal Ilustrado,* Nov. 5, 1925, pp. 20–21.

FA62 ———. "Lichnost' Edgara Poe" [The personality of Edgar Poe]. *Vestnik inostrannoi literatury,* No. 9 (1897), pp. 357–59.

FA63 ———. "Marginalia." *Ausonia,* V (Jan. 1950), 55.

FA64 ———. "Nel centenario di Poe." *Roma,* Nov. 17, 1949, p. 3.

FA65 ———. "Nog eens 'The Raven'." *Litterair paspoort,* V (1950), 155.

FA66 ———. "Notícia sobre Poe." *Els poemes d'Edgar Poe.* Trans. A. Esclasans. Barcelona: Editorial Barcino, 1934, pp. 5–8.

FA67 ———. "Notiziario letterario." *Messaggero* (Feb. 9, 1950), p. 3.

FA68 ———. "Novaia biografia i novoe izdanie sochinenii E. A. Poe" [A new biography and a new edition of the works of E. A. Poe]. *Ezhenedel'noe novoe vremia,* Vol. V, No. 63 (1880), 702–4.

FA69　Deleted.

FA70　————. "Patologicheskaia literatura i bol'nye pisateli. Edgar Allan Poe" [Pathological literature and sick writers. Edgar Allan Poe]. *Novyi zhurnal inostrannoi literatury,* No. 2 (1898), pp. 190–200.

FA71　————. "Po." *34—i.e. Tridtsat' chetyre—biografii izvestneishikh russkikh i inostrannykh pisatelei* [34 biographies of the best-known Russian and foreign writers]. St. Petersburg, 1913, pp. 35–36.

FA72　————. "Poe Allan Edgar—Ingram H. Jánostól." *Budapesti Szemle,* 1881, pp. 93–108.

FA73　————. "Poe Edgar végpercei. J. J. Moran közleménye a New York Heraldból." *Otthon,* I (1876), 173–79.

FA74　————. [Review of *Oeuvres choisies d'Edgar Allan Poe*]. *Bibliothèque Universelle de Genève,* XXXI (Feb. 1856), 278–80.

FA75　————. "Rodonachal'nik simvolizma Edgar Poe" [Edgar Poe, the originator of symbolism]. *Russkii vestnik,* No. 9 (1897), pp. 316–23.

FA76　————. "Il romanzo poliziesco è frutto della civiltà moderna." *Illustrazione italiana,* NS IX (July 1953), 56–60.

FA77　————. "Segnalazioni." *Studium,* XLIII (Oct. 1947), 353.

FA78　————. "William Wilson." *Civiltà cattolica,* XCIX (Sept. 4, 1948), 529.

FA79　————. "Zum 100. Todestage E. A. Poes." *Die Zeit, Wochenzeitung für Politik, Wirtschaft, Handel und Kultur* (Hamburg), IV, No. 40 (1949), 1–5.

FA80　Anttila, Aarne. "Edgar Allan Poen 'Korppi'-runon kaikua suomalaisessa runoudessa." *Kirjallisuudentutkijain seuran vuosikirja,* 8 (1945), pp. 36–39.

FA81　Apostolov, N. "Edgar Po" *Impressionizm i modernizm* [Impressionism and modernism]. Kiev, 1908, pp. 43–44.

FA82　Ara, Masato. "Poe, a Detective Story Writer." *Eigo Seinen* [The rising generation], CV, No. 5 (May 1959), 2–3.

FA83　Araripe Junior, T. A. "Estética de Poe." *Revista Brasileira,* I, II, V, VI, XI, XII (1895–97).

FA84　Araujo, Fernando. "Edgar Poe y Julio Verne." *La España Moderna,* XXI (Sept. 1909), 148–54.

FA85　Arbib, Rodolfo. *Nuovi racconti straordinari di Edgardo Poe.* Milano: E. Sonzogno, 1885.

FA86　Arnavon, Cyrille. "Edgar Allan Poe." *Histoire littéraire des Etats-Unis.* Paris: Hachette, 1953, pp. 109–15.

FA87   ———. *Les Lettres américaines devant la critique française* (*1887–1917*). Paris: Belles Lettres, 1951.

FA88   ———. "Poe cent ans après." *Langues Modernes,* No. 5 (Sept.–Oct. 1949), pp. 28–39.

FA89   Arnould, Arthur. "Edgar Poe: L'Homme, l'artiste, el l'oeuvre." *Revue Moderne,* XXXIV (April 1, June 1, 1865), 65, 475; XXXV (July 1, 1865), 68.

FA90   ———. "Edgar Poe: Un Mystère de sa vie, ses ouvrages." *L'Intermediaire des Chercheurs et Curieux,* June 15, 1864, p. 100.

FA91   Asselineau, Charles. "Edgar Poe, ses ouvrages." *L'Intermédiaire des Chercheurs et Curieux,* July 15, 1864, p. 127.

FA92   Asselineau, Roger. "Introduction." *Edgar Allan Poe: Histoires extraordinaires.* Trans. Charles Baudelaire. Paris: Garnier-Flammarion, 1965, pp. 17–24.

FA93   ———. "Introduction." *Histoires grotesques et sérieuses.* Paris: Garnier-Flammarion, 1966, pp. 15–23.

FA94   ———. "Rev. of *Die erzählende Prosa E. A. Poes* by Kuno Schuhmann." *EA,* XIII (Jan.–March 1960), 84–85.

FA95   ———. "Rev. of *The French Face of Edgar Poe* by Patrick F. Quinn." *RLC,* XXXIII (Oct.–Dec. 1959), 597–99.

FA96   ———. "Rev. of *Poe: A Critical Study* by Edward Davidson." *RLC,* XXXIII (Oct.–Dec. 1959), 599–600.

FA97   ———, ed. *Edgar Poe: Choix de contes.* Paris: Aubier, 1958. Reviewed: Patrick F. Quinn, *EA,* XII, 89.

FA98   Astaldi, Maria Luisa. "Poe in italiano" *Giornale d'Italia,* IX (June 15, 1954), 3. Review of F. O. Matthiessen, *American Renaissance.*

FA99   Aste, Luigi. "Il calderone dell' arte nel paese del dollaro." *Giornale dell' Emilia* (Nov. 16, 1947), p. 3.

FA100   Atsumi, Akio. "Terror in Poe's Works—An Analysis of Its Aspects." *Annual Report of Researches of Gakushūin University* (*Kenkyu Nempō*) (Tokyo), I (March 1953), 345–52.

FA101   Attal, Jean-Pierre. "L'Image métaphysique." *MdF,* CCCLI (June 1964), 270–95.

FA102   Auriant. "Emile Hennequin, traducteur d'Edgar Poe; Documents inédits." *MdF,* CCLXI (Aug. 1, 1935), 626–31.

FA103   Azzali, Ferrante. "Bellezza e morte per Poe furono un affascinante contrasto." *Giornale dell' Emilia,* Oct. 18, 1949, p. 3.

FA104   ———. "Dormiva con un gatto accovacciato sul petto." *Momento,* Sept. 6, 1950, p. 3.

FA105 ———. "Enigmi sentimentali di Edgar Allan Poe." *Giornale,* Oct. 14, 1949, p. 3.

FB

FB1 B. "Edgar Poe's Tales." *Rev Suisse* (*Bibliothèque Universelle de Genève*), XX (1852), 106.

FB2 Bab, Julius. *Amerikas Dichter.* Berlin, 1949, pp. 22–26.

FB3 Bachelard, Gaston. *L'Air et les songes.* Paris: José Corti, 1943, pp. 112–23.

FB4 ———. *L'Eau et les rêves.* Paris: Librairie José Corti, 1942.

FB5 ———. "Introduction." *Aventures d'Arthur Gordon Pym.* Paris: Stock, Delamain, et Boutelleau, 1944.

FB6 ———. *La Psychanalyse du feu.* Paris, 1938.

FB7 Baldini, Gabriele. "Centenario di Poe. Un poeta della nostra epoca." *FLe,* IV (Oct. 9, 1949), 1.

FB8 ———. *Edgar A. Poe, studi.* Brescia: Morcelliana, 1947. Reviewed: N. Orsini, *AL,* XIII, 389–90.

FB9 ———. "La filosofia della composizione." "Roderick Usher e la poetica del sistema nervoso." *Narratori americani dell' 800.* Turin: ERI, 1956, pp. 14–17, 18–28.

FB10 ———, comp. and ed. *Poe.* With introd. Milan: A. Garzanti, 1949.

FB11 ———. "Il poeta escluso." *Mondo,* I (Oct. 29, 1949), 9–10.

FB12 ———. "Prospettiva europea della letteratura d'oltre-atlantico." *FLe,* II (June 12, 1947), 10.

FB13 ———, ed. *La relazione di Arthur Gordon Pym da Nantucket.* Turin: Einaudi, 1943.

FB14 ———, trans. *William Wilson.* With notes. Brescia: Morcelliana, 1947.

FB15 Bal'mont, K. "Edgar Po, 1809–1849." Poe, *Sobranie sochinenii* [Collected works]. Vol. I. Moscow, 1901, pp. vii–xii.

FB16 ———. "Ocherk zhizni Edgara Po. Posleslovie perevodchika" [A sketch of the life of Edgar Poe. An afterword from the translator]. Poe, *Sobranie sochinenii* [Collected works]. Vol. V. Moscow, 1912, pp. 1–107, 303–11.

FB17 ———. "Predislovie" [Foreword]. Poe, *Ballady i fantasii* [Ballads and fantasies]. Moscow, 1895, pp. iii–xiv.

FB18 Bandy, W. T. "Amédée Pichot: Premier traducteur de Poe." *Bulletin Baudelairien*, II, No. 1 (1966), 12.

FB19 ———. "Baudelaire et Edgar Poe: Vue retrospective." *RLC*, XLI (April–June 1967), 180–94.

FB20 ———. "Baudelaire et Poe: Vers une nouvelle mise au point." *Revue d'Histoire Littéraire de la France*, LXVII (April–June 1967), 329–34.

FB21 ———. "Edgar Poe et la dédicace des *Fleurs du Mal.*" *RSH*, No. 85 (Jan.–March 1957), pp. 97–100.

FB22 ———. "Editions originales et éditions critiques des *Histoires extraordinaires* d'Edgar Poe." *Bulletin du Bibliophile*, IV (1953), 184–94.

FB23 Banville, Théodore de. *Mes souvenirs*. Paris: Charpentier, 1882.

FB24 Baralt, Blanca Z. de. "El centenario de Poe (con retrato)." *Cuba y América*, XIII (Feb. 1909), 57–58.

FB25 ———. "Edgar Allan Poe." *Estudios de Arte y de Vida*. Paris: n.d. [1914?], pp. 72–79.

FB26 Baratono, Pierangelo. *Edgar Poe.* Rome: Formiggini, 1924. Reviewed: Merritt Y. Hughes. *SatRL*, II (Feb. 6, 1926), 546.

FB27 Barbey d'Aurevilly, Jules A. *Littérature etrangère*. Paris: Lemerre, 1890.

FB28 Barine, Arvède (Mme. C. Vinciens). *Edgar Poe: Saggio di arte patologica.* Trans. and introd. Giacinto de Thomasis. Rome: Edizioni Del Secolo, 1938.

FB29 ———. "Essais de littérature pathologique: III. L'Alcool: Edgar Poe." *RDM*, CXLII (July 15, Aug. 1, 1897), 336–73, 552–91. Reprinted in her *Poètes et nevrosés* (Paris, 1908).

FB30 ———. *Névrosés: Hoffmann, Quincey, Edgar Poe, G. de Nerval.* Paris, 1898.

FB31 Bartres, J. Raymundo. "De Poe a Hemingway pasando por Baroja." *La Torre*, VIII (July–Sept. 1960), 165–71.

FB32 Baudelaire, Carlos [Charles]. "Edgardo Poe: su vida y sus obras." *Letras del Ecuador*, Nos. 50–52 (1949), pp. 10–13.

FB33 Baudelaire, Charles, trans. *Aventures d'Arthur Gordon Pym.* With imaginary conclusion by Jules Verne in *Le Sphinx des glaces.* Club des libraires de France, 1960.

FB34 ——, trans. *Choix de contes.* Introd. and notes by Roger Asselineau. Followed by a grotesque tale and an essay on the art of the short story, trans. and annotated by Roger Asselineau. Paris: Aubier, 1958.

FB35 ——. "Edgar Allan Poe, sa vie et ses ouvrages." *RdP,* Nos. 6 and 7 (March–April 1852), pp. 138–56, 90–110.

FB36 ——. "Edgar Allan Poe, su vida y su obra." *Historias extraordinarias.* Trans. Emilio Carrere and others. 7 vols. Madrid: Matev, n.d.

FB37 ——, trans. Edgar Poe, *Histoires extraordinaires.* Paris: Michel Lévy frères, 1856.

FB38 ——. "Edgar Poe, sa vie et ses oeuvres." *Oeuvres complètes.* Vol. VI. Paris: Conard, 1932, pp. vii–xxx.

FB39 ——. "Edgar Poe, sa vie et ses oeuvres." *Le Pays,* Feb. 25, 1856.

FB40 ——, trans. *Histoires extraordinaires.* Montréal: Les Éditions Variétés, 1945.

FB41 ——. *Lettres à sa mère.* Paris: Calmann-Lévy, 1932.

FB42 ——. *Lettres, 1841–1866.* Paris: Mercure de France, 1907.

FB43 ——. "Notes nouvelles sur Edgar Poe." *Nouvelles Histoires par Edgar Poe.* Paris: Michael Lévy frères, 1857.

FB44 ——. "Notes nouvelles sur Edgar Poe." *Oeuvres complètes.* Vol. VII. Paris: Conard, 1933, pp. v–xxiii.

FB45 ——. *Oeuvres complètes.* Ed. Yves Florenne. Paris: Le Club Français du Livre, 1966. Reviewed: Richard, *PN,* I, 11–12.

FB46 ——. *Les Plus Beaux Contes d'Edgar Poe.* Paris: G. Crès, 1917.

FB47 ——, trans. *Quatre histoires extraordinaires.* Illus. Henri Evenepoel. Bruxelles: Aux dépens des Éditions Lumière, 1944.

FB48 ——, trans. *La Scarabée d'or et autres contes.* Paris: Librairie Gründ, 1959.

FB49 ——. *Selected Critical Studies.* Ed. and introd. by D. Parmée. Cambridge: University Press, 1949.

FB50 ——. *Souvenirs, correspondance.* Paris: Pinceborde, 1872.

FB51 Bazán, Armando. "Prólogo." *Edgard Allan Poe: Obras completas.* Vol. I. Buenos Aires: Editorial Claridad, 1944, pp. 7–19.

FB52 Beaupré, Barbara. *Nowelle.* Trans. and introd. Barbara Beaupré. Cracow, 1909.

FB53 Béguin, Albert. *L'ame romantique et le rêve.* Paris: Corti, 1939.

FB54 ——. "Il centenario di Edgar Allan Poe." *Ponte,* V (Dec. 1949), 1497–1500.

FB55 ——. "Grandeur d'Edgar Poe." *Nouvelles Littéraires,* No. 1156 (Oct. 1949), p. 5.

FB56 ——. "Para el centenario de Edgard Allan Poe." *Letras del Ecuador,* Nos. 50–52 (1949), p. 13.

FB57 Bellanger, Charles, trans. *Le Principe de la poésie,* by Edgar Allan Poe. With notes. Paris: Editions du Myrte, 1945.

FB58 Bellonci, Goffredo. "Il centenario di Poe." *Giornale d'Italia,* Oct. 4, 1949, p. 3.

FB59 ——. "Edgar Poe in Italia." *Messaggero,* March 20, 1954, p. 3.

FB60 Benjamin, Walter. *Schriften.* 2 vols. Frankfurt am Main: Suhrkamp Verlag, 1955. See vol. I for Poe.

FB61 Bense, Max. *Literaturmetaphysik: Der Schriftsteller in der technischen Welt.* Stuttgart: Deutsche Verlagsanstalt, 1950. Poe: pp. 26–29, 68–71, 88–91.

FB62 Bentzon, Th. "Les Poetes américains." *RDM,* May 1, 1886.

FB63 Benzmann, Thalès. [The Poetical Works of Poe.] *L'Athenaeum Français,* Sept. 10, 1853.

FB64 Berisch, Karl. "Der Analytiker des Grauens: Zu Edgar Allan Poes 100. Todestage." *Rheinischer Merkur,* IV, No. 41 (1949), 7–8.

FB65 Bernárdez, F. L. "Vestigios de España en Poe." *La Nación* [Buenos Aires], June 15, 1952.

FB66 Berne-Joffroy, André. *Présence de Valéry.* Paris: Librairie Plon, 1944.

FB67 Bernson, Bernhard, ed. and trans. *Erzählungen.* Ulm: Aegis-Verlag, 1946.

FB68 Berti, Luigi. *Boccaporto secondo.* Florence: Parenti, 1944.

FB69 ——, trans. *Marginalia.* With preface. Milan: Mondadori, 1949.

FB70 ——. "Il Poe critico." *Inventario,* II (Summer 1949), 1–11.

FB71 ——. "Tra Melville e Poe un'affascinante parentela." *FLe,* VII (Oct. 26, 1952), 1.

FB72 Betz, Louis P. "Edgar Poe in der französischen Literatur." *Studien zur vergleichenden Literaturgeschichte der neueren Zeit.* Frankfurt, 1902, pp. 16–82.

FB73 ——. "Edgar Poe in Deutschland." *Zeit,* XXXV (1903).

FB74 Bianchi, Ruggero. "Corollari di una poetica del' l'effetto: I *Marginalia* di E. A. Poe." *Rivista di Estatica* (Univ. of Padua), XI (1966), 408–22.

FB75 Biancotti, Angiolo. *Dalle avventure d'Arthur Gordon Pym.* Turin: Paravia, 1924.

FB76 Bienenstein, K. "Edgar Poe." *Ostdeutsche Rundschau* (Vienna), No. 28 (1903).

FB77 Bignami, Marialuisa. "Edgar Allan Poe di fronte alla natura." *SA,* XI (1965), 105–15.

FB78 Bigongiari, Piero. "Il caso letterario assoluto." *Letteratura e arte contemporanea,* XIV (Nov.–Dec. 1950), 56–58.

FB79 ———. "Centenario di Poe." *Popolo,* Nov. 10, 1949, p. 3.

FB80 ———. "Edgar Poe: Il caso letterario assoluto" (1949). *Il senso della lirica italiana e altri stud.* Florence: Sansoni, 1952, pp. 257–61.

FB81 Binder, Sr. M. Claudia. "Studien zur Charakterisierungstechnik in Kurzgeschichten Irvings, Poes und Hawthornes." Graz: Diss., 1950.

FB82 Bizzarri, Aldo. "Estetica del decadente Poe." *FLe,* No. 43 (Oct. 23, 1949). Reprinted in *Mondo,* I (Dec. 10, 1949), 9.

FB83 Bjerke, André. "Edgar Allan Poe." *Drømmen I En Drøm.* Oslo: H. Aschehoug, 1967, pp. 64–73.

FB84 Bjørnvig, Thorkild. "Edgar Allan Poe som tidskritiker." *Vindrosen,* X (1963), 590–607.

FB85 Bjurman, Gunnar A. *Edgar Allan Poe, en litteraturhistorisk studie.* Lund: Gleerup, 1916.

FB86 ———. "Edgar Allan Poe och Sverige." *Edda,* 1916, pp. 246–57.

FB87 Bleibtreu, Karl. "Edgar Allan Poë (geb. 19 Januar 1809)." *Allgemeine Zeitung,* Jan. 16, 1909.

FB88 Blöcker, Günther. *Die neuen Wirklichkeiten: Linien und Profile der modernen Literatur.* Berlin: Argon Verlag, 1957. Poe: pp. 124–32.

FB89 ———, ed. *Meistererzählungen.* With intro. Bremen: Carl Schunemann, 1960.

FB90 Bloem, J. C. "E. A. Poe: Een dichter over gedichten naar aanleiding van A. Huxley: 'Vulgarity in Literature.'" *Elsevier,* June 30, 1951.

FB91 Bobrova, M. N. "O proze Edgara Po" [Concerning Edgar Poe's prose]. *Izvestiia Irkutskogo Pedagogicheskogo instituta,* III (1937), 23–63.

FB92 ———. "Predislovie" [Foreword], and M. Bekker, "Komentarii" [Commentary]. Poe, *Izbrannoe* [Selections]. Moscow, 1958, pp. 3–15, 334–341. 2nd ed. Moscow, 1959.

FB93 Bodler, Sh. [Baudelaire, Ch.]. "Edgar Ellen'-Poe. Severoamerikanskii poet" [Edgar Allan Poe. A North American Poet]. *Panteon*, No. 9, Part III (1852), pp. 1–34.

FB94 ———. *Edgar Po. Zhizn' i tvorchestvo* [Edgar Poe. Life and work]. Odessa, 1910.

FB95 Bogardo, Alfredo. "Prefazione." *Le tre inchieste di Dupin di Edgar Allan Poe.* Ed. Bogardo. Universale Economica. Milan: Via Solferino, 1949, pp. 5–7.

FB96 Bohnhof, Anna. "Edgar Allan Poe." *Valvoja*, 1910, pp. 537–51.

FB97 Boisjollin, S. de. "Hoffmann, Poe. . . ." *Rev des Études Historiques* (Paris), June–July 1899.

FB98 Bolle, Jacques. *La Poésie du cauchemar.* Paris: Presse française et étrangère, 1946.

FB99 Bonaparte, Marie. *Edgar Poe: Eine psychoanalytische Studie . . . mit einem Vorwort von Sigmund Freud.* 3 vols. Vienna: Internationaler Psychoanalytischer Verlag, 1934.

FB100 ———. *Edgar Poe, étude psychanalytique.* 2 vols. Paris: Denoël et Steele, 1933. Reviewed: J. Grenier, *NRF,* Oct. 1934, pp. 610–12; F. Lot, *Rev Politique et Litteraire,* LXXII (Dec. 1, 1934), 901–4; V. O'Sullivan, *DM,* IX, 58; G. Marcel, *L'Europe Nouvelle* (Paris), XVI (Aug. 5, 1933), 738–39.

FB101 ———. *Edgar Poe, sa vie—son oeuvre: Étude analytique.* 3 vols. Paris: Presses universitaires de France, 1958.

FB102 Bonsanti, Alessandro. "Commenti." *Letteratura e arte contemporanea,* XIV (Jan.–Feb. 1950), 51–52.

FB103 ———. "Commenti." *Letteratura e arte contemporanea,* XIV (July–Aug. 1950), 65–66.

FB104 Borges, Jorge Luis. "Edgar Allan Poe." *La Nación* [Buenos Aires], Oct. 2, 1949, sec. 2, p. 1.

FB105 ———. "La génesis de 'El cuervo.'" *La Prensa* [Buenos Aires], Aug. 25, 1935, sec. 4, p. 2.

FB106 Borgese, G. A. "La poesia di Edgardo Poe." *Corriere della sera,* Jan. 2, 1913.

FB107 Bourget, Paul. *Le Parlement,* Nov. 3, 1882.

FB108 Boussoulas, Nicholas I. "La Peur et l'univers dans l'oeuvre d'Edgar Poe." Diss., Paris, 1950.

FB109 ———. *La Peur et l'univers dans l'oeuvre d'Edgar Poe* (une métaphysique de la peur). Paris: Presses universitaires de France, 1952.

FB110 Brachvogel, U. "Poe, Longfellow, und Tennyson." *Nord und Süd* (Breslau), LXXVII (1896), 87–96.

FB111 Brassai, Sámuel. "Adalékok Edgar Poe (amerikai költo) ismertetéséhez." *S Zépirodalmi Közlöny,* Nos. 5–8 (1858).

FB112 Brazolenko, B. "Edgar Po. (1809–1849–1909)." *Vestnik znaniia,* No. 3 (1909), pp. 348–52.

FB113 Bresciano, Raffaele. *Il vero Edgardo Poe.* Rome: Fr. Ganguzza-Lajosa, 1904.

FB114 Brisson, Adolphe. *Portraits intimes.* [Paris?], 1899.

FB115 Brisson, Firmin. [Edgar Allan Poe.] *Polybiblion,* 52 (1888).

FB116 Briusov, V. "Edgar Po." *Istoriia zapadnoi literatury* [A history of Western literature]. Vol. III. Moscow, 1914, pp. 328–44.

FB117 ———. "Predislovie perevodchika.—Edgar Po. Biograficheskii ocherk; Kritiko-bibliograficheskii kommentarii" [Translator's foreword. —Edgar Poe. Biographical sketch; Critical-bibliographic commentary]. Poe, *Polnoe sobranie poem i stikhotvorenii* [Complete collection of poems and verse]. Moscow, Leningrad, 1924, pp. 5–16, 107–25.

FB118 Brunel, Pierre. "Claudel et Edgar Poe." *La Rev des Lettres Modernes,* No. 103 (1964), pp. 99–130.

FB119 Brunner, Const. "Die Technik des künstlerischen Schaffens." *Der Zuschauer* (Hamburg), 1893, pp. 110–15, 135–40, 169–75, 212–20.

FB120 Bukowski, Kazimierz. "Edgar Allan Poe." *Sylwetki. Studya z literatury i sztuki.* Lvov, 1914, pp. 100–138.

FB121 Bulgheroni, Marisa. "Poe e il demone americano." *SA,* IX (1964), 69–82.

FB122 Buranelli, Vincent. *Edgar Allan Poe.* Trans. Livia Deac. Bucharest: Editura Pentru Literatură Universală, 1966.

FB123 Butor, Michel. *Histoire extraordinaire: Essai sur un rêve de Baudelaire.* Paris: Gallimard, 1961.

FC

FC1 Cabau, Jacques. *E. A. Poe (Edgar Poe par lui-même).* Trans. Giulia Veronesi. Milan: Mondadori, 1961.

FC2 ———, ed. *Edgar Poe par lui-même.* Paris: Éds. du Seuil, 1960.

FC3   Cabrera, Romulo F. "Edgardo Allan Poe." *El Hogar,* No. 773 (Aug. 8, 1924), p. 11.

FC4   Cacho, Miguel Bolaños. "Después de la lectura—Edgar Poe." *El Renacimiento,* 1894, pp. 122–24. Reprinted as "Edgardo Poe," *El Mundo,* I (May 16, 1897), 323–24.

FC5   Cain, Lucienne (Daniel-Mayer). "Edgar Poe et Valéry." *MdF,* No. 1041 (May 1950), 81–94.

FC6   ———. *Trois essais sur Paul Valéry: Valéry et l'utilisation du monde sensible, Edgar Poe et Valéry, et L'Être vivant selon Valéry.* Paris: Gallimard, 1958.

FC7   Cajumi, Arrigo. "Poe cent'anni dopo" (1949). *Colori e Veleni: Saggi di varia letteratura.* Preface by Pietro Paolo Trompeo. Naples: Ed. Scientif. Ital., 1956, pp. 139–43.

FC8   ———. "Poe cent'anni dopo." *Stampa,* Oct. 6, 1949, p. 3.

FC9   Calinescu, Matei. "Structura Fantasticului in Proza lui E. A. Poe." Preface to Poe, *Scrieri in Proză.* 2 vols. Bucharest: Editura pentru Literatura, Biblioteca pentru Toți, 1965.

FC10   Calvo, Francisco Soto y. "Prôlogo." *Joyario de Poe.* Buenos Aires, 1927.

FC11   Calvocoressi, M. D. "Edgar Poe, ses biographies, ses editeurs, ses critiques." *MdF,* LXXVII (Feb. 1, 1909), 385–403.

FC12   Cano y Cueto, Manuel. "Noticia sobre Poe y sus obras." *Historias extraordinarias.* Sevilla, 1871.

FC13   Cardoso, Lúcio. "Edgar Poe." *Revista do Instituto Brasil Estados Unidos,* II (Sept. 6, 1944), 68–76.

FC14   Carpitella, M. "Liricità di Poe." *Studium,* L (Feb. 1954), 119–20. Review of A. Colling, *E. A. Poe* (Paris, 1952).

FC15   Carreño, Eduardo. "Apostilla sobre 'El cuervo.'" *Bitacora,* No. 4, pp. 19–21.

FC16   Carrère, B. *Dégénérescence et dipsomanie d'Edgar Poe.* Toulouse, 1907.

FC17   Carrere, Emilio. "Edgar Poe, ocultista." *Las ventanas del misterio.* Madrid, n.d. [1913?], pp. 37–42.

FC18   ———. "La última copa Edgard Poe." *El dolor de la literatura.* Madrid, n.d., pp. 68–71.

FC19   Carrion, Alejandro. "Danza macabra en la muerte de Poe." *Letras del Ecuador,* Nos. 50–52 (1949), pp. 9–10.

FC20   Carstens, Erik. "Trangen til at gøre det man ikke skulle." *Tvesind og neurose,* 1949, pp. 106–10.

FC21   Cartier, Léon. "Edgar Poe, romancier américain." *Le Figaro,* March 27, 1856.

FC22   Casanove, Maurice de. *Edgar Allan Poe.* Portraits d'hier, 27. Paris: Fabre, 1910, pp. [67]–96.

FC23   Casnati, Francesco. "Studi su Poe." *Popolo,* June 13, 1948, p. 3.

FC24   Caspari, Heinz. *Edgar Allan Poes Verhältnis zum Okkultismus; eine literarhistorische Studie.* Hanover: W. A. Adams, 1923. Reviewed: B. Fehr, *Deutsche Literaturztg,* II, 1997–99; W. Fischer, *Literaturblatt,* XLVI, 91–93; *Zeitschrift für französischen und englischen Unterricht,* XXV, 373–74.

FC25   Castelnau, Jacques Thomas de. *Edgar Poe.* Paris: J. Tallandier, 1945.

FC26   Castelnuovo, G. "Il nuovo realismo americano." *Comunità,* No. 17 (Aug. 9, 1947), p. 5.

FC27   Castillo, Domingo B. "Edgar Allan Poe." *El cojo illustrado,* XI (Aug. 15, 1902), 508–10.

FC28   Castro, Federico de Córdova. "Edgar Allan Poe." *Revista Bimestre Cubana,* XXX (Nov.–Dec. 1932), 375–85.

FC29   Castro, Humbetto de. "Whitman y Poe en la poesía de Rubén Darío." *Boletín Cultural y Bibliográfico* (Bogotá), X (1967), 90–104.

FC30   Castro, José di y Seraío. *Historias vulgares.* Madrid, 1868.

FC31   Catá, Alfonso Hernández. "Nota biográfica." *Narraciones extraordinarias.* Madrid, n.d. [1908?].

FC32   Cavazutti, Esteban M. "Del epistolario de Edgardo Poe y de sus amores." *Nosotros,* XXXIV (Feb. 1920), 204–45.

FC33   Cealîc, M. *Influenţe Morbide in Literatura: Edgar Poe, Viaţa şi Opera Sa.* Bucharest, 1906.

FC34   Cecchi, Emilio. "Aneddotica del 'Corvo' " (1945). *Scrittori inglesi e americani,* Milan: Saggiatore, 1962, pp. 80–82.

FC35   ——. "Il centenario del *Corvo*" (1945). *Scrittori inglesi e americani.* Milan: Mondadori, 1947, pp. 66–69.

FC36   ——. "Il centenario di Poe" (1950). *Scrittori inglesi e americani.* Vol. I. Milan: Saggiatore, 1962, pp. 85–87.

FC37   ——. "Il corvo di Poe sul berretto da notte di Baldini." *Europeo,* IV (Dec. 19, 1948), 7.

FC38   ——. "Lettere amorose di E. A. Poe" (1925). *Scittori inglesi e americani.* Vol. I. Milan: Saggiatore, 1962, pp. 71–77.

FC39   ——. "Miscellanea poeiana" (1948). *Scrittori inglesi e americani.* Vol. I. Milan: Saggiatore, 1962, pp. 82–84.

FC40 ——. "Poe e Manzoni" (1923). *Scrittori inglesi e americani.* Vol. I. Milan: Saggiatore, 1962, pp. 77–79.

FC41 ——. "Poe sotto processo" (1954). *Scrittori inglesi e americani.* Vol. I. Milan: Saggiatore, 1962, pp. 87–92.

FC42 ——. "Il processo a Edgar Poe." *Il Corriere della sera,* March 13, 1954, p. 3.

FC43 ——. "Processo a Poe." *Europeo,* VI (Jan. 15, 1950), 9.

FC44 ——. *Scrittori inglesi e americani.* Milan: A Mondadori, 1947.

FC45 Cederberg, Eino. "Edgar Allan Poe." *Ilta-Sanomat,* No. 14 (1959).

FC46 Cerretani, Arturo. "Edgard Allan Poe, el niño de la frente grande." *El Hogar,* No. 1378 (March 13, 1936), p. 80.

FC47 Cestre, Charles. "Poe et Baudelaire." *Revue Anglo-Américaine,* XI (April 1934), 322–29.

FC48 Chanut, J. "Edgar A. Poe." *Nouvelle biographie générale.* Paris: Didot Frères, 1852.

FC49 Charbonnel, Victor. *Les Mystiques dans la literáture présente.* Paris: Mercure de France, 1897.

FC50 Chasles, Philarète. "Cornelius Mathews." *Rev Contemporaine,* I (1852), 420.

FC51 ——. "Revue etrangère." *Jour des Debats,* April 20, 1856.

FC52 Chassé, Charles. "Edgar Poe et la France." *Figaro,* Jan. 20, 1934.

FC53 ——. "Essai d'une interprétation objective du tombeau d'Edgar Poe." With text, trans., and notes in English by Mallarmé. *RLC,* XXIII (Jan. 1949), 97–109.

FC54 ——. *Lueurs sur Mallarmé.* Paris, 1927.

FC55 Chauvet, Paul. *Sept essais de littérature anglaise.* Paris: Figuière, 1931. Reviewed: *New Statesman,* II (Oct. 3, 1931), 412.

FC56 Chiaramonte, Nelly. "Origini e cronache del 'pesce d'aprile.'" *Mattino d'Italia,* April 1, 1951, p. 3.

FC57 Chikara, China G. [List of Writings on Poe.] *Japan Society of Comparative Literature Bulletin,* No. 4 (Jan. 1, 1956), No. 21 (1960).

FC58 Chinard, Gilbert. "La Littérature française dans le sud des Etats-Unis après le 'Southern Literary Messenger,' 1834–64." *RLC,* VIII (Jan. 1928), 87–99.

FC59 Christ, Ernst. "E. A. Poe, der Dichter des Grauens." *Weltstimmen,* XIX (1949/50), 1ff.

FC60 Chu, Limin. *American Literature, 1607–1860.* [Taipei, Taiwan?]: Lien Ho Publishing Co., 1962.

FC61 Chudoba, F. *Pod listnatym Stromem* [A collection of essays]. Prague, 1932, pp. 145–67.

FC62 Claretie, Jules. "Edgar Poe." *Letras* (Asunción), I (Nov. 1915), 284–86.

FC63 ———. "Edgar Poe el genio del espanto." *Revista de Revistas,* No. 906 (Sept. 18, 1927), p. 62.

FC64 Clerban, Noël. "Le Centenaire d'Edgar Poe." *Les Nouvelles,* Nos. 24, 25 (Jan. 21, 22, 1909).

FC65 Coeuroy, André. "Philosophie et poétique musicale d'Edgar Poe." *Musique et littérature—Etudes de musique et de littérature comparées.* Paris: Bloud & Gay, 1923, pp. 173–89.

FC66 Colling, Alfred. *Edgar Poe.* Paris: Michel, 1952. Reviewed: F. C. Danchin, *EA,* V, 374–75.

FC67 Confalonieri, Giulio. "Due centenari." *Giornale dell'Emilia,* Feb. 12, 1949, p. 3.

FC68 Cordero y Leon, Rigoberto. "Edgar Allan Poe, genio del misterio." *Anales de la Universidad de Cuenca,* X (1954), 111–20.

FC69 Corrêa, Manuel Tanger. "Mallarmé e Fernando Pessoa perante o 'Corvo' de Edgar Allan Poe." *Ocidente,* LXV (1963), 4–20.

FC70 Cortázar, Julio, trans. and ed. *Obras en prosa* by Edgar Allan Poe. With introd. and notes. Madrid: Ediciones de la Universidad de Puerto Rico, 1956.

FC71 Cortina-Aravena, A. "Al margen de La Bella Durmiente." *Proa,* No. 9 (Oct. 1927), pp. 16–19.

FC72 La Cour, Tage. "Detektiven Edgar Allan Poe." *Bonniers Litterära Magasin,* XXVI (Oct. 1957), 704–7.

FC73 ———. "Detektiven Edgar Allan Poe." *Rejsen til månen og andre udflugter i den lettere bogverden.* Copenhagen, 1965, pp. 71–79.

FC74 Covert, John Cutler. *Quelques poètes américains: Longfellow, Whitman, Poe.* Lyon: Cumin and Masson, 1903.

FC75 Crépet, Jacques. "Eclaircissements." Baudelaire, *Oeuvres.* Vol. VII. Paris: Conard, 1933, pp. 317–503.

FC76 ———. "Eclaircissements et variantes." Baudelaire, *Oeuvres.* Vol. VIII. Paris: Conard, 1934, pp. 273–322.

FC77 ———. "Eclaircissements et variantes." Baudelaire, *Oeuvres.* Vol. IX. Paris: Conard, 1936, pp. 269–329.

FC78 ———. "Eclaircissements et variantes." Baudelaire, *Oeuvres.* Vol. XIV. Paris: Conard, 1937, pp. 247–316.

FC79 ——. "Edgar Poe et Anne de Geierstein." *Figaro,* Dec. 14, 1932.

FC80 ——. "Histoire de la traduction d'*Eureka.*" Baudelaire, *Oeuvres.* Vol. IX. Paris: Conard, 1936, pp. 207–65.

FC81 ——. "Histoire des *Aventures d'Arthur Gordon Pym.*" Baudelaire, *Oeuvres.* Vol. VIII. Paris: Conard, 1934, pp. 247–67.

FC82 ——. "Histoires des *Histoires extraordinaires.*" Baudelaire, *Oeuvres.* Vol. VI. Paris: Conard, 1933, pp. 349–85.

FC83 ——. "Histoire des *Histoires grotesques et sérieuses.*" Baudelaire, *Oeuvres.* Vol. XIV. Paris: Conard, 1937, pp. 215–45.

FC84 ——. "Histoire des *Nouvelles histoires extraordinaires.*" Baudelaire, *Oeuvres.* Vol. VII. Paris: Conard, 1933, pp. 307–16.

FC85 ——. "Notes et eclaircissements." Baudelaire, *Oeuvres.* Vol. VI. Paris: Conard, 1932, pp. 391–496.

FC86 ——. "Travaux sur Poe: Tableau chronologique de publication du vivant du traducteur." Baudelaire, *Oeuvres.* Vol. VI. Paris: Conard, 1932, pp. 387–90.

FC87 Croce, Benedetto. "Intorno ai saggi del Poe sulla poesia" (1947). *Letture di poeti e riflessioni sulla teoria e la critica della poesia.* Bari: Laterza, 1950, pp. 209–15.

FC88 Cross, Leland W. "Poe y Silva: Unas palabras de disensión." *Hispania* (Univ. of Conn.) XLIV (Dec. 1961), 647–51.

FC89 Cruz Monclova, Lidio. "Edgar Allan Poe y Puerto Rico." *Asomante,* XIV (Oct.–Dec. 1958), 64–69.

FC90 Curi Miguel, Neify Yolanda. *La mujer en la obra de Edgar Allan Poe.* Mexico, 1965.

FD

FD1 Dabrowski, Wojciech. "Edgar Allan Poe." *Tydzien,* Nov. 4–6 (1897), pp. 25–26, 33–35, 46–47.

FD2 ——. "Poeta lęku i trwogi. Z powodu setnejrocznicy urodzin E. A. Poe 1809–1909." *Słowo Polskie,* No. 38 (1909), pp. 4–5.

FD3 D'Agostino, Nemi. "Poe, Whitman, Dickinson." *Belfagor,* VIII (Sept. 1953), 517–38.

FD4 Darío, Rubén. "Edgar Allan Poe." *La Nación* (Buenos Aires), 1893. Reprinted in *Los raros* (Buenos Aires, 1893); and as prologue to Poe, *Poemas* (Madrid: Primitivo Fernández, 1909).

FD5 ———. "Edgar Allan Poe." *Los raros.* Madrid: Editorial Mundo Latino, 1918. See Vol. VI in his *Obras completas.*

FD6 ———. "Edgar Allan Poe." *La Semana,* No. 6 (Oct. 8, 1960), pp. 8–9, 15.

FD7 ———. "Prólogo." *Poemas,* by Poe. With a study by Baudelaire. Montevideo: C. Garcia, 1938.

FD8 da Silva, A. Casimiro. "Divagações sôbre Edgar Poe." *Correio da Manhã* (Rio), Oct. 28, 1945.

FD9 Dávalos, Balbino. *Los grandes poetas norteamericanos.* Mexico City, 1901, pp. 14–17.

FD10 Da Via, Gualtiero. "Il romanzo americano." *Popolo,* Aug. 7, 1948, p. 3.

FD11 Dávila, Carlos. "Poe y el centenario de la novela policíaca." *America,* XXXIII (April–June 1947), 21–23.

FD12 Debout-Oleszkiewicz, Simone. "L'Analogie ou 'Le Poème mathématique' de Charles Fourier." *Revue Internationale de Philosophie* (Brussels), XVI (1962), 176–99.

FD13 de Calys, Rurico. "Historias extraordinarias de Edgar Allan Poe." *El Hogar,* No. 537 (Jan. 23, 1920).

FD14 DeFosse, Marcel. *La Méthode intellectuelle d'Edgar Poe,* by Denis Marion [pseud.]. Paris: Éditions de Minuit, 1952.

FD15 De Graf, D. A. "Poe en Dickens." *Levende Talen,* No. 195 (June 1958).

FD16 Delarus-Mardus, L. "Oeuvre, vir, amours d'Edgar Poe." *RdP,* XXXII (Nov. 15, Dec. 1, 1925), 270–301, 578–600.

FD17 Delaunay. "Alcooliques et névrosés: Silhouettes d'ecrivains: Edgar Poe." *Jour de Médicine de Paris,* 2nd ser., XV (1903), 143–54.

FD18 Deleito y Piñuela, José. "La tristeza del horror—Edgard Poe." *El sentimiento de tristeza en la literatura contemporánea.* Barcelona, 1922, pp. 153–56.

FD19 De Marco, Sergio. " 'Eureka' di Edgar Allan Poe." *Rivista di letterature moderne e comparate,* XVII (1964), 265–84.

FD20 Depken, Friedrich. *Sherlock Holmes, Raffles und ihre Vorbilder: Ein Beitrag zur Entwicklungsgeschichte und Technik der Kriminalerzählung.* Heidelberg: C. Winter, 1914.

FD21 De Ritis, Beniamino. "Anime profetiche. Il gatto che ride." *Messaggero,* March 17, 1950, p. 3.

FD22 de Vries, H. "Edgar Allan Poe, dichter en proza—dichter, vergeleken met zijn Tijdenoot Frederic Chopin." *Kroniek van Kunst en Cultur,* 10 (1949), pp. 309–13.

FD23   Diddi, Raoul. "Due gatti neri." *Mattino,* Dec. 13, 1950, p. 3.

FD24   Diez-Canedo, Enrique. "Poe, traducido . . . del español." *El Sol* (Madrid), Nov. 22, 1931.

FD25   DiMarco, Sergio. " 'Eureka' di Edgar Allan Poe (per eina interpretazione)." *RLMC,* XVII (1964), 265–84.

FD26   Dinamov, S. "Edgar Po—khudozhnik smerti i razlozheniia" [Edgar Poe—an artist of death and decay]. *Oktiabr',* No. 4 (1934), pp. 160–71. Reprinted, enlarged and with title "Tvorchestvo Edgara Po" [The work of Edgar Poe], Poe, *Izbrannye proizvedeniia* [Selected works] (Moscow, 1935), pp. 5–51.

FD27   ———. "Nauchno-fantasticheskie novelly Edgara Po" [The science fiction short stories of Edgar Poe]. *Literatura i marksizm,* No. 3 (1931), pp. 51–64.

FD28   ———. [Review of] "Poe, E. A. Polnoe sobranie poem i stikhotvorenii" [Complete collection of poems and verse]. *Knigonosha,* No. 34 (1924), p. 8.

FD29   Donoso, Armando. "Al margen de Edgard Poe." *Atenea* [Argentina], I (1918), 19–27.

FD30   Doorn, Willem Van. "Edgar Poe en Ulalume." *Levende Talen* (Groningen), No. 151 (1949).

FD31   ———. "Poe's Ulalume." *Rev des Langues Vivantes,* XXIV (Sept.–Oct. 1958), 395–404.

FD32   Dornis, Jean. *La Sensibilité dans la poésie française contemporaine (1885–1912).* Paris, 1912.

FD33   Dostoevskii, F. M. "Tri rasskaza Edgara Poe" [Three tales of Edgar Poe]. *Vremia,* I (1861), 230–31. (Signed: Red.). Reprinted in Dostoevskii, *Polnoe sobranie sochinenii* [Complete collected works], XIII (Moscow, Leningrad, 1930), 523–24.

FD34   Dovski, Lee van (pseud.). *Genie und Eros.* Bern: 1947. 2 vols., with new illus., Olten: 1950.

FD35   Dromundo, Baltasar. "Edgar Poe y la poesía." *Todo,* July 23, 1935.

FD36   D'Sola, Juan. "Heráldica (Poe y Baudelaire)." *El Cojo Ilustrado,* XIV (Feb. 1, 1905), 101.

FD37   Dubedout, E. J. "Edgar Poë et Alfred de Musset." *MLN,* XXII (March 1907), 71–76.

FD38   Dumitrescu-Bușulenga, Zoe. "Edgar Allan Poe." Preface to Poe, *Scrieri Alese.* Bucharest: Editura pentru Literatură Universală, 1963.

FD39   Dumolin, Mauricio. "Edgardo Poe, autor y marido." *La Revista Blanca,* VII (Aug. 15, 1904), 126–28.

FD40   Dupouy, R. "L'Opiumisme d'Edgar Poe." *Annales Médico-Psychologiques* (Paris), 9th ser., XIII (1911), 5–18.

FD41   Durini, Emilia. "Vita tragica di Edgar Poe." *Popolo,* June 11, 1949, p. 3.

FD42   Dzięciołowski, Alfons. "Cieniom Edgara Poego." *Widnokragx,* No. 26 (1914), p. 12.

FE

FE1   E., L. "[Zum 50. Todestage] E. A. Poe[s]." *Norddeutsche allgemeine Zeitung* (Berlin), Supplement, No. 236 (1899).

FE2   Eastman, Max Forrester. "Poe, Whitman et la poésie des temps nouveaus." *Europe,* XV (Dec. 15, 1928), 443–62.

FE3   Eben, Karl Theodor, trans. *Der Rabe: Ein Gedicht von Edgar Allan Poe.* With a biog. sketch. Philadelphia: Barclay and Co., 1869.

FE4   Echaqüe, J. P. "El amor en la literatura." *Boletín de la Academia Argentina de Letras,* IX (July–Sept. 1941), 373–499.

FE5   Eck, Dr. Marcel. "L'Angoisse d'Edgar Allan Poe et son univers fantastique." *L'Homme et l'angoisse.* Paris: Arthème Fayard, 1964, pp. 217–32.

FE6   Edinger, Kurt. "Das Ende des Edgar Allan Poe." *Germania,* CVII (1929).

FE7   Edlund, Mårten. "Inledning." *Den Svarta Katten.* Stockholm: Bokförlaget Prisma, 1964, pp. 7–11.

FE8   Edward, Georg. "Die Rehabilitation Poes." *Beilage zur allgemeinen Zeitung* (Munich), No. 23 (1903).

FE9   Eguchi, Yuko. "The Change of Poe's Reputation in the United States." *Publications of the Institute for Comparative Studies of Culture (Kiyo)* (Tokyo Woman's Christian College), V, No. 1. (1957), 59–87.

FE10   ———. "Death Associated with Love as Expressed in Poe's Poetical Works." *Essays and Studies (Ronshu)* (Tokyo Woman's Christian College), III, No. 3 (1953), 17–42.

FE11   ———. *Edgar Poe: Ryunosuke Akutagawa and Edgar Poe.* Publications of the Academic Society of Tokyo Woman's Christian College.

Tokyo: Sobunsha, 1968. Part I, The Reconsideration of Edgar Poe in the Twentieth Century. Part II, A Comparative Study of Ryunosuke Akutagawa and Edgar Poe.

FE12 ——. "Houses and Monuments of Edgar A. Poe in the United States." *Comparative Studies of Culture (Hikaku Bunka)* (Tokyo Woman's Christian College), No. XIII (1967), pp. 11–25.

FE13 ——. "The Literary Environment of Edgar A. Poe." *Publications of the Institute for Comparative Studies of Culture (Kiyo)* (Tokyo Woman's Christian College), XII (1961), 89–112.

FE14 ——. "Ryunosuke Akutagawa and Edgar Poe: Their Artistic Viewpoints and Self-conscious Technique." *Publications of the Institute for Comparative Studies of Culture (Kiyo)* Toyko Woman's Christian College), XV (1963), 1–21.

FE15 ——. "Ryunosuke Akutagawa and Edgar Poe: Their Taste for the Strange and the Bizarre." *Publications of the Institute for Comparative Studies of Culture (Kiyo)* (Tokyo Woman's Christian College), XVIII (1964), 39–66.

FE16 ——. "Ryunosuke Akutagawa and Edgar Poe: Their Technique of Short Story Writing." *Publications of the Institute for Comparative Studies of Culture (Kiyo)* (Tokyo Woman's Christian College), XVI (1963), 61–89.

FE17 ——. "Southern Traits of Poe as Critic." *Publications of the Institute for Comparative Studies of Culture* (Tokyo Woman's Christian College), X (Nov. 1960), 63–80.

FE18 Ehrenstein, Albert. "Martyrdom of Poe." *Internationale Zeitschrift für Individualpsychologie,* VIII (July–Aug. 1930), 389–400.

FE19 ——. "Das Martyrium des Edgar Allan Poe." *Die denkwürdigen Erlebnisse des Gordon Pym.* Illus. Albert Kubin. Berlin: Deutsche Buch. Gemeinschaft, G.m.b.H., [1928?], pp. 365–84.

FE20 Eishiskina, N. "Edgar Po, ego zhizn' i tvorchestvo" [Edgar Poe, his life and work]. *Voprosy literatury,* No. 10 (1963), pp. 206–11.

FE21 ——. "Novoe izdanie Edgara Po" [A new edition of Edgar Poe]. *Inostrannaia literatura,* No. 9 (1959), pp. 267–68. Review of *Izbrannoe* [Selections] (Moscow, 1958).

FE22 Ekelund, Vilhelm. "Till Edgar Poes hundraårsdag." *Arbetet,* Jan. 19, 1909. Reprinted in *Böcker och vandringar* (Malmö, 1910), pp. 142–49.

FE23 Elek, Artúr. "Edgar költernényei." *Nyugat,* I, Nos. 13–17 (1909).

FE24 ——. *Poe Edgar (Két Tanulmány).* Budapest: a Nyugat Kiadása, 1910.

FE25 ———. "Poe Hollójának legújabb fordítása." *Nyugat,* II (1913).

FE26 ———. *Úp Poe-fordítások.* Figyelö, 1905.

FE27 Elek, Oszkár. "Artúr Elek: Poe Edgar." *EPhK,* 1910.

FE28 Elektorowicz, Leszek. "Edgar Allan Poe i współczesność." *Zycie Liter,* 28 (1957), p. 6.

FE29 Eliot, Thomas Stearns. "Da Poe a Valéry." *Inventario,* III (Spring 1950), 40–52.

FE30 ———. "Edgar Poe et la France." *TR,* No. 12 (Dec. 1948), pp. 1973–92.

FE31 ———. "Note sur Mallarmé et Poe." *NRF,* XXVII (Nov. 1926), 524–26.

FE32 ———. "Von Poe zu Valéry." *Merkur,* IV, No. 12 (1950), 1252–67.

FE33 Eloesser, A. "E. A. Poe." *Sonntagsbeilage der vossischen Zeitung* (Berlin), Nos. 15 and 16 (1905).

FE34 Elwall, Georges. [Edgar Allan Poe?] *Rev Blanche,* XVII (1898), 200.

FE35 Emerenciano, Jordão. *Edgard Allan Poe, o homem, o temperamento.* Recife: Diretoria de Documentação e Cultura, 1950.

FE36 Engel, Claire-Eliane. "L'Etat des travaux sur Edgar Allan Poe en France." *MP,* XXIX (May 1932), 482–88.

FE37 Engel, Eduard. "Edgar Allan Poe, ein Essay." *Neue Monatshefte für Dichtkunst und Kritik,* II (Nov. 1875), 377–89.

FE38 ———. "Edgar Poe." *Bühne und Welt,* II (July 1904), 837–44. Reprinted in *Blätter für Handel und Gewerbe und soziales Leben,* Supplement to *Magdeburger Zeitung,* Nos. 34, 35 (1904); *Tagesbote* (Brno), No. 384 (1907).

FE39 ———. "Eine neue Gesammtausgabe von Edgar Poes Werken." *Magazin für die Literatur des Auslandes,* XLIX (Feb. 28, 1880), 119–21.

FE40 Engel'gardt, M. "Edgar Po. Ego zhizn' i proizvedeniia" [Edgar Poe. His life and works]. Poe, *Sobranie sochinenii* [Collected works]. 2nd ed., vol. I. St. Petersburg, 1909, pp. vii–xxxi.

FE41 Englekirk, John E. "El divino Edgardo." *Leitura* (Rio), 39 (1946).

FE42 ———. *A literatura norteamerican no Brazil.* Mexico: 1950.

FE43 Enguídanos, Miguel. "El encuentro de Edgar Allan Poe y Luis Palés Matos." *Insula,* XVI (1961), 7.

FE44   Ernouf (Baron). "Revue Critique." *Rev Contemporaine,* XXVIII (July 15, 1862), 409–10. A review of *Contes inédits d'Edgar Poe,* trans. W. Hughes.

FE45   Erskine, John. "Introduction." Trans. Carmen Torres Calderón de Pinillos. *Biblioteca Interamericana.* II: *Cuentos clásicos del Norte.* 1st ser. New York, 1920, pp. v–xvi.

FE46   Estlander, C. G. [Review of] "Edgar Allan Poe, Underliga historier" [Strange stories], "Valda noveller" [Selected short stories]. *Finsk tidskrift,* No. 13 (1882), pp. 448–49.

FE47   Estrada, Ezequiel M. "Balzac, Poe y Dostoiewsky." *Revista do Livro,* No. 7 (Sept. 1957), pp. 23–28.

FE48   Etienne, Louis. "Les Conteurs americains, Edgar Poe." *Rev Contemporaine,* XXXII (July 15, 1857), 492–525.

FE49   Etze, Gisela [Gisela Etzel.] *Der Doppelmord in der Rue Morgue, und andere Verbrechergeschichten.* Vienna: Ullstein, 1946.

FE50   Etzel, Theodor. "Einleitung." Poe, *Gedichte.* Munich and Leipzig: Müller, 1909. Reprinted Berlin: Im Propyläenverlag, 1921–22. Reviewed: Gustav Noll, *Beiblatt zur Anglia,* XXI (Sept. 1910), 279–81.

FE51   Evans, E. P. "Edgar Allan Poe. Am fünfzigsten Todestage des Dichters." *Beilage zur allgemeinen Zeitung* (Munich), No. 229 (Oct. 7, 1899).

FE52   Ewers, Hanns H. *Edgar Allan Poe.* Berlin, 1905.

FE53   ———. "Edgar Allan Poe. Zum 100jährigen Geburtstage." *Nord und Süd* (Berlin), III (March 1909), 501–7.

FF

FF1   Fabiani, Edmea. "Il padre dei 'gialli'morì come un suo personaggio." *Mattino d'Italia e Momento,* May 6, 1953, p. 3.

FF2   Fabri, Albrecht. "Über E. A. Poe." *Deutsche Beiträge,* I (1946/47), 560–68.

FF3   ———, trans. *Vom Ursprung des Dichterischen und zwei andere Essays.* With introd. Cologne: Staufen, 1947.

FF4   Faleński, Felicjan. "Edgar Allan Poe i jego nowelle." *Bibl. Wwska,* IV, No. 1 (1861), 1–44.

FF5   Farrán y Mayoral, J. "El arte de Edgar Poe." *Narraciones extraordinarias.* Barcelona: Muntaner, 1942, pp. 7–15.

FF6 ———. [A Critical Study of Poe.] *Letras a una amiga estrangera.* Barcelona: *La Revista,* 1920.

FF7 ———, trans. *Narraciones extraordinarias, completas y seguidas de varios poemas.* 2 vols. Barcelona: Diamante, 1958.

FF8 Faures, André. "Edgar Poe." *Nouvelles Littéraires,* April 7, 1934, p. 22.

FF9 Ferenczi, Zoltán. *Költeméntyei.* Budapest: Franklin-Társulat, 1895.

FF10 ———. "Poe A. Edgar elbeszélései." *Az Erdélyi Múzeum Egylet Kiadványai* (Cluj), 1899, pp. 344–56, 440–61.

FF11 ———. "Poe Edgar Költemenyei." *Az Erdélyi Múzeum Egylet Kiadványai* (Cluj), 1888, pp. 115–31.

FF12 Fernandat, R. "Paul Valéry et les marginalia de Poe." *Muse Française,* July 10, 1929.

FF13 Ferran, André. *L'Esthétique de Baudelaire.* Paris: Hachette, 1933.

FF14 ———. *L'Esthétique de Baudelaire.* Paris: Nizet, 1968.

FF15 Ferrari, Santiago A. *Edgar Allan Poe.* n.p., [196–?].

FF16 Ficowski, Tadeusz, *Kruk. Milczenie. Presklady Czeslawa Koslowskiego . . . Odbitka z "Piora."* Kiev: Czcionkami Drukarni Polskiej, 1915.

FF17 Field, Jay C. "Edgard Allan Poe." *Sphinx,* No. 9 (April–May 1940), pp. 81–86.

FF18 Filloux, J. C. "Psychanalyse et critique: Edgar Poe." *Confluences,* March–April 1944, pp. 207–16.

FF19 Fiorino, Salvatore. "L'essenza della lirica di E. A. Poe." *Davide,* V, No. 1 (Jan.–Feb. 1955), 40–56.

FF20 Fiumi, Lionello. "Nel vivo d'una tragedia." *Vite appassionate e avveturose.* Osimo: Barulli, 1943, pp. 55–60.

FF21 Fleury, Jules. *Souvenirs et portraits de jeunesse.* Paris, 1872.

FF22 Fontainas, André. "Ce qu'ont pensé d'Edgar Allan Poe ses contemporains." *MdF,* CCXXV (Jan. 15, 1931), 312–24.

FF23 ———, trans. *Edgar A. Poe: Lettres à John Allan, son père adoptif.* Paris: G. Crès, 1930.

FF24 ———. "Edgar Poe adolescent et John Allan, son père adoptif." *MdF,* CLXXXVII (April 15, 1926), 324–36.

FF25 ———. "Edgar Poe et la poesie française." *Muse Française,* July 15, 1933.

FF26 ———. "Un Témoignage sur Edgar Poe." *Figaro,* June 21, 1930.

FF27 ———. *La Vie d'Edgar Poe, avec un portrait en héliogravure.* Paris: Mercure de France, 1919.

FF28 Foppema, Yge. "Poe, de libbene." *Tsjerne,* IV (1949), 304–10.

FF29 Forclaz, Roger. "Un Voyage aux frontieres de l'inconnu: *Les Aventures d'A. G. Pym,* d'Edgar Poe." *Études de Lettres* (University de Lausanne), VII (1964), 46–58.

FF30 Forgues, E. D. "Les Contes d'Edgar Poe," in "Etudes sur le roman anglais et américain," *RDM,* NS V (Oct. 15, 1846), 341–66.

FF31 ———. "La Fantasie aux Etats-Unis," *RDM,* July 15, 1860.

FF32 ———. "Poètes et romanciers américains: Nathaniel Hawthorne," *RDM,* II (April 5, 1852), 337–65.

FF33 Fournel, Victor. "Les Conteurs fantastiques." *Rev Française,* III (May 1856), 449.

FF34 Fox, Lucia Ungaro de. "El parentesco artístico entre Poe y Darío." *Revista Nacional de Cultura* (Caracas), XXVII (1966), 81–83.

FF35 Françon, Marcel. "Poe et Baudelaire." *PMLA,* LX (Sept. 1945), 841–59.

FF36 Frank, Max. "Melville und Poe: Eine Quellenstudie zu 'Fragments from a Writing Desk No. 2,' 'Redburn' und 'The Assignation.'" *Kleine Beiträge zur amerikanischen Literaturgeschichte: Arbeitsproben aus deutschen Seminaren und Instituten.* Ed. Hans Galinsky and Hans-Joachim Lang. Heidelberg: Winter 1961, pp. 19–23.

FF37 Frattarolo, Renzo. "Marginalia," *Italia che scrive,* XXXIII (March 1950), 30.

FF38 ———. "Poe." *Italia che scrive,* XXXIII (March 1950), 30.

FF39 Friedrich, Hugo. *Die Struktur der modernen Lyrik: Von Baudelaire bis zur Gegenwart.* Hamburg: Rowohlt, 1956.

FF40 Frunzetti, Ion. "Poezia lui Edgar Allan Poe." *Revista româno-americană,* I (1946), 232–36.

FF41 Fuhara, Yoshiaki. "Life of E. A. Poe." *Eigo Kenkyu* [The study of English], Poe Number (Oct. 1949), pp. 3–8.

FF42 Fukuda, Rikutaro. "Escape from the Moving Walls—A Study of Poe." *Eigo Seinen* [The rising generation], CXIII, No. 8 (Aug. 1967), 514–15.

FF43 ———, trans. *The Poetic Principle.* With notes. Tokyo: Kenkyusha, 1968.

FF44 Fumet, Stanislas. "Edgar Poe." *La Poesie au rendez-vous.* Paris: Desclée de Brouwer, 1967, pp. 65–98.

FF45   Futami, Kohei. "Poe and Music." *Eigo Seinen* [The rising generation], XCVI, No. 8 (Aug. 1950), 20–21.

FG

FG1   Gabrieli, Vittorio. *"Edgar A. Poe: Studi,* di Gabriele Baldini." *Italia che scrive,* XXXI (April 1948), 78.

FG2   Gadler, Diego. "Qualche pensiero sulla poesia pura." *Via,* II (May 27, 1950), 6.

FG3   Gale, Robert L. "Evil and the American Short Story." *Annali Istituto Universitario Orientale, Napoli, Sezione Germanica,* I (1958), 183–202.

FG4   Galinsky, Hans. "Beharrende Strukturzüge im Wandel eines Jahrhunderts amerikanischer Kurzgeschichte (dargelegt an E. A. Poes 'The Masque of the Red Death' und Ernest Hemingways 'The Killers')." *NS,* Supplement III (1958), 5–45.

FG5   García, Oton M. "Edgar Poe—Anti-romântico." *Ribeu,* III (Jan. 7, 1945), 25–31.

FG6   Gargiulo, Alfredo. [Review of Lauvrière, *Edgar Poe, sa vie et son oeuvre,* and Bresciano, *Il vero Edgardo Poe.*] *La critica,* IV (July 1905), 309–19.

FG7   Garrone, Federico, and Ernesto Ragazzoni, eds. *Edgar Allan Poe.* Turin: Roux Frassati, 1896.

FG8   Gaucher, Maxime. [Edgar Allan Poe.] *Rev Politique et Litteraire,* Dec. 2, 1882, p. 730.

FG9   Gautier, Théophile. "Introduction." *Les Fleurs du Mal,* by Charles Baudelaire. Paris: Callmann—Lévy, 1868.

FG10   Gel'strem, V. A. "Literaturnaia khronika. Kul't Edgara Po" [Literary chronicle. The cult of Edgar Poe]. *Novoe vremia,* Jan. 8/21, 1903.

FG11   Genneken, E. "Zhizn' Edgara Allena Poe" [The life of Edgar Allan Poe]. Poe, *Ocherki, rasskazy i mysli* [Essays, stories and thoughts]. Moscow, 1885, pp. i–lxiv.

FG12   Georges-Bazile, Cecil. *Lettres d'amour à Helen.* Paris: Emile-Paul Frères, 1924.

FG13   Getto, Giovanni. "Pascoli e l'America." *Nuova antologia,* XCI (Oct. 1956), 159–78.

FG14   Gheorghiu, Mihnea. "Edgar Allan Poe Calomniatul." *Orientări în Literatura Străină.* Bucharest: Editura pentru Literatura, 1958.

FG15   Ghysbrecht, P. F. R. M., and R. J. G. Venneman. "Een Fantasieproduct, 'The Raven' van E. A. Poe." *Rev des Langues Vivantes,* XXII (Jan.–Feb. 1956), 79–84.

FG16   Giaccari, Ada. "La fortuna di E. A. Poe in Italia." *SA,* V (1959), 91–118.

FG17   ———. "Poe nella critica italiana." *SA,* V (1959), 51–89.

FG18   Giordano-Orsini, G. N. "Gli ultimi giorni di E. Poe." *Nuova Italia,* Jan. 1935.

FG19   Giovannetti, Eugenio. "Il centenario del 'Corvo.'" *Poesia,* I (April 28, 1945), 374.

FG20   Gómez de la Serna, Julio. "Colofón explicativo al poema 'El cuervo.'" *Edgar Allan Poe: Narraciones completas.* Madrid: Aguilar, 1958, pp. 84–94.

FG21   ———, *et al.,* trans. *Narraciones completas.* With a prologue by Charles Baudelaire. With notes. 3rd ed. Madrid: Aguilar, 1958.

FG22   Gómez de la Serna, Ramón. "Las campanas de Poe." *Revista de Revistas,* No. 1867 (March 24, 1946).

FG23   ———. "Edgar Poe." *Efigies.* Madrid: Oriente, 1929.

FG24   ———. *Edgar Poe, el genio de América.* Buenos Aires: Editorial Losada, 1953.

FG25   ———. "Visión de Poe en su centenario." *Revista Nacional de Cultura,* No. 76 (Sept.–Oct. 1949), pp. 12–22.

FG26   Gomperts, H. A. *De Schok der Herkenning.* Amsterdam: van Oorschot, 1960.

FG27   Goncourt, Edmond and Jules. [Occasional Articles on Poe.] *Jour* (Paris), July 16, 1856, Jan. 19, 1866, March 23, 1868, July 17, 1875.

FG28   ———. "Memorias de la vida literaria." *Revista Cubana,* XII (1890), 467–75.

FG29   Gorlenko, V. Novyi trud ob Edgare Poe" [A new work about Edgar Poe]. *Otbleski* [Reflections]. St. Petersburg, 1906, pp. 86–97.

FG30   Gorlier, Claudio. "Il romanzo e la scienza." *Ulisse,* X, Nos. 24–25 (1957), 1020–27.

FG31   Gosse, E. "K stoletiiu so dnia rozhdeniia Edgara Po. Ocherk" [On the centenary of the birth of Edgar Poe. Essay]. *Novoe slovo,* No. 4 (1909), pp. 107–9.

FG32 Götzfried, H. L. "Nachwort." *Novellen.* Trans. Liselotte Hahlweg, illus. Leo Blaser. Nuremberg: Dipax, 1946.

FG33 Gourmont, Rémy de. [Edgar Allan Poe.] *Le Contemporain,* Jan. 1884, p. 38.

FG34 ———. "Marginalia sur Edgar Poe et sur Baudelaire." *Promenades Littéraires.* 1st ser. Paris: Mercure de France, 1904.

FG35 ———. "Notes sur Edgar Poe et Baudelaire." *Flegrea* (Naples), July 5, 1900.

FG36 Graaf, D. A. de. "E. A. Poe en Dickens." *Levende Talen,* No. 195 (June 1958), pp. 351–56.

FG37 Grabiński, Stefan. "Książe fantastów." *Lwowskie Wiad. Muz. i Lit.,* No. 6 (1931), pp. 64–66.

FG38 Gracq, Julien. "Edgar Poe et l'Amérique." *Préférences.* Paris: José Corti, 1961, pp. 177–82.

FG39 Grana, Gianni. "Interpretazioni di Poe." *Fle,* XI (July 1, 1956), 6.

FG40 Grava, Arnolds. *L'Aspect métaphysique du mal dans l'oeuvre littéraire de Charles Baudelaire et d'Edgar Allan Poe.* Ann Arbor: University Microfilms, 1954.

FG41 ———. "L'Aspect métaphysique du mal dans l'oeuvre littéraire de Charles Baudelaire et d'Edgar Allan Poe." *DA,* XIV (1954), 1238.

FG42 ———. *L'Aspect métaphysique du mal dans l'oeuvre littéraire de Charles Baudelaire et d'Edgar Allan Poe.* University of Nebraska Studies, No. 15 (June 1956).

FG43 ———. "L'Aspect métaphysique du mal dans l'oeuvre littéraire de Charles Baudelaire et d'Edgar Allan Poe." Diss., University of Nebraska, 1954.

FG44 Grech, A. [Review of] *Zolotoi zhuk* [The Gold Bug] (St. Petersburg, 1922). *Pechat' i revoliutsiia,* No. 2 (1923), pp. 247–48.

FG45 Gridinskii. "Edgar Po (1809–1849)." *Ezhemesiachnye sochineniia,* No. 10 (1900), pp. 109–13.

FG46 Griffis, William Elliot. "El misterio de 'El cuervo' de Edgar Poe." *Revista de Revistas,* No. 718 (Feb. 10, 1924), pp. 32–33. Translated from *NYTBR,* Feb. 10, 1924.

FG47 Grigor'ev, Ap. "Obzor inostrannoi zhurnalistiki. (Edgar Po)" [A survey of foreign journals. (Edgar Poe)]. *Moskvitianin,* No. 22, Part VI (1852), pp. 13–15.

FG48 Grolig, Moriz. "Bibliographie." *Worte Poes.* Minden: J. C. C. Bruns, 1907.

FG49   Gross, Ferdinand. *Seltsame Geschichten von Edgar Allan Poe.* Berlin and Stuttgart: Speman, 1881.

FG50   Guerra, Angel. "El centenario de Edgard Allan Poe." *La España Moderna,* XXI (April 1909), 130–44.

FG51   Guidi, Augusto. "E. A. Poe critico" (1949). *Occasioni americane.* Rome: Edizioni Moderne, 1958, pp. 17–21.

FG52   ———. "L'Italia di E. A. Poe" (1949). *Occasioni americane.* Rome: Edizioni Moderne, 1958, pp. 9–16.

FG53   ———. "Recenzione a Edgar A. Poe di G. Baldini." *Letterature moderne,* I (1950), 80–81.

FG54   ———. "Recensione a *Poesie* (Poe-Mallarmé, 1947)." *Fle,* II (Oct. 16, 1947), 6.

FG55   Gulian, Emil. "Prefața." *Poemele lui Edgar Allan Poe.* Bucharest: Editura Fundațülor Regale, 1938.

FG56   Gündel, G. Edmund. *Edgar Allan Poe: Ein Beitrag zur Kenntnis und Würdigung des Dichters.* Freiberg: Verlachsche Buchdruckerei, 1895.

FG57   Gusanma, Francisco, trans. *Poemas en prosa.* Barcelona: Editorial Apolo, 1946.

FG58   Gutiérrez, Fernando, trans. *Aventuras de Arturo Gordon Pym.* Barcelona: Mateu, 1956.

FG59   Güttinger, Fritz. [Introduction.] *Unheimliche Geschichten.* Zurich: Artmis, 1958.

FH

FH1   H., T. "Zum 50. Todestage E. A. Poes." *Leipziger Tageblatt und Anzeiger,* No. 516 (1899).

FH2   de Haan, Tj. W. R. "Nochris 'The Raven.'" *Tsjerne,* VI (1951), 95–96.

FH3   Haines, Charles. *E. A. Poe.* Milan: La Goliardica, 1958.

FH4   Hallberg, Louis Eugène. *Histoires des littératures etrangères.* 5 vols. Paris: A. Lemerre, 1878. See vol. II.

FH5   Halmar, Augusto d'. "Edgard Poe y el álgebra del terror." *Los 21.* Santiago de Chile: Editorial Bachillerato, 1962.

FH6   Hamada, Masajiro. "Pluto in 'The Black Cat.'" *Eigo Seinen* [The rising generation], CXII, No. 12 (Dec. 1966), 826–27.

FH7   Hansson, Ola. "Edgar Allan Poe." *Tolkare och siare.* Vol. X of *Samlade skrifter.* Stockholm, 1921, pp. 13–87. Previously published in German, Danish, Norwegian, and Polish translations.

FH8   ———. "Edgar Allan Poe." *Tolke og Seere,* 1893, pp. 1–71. Abridged version.

FH9   ———. *Jasnowidze i Wrözbici.* Warsaw: Gebethner i Wolff, 1905.

FH10   ———. *Seher und Deuter.* Berlin: Rosenbaum S. Hart, 1895.

FH11   Harry, S. J. "Edgar Allan Poe, genio de la pesadilla." *La Semana,* No. 14 (Sept. 19, 1959), pp. 1, 15.

FH12   Héduin, H. "Poets and Poetry of America." *L'Athenaeum Français,* July 1, 1854, p. 595 (col. 1) and p. 597 (col. 3).

FH13   Hellens, Frans. "Edgar Poe et Melville." *Le Fantastique réel.* Brussels-Amiens: "Sodi," 1967, pp. 33–45.

FH14   Helling, C. "Een onbekende short-story van Poe." *Litterair pasport,* V (1950), 78–80.

FH15   ———. "Poe en Zijn laatste Uren." *Litterair pasport,* July 1947.

FH16   Hello, Ernest. [Concerning Hawthorne and Poe.] *Rev du Monde Catholique,* Feb. 25, 1862, p. 711.

FH17   ———. "Du Genre fantastique." *Rev Français,* Oct. 1858, p. 39.

FH18   Hennel, Adolf. "Edgar Poe, jego życie i pisma." *Gazeta Codz* (1858), No. 61, pp. 3–4; No. 62, p. 5; No. 63, p. 4; No. 96, p. 3.

FH19   Hennequin, Émile. "Edgar Allan Poe." *Écrivains Françaisés.* Paris: Perrin, 1889, pp. 117–61. Reprinted from *Rev contemporaine,* Jan. 25, 1885.

FH20   ———. *Études de critique scientifique. Écrivains Françaisés: Dickens-Heine-Tourguénef-Poe-Dostoïewski-Tolstoi.* Paris: Perrin, 1889.

FH21   ———. "Vie d'Edgar Allan Poe." *Contes grotesques,* by Edgar Poe. 4th ed. Paris: Paul Ollendorf, 1882. Reviewed: Emile Bergerat, *Le Voltaire,* March 6, 1883.

FH22   Hinatsu, Konosuke. *The Romantic and Symbolic Schools of English Poetry.* Tokyo: Hakusiusha, 1940–41.

FH23   Hippe, Fritz. "Vorgelegt." *Edgar Allan Poes Lyrik in Deutschland.* Borna-Leipzig: Robert Noske, 1913.

FH24   Hitchcock, Alfred. "Förord." *Edgar Allan Poe Sällsamma historier.* Stockholm: Rabén and Sjögren, 1964, pp. 7–10.

FH25   Hittmair, Hans. "E. A. Poe und E. T. A. Hoffmann—ein Vergleich." Diss., Innsbruck, 1952.

FH26   Holthusen, Hans Egon. "Das lyrische Kunstwerk." *Deutsche Philologie im Aufriss*. Berlin, 1951, III, 962, 969.

FH27   Honda, Sanshiohi. "Ryunosuke Akutagawa and Edgar Allan Poe." *Kobe Gaidai Ronsô* [Kobe City Univ. Jour.], VII, Nos. 1–3 (June 1956), 93–102.

FH28   Horta, Eulogio. "Rápidas notas sobre Casal, Poe, etc." *Bronces y rosas* (Havana), 1908.

FH29   Hosoiri, Totaro. "Poe as a Journalist." *Eigo Seinen* [The rising generation], XCIII, No. 1 (Jan. 1947), 53–54.

FH30   Hughes, William L., trans. *Contes inédits d'Edgar Poe*. Paris: Hetzel, n.d.

FH31   Huguenin, Daniel. "Baudelaire et Edgar Poe." *Poésie et monde humain: Essai sur les cheminements de l'imagination dans la poésie française moderne*. Paris: Le Soleil dans la Tête, 1960, pp. 15–34.

FH32   Huret, Jules. *Enquête sur l'evolution littéraire*. Paris: Charpentier, 1891.

FI

FI1   Ibels, A. "La vida y la muerte de Poe." *La Razón*, Sept. 1, 1926.

F12   Ichiriki, Hideo. *Edgar Allan Poe*. Vol. I. Tokyo: Kwobundo, 1960.

FI3   ———. "Maternal Influence on Poe." *Essays on English and English and American Literature for the Celebration of Dr. Minoru Toyoda's 70th Birthday*. Fukuoka: University of Kyushu, 1956.

FI4   ———. "On the Style of Edgar Poe." *Essays for the Celebration of the 75th Anniversary of Waseda University* (Dec. 1957). Tokyo: Waseda University, 1957.

FI5   ———. "One Aspect of E. Poe." *Eigo Eibungaku Ronsô* (Fukuoka: Univ. of Kyushu), No. 3 (1953).

FI6   ———. "Poe vs. Griswold." *Kyudai Ronsô*, No. 2 (1952).

FI7   ———. "Poe's Characters—On Plagiarism." *Kyudai Ronsô*, No. 3 (1953).

FI8 ——. "Reconsideration of 'The Fall of the House of Usher.'" *Waseda Hogakukai Shi* (Tokyo: Waseda Univ.), IX (Jan. 1959).

FI9 ——. "Thoughts on Edgar Poe." *Waseda Hôgakukai Shi* (Tokyo: Waseda Univ.), No. 7 (Jan. 1957).

FI10 Ingram, John H. "Ein Dichterleben: Biographische Skizze." Trans. Leopold Katscher. *Literatur, Kunst und Gesellschaft*, VII (1884), 26–39.

FI11 ——. *Edgar A. Poe, vida y obra*. Buenos Aires: Lautaro, 1944.

FI12 ——. "Edgar Allan Poe: Eine biographische Skizze." *Blätter für Handel, Gewerbe, und soziales Leben*, 38, 39, and 40 (Sept. 23, Sept. 30, and Oct. 7, 1878), pp. 293–95, 301–2, 309–10.

FI13 ——. "Edgar Poe et ses amis." Trans. Henry Dovray. *MdF*, LXXVII (Jan. 16, 1909), 208–19.

FI14 ——. *Edgar Poe: Poésies complètes*. Trans. Gabriel Mourey. With a letter from John H. Ingram, "La Philosophie de la composition," and biog., and bibliog. notes. Paris: Mercure de France, 1910.

FI15 ——. *Edgar Poes Werke*. Trans. Hadda Moeller-Bruck and Hedwig Lachmann. Minden: J. C. C. Bruns, 1911–14.

FI16 ——. *Edgardo Allan Poe, su vida, cartas y opiniones*. Trans. Edelmiro Máyer. Buenos Aires: J. Peuser, 1887.

FI17 ——. "Poe Allan Edgar." *Budapesti Szemle*, XLIX (Jan. 1881), 93–108.

FI18 Inomata, Hiroshi. "The Depths of the Woodland of Weir— an Approach to Edgar Poe." *Essays* (Tokyo), No. 4 (April 1957), pp. 10–19.

FI19 Izzo, Carlo. [Introductory Notes, Biography, Bibliography, Excerpts from Poe.] *Tutti i racconti e le poesie*. Gherardo Casini editore, n.d., pp. v–xxv, 1203–17.

FJ

FJ1 Jackowska, Suzanne d'Olivera. *Le Corbeau de Edgar Poe: Deuxième volume de ses plus beaux poemes en vers français avec texte anglais en regard*. Preface by M. C. Cestre. Paris: Les Amis d'Edgar Poe, 1933. Reviewed: B. Matulka, *RR*, XXVI (July–Sept. 1935), 266–67.

FJ2   ——. "La Réhabilitation d'Edgar Poe." *NRF* (March and April 1933), pp. 103–15, 187–96.

FJ3   ——. *La Réhabilitation de Edgar Poe, et ses plus beaux poèmes en vers français, avec texte anglais en regard.* Preface by M. le Professeur C. Cestre. New York: Stechert; Paris: Les Amis d'Edgar Poe, 1933. Reviewed: B. Matulka, *RR*, XXVI, 266–67.

FJ4   Jacobs, Monty. "Poe." *Die Nation* (Berlin), I, No. 34 (1901).

FJ5   Jaloux, Edmond. *Edgar Poe et les femmes.* Geneva: Éditions du Milieu du Monde, 1942.

FJ6   ——. "Recontres avec Edgar Poe." *1935,* March 27, 1935, p. 9.

FJ7   Jannaccone, Pasquale. "L'estetica di Edgardo Poe." *Nuova antologia* (Rome), July 15, 1895.

FJ8   Jiménez Rueda, Julio. "Edgar A. Poe y nosotros." *Revista de Revistas,* No. 2048 (Oct. 23, 1949), p. 7.

FJ9   Jørgensen, Johannes. "Indledning." *Arthur Gordon Pyms Haendelser.* Copenhagen: Lehmann & Stages Forlag, 1892.

FJ10   ——. "En ny Digtning: I. Edgar Poe." *Tilskueren,* X (1893), 375–86.

FJ11   Johansons, Andrejs, trans. *Melnais Kakis.* Stockholm: Vegastiftelsens förlag, 1946.

FJ12   Jünger, Ernst. *Strahlungen.* Tübingen: 1949, pp. 9, 65, 82, 83f., 118, 349, 435, 464. A novel.

FJ13   ——. *Der Waldgang.* Frankfurt: 1950, pp. 43, 67, 121.

FJ14   Just, Klaus G. "Edgar Allan Poe und die Folgen." *Übergänge: Probleme und Gestalten der Literatur.* Bern: Francke, 1966, pp. 58–78.

FJ15   Just, Walter. *Die romantische Bewegung in der amerikanischen Literatur, Brown, Poe, Hawthorne: Ein Beitrag zur Geschichte der Romantik.* Berlin: Mayer and Müller, 1910.

FK

FK1   K., L. "Galeria zagranicznych pisarzy 'Edgar Allan Poe.'" *Dziennik liter,* Nos. 31–32 (1868), pp. 496–97, 515–16.

FK2   Kagami, Eizo. *The Black Cat & The Gold-Bug.* Trans. with notes by Motoshi Karita. Tokyo: Ōbunsha, May 1966. Contains "The Masque of the Red Death," "The Fall of the House of Usher," "The Murders in the Rue Morgue," "William Wilson."

FK3 ———. "The Intellectual Narcissism in Edgar Allan Poe." *Annual Report of Gifu College of Education (Jinbun Kagaku)* (Gifu), No. 12 (Feb. 1964), pp. 1–9.

FK4 ———. "On the Problem of Mortality in Poe." *Annual Report of Gifu College of Education (Jinbun Kagaku)* (Gifu), No. 3 (Feb. 1955), pp. 33–39.

FK5 Kahn, Ernst. *Edgar Allan Poe und Charles Baudelaire: Ein Vergleich ihrer Weltanschauung und Kunstlehre.* Diss., University of Heidelberg, 1921.

FK6 Kahn, Gustave. "Les Poèmes de Poe traduits par Stéphane Mallarmé." *Revue Indépendante,* VIII (Sept. 1888), 435–43.

FK7 ———. *Silhouetts littèraries.* Paris, 1925.

FK8 Kalma, D. "Poe en Melville." *Tsjerna,* VI (1951), 245–50.

FK9 Kamegulov, A. "Edgar Po. (Predislovie)" [Edgar Poe. (Foreword)]. Poe, *Ubüstvo v ulitse Morg* [The murders in the Rue Morgue]. Leningrad, 1927, pp. 3–9.

FK10 Kameński, Henryk S. "Edgar Allan Poe." *Społeczeństwo,* Nos. 20–21 (1909), pp. 240–41, 249–51.

FK11 Kardos, L. "Edgar A. Poe." *Edgar Allan Poe ösezes versei.* Budapest, 1949.

FK12 Kartzke, Georg. "Eingeleitet." *Phantastische Erzählungen.* Trans. Günther Steinig. Leipzig: Dietrich, 1953.

FK13 Kasegawa, Koh. "An Interpretation of 'The Fall of the House of Usher.'" *Aoyáma Journal of General Education* (Tokyo: Aoyama Gakuin Univ.), No. 3 (Nov. 1962), pp. 1–31.

FK14 Kasiński, Władysław Jerzy. "Gorączka zwana życiem." *Życie i Myśl,* Nos. 11–12 (1960), pp. 100–117.

FK15 ———. "Kobiety Edgara Allana." *Kierunki,* No. 33 (1960), pp. 7, 11.

FK16 Kass, Werner. *"The Raven:* Ein Beitrag zur lautklanglichen Harmonik der Poesie." *Schweizer Monatshefte* (Zürich), XXVII (1947), 224–41.

FK17 Kassner, Rudolf. "Edgar Allan Poe." *Die Mystik, die Künstler und das Leben.* Leipzig: Diederichs, 1900.

FK18 Katayama, Tadao. "Poe and Allegory." *Anglo-American Studies,* I (Oct. 1958), 79–85.

FK19 ———. "Poe's Conception of Immortality." *Jour of Osaka University of Foreign Studies,* VII (April 1959), 1–10.

FK20 ———. "A Study of 'Ligeia.'" *Jour of Osaka University of Foreign Studies,* VI (April 1958), 1–18.

FK21 ———. "Verisimilitude and Poe's Stories." *Eibei Kenkyu*, No. 3 (July 1962), pp. 71–91.

FK22 Kato, Akihiko. "A Study of Poe." *Memoirs of the Mejiro Gakuen Woman's Junior College* (Tokyo), II (Nov. 1965), 153–57.

FK23 Katscher, Leopold. "Edgar Allan Poe." *Hannoverscher Courier*, No. 27,851 (Jan. 19, 1909), pp. 1–2.

FK24 Katsurada, Rikichi. "Some Notes on the Studies of Essays on Poetry by Coleridge and Poe." *Studies in English Language and Literature* (Tokyo: Hosei Univ.), IV (March 1961), 14–20.

FK25 Kayser, Wolfgang. *Das Groteske: Seine Gestaltung in Malerei und Dichtung*. Hamburg: 1957, pp. 81–86.

FK26 Kelemen, Mór. "Edgar A. Poe élete." *Hölgyfutár*, No. 212 (1856).

FK27 Kersten, Kurt. "E. A. Poe und E. Th. Hoffmann." *Fränkische Blätter für Geschichtsforschung und Heimatpflege* (Bamberg), VII, No. 3 (1955), 1–11.

FK28 ———. "E. A. Poe und E. Th. Hoffmann." *Welt und Wort, Literarische Monatsschrift* (Tübingen), IV (1949).

FK29 Kijima, Heijiro. "Time and Place Did Not Favor Poe." *Eigo Seinen* [The rising generation], CV, No. 5 (May 1959), 4–5.

FK30 Kildal, Arne. "Edgar Allan Poe." *Vor Verden*, 1929, pp. 361–68.

FK31 Killy, Walther. "Künstliche Abenteuer: Poe: 'Narrative of A. Gordon Pym.'" *Wirklichkeit und Kunstcharakter—Neun Romane des 19. Jahrhunderts*. Munich: C. H. Beck'sche Verlagsbuchhandlung, 1963, pp. 125–145.

FK32 Kimura, Takeshi. "Poe and Japanese Literature in Meiji Era." *Eigo Seinen* [The rising generation], CIII, No. 7 (July 1957), 2–3; No. 8 (Aug. 1957), 28–29; No. 9 (Sept. 1957), 26–27; No. 10 (Oct. 1957), 30–31; No. 11 (Nov. 1957), 28–29; No. 12 (Dec. 1957), 29–30.

FK33 Kipling, Rudyard, and Edgar Allan Poe. *Rudyard Kipling—Edgar Allan Poe (Versei-Poems)*. Trans. József Szebenyei and Árzád Pásztor. Nazyvárad, Hungary, 1904.

FK34 Kiss, Béla Zilahi. *Edgar A. Poe*. No. 344. Budapest: Hírlap, 1904.

FK35 Kitamura, Tatsuzo. "A Study on the Peculiarity of Poe's Literature." *Bulletin of the Faculty of Education of Shinshu University*, IV (March 1954), 9–19.

FK36 Kjaer, Nils. "Edgar Allan Poe." *Kjaer: Kuvia ja esseitä* [Pictures and essays]. Helsinki, 1910, pp. 7–34.

FK37 ———. "Edgar Poe." *Essays, Fremmede Forfattere.* Oslo, 1895, pp. 19–48.

FK38 ———. "Poe og Emerson: Fragment." *Tids-signaler,* 1895, pp. 571–72.

FK39 Kleinstück, J. [Essay and Bibliography.] *Der Mord in der Rue Morgue: Geschichten zwischen Tag, Traum und Tod.* Trans. Fanny Fitting und Walter Hess. Hamburg: Rowohlt, 1959.

FK40 Klepatskii, G. "Predislovie" [Foreword]. Poe, *Polnoe sobranie sochinenii* [Complete collected works]. Kishinev, 1895, pp. 1–11.

FK41 Kohut, Adolf. "Edgar Allan Poe: Zum 100. Geburtstage des Dichters am 9. Januar 1909." *Reclams Universum moderne illustrierte Wochenschrift,* XVI (Jan. 27, 1909), 383–84.

FK42 Komarov, A. "Edgar Allan Poe, ego zhizn' i tvoreniia" [Edgar Allan Poe, his life and writings]. *Ezhenedel'noe novoe vremia,* V, Nos. 61–62 (1880), 548–58, 626–39.

FK43 Koskimies, Rafael. *Maailman kirjallisuus* [World literature]. Vol. IV. Helsinki, 1965, pp. 119–23.

FK44 Köstlein, Karl, trans. *Geschichten aus dem Dunkel: Fünf Erzählungen.* With introd. Die Perlenkette, 32. Stuttgart: Riederer, 1954.

FK45 Kotliarevskii, N. "Edgar Poe i Sharl' Bodler" [Edgar Poe and Charles Baudelaire]. *Deviatnadtsatyi vek* [The nineteenth century]. St. Petersburg, 1921, pp. 188–97.

FK46 Krasnosel'skii, A. "V bor'be s prozoi zhizni. (K psikhologii neopredelennykh stremlenii). II. Edgar Po" [In the struggle against the prose of life. (On the psychology of unfocussed strivings). II. Edgar Poe]. *Russkoe bogatstvo,* No. 11, Part II (1900), pp. 46–55.

FK47 Kristensen, Tom. "Edgar Allan Poe." *Til dags dato,* 1953, pp. 295–301.

FK48 Krzhizhanovskii, S. "Edgar Allan Po." *Literaturnaia gazeta,* Oct. 26, 1939.

FK49 Kudo, Yoshimi. "Edgar Allan Poe." *Studies in English Literature.* Tokyo: Asahi-Shinbun-Sha, 1948, pp. 31–42.

FK50 Kühnelt, Harro H. "Die Aufnahme und Verbreitung von E. A. Poes Werken im Deutschen." *Festschrift für Walther Fischer.* Heidelberg: C. Winter Verlag, 1959, pp. 195–224.

FK51 ———. *Die Bedeutung von E. A. Poe für die englische Literatur.* Innsbruck: E. Schumacher, 1949. Reviewed: T. O. Mabbott, *AL,*

XXIII, 260; F. W. Lorch, *JEGP*, L, 283–84; C. Wegelin, *MLN*, LXVI, 356–57; L. Von Hibler, *MLR*, XLVII, 229–30; A. J. Farmer, *RLC*, XXV, 283–85.

FK52 ——. "Deutsche Erzähler im Gefolge von E. A. Poe." *RLMC*, II (Oct.–Dec. 1951), 457–65.

FK53 ——. "E. A. Poe und Alfred Kubin: Zwei künstlerische Gestalter des Grauens." *Wiener Beiträge zur englischen Philologie*, LXV (1957), 121–41.

FK54 ——. "E. A. Poe und die phantastische Erzählung im österreichischen Schrifttum." *Schlern-Schriften* (Innsbruck), CIV (1953), 131–43.

FK55 ——. "Edgar Allan Poe und Dante Gabriel Rossetti." Diss., Innsbruck, 1948.

FK56 ——. "Nachwort." *Edgar Allan Poe: Gedichte Essays*. Trans. Theodor Etzel (*Gedichte*, "Die Philosophie der Komposition") and Hedwig Lachmann (*Heureka*). Munich: Winkler-Verlag, 1966, pp. 205–35.

FK57 ——. "T. S. Eliot als Poe Kritiker." *NS*, V (March 1956), 105–12.

FK58 Kuroda, Kenjirô, ed., *Edgar Allan Poe: The Fall of the House of Usher & Other Pieces*. Annotated together with Haruzô Demizu. Kyoto: Seki-shoten, 1953.

FK59 ——. "The Evil Heart in Poe." *The Helicon* (Matsuyama: Ehime Univ., No. 5 (1953).

FK60 ——. "Perverseness in Poe." *The Helicon* (Matsuyama: Ehime Univ., No. 5 (Nov. 1953), pp. 4–10.

FK61 Kurokawa, Nobuo. "E. A. Poe and Arthur Rimbaud." *English Literature in Hokkaido* (Sapporo: Univ. of Hokkaido), No. 5 (June 1959), pp. 78–86.

FK62 ——. "A Preliminary Essay on E. A. Poe." *Hokkaido Eigo Eibungaku* (Sapporo: Univ. of Hokkaido), No. 5 (June 1959).

FK63 Kusenberg, Kurt. "Der Dichter im höllischen Sog." *Deutsche Zeitung und Wirtschaftszeitung* (Stuttgart), IV, No. 80 (Oct. 5, 1949).

FK64 Kuz'ko, P. "Poet bezumiia i uzhasa—Edgar Poe. (1809–1849)" [A poet of insanity and horror—Edgar Poe, 1809–1849]. *Na Kavkaze* (Krasnodar), No. 1 (1909), pp. 86–89.

FK65 Kuzuoka, T. "Poe's Wife." *Present-day English*, No. 6 (1950).

FL

FL1   L., E. "Der Dichter, der den Detectiv erfand: Das seltsame Leben des Edgar Allan Poe." *Kasseler neueste Nachricht,* No. 5 (1934).

FL2   Labra, Rafael M. de. "La literatura norteamericana en Europa: J. Fenimore Cooper, Harriet Beecher Stowe, Edgar A. Poe." *Revista de España,* XLVII (April 28, 1879), 457–89.

FL3   Lacan, Jacques. "Le Séminaire sur la lettre volée." *Ecrits* (Paris, 1966), pp. 11–61.

FL4   Lacerda, Aurélo, trans. *Contos de imaginação e mistério.* Rio de Janeiro: Edições Pinguim, 1947.

FL5   Lachize, Samuel. "W sto pięćdziesiątą rocznicę urodzin Edgara Allana Poe genialnego mistyfikatoraa." *Widnokręgi,* No. 2 (1959), pp. 42–50.

FL6   Lachmann, Hedwig. *Ausgewählte Gedichte.* Berlin: Verlag des Bibliographischen Bureaus, 1891, pp. 5–78.

FL7   Lachowicz, Bogdan. "Poe, mistrz grozy i niesamowitości." *Kurier Codz,* No. 39 (1947), p. 10.

FL8   Lalou, René. "Edgar Poe et la France." *Bulletin de l'Education Nationale,* No. 4 (Jan. 26, 1950), pp. 7–8.

FL9   Lancellotti, Arturo. "Il centenario di Edgardo Poe." *Popolo,* Sept. 17, 1949, p. 3.

FL10   ——. "Edgar Poe e le sue allucinanti novelle." *Momento,* Oct. 31, 1946, p. 3.

FL11   Lancelotti, Mario A. *De Poe a Kafka: para una teoría del cuento.* Buenos Aires: Editorial Universitaria de Buenos Aires, 1965.

FL12   Lanckrock, Rik. "Edgar Allan Poe, zes vertellingen vertaald door J. F. Ankersmit." *Arsenaal,* VI (1950), 40.

FL13   Landa, Dr. Nicasio. "Prólogo crítico-biográfico." *Historias extraordinarias.* Madrid: Luis García, 1858, pp. i–xxviii.

FL14   Lang, Hans-Joachim. "Die Prosaerzählungen des 'Atlantic Souvenir:' Zur Situation der Kurzgeschichte zwischen Irving und Poe." *Jahrbuch für Amerikastudien* (Heidelberg), X (1965), 78–105.

FL15   Lang, S. "Edgar Poe und die neuere Dichtung." *Neue Schweizer Rundschau,* XXI (1928), 188–97.

FL16   Laplaza, Francisco P. "Edgar Allan Poe, la novela policial y la crimonología." *Pórtico,* No. 10 (1944), pp. 12–14.

FL17 Lara, Justo de [José de Armas y Cárdenas, pseud.]. "Edgar A. Poe." *Historia y literatura.* Havana, 1915, pp. 225–30.

FL18 Larsen, Alf. "De stora dødsdiktere." *Den kongelige kunst.* 3rd ed. Oslo, 1960, pp. 15–35.

FL19 Lashiz, S. "Edgar Allan Po—genial'nyi mistifikator" [Edgar Allan Poe—a mystifier of genius]. *V zashchitu mira,* No. 93 (1959), pp. 72–78.

FL20 Lauvrière, Émile. "A propos d'Edgar Poe." *Rev Anglo-Américaine,* April 1928, pp. 340–42.

FL21 ———. "L'Alcoolisme d'Edgar Poe." *Clairière* (Brussels), IV (1903), No. 80.

FL22 ———, trans. and ed., *Contes et poésies,* by Edgar Allan Poe. With introd. Paris: La Renaissance du Livre, 1917, 1925.

FL23 ———. *Edgar Poe.* Paris: Bloud, 1911.

FL24 ———. "Edgar Poe et le freudisme." *Grande Rev,* CXLIII (Oct. 1933), 565–87.

FL25 ———. *Edgar Poe, sa vie et son oeuvre: Étude de psychologie pathologique.* Paris: F. Alcan, 1904.

FL26 ———. *L'Etrange vie, les etranges amours d'Edgar Poe.* Paris: Desdée de Brouwer, 1934. Reviewed: Schmitz, *AL,* VI, 366–67; V. O'Sullivan, *Dublin Mag,* IX, 58; E. J. Breen, *Cweal,* XXIII (Dec. 27, 1935), 250–51; W. R. Benet, *American Mercury,* XXVII, 375–77; J. Cournos, *NYTBR,* Feb. 9, 1936, p. 16; E. Jaloux, *Nouvelles Littéraires,* April 14, 1934; J. S. Wilson, New York *Herald Tribune,* Book Review sec., Feb. 9, 1936, p. 12.

FL27 ———. *Le Génie morbide d'Edgar Poe: Poésies et contes.* Paris: Desclée, de Brouwer, 1935.

FL28 ———. "La Vie et les amours d'Edgar A. Poe." *Rev Universelle,* XXXV (Nov. 15, Dec. 1, 1928), 420–58, 538–76.

FL29 Le Breton, Maurice. "Edgar Poe et Macaulay." *Rev Anglo-Américaine* (Oct. 1935), pp. 38–42.

FL30 Lécuyer, Raymond. "Le Centenaire d'Edgar Poe." *Le Gaulois,* Jan. 18, 1909.

FL31 Le Dantec, Yves-Gérard. "Baudelaire et Edgar Poe." *L'Education Nationale* (Paris), June 14, 1956, pp. 22–23.

FL32 ———. "Baudelaire traducteur." *Correspondant,* Jan. 10, 1932.

FL33 ———, ed. Edgar Allan Poe, *Histoires.* Trans. Ch. Baudelaire. Paris: La Pléiade, 1932.

FL34 Legendre. "Le Livre d'Edgar Poe." *Le Figaro,* April 10, 1856.

FL35   Lemaitre, Jules. [Edgar Allan Poe.] *Les Lettres et les arts,* Jan. 1886.

FL36   Lemnaru, Oscar. "Nuvele Fantastice ale lui Poe." *Revista Romăno-Americană,* I (1946), 242–44.

FL37   Lemonnier, Léon. "Baudelaire et Mallarmé traducteurs de Poe." *Langues Modernes,* XLIII (Jan.–Feb. 1949), 47–57.

FL38   ——. "Baudelaire, traducteur du Corbeau." *Muse Française,* VIII (Dec. 10, 1929), 701–5.

FL39   ——. "Baudelaire: Tuteur et traducteur d'Edgard Poe." *Rev Hebdeomadaire,* XXXV (Oct. 9, 1926), 210–25.

FL40   ——. *Edgar Poe et la critique française de 1845 à 1875.* Paris: Presses Universitaires de France, 1928. Reviewed: F. Delatte, *Rev Belge de Philologie et d'Histoire,* VIII, 597–99.

FL41   ——. "Edgar Poe et le bon sens français." *Grande Rev,* CXII (May 1928), 458–66.

FL42   ——. "Edgar Poe et le roman scientifique français." *Grande Rev,* CXXXIII (Aug. 1930), 214–23.

FL43   ——. "Edgar Poe et le théâtre de mystère et de terreur." *Grande Rev,* CXXX (May 1929), 379–96.

FL44   ——. *Edgar Poe et les conteurs françaises.* Paris: Aubier, 1947.

FL45   ——. "Edgar Poe et les origines du roman policier en France." *MdF,* CLXXXIII (Oct. 15, 1925), 379–91.

FL46   ——. "Edgar Poe et les Parnassiens françaises." *RLC,* IX (Oct. 1929), 728–36.

FL47   ——. *Edgar Poe et les poètes francaises.* Paris: Nouvelle Revue Critique, 1932. Reviewed: C. Cestre, *Rev Anglo-Américaine,* April 1933, 360.

FL48   ——. "Edgar Poe et Théodore de Banville." *RLC,* VI (Oct. 1926), 688–90.

FL49   ——. "Edgar Poe, illuminé français." *MdF,* CCI (Jan. 15, 1928), 367–74.

FL50   ——. "L'Influence d'Edgar Poe sur Baudelaire." *Rev de France,* IX (Oct. 15, 1929), 689–713.

FL51   ——. "L'Influence d'Edgar Poe sur les conteurs françaises symbolistes et decadents." *RLC,* XIII (Jan.–March 1933), 102–33.

FL52   ——. "L'Influence d'Edgar Poe sur Mallarmé." *Rev Mondiale,* Feb. 1929.

FL53 "L'Influence d'Edgar Poe sur quelques conteurs réalistes, Erckmann-Chatrian, Henri Rivière, Eugène Mouton." *RLC,* XI (July–Sept. 1931), 451–65.

FL54 ———. "L'Influence d'Edgar Poe sur quelques poètes symbolistes et décadents." *MdF,* CCXII (June 15, 1929), 513–56.

FL55 ———. "L'Influence d'Edgar Poe sur Verlaine et Rimbaud." *Le Figaro,* Jan. 19, 1929.

FL56 ———. "L'Influence d'Edgar Poe sur Villiers de L'Isle-Adam." *MdF,* CCXLVI (Sept. 15, 1933), 604–19.

FL57 ———. "Introduction." *Histoires grotesques et sérieuses.* Trans. Charles Baudelaire. Paris: Garnier Frères, 1950, pp. i–xxiii.

FL58 ———. "Introduction." *Nouvelles Histoires extraordinaires.* Preface and trans. Charles Baudelaire. Paris: Garnier Frères, 1961, pp. i–xxix.

FL59 ———. "Paul Valéry et Edgar Poe." *Nouvelles Littéraires.* August 24, 1929.

FL60 ———. *Les Traducteurs d'Edgar Poe en France de 1845 à 1875: Charles Baudelaire.* Paris: Presses Universitaires de France, 1928. Reviewed: Victor Klemperer, *Deutsche Literatureztg.,* 1929, pp. 808–10; "M. E. I. R.," *MLR,* XXV, 387–88; Y.-G. Le Dantec, *RLC,* X, 375.

FL61 ———. "La Vocation fantastique d'Edgar Poe." *Rev des Vivants,* pp. 1237–51.

FL62 ———, trans. *Poèmes d'Edgar Poe.* With preface notes. Paris: Corti, 1949.

FL63 Lennig, Walter, ed. "Edgar Allan Poe." *In Selbstzeugnissen und Bildokumenten.* Hamburg: Rowohlt, 1959. Reprinted 1963.

FL64 LeRoy, Albert. [Of a National Literature from the United States.] *RdP,* July 1854, p. 32.

FL65 Levi, Fritz, comp. and ed. *Aus den Tiefen der Seele: Phantastische Geschichten.* Illus. Vladimir Kirin. Wiesbaden: Der Greif, 1956.

FL66 ———, comp. and ed. *Phantastische Geschichten.* Illus. Vladimir Kirin. Zürich: Buchklub Ex Libris, 1955.

FL67 Lillo Catalán, Victoriano. *Trilogía doliente: Musset, Chopin, Bécquer. Dos grandes sinfonistas opuestos: Ruben Darío y Edgar Poe.* Buenos Aires: Revista Americana de Buenos Aires, 1935.

FL68 Lindsay, Philip. *E. A. Poe [The Haunted Man: A Portrait of E. A. Poe].* Trans. Maria Gallone. Milan: Rizzoli, 1956.

FL69 Link, Franz H. "Die Burlesken Edgar Allan Poe." *NS,* NS 16 (Oct. 1967), 461–71.

FL70 ———. " 'Discovery' und 'Destruction:' Eine Interpretation von Edgar Allan Poes 'MS. Found in a Bottle.' " *NS*, NS X (Jan. 1961), 27–38.

FL71 ———. "Edgar Allan Poes 'Ligeia' und das Paradoxon der modernen Dichtung." *Deutsche Vierteljahrsschrift für Literaturwissenschaft und Geistesgeschichte*, XXXVII (Aug. 1963), 363–76.

FL72 Lipparini, Giuseppe. "Poetica di Poe." *Messaggero* (Dec. 15, 1949), p. 3.

FL73 Liszka, Béla. "Poe Allan Edgar—Engel Eduard után." *Fövárosi Lapok,* No. 233 (1879).

FL74 Locard, Edmond. "Edgar Poe, Detective: Étude de technique policiere." *Rev Hebdeomandaire*, XXX (July 30, 1921), 527–44.

FL75 Lockspeiser, Edward, comp. and ed. *Debussy et Edgar Poe; Manuscrits et documents inédits.* Preface by André Schaeffner. Monaco: Editions du Rocher, 1962.

FL76 Löhrer, Frieda. "Poe und Baudelaire." *Die Sammlung: Monatsschrift für Erziehung und Kultur* (Göttingen), IV (1949), 689–84.

FL77 Lombardo, Agostino. "L'America e la letteratura." *Criterio*, I, No. 5 (May 1957), 377–82.

FL78 ———. *La poesia inglese dall'estetismo al simbolismo.* Rome: Ed. di Storia e Lett., 1950, pp. 59–60, 227–28.

FL79 Lopushinskii, E. "Edgar Poe (Amerikanskii poet)" [Edgar Poe. (An American poet)]. *Russkoe slovo,* No. 11, Part III (1861), pp. 1–30.

FL80 Lot, Fernand. "Edgar Poe mis a nu?" *Rev Bleue,* XXIII (Dec. 1934), 901–5.

FL81 Lubbers, Klaus. *Die Todesszene und ihre Funktion im Kurzgeschichtenwerk von Edgar Allan Poe.* Mainzer amerikanistische Beiträge, IV. Munich: Max Hueber, 1961. Reviewed: Lorch, *AL*, XXXV, 94–95; Moore, *YWES*, XLII, 282.

FL82 Lucka, Emil. "Poe und die romantische Kunst." *Österreichische Rundschau*, XVIII (Jan. 15, 1909), 110–16.

FL83 Lüdeke, Henry. "American Literature in Germany." *Geschichte der amerikanischen Literatur.* Bern: A. Francke, 1952, pp. 122–31.

FL84 ———. "Rev. of *Choix de Contes,* trans. by Charles Baudelaire and Roger Asselineau." *English Studies* (Amsterdam), XL (Aug. 1959), 327–28.

FL85 Luzi, Mario. "Poe come uomo." *Giornale del Mattino,* May 30, 1956, p. 3.

FL86 L'vov-Rogachevskii, V. "Edgar Po i Leonid Andreev" [Edgar

Poe and Leonid Andreev]. *Dve pravdy. Kniga o Leonide Andreeve* [Two truths. A book about Leonid Andreev]. St. Petersburg, 1914, pp. 169–186.

FMc

FMc1   McCormick, John O. "Die Feuer des Willens: Eine Deutung Poescher Prosa-Dichtung." Epilogue to Poe, *Erzählungen.* Munich: Winkler, 1959.

FMc2   McKenzie, Kenneth. "Poe." *Conferenza sulla letterature americana.* Bari: Editorial Laterza, 1922.

FM

FM1   Macchioni, Rodolfo. "Tre saggi sulla poesia." *Ponte,* II (Sept. 1946), 827–829.

FM2   Maeno, Shigeru. "Edgar Poe and His Time." *Kindai* (Kobe: Kobe Univ.), I (Dec. 1952), 27–33.

FM3   ———. "Some Problems in Baudelaire's Criticism on Poe." *Kindai,* X (Jan. 1955), 53–63.

FM4   ———. "Some Sources of Baudelaire's Criticism on Poe." *Kindai,* XIII (Dec. 1955), 19–29.

FM5   Maggi, Maria. *"Le avventure di Gordon Pym." "Il corsaro rosso." Nuova antologia,* LXXXIII (March 1948), 377–78.

FM6   Malgrat, Jaime, trans. *Aventuras de Arturo Gordon Pym.* Barcelona: Arimany, 1956.

FM7   Mallarmé, Stéphane. *Divagations.* Paris: Charpentier, 1897.

FM8   ———, trans. *Les Poèmes d'Edgar Poe.* Firenze: Sansoni, 1957.

FM9   ———, trans. *Les Poèmes d'Edgar Poe.* Paris: Gallimard, 1928. First appeared in 1880.

FM10   ———. *Poesie—Versione francese di S. Mallarmé.* With English text. Ed. Gabriele Baldini. 2 vols. Firenze: Fussi Editore, 1947.

FM11   ———. "Pomnik Edgara Poe." Trans. M. Jastrun. *Twórczość,* No. 3 (1946), p. 33.

FM12   Mandolini, Hernano. "Los maestros de la muerte, Poe, Maupassant, Tolstoi." *Nosotros,* XLVIII (Nov. 1924), 291–99.

FM13   ——. "La psiquiatría en la obra de Edgar Poe." *Revista Argentina de Neurología, Psiquiatría y Medicina Legal,* XXI (March–April 1929), 178–80.

FM14   Marcellini, Giovanni. "Si collegano al poeta del 'Corvo' le correnti di letteratura moderna." *Roma,* Feb. 20, 1954, p. 3.

FM15   Marco, Sergio de. " 'Eureka' di Edgar Allan Poe (per una interpretazione)." *RLMC,* XVII (1965), 265–84.

FM16   Marion, Denis [Marcel Defosse]. "La Méthode intellectuelle de Poe." *Mesures,* VI (April 1940), 89–127.

FM17   Markus, Dr. G. "Feuilleton; Edgar Allan Poe: Zu seinem hundertsten Geburtstag." *Neue Zürcher Zeitung* (Zürich), CXXX, Nos. 19, 20, 21 (Jan. 19, 20, 21, 1909).

FM18   Marsilia, Antonio. "Romanticismo in America." *Mattino d'Italia,* Feb. 3, 1954, p. 3. Review of Baldini's lecture on Poe.

FM19   Marussi, Garibaldo. "E. A. Poe, o del bene perduto." *Radio Corriere,* NS IV (Aug. 1–7, 1948), 16.

FM20   Masson, Gustave. [Edgar Allan Poe.] *La Correspondence littéraire,* May 1860, p. 301.

FM21   Masuda, Michizo. "Edgar Allan Poe and 'Undine.' " *Studies in Humanities,* IV, No. 10 (Oct. 1953), 17–29.

FM22   ——. "A Portrait of E. A. Poe." *Eigo Kenkyu* [The study of English], XLVI, No. 8 (Aug. 1957), 12–16.

FM23   ——. "Utopian Senses in the Works of E. A. Poe." *Studies in Humanities* (Osaka: The Literary Association, Osaka City Univ.) III, No. 9 (Sept. 1952), 1–8.

FM24   Mathews, Frances Aymar. "Hvorledes Poe's 'Ravnen' blev til." *Kringsjaa,* IX (1897), 264–67.

FM25   Matsumura, Tatsuo. "Poe's Profile." *Eigo Kenkyu* [The study of English], Poe Number (Oct. 1949), pp. 28–31.

FM26   Maucher, Gisela Maria. *Das Problem der dichterischen Wirklichkeit im Prosawerk von E. T. A. Hoffman und E. A. Poe.* Ann Arbor, Michigan: University Microfilms, 1964.

FM27   ——. "Das Problem der dichterischen Wirklichkeit im Prosawerk von E. T. A. Hoffmann und E. A. Poe." *DA,* XXVI (July 1965), 356–57.

FM28   ——. "Das Problem der dichterischen Wirklichkeit im Prosawerk von E. T. A. Hoffmann und E. A. Poe." Diss., University of Washington, 1964.

FM29   Mauclair, Camille. "Edgar Poe, idéologue." *La Quinzaine,* LXXVIII, LXXIX (1898), 203–14, 301–17. Reprinted in his *L'Art en silence* (Paris: Ollendorff, 1901).

FM30   ———. *Le Génie d'Edgar Poe: La Légende et la vérité, la méthode, la pensée, l'influence en France.* Paris: A. Michel, 1925. Reviewed: Brander Matthews, *Literary Digest International Book Rev,* IV, 478–80.

FM31   ———. "Le Génie d'Edgar Poe; le peintre et l'aquafortiste." *Rev Politique et Litteraire,* LXIII (Oct. 3, 1925), 640–44.

FM32   ———. *Louis Legrand, peintre et graveur.* Paris: H. Floury, 1910. See chap. 6.

FM33   ———. *Princes de l'esprit.* Paris: A. Michel, 1930.

FM34   Medrano, Higinio J. *En el país de Poe.* Philadelphia, 1920.

FM35   Mejia Sánchez, Ernesto. "Edgar Allan Poe en México." *Repertorio Americano,* No. 1129 (Aug. 15, 1951), p. 144.

FM36   Mendés, Catulle. [Introduction to Excerpts from Poe's *Marginalia.*] *La Republique des Lettres,* March 20, 1876, pp. 131–32.

FM37   Mendes, Oscar, and Milton Amado, trans. *Poesia e prosa, obras completas,* by Edgar Allan Poe. Pôrto Alegre: Livraria do globo, 1944.

FM38   Menz, Lotte. *Die sinnlichen Elemente bei Edgar Allan Poe und ihr Einfluss auf Technik und Stil des Dichters.* Marburg: N. G. Elwert'sche Verlagsbuchhandlung, 1915.

FM39   Messac, Régis. *Le "Detective Novel" et l'influence de la pensée scientifique.* Paris, 1929.

FM40   ———. *Influences francaises dans l'oeuvre d'Edgar Poe.* Paris: Picart, 1929.

FM41   Meurer, Kurt Erich, ed. *Das goldene Zeitalter: Nordamerikanische Lyrik des 19. Jahrhunderts.* Heidelberg: Meister, 1948. Nineteen poems by Poe included.

FM42   Meyer, E. "Consultation d'Edgar Poe sur un crime: Edgar Poe à M. le directeur de 'La Grande Revue.' Du pays de la soif eternelle." *Grande Rev,* CXLIV (March 1934), 114–18.

FM43   Michaud, Guy. *Message poétique du symbolisme.* 4 vols. Paris, 1947.

FM44   Michaud, Régis. "Baudelaire et Edgar A. Poe: Une Mise au point." *RLC,* XVIII (Oct.–Dec. 1938), 666–83.

FM45   Micheli, Silvio. "Una giornata di Edgar Poe." *Vie nuove,* V (Feb. 19, 1950), 15.

FM46 Miedzyrzecki, Artur. "Edgar Allan Poe po polsku." *Nowe Książki,* No. 15 (1960), pp. 903–5.

FM47 Mikami, Tadashi. "E. A. Poe and His Masochism—Centering on His 'The Black Cat.'" *Daito Bunka University Literature Department Bulletin* (Tokyo), V (Dec. 1966), 39–60.

FM48 ——. "An Essay on Poe's 'The Haunted Palace.'" *Daito Bunka University Literature Department Bulletin* (Tokyo), VI (Jan. 1968), 23–34.

FM49 ——. "An Essay on Poe's 'The Masque of the Red Death.'" *Daito Bunka University Collection of Economic Treatises* (Tokyo), VIII (June 1967), 165–81.

FM50 ——. "Poetic Intuition and Poetic Calculation." *Daito Bunka University Literature Department Bulletin* (Tokyo), IV (Feb. 1966), 71–86.

FM51 Milner, Max. *Le Diable dans la littérature française de Cazotte à Baudelaire, 1772–1861.* 2 vols. Paris: J. Corti, 1960.

FM52 Minagawa, Soichi. "Poe as a Poet." *Eigo Kenkyu* [The study of English], Poe Number (Oct. 1949), pp. 32–33.

FM53 Moeller-Bruck, Arthur. "Poes Leben und Schaffen." *Edgar Allan Poes Werke.* Ed. Hedda and Arthur Moeller-Bruck. Minden: J. C. C. Bruns, 1904. See I, 123–48.

FM54 Möllenhoff, J. *Ausgewählte Novellen von Edgar Allan Poe.* 3 vols. Leipzig: P. Reclam, 1883–86.

FM55 Møller, Niels. "Edgar Poe." *Tilskueren,* XII (1895), 589–615. Reprinted in *Nattevagter, Udvalgte Afhandlinger* (Copenhagen and Oslo, 1923), pp. 229–54.

FM56 Mönch, Walter. "Poe und Baudelaire: An der Schwelle der modernen Dichtung." *Das Gastmahl: Begegnungen abendländischer Dichter und Philosophen.* Hamburg: Hugo, 1947, pp. 331–407.

FM57 Mondor, Henri. "Quincey, Dickens, Poe, Ruskin . . . parmi bien d'autres: Comme les voyait Mallarmé." *FLe,* Nov. 18, 1961, p. 4.

FM58 ——. *Vie de Mallarmé.* Paris, 1946.

FM59 Monin, E. "Essai médical sur Edgar Poë." *Praticien* (Paris), IV (1881), 253–57.

FM60 Monner Sans, José Maria. "Edgar Allan Poe: algunos aspectos de su obra." *Cursos y Conferencias,* XXXVII (1950), 1–12.

FM61 Montalvo, Antonio. [Review of *Los poemas de Edgar Poe,* trans. by Carlos Obligado (Buenos Aires: Viau y Zona, 1932).] *América,* No. 54 (1934), pp. 115–19.

FM62   Montégut. [On Literature in Europe and America.] *RDM*, Oct. 15, 1849.

FM63   Montenegro, Ernesto. "Edgardo Poe: una rehabilitación científica." *Revista Chilena,* XV (March–April 1923), 548–53.

FM64   Montesi, Gotthart, "E. A. Poe: Der Prophet des Schreckens." *Wort und Wahrheit* (Vienna), IV (1949), 772–77.

FM65   Montesions Malo, Arturo. "Primer centenario de la muerte de Poe: La añoranza de lo que nunca fue." *Letras del Ecuador,* Nos. 50–52 (1949), pp. 6–8.

FM66   Monti, Argia, trans. *Racconti straordinari.* With introd. 2nd ed. Modena: Edizioni Paoline, 1959.

FM67   Montoliu, Manuel de. "Un jucio crítico." *Poesías de Edgar Poe.* Las mejores poesías [líricas] de los mejores poetas, XLVII. Barcelona: Editorial Cervantes, 1924, pp. 5–21.

FM68   Morand, Paul. "Préface." *Le Sphinx, et autres contes bizarres,* by Poe. Trans. Marie Bonaparte, Matilda C. Ghyka, et Maurice Sachs. Paris: Gallimard, 1934.

FM69   Moreau, P. "Edgar Poe, étude de psychologie morbide." *Annales Médico-Psychologiques* (Paris), 73rd ser., XIX (1894), 5–26.

FM70   Morice, Charles. *La Littérature de tout à l'heure.* Paris: Perrin, 1889.

FM71   Moriyasu, Yukio. "The Prose Style of E. A. Poe—Some Notes on 'The Fall of the House of Usher.' " *Studies in Humanities* (Osaka: The Literary Association, Osaka City Univ.), III, No. 3 (March 1952), 18–34.

FM72   Morris, George D. "Edgar Poe d'après la critique française du dix-neuvième siècle." *Fenimore Cooper et Edgar Poe d'après la critique française du Dix-Neuvième Siècle.* Paris: Emile Larose, 1912.

FM73   Morrisette, Bruce. *Les Aspects fondamentaux de l'esthétique symboliste.* Clermont-Ferrand, 1933.

FM74   Mortensen, Johan. "Edgar Allan Poe." *Svensk tidskrift,* III (1894), 160–80. Reprinted in *Likt och loikt: Studier och kritik* (Stockholm, 1908), pp. 3–48.

FM75   Mostovich, Ch. "Amerikanskii Gofman" [An American Hoffmann]. *Knizhki nedeli,* No. 11 (1899), pp. 226–28.

FM76   Mourey, Gabriel. "Un Amour d'Edgar Poë." *Rev Politique et Litteraire,* XLVII (March 6, 1909), 307–11.

FM77   Moüy, Chs. de "Edgar Poe." *Rev Française,* VI (Oct. 1, 1863), 145–58.

FM78   Mucci, Renato. "Recenti studi su Edgar Poe." *Popolo,* Jan. 15, 1954, p. 3.

FM79   ———. " 'Science fiction' antica e moderna." *Popolo,* Sept. 19, 1954, p. 3.

FM80   Mummendey, Richard, trans. *Das verräterische Herz: Erzählungen.* With notes and epilogue. Hattingen: Hundt, 1953.

FM81   Murakami, Fujio. "The Truth about the Griswold Memoir." *Studies in Humanities,* IV, No. 4 (April 1953), 18–32.

FM82   Murao, Hozumi. "The Background of E. Poe's Work." *Kenkyu Hôkoku* (Takamatsu: College of Education, Kagawa Univ.), No. 5 (March 1955), pp. 1–20.

FM83   ———. "E. Poe in France." *Kenkyu Hôkoku* (Takamatsu: College of Education, Kagawa Univ.), No. 9 (July 1957), pp. 32–43.

FM84   ———. "Miscellanea of E. A. Poe." *Kenkyu Hôkoku* (Takamatsu: College of Education, Kagawa Univ.), August 1959, pp. 53–71.

FM85   ———. " 'The Mysterious Years' of E. A. Poe." *Kenkyu Hôkoku* (Takamatsu: College of Education, Kagawa Univ.), No. 14 (Sept. 1961), pp. 1–18.

FM86   ———. "On E. Poe's Prose." *Kenkyu Hôkoku* (Takamatsu: College of Education, Kagawa Univ.), April 1954, pp. 35–37.

FM87   Murena, H. A. "Los parricidas: Edgar Allan Poe." *Realidad,* Nos. 17–18 (1949), pp. 129–53.

FN

FN1   Nadeau, Maurice. "Préface" to "De Joseph de Maistre à Edgar Poe." *Oeuvres complètes de Baudelaire.* Vol. I. Paris: Le Club du meilleur livre, 1955, pp. [337–52].

FN2   Naerup, Carl. "Edgar Poe." *Kringsjaa,* XXXIII (1909), 273–77.

FN3   Naganuma, Kohki. *Introductory Seminar of Mystery Stories on Edgar Allan Poe.* Tokyo: Kohdan-sha, 1962.

FN4   Nakamura, Jyun-ichi. *Edgar Allan Poe's Relations with New England.* Tokyo: Hokuseido, 1958.

FN5   Nakamura, Tôru. "Some Problems in Poe's Literary Criticism." *Bulletin of the Faculty of Arts and Sciences* (Mito: Ibaraki Univ.), No. 17 (Dec. 1966), pp. 149–62.

FN6 Nakano, Yoshio. "On E. A. Poe." *Eigo Kenkyu* [The study of English], Poe Number (Oct. 1949), pp. 9–12.

FN7 Deleted.

FN8 Nakazato, Haruhiko. "The Early Poetic Theories of Edgar Allan Poe." *Rikkyo Rev* (Tokyo: St. Paul's Univ.), No. 22 (March 1961), pp. 55–78.

FN9 ———. "Edgar A. Poe and Shohei Ohoka." *St. Paul's Review* (Tokyo: St. Paul's Univ.), No. 23 (March 1968), pp. 48–72.

FN10 ———. "On *The Narrative of Arthur Gordon Pym* of Edgar A. Poe." *St. Paul's Review* (Tokyo: St. Paul's Univ.), No. 21 (May 1967), pp. 23–41.

FN11 Nalimov, A. [Review of] "Poe, E. A. Sobranie sochinenii" [Collected works] (vol. II, Moscow, 1906). *Rus'*, March 3, 1906 (Supplement).

FN12 Nania, Salvatore. *Il dramma e il pensiero estetico russo nei saggi critici di Edgar Allan Poe: Il crollo di un mito.* Naples: Libreria Intercont, 1957.

FN13 Napolitano, Felice. "Ritorno del terrore (Edgar Allan Poe un parente terribile)." *Mattino d'Italia*, March 31, 1954, p. 3.

FN14 Nardi, Dino. "La rivelazione di Poe." *FLe*, No. 28 (1956).

FN15 Narita, Shigehisa. "On Poe's Short Stories." *Senior English*, No. 6 (1947).

FN16 ———. "Poe's Critical Essays." *Eigo Kenkyu* [The study of English], Poe Number (Oct. 1949), pp. 20–23.

FN17 ———. "Poe's Style." *Study and Teaching of English*, No. 10 (1946).

FN18 Nass, L. "Un Alcoolique de génie." *Paris Médical*, XXXIII (appendix) (1919), 122–24.

FN19 Navarro, Diego, trans. *Historias extraordinarias; Poemas,* by Poe. With prologue. Barcelona: Janés, 1952.

FN20 Nebel, Gerhard. "Nachwort." *Wirbel und Nacht: Drei Novellen.* Trans. Th. and G. Etzel. Anker-Bücherei, No. 49. Stuttgart: Klett, 1949.

FN21 Nemésco, Vitorino. "No centenário de Unamuno." *Colóquie,* No. 31 (1964), pp. 41–43.

FN22 Nicoletti, Gianni. "La poesia dell'impostura." *Giornale,* Feb. 20, 1950, p. 3.

FN23 Nigot, G. "Edgar Poe devant la critique." *Rev de l'Enseignement des Langues Vivantes,* Nov. 1926, pp. 393–400.

FN24 Niiniluoto, Y. E. "Edgar Allan Poen käsitys runollisesta luomistyöstään" [Edgar Allan Poe's idea of his poetic work]. *Valvoja-Aika*, III (1925), 320–24.

FN25 Nikoliukin, A. [Review of] "Moss, S. P. *Poe's Literary Battles*. 1963." *Sovremennaia khudozhestvennaia literatura za rubezhom* No. 12 (1963), pp. 104–6.

FN26 Nishimura, Kôji. "Edgar Allan Poe." *Sekai Bungaku* (Tokyo), April 1947.

FN27 Nishimura, Tôru. "The Method of Poe's Fiction." *Jour of Literature of Osaka Woman's College*, IV (July 1952), 18–30.

FN28 Nist, John. "A projeção mitica de Edgar Poe." *O Estado de São Paulo, Suplemento Literário*, Dec. 24, 1959, p. 7.

FN29 Nomura, Akichika. *A Study of E. A. Poe*. Tokyo: Fukumura-Shoten, 1949.

FN30 Noulet, E. "L'Influence d'Edgar Poe sur la poésie française." *Études Littéraires* (Mexico), 1945, pp. 79–126.

FN31 ———. *L'Oeuvre poétique de Stéphane Mallarmé*. Paris, 1940.

FN32 Nousiainen, Oskari. "E. A. Poe: Rakkauden ja kuoleman lauluja" [Songs of love and death]. *Edgar Allan Poen kirjallinen tuotanto* [The literary production of Edgar Allan Poe]. Helsinki, 1946, pp. 5–51.

FN33 Nuñez, Estuardo. "Poe en el Perú." *IPNA*, No. 24 (1954), pp. 25–29.

FO

FO1 Obligado, Carlos, trans. *Los poemas de Edgar Poe*. With prologue and notes. 3rd ed. Buenos Aires: Viau y Zona, 1944.

FO2 ———. "Prólogo." *Los poemas de Edgar Poe*. Buenos Aires: Espasa-Calpe Argentina, 1944, pp. 1–24.

FO3 Obligado, P. M. "La tragedia de Edgar Poe." *La Nación*, June 12, 1927. Reprinted in his *La tristeza de Sancho y otros ensayos* (Buenos Aires: AGLP, 1927).

FO4 Ochoa, F. Salcedo. "Edgar Allan Poe (Una visita a su tumba)." *El Cojo Ilustrado*, XIV (March 15, 1905), 200–202.

FO5 Ogata, Toshihiko. "On E. A. Poe." *Jour of Literature of Osaka Woman's College*, XIII (March 1961), 68–90.

FO6   ——, ed. *The Poetic Principle and Others.* With notes. Kyoto: Apollon-sha, 1962; 1966.

FO7   Ogawa, Kazuo. "On 'Eureka.'" *Intelligence and Modern English Literature.* Tokyo: Kenkyusha, 1952, pp. 249–66.

FO8   ——. "Poe, an Originator." *Intelligence and Modern English Literature.* Tokyo: Kenkyusha, 1952, pp. 267–87.

FO9   Oguiza, Tomás. "Baudelaire, Poe, Goya: Un cietro extramundo." *Cuadernos Hispanoamericanos* (Madrid), LXX (1967), 29–35.

FO10   Ohsawa, Mamoru, trans. "Walt Whitman: Edgar Poe's Significance." With notes. *Eigo Seinen* [The rising generation], XCV, No. 8 (Aug. 1949), 303–6.

FO11   Oi, Koji. "Poe's Income." *Eibei Kenkyu,* No. 3 (July 1962), pp. 92–113.

FO12   Okamoto, Masao. "Coleridge's Influence in Poe's Poetic Theory." *Eigo Seinen* [The rising generation], XCVII, No. 1 (Jan. 1951), 12–14.

FO13   Okui, Kiyoshi. "A Eulogy on Poe—on 'William Wilson.'" *Comparative Literature and Comparative Culture.* Tokyo: Kobundo, 1961, pp. 201–20.

FO14   Olenjeva, B. "Amerikans'ka novela epoxy romantyzmu." *Radjans'ke Literaturoznavstvo* (Kiev), XI (1967), 45–55.

FO15   Oliver, Miguel S. "Poe, revisiones y centenarios." *Hojas del Sábado* (Barcelona), 1918, pp. 245–52.

FO16   Olivera, Carlos. "La infancia de Edgar Poe." Buenos Aires, n.d. [1884?].

FO17   Olivero, Federico. *Edgar Allan Poe.* Turin: Edizioni de "L'Erma," 1939.

FO18   ——. *Nuovi saggi di letteratura inglese.* Turin: Libreria Editrice Internazionale, 1918.

FO19   ——, trans. *La poesie.* Bari: Laterga, 1912.

FO20   ——. *Studi britannici.* Turin: Bocca, 1931.

FO21   ——. *Studi sul romanticismo inglese.* Bari: Laterza, 1914.

FO22   Oppel, Ilse. "Poe und Baudelaire." Diss., Vienna 1950.

FO23   Oras, Ants. "'The Bells' of Edgar Allan Poe and 'A Prophecy' by John Keats." *Apophoreta Tartuensia* (Stockholm), II (1949), 88–94.

FO24   Ortensi, Ulisse, trans. *Il libre dei poemi.* With preface. Turin-Rome: Roux e Viarengo, 1902.

FO25 ——. "Nel centenario di Edgar Poe: L'uom e l'idealogo." *La Tribuna,* Jan. 20, 1909.

FO26 ——. *Poemetta e liriche di Edgar Poe.* Lanciano: G. Garabba, 1930.

FO27 ——. *Poesie di Edgar Poe: Prima versione italiana in prosa.* With biog. and bibliog. of Poe. Lanciano: Rocca Carubba, 1892.

FO28 O'Sullivan, Vincent. "Edgar Poe et ses compatriotes." *Rev de l'Enseignement des Langues Vivantes,* Dec. 1928, pp. 441–57.

FO29 ——. "Edgar Poe, O'Brien et Thomas De Quincey." *MdF,* CCLX (June 1, 1935), pp. 445–48.

FO30 Oyamada, Yoshifumi. "The Grotesque in American Literature. Edgar Poe and His Contemporaries." *Bul. of Kanto Gakuim Univ.* (Yokohama), No. 4 (Dec. 1963), pp. 47–56.

FO31 ——. "The World of Edgar A. Poe." *Essays Dedicated to Prof. Iwasaki in Honor of His 60th Birthday.* Tokyo: Kenkyusha, 1954, pp. 453–70.

FO32 Ozaki, Yasushi. "Some Problems on 'Effect' Used by E. A. Poe." *Literary Review of Seinan Gakuin University* (Fukuoka), II, No. 1 (Nov. 1955), 1–8.

FP

FP1 Paleólogo, Constantino. *Machado, Pöe e Dostoievski.* Rio de Janeiro: Revista Branco, 1950.

FP2 Pannwitz, Rudolf. *Der Nihilismus und die werdende Welt.* Nuremberg: H. Carl, 1951. Poe: "Ulalume," pp. 186–92.

FP3 Papini, Giovanni. "Un centenario." *Messaggero,* Oct. 8, 1949, p. 3.

FP4 ——. "Un centenario: Edgar Poe." *Secolo XIX nuovo,* Oct. 21, 1949, p. 3.

FP5 ——. "Edgar Poe" (1949). *La loggia dei busti: pensieri sopra uomini di genio, d'ingegno, di cuore.* Florence: Vallecchi, 1955, pp. 119–23.

FP6 Papp, Dániel. "Edgar A. Poe." *A Hét,* No. 44 (1899).

FP7 Pardo, Aristobulo. "La actitud crítica de Edgar Allan Poe." *Revista de las Indias,* No. 111 (Oct.–Dec. 1949), pp. 353–71.

FP8   Parks, E. W. "Edgar Allan Poe como critico." *Diario de São Paulo* (Brazil), Oct. 1949, p. 3.

FP9   Pascual-Leone, Blanca. *Posibles influencias de Edgar Allan Poe sobre Gustavo Adolfo Bécquer.* Mexico, 1963.

FP10   Pasolini, Desideria. "Traduzione e scelta dai Marginalia di E. A. Poe." *L'Immagine,* No. 12 (March–April 1949).

FP11   Pásztor, Árpád. "Beszélgetés Poe Edgarral." *Pesti Naptó,* No. 15 (1909).

FP12   ——. *Találkozásom Poe A. Edgarral.* Budapest: M. Dick, 1916.

FP13   Patterson, A. S. *L'Influence d'Edgar Poe sur Charles Baudelaire.* Grenoble: Allier Frères, 1903.

FP14   Deleted.

FP15   Paustovskii, K. "Edgar Po." Poe, *Zolotoi zhuk* [The gold bug]. Moscow, 1946, pp. 3–8.

FP16   Pavolini, Emily Cook. *Edgar Poe: Lettere d'amore con uno studio.* Florence: Rinascimento del Libro, 1931.

FP17   Péladan, Joséfin. "Introduction." *Poésies complètes. Trans. Gabriel Mourey.* Paris: Dalou, 1888, 1889.

FP18   Pellegrini, Lino. "Lettera a Poe." *Illustrazione italiana,* NS I (Jan. 21, 1945), 906.

FP19   Pérez Triana, Santiago. "Introducción." *The Raven,* trans. Pérez-Bonalde. New York, 1887.

FP20   Persico, Federico. "Edgardo Poe." *Conferenza Tenuta nel Circolo Filologica Il di 24.* Naples, 1876.

FP21   Pesce, Cesare. "La vita tormentosa e la tragica fine di E. A. Poe." *Momento,* Oct. 7, 1949, p. 3.

FP22   Pesce, Hugo. "Poe, precursor de Einstein." *Amauta* (Lima), III (March 1928), 25–26. Reprinted in *IPNA,* No. 24 (1954), pp. 21–24.

FP23   Petacco, Arrigo. "Il delirium tremens uccise il precursore del brivido." *Avanti!,* Oct. 20, 1949, p. 3.

FP24   Peters, H. F. "El interés de Ernest Jünger por Edgar Allan Poe." *Armas y Letras,* IV, No. 3 (1961), 53–61. Trans. by Hugo Padilla from *CL.*

FP25   Petit, Georges. *Étude médico-psychologique sur Edgar Poe.* Paris and Lyon: A. Maloine, 1906.

FP26   Petrascincu, Dan. "E. A. Poe: la verità, la poesia." *FLe,* VIII (Oct. 25, 1953), 2.

FP27 ———. *Edgar Poe, Iluminatul.* Bucharest: Editura Cultura Românească, 1942.

FP28 ———. " 'Eureka.' " *Popolo,* Jan. 27, 1954, p. 3.

FP29 ———. "Il grande dannato." *FLe,* IX (March 21, 1954), 4, 6.

FP30 Petriconi, Hellmuth. "Abenteur und kein Ende II: *Aventures d'Arthur Gordon Pym.*" *Romanistiches Jahrbuch,* XV (1964), 160–71.

FP31 Petrucciani, Mario. "Poe teoretico della poesia." *Idea,* VI (Jan. 29, 1950), 4.

FP32 ———. *Poetica dell'ermetismo italiano.* Turin: Loescher, 1955.

FP33 ———. "I postulati di poetica pura del Poe." *Poetica dell'ermetismo italiano.* Turin: Loescher, 1955, pp. 23–26.

FP34 Petsch, R. "Die Kunsttheorie von Edgar Allan Poe." *NS,* XXXIX (1931), 488–97.

FP35 Philippide, Alexandru. "Introducere in Poezia lui Edgar Allan Poe." *Scriitorul şi Arta lui.* Bucharest: Editura pentru Literatură, 19.

FP36 Piast, V. [Review of] "Poe, E. A. Sobranie sochinenii [Collected works]. Vol. 5. Moscow, 1912." *Apollon,* No. 6 (1912), pp. 49–50.

FP37 Pichois, Claude, "De Poe à Dada." *Rev d'Histoire Littéraire de la France,* LXVII (April–June 1967), 450–60.

FP38 ———, ed. *Aventures d'Arthur Gordon Pym.* With the imagined conclusion by Jules Verne in *Le Sphinx des Glaces.* With introd. Paris: Club des Libraries de France, 1960.

FP39 Piñeyro, Enrique. "Notas críticas." *Revista Cubana,* VIII (1888), 563–68. Review of Poe's *Poésies complètes.*

FP40 ———. "Otro centenario de poeta. (Edgard Allan Poe) (con retrato)." *El Fígaro* (Havana), XXV (March 14, 1909), 133.

FP41 Pissin, Raimund. "E. A. Poe." *Berliner Hefte für geistiges Leben,* IV (1949), 453–67.

FP42 Pistelli, L. "Donne e lettere di Poe." *La stampa,* Dec. 22, 1956, p. 3.

FP43 Pitollet, Camille. "Edgar Poe, critique littéraire." *Rev de l'Enseignement des Langues Vivantes,* Jan. 1926, pp. 10–17.

FP44 Pittaluga, M. C., ed. *Racconti.* With introd. Turin: Unione Tipografico-Editrice Torinese, 1958.

FP45 Poe, Edgar Allan. *Aventuras de Arthur Gordon Pym.* Bibliog. essay by Eloy Pontes. Rio de Janeiro: Ed. de Ouro, 1967.

FP46 ———. *Aventures d'Arthur Gordon Pym.* Trans. Charles Baudelaire. Introd. by Henriette Guex-Rolle. Lausanne: Edit. Rencontre, 1957.

FP47 ———. *Aventures d'Arthur Gordon Pym.* Trans. Charles Baudelaire. Notes by René Louis Doyon. Paris: E. Rasmussen, 1946.

FP48 ———. *Les Aventures d'Arthur Gordon Pym.* Trans. Charles Baudelaire. Preface by Jacques Perret. Paris: Livre de Poche, 1959.

FP49 ———. *Les Aventures d'Arthur Gordon Pym.* Trans. Charles Baudelaire. Preface by Jules Romains. Paris: Editions de la Banderolle, 1921.

FP50 ———. *Les Aventures d'Arthur Gordon Pym.* Trans. Charles Baudelaire. Preface by Pierre MacOrlan. Paris: Edit. de la Bibliothèque Mondiale, 1956.

FP51 ———. *Les Aventures de Gordon Pym.* Preface by Jacques de la Cretelle. Paris: A. Fayard, 1948.

FP52 ———. *Le avventure di Gordon Pym.* Trans. E. Vittorini and D. Cinelli. Preface by A. Canale. Milan: Club degli editori, 1963. Includes *The Narrative of A. G. Pym,* "The Gold Bug," "MS Found in a Bottle."

FP53 ———. *Cartas de amor a Helen.* Trans., prologue, and notes by Carlos Martínez-Barbeito. Metropolitana, 1943.

FP54 ———. *"Il corvo," altre poesie e "La filosofia della composizione."* Trans. Franco De Poli, introd. Charles Baudelaire. Parma: Guanda, [ca. 1964].

FP55 ———. *Cuentos escogidos.* Introd. Arturo Souto. Mexico: [Universidad Nacional Autónoma de México], 1958.

FP56 ———. *Edgar Allan Poe összes költeményei.* Introd. and notes by L. Kardos. Budapest, 1949.

FP57 ———. *Edgar Allan Poe összes versei.* Introd. Tibor Lutter and notes by György Radó. Budapest, 1959—.

FP58 ———. *Edgar Poe; présentation par Jean Rousselot: Choix de textes, bibliographe, dessins, portraits, fac-similés.* Paris: P. Seghers, 1962.

FP59 ———. *Epistolario.* Comp. John W. Ostrom. Preface, biog. of principal personages, and bibliog. of Italian trans. of Poe by Henry Furst. Trans. Henry Furst. Milan: Longanesi, 1955. Trans. of *The Letters of E. A. Poe* (Cambridge, 1948).

FP60 ———. *Erzählungen.* Illus. Alfred Kubin. Munich: Nymphenburger Verlagshandlung, 1965.

FP61 ———. *Eureka. La Genese d'un poëme, Le Corbeau; méthode de composition.* Prefatory comment, notes, and explanations by Jacques Crépet. Paris: L. Conard, 1966.

FP62 ———. *Gedichte; Essays.* Trans. Theodor Etzel and Hedwig Lackmann. Epilogue by Harro H. Kühnelt. Munich: Winkler, 1966.

FP63 ——. *The Gold-Bug.* Introd., comment, and notes by Anna Benedetti. Turin: Chiantore, 1946.

FP64 ——. *Gordon Pym.* Trans. Elio Vittorini. Introd. Delfino Cinelli. Milan: Mondadori, 1950.

FP65 ——. *Gruwelijke verhalen.* Foreword and introd. by S. Vestdijk. Amsterdam, 1965.

FP66 ——. *Histoires grotesques et sérieuses.* Trans. and comments by Charles Baudelaire. Prefatory comments and notes by Geneviève Bulli. Paris: Le Livre de Poche, 1967.

FP67 ——. *Im Wirbel des Maelstroms und andere seltsame Geschichten.* Trans. Carl W. Neumann. Epilogue by Ludwig Tügel. Stuttgart: Reclam, 1966.

FP68 ——. *Marginalia.* Preface and trans. by L. Berti. Milan: Mondadori, 1949.

FP69 ——. *Narraciones extraordinarias.* Barcelona: Editorial Juventud, 1957.

FP70 ——. *Nevelmeer.* Introd. S. S. Ewers, illus. Alfred Kubin. Munich: G. Müller, n.d.

FP71 ——. *Nuovi racconti straordinari; Poesie scelte.* Trans. F. Della Pergola and Renato Ferrari. Introd. Charles Haines. Milano: Edizioni per il Club del Libro, [ca. 1961].

FP72 ——. *Obras completas.* Comp. and prologue by Armando Bazán. 3rd ed. Mexico: D. F. Editorial Continental, 1958.

FP73 ——. *Oeuvres complètes.* Trans. Charles Baudelaire. Paris: Gilbert, 1956.

FP74 ——. *Oeuvres complètes de Charles Baudelaire.* Trans., prefatory comments, notes, and explanations by Jacques Crépet. Paris: Conard, 1932–66.

FP75 ——. *Oeuvres en prose.* Trans. Charles Baudelaire. Ed. Y.-G. Le Dantec. Bibliothèque de la Pléiade. Paris: Gallimard, 1951.

FP76 ——. *Oeuvres imaginatives et poétiques complètes d'Edgar Allan Poe.* Ed. Charles Moulin. Paris: Editions Vialatay, 1966. Reviewed: Bonnet, *PN,* I, 12–13.

FP77 ——. *Összes versei.* Budapest: Corvina, 1959.

FP78 ——. *Poe.* Introd., comp., and trans. G. Baldini. Milan: Garzanti, 1949. Poe's main works.

FP79 ——. *Los poemas de Edgar Poe.* Trans., prologue, and notes by Carlos Obligado. 2nd ed. Buenos Aires: Espasa-Calpe, 1942.

FP80 ——. *Poems by Poe.* Trans. Tamotsu Abe. Tokyo: Shinchâsha, 1957.

FP81 ———. *Poe's Works.* 6 vols. Trans. Seiji Tanizaki. Tokyo: Shunyodo, 1955.

FP82 ———. *Poésies complètes.* Trans. Gabriel Mourey. Paris: Mercure de France, 1910.

FP83 ———. *Poesias e prosa.* Trans. Oscar Mendes and Milton Amado. Bibliog. comment by Hervey Allen and critical essay by Charles Baudelaire. Pôrto Alegre: Globo, 1960.

FP84 ———. "Quelques fragments des marginalia." Trans. and notes by Paul Valéry. *Commerce,* XIV (Winter 1927), 11–41.

FP85 ———. *Der Rabe: ein Gedicht von Edgar Allan Poe.* Trans. Carl Theodor Eben. With a biog. sketch of the author. Illus. David Scattergood. Philadelphia: Barclay & Co., 1869.

FP86 ———. *Racconti.* Preface by Marìa C. Pittaluga. Trans. Lidia Rho Servi and Beatrice Boffito Serra. Turin: UTET, 1958.

FP87 ———. *Racconti fantastici.* Preface by Orio Vergani. Milan: IEI, 1959.

FP88 ———. *Racconti straordinari.* Introd. Liana Johnson. Trans. Paola Ferruzzi, Rome: Curcio, 1962.

FP89 ———. *Racconti straordinari.* Trans. and introd. by Argia Monti. Modena: Ed. Paoline, 1958. 2nd ed., 1959.

FP90 ———. *Racconti straordinari; Genesi di un poema; Racconti grotteschi e seri.* Ed. Franco Della Pergola. Trans. F. Della Pergola, M. S. Battaglia, R. Ferrari. With Baudelaire's *Edgar Poe: La sua vita e le sue opere.* Milan: Edizioni per il Club del Libro, 1957.

FP91 ———. *The Raven.* English text and French trans. by S. Mallarmé. Interpretation by Ettore Serra. Rome: Ed. Prometeo, 1945. Reprinted with an essay by Emilio Cecchi, Milan: Ceschina, 1956.

FP92 ———. *Scrieri alese în doua volume.* Introd. Zoe Dumitrescu-Buşulenga. Bucharest: Editura pentru Literatură Universală, 1963.

FP93 ———. *Sette racconti.* Comp. and commentary by Giorgio Milesi. Bergamo: Minerva Italica, 1966.

FP94 ———. *Storia di Gordon Pym.* Trans. and notes by M. Gallone. Milan: Rizzoli, 1957.

FP95 ———. *Le tre inchieste di Dupin.* Ed. Alfredo Bogardo. Milan: Universale Economica, 1949.

FP96 ———. *Tre saggi sulla poesia.* Ed. Elio Chinol. Padua: Le Tre Venezie, 1946.

FP97 ———. *Ulalume.* English text and French trans. by S. Mallarmé. Introd. Emilio Cecchi. Illus. Dario Cecchi. Rome: Bestetti, 1949.

FP98 ———. *Venti racconti umoristici.* Trans. A. Traverso and A. C. Rossi. Preface by Marisa Bulgheroni. Milan: Club degli Editori, 1961.

FP99 ——. *William Wilson.* Trans. and notes by G. Baldini. Brescia: Morcelliana, 1947.

FP100 Polt, Robert, trans. *Der Goldkäfer und andere seltsame Geschichten.* With foreword. Vienna: Kremayr und Scheriau, 1955.

FP101 Pommier, Jean. *Dans les chemins de Baudelaire.* Paris: José Corti, 1945.

FP102 ——. *La Mystique de Baudelaire.* Paris, 1932.

FP103 Pontes, Eloy, trans. *Aventuras de Artur Gordon Pym.* With bibliog. essay. Rio de Janeiro: Irmãos Pongetti, 1944.

FP104 Pontmartin, A. de. "Le Roman terrible." *Jour des Débats,* Nov. 12, 1856.

FP105 Poppenberg, F. "Bemerkungen zu E. A. Poe." *Neue deutsche Rundschau* (Berlin), XII (1901), 669–70 (Part 2).

FP106 ——. "Poe-Probleme." *Der Türmer* (Stuttgart), VII, No. 2 (1905), 674–79.

FP107 Porché, François. *Baudelaire: Histoire d'une âme.* Paris: Flammarion, 1945.

FP108 Portizky, J. E. "E. A. Poe." *Zeitgeist, supplement to Berliner Tageblatt,* Nov. 23, 1903.

FP109 Potez, Henri. "Edgar Poe et Jules Verne." *La Rev* (Paris), May 15, 1909, pp. 191–97.

FP110 Poulet, Georges, "Edgar Poe." *Les Métamorphoses du cercle.* n.p.: Libraire Plon, 1961, pp. 269–304.

FP111 ——. "L'Univers circonscrit d'Edgar Poe." *Les Temps Modernes,* CXIV–CXV (June–July 1955), 2179–2204.

FP112 Poulet-Malassis. "Edgar Allan Poe." *Journal d'Alençon,* Jan. 9, 1853.

FP113 Praz, Mario. "Gli alti e bassi di Poe." *Tempo,* Feb. 5, 1954, p. 3.

FP114 ——. "Disse il corvo: 'Mai più.'" *Nuova Europa,* II (April 15, 1945), 7. Reprinted in *Lettrice notturna* (Rome: Casini, 1952), pp. 56–59.

FP115 ——. "Il dramma di un'anima eccezionalmente condizionata." *Fle,* V (Jan. 29, 1950), 4.

FP116 ——. "Fare il punto su Poe" (1954). *Cronache letterarie anglosassoni.* 2nd ser., 2 vols. Rome: Ed. di Storia e Letteratura, 1966, II, 227–31.

FP117 ——. "Il fiabesco quotidiano." *Il Tempo,* Feb. 21, 1958, p. 3.

FP118 ——. "Fortuna di Poe." *Il Tempo,* Oct. 7, 1949. Reprinted as "Fortuna de Poe nel primo centenario della morte," *Cronache* *letterarie anglosassoni* (2 vols., Rome: Ed. di Storia e Letteratura, 1951), II, 144–48.

FP119 ———. "Poe, genio d'esportazione." *Approdo letterario,* IV, No. 3 (July–Sept. 1958), 3–15.

FP120 ———. *Studi e svaghi inglesi.* Florence: Sansoni, 1937.

FP121 Press, A. "Edgar Allen Po. (Kharakteristika)" [Edgar Allan Poe. (A character sketch)]. *Kosmopolis,* No. 2 (1897), pp. 102–30.

FP122 Prezzolini, Giuseppe. "Novità americane." *Illustrazione italiana,* NS V (Feb. 6, 1949), 203. A review of *The Letters of E. A. Poe.*

FP123 Prieto, Juan. "Edgard Poe: Escritores norteamericanos." *Revista Hispano-Americana,* VI (Jan. 15, 1867), 22–31. Reprinted as "Edgar A. Poe III: La literatura norteamericana en Europa," [ed.] Rafael M. de Labra, *Revista de España,* LXVII (April 1879), 457.

FP124 Probst, Ferdinand. *Edgar Allan Poe.* Munich: Ernst Reinhardt, 1908.

FP125 Prouteau, Gilbert. *Les Dieux meurent le matin.* Paris: Grasset, 1962.

FP126 Provenzal, Dino. "Le fonti dell'ispirazione." *Mattino,* April 8, 1954, p. 3.

FP127 Przesmycki, Zenon. "Edgar Allan Poe. Poeci północnoamerykańscy. Podług szkicu Engla." *Zycie,* Nos. 22–23 (1887), pp. 345–47, 361–63.

FP128 Puccini, Dario. "Edgar Poe." *Unità,* Oct. 21, 1949, p. 3.

FP129 Pujals, Esteban. "El efectismo visionario de Edgar Allan Poe." *Drama, pensamiento y poesía en la literatura inglesa.* Madrid: Rialp, 1965, pp. 304–26. Previously appeared in *Forjadores del mundo contemporáneo* (Planeta: Barcelona, 1959).

FP130 Putterlik, D. [, ed.?]. *The Gold-Bug.* Adapted for classroom use with commentary. Vienna: Universum, 1946.

FQ

FQ1 Queneau, Raymond. "Poe et l'analyse." *Bards—Mathématiciens, précurseurs, encyclopédistes.* Paris: Hermann, 1963, pp. 69–80.

FQ2 Quesnel, Léo. "La Littérature d'imagination aux Etats-Unis." *Rev Politique et Littéraire,* XII (Feb. 14, 1874), 777–82.

FQ3 ——. "Poètes américains: Edgar Allan Poe." *Revue Politique et Littéraire,* XVI (Feb. 8, 1879), 751–56.

FQ4 Quinn, Patrick. "Rev. of *Choix de contes.* Trans. Charles Baudelaire and Roger Asselineau." *EA,* XXII (Jan.–March 1959), 89.

FR

FR1 R., F. S. "Edgar Allan Poe." *Fantasias humorísticas.* Madrid: Aguilar, 1951, pp. 11–14.

FR2 Raabe, Paul. *Alfred Kubin: Leben—Werk—Wirkung.* Collected under the supervision of Kurt Otte, Kubin Archives. Hamburg: Rowohlt, 1957. Presents illus. by Kubin appearing in fourteen German editions of Poe.

FR3 Rabbe, F. *Edgar Poe: Derniers Contes.* Paris: Stock, 1906.

FR4 Railo, Eino. *Yleisen kirjallisuuden historia* [History of general literature]. Vol. V. Porvoo, 1937, pp. 165–66.

FR5 Raimondi, Ezio. "Note sulla narrativa americana contemporanea." *Convivium,* XVI (1947), 65–77.

FR6 Raimondi, Giuseppe. "Idea di Poe." *Giornale, ossia taccuino: 1925–1930.* Florence: Le Monnier, 1942, pp. 79–83.

FR7 Rasmussen, Egil. *Angstens dikter Edgar Allan Poe.* Oslo: Gyldendal, 1949.

FR8 ——. *Kunstneren og samfunnsbildet.* Oslo, 1949. Passages on Poe.

FR9 Rat, Maurice. "Baudelaire a recréé Poe plus qu'il ne l'a traduit." *Figaro Littéraire,* Jan. 5, 1952.

FR10 Rauter, Herbert. "Edgar Allan Poes *The Man of the Crowd:* Interpretation und Einordnung ins Gesamtwerk." *NS,* XI (Nov. 1962), 497–509.

FR11 ——. "Zeit, Zeitmessung und Bewusstsein bei E. A. Poe." *Anglia,* LXXXV (1967), 363–89.

FR12 Raymond, Marcel. *De Baudelaire au Surréalisme.* Paris, 1947.

FR13 Reichenberger, Kurt. "Baudelaire und die Dichtung Edgar Allan Poes: Kritische Bemerkungen zur Methodik eines Deutungsversuchs." *Literaturwissenschaftliches Jahrbuch* (Berlin), VI (1965), 321–24.

FR14   Reményi, Jozsef. *Amerikai írók.* Budapest, n.d. Chapter on Poe.

FR15   ——. "Edgar Allan Poe nyomán." *Nyugat,* I (1939), 175–81.

FR16   Renaud, Armand. "Edgar Poe, d'après ses poésies." *Nouvelle Rev de Paris,* IV (1864), 537–53.

FR17   Rentero, Manuel Genaro. *Edgard Poe: Drama en un acto y en verso.* . . . Madrid: J. Rodríguez, 1875.

FR18   Riba, Charles. "Pròleg." *El assassinats del carrer de la morgue.* Barcelona: Editorial Selecta, 1953, pp. 9–15.

FR19   Ricardou, Jean. "Le Caractère singulier de cette eau." *Critique* (Paris), NS XIV (Aug.–Sept. 1967), 718–33.

FR20   ——. "L'Histoire dans l'histoire." *Critique,* LCXXXI–LCXXXII (Aug.–Sept. 1966), 711–29.

FR21   ——. *Problemes du noveau roman.* Paris: Editions du Seuil, 1967.

FR22   Richard, Claude. "André Breton et Edgar Poe." *NRF,* CLXXII (April 1967), 926–36.

FR23   Richepin, Jean. "L'Ame américaine à travers quelques-uns de ses poètes, penseurs et écrivains, Edgar Poe." *Jour de L'Université des Annales,* XII (June 1919), [3]–21.

FR24   ——. "Edgar Poe." *L'Âme américaine à travers quelques-uns de ses interprètes.* . . . Paris: E. Flammarion, 1920.

FR25   Richie, Donald. "Edgar Allan Poe." *Jiji Eigo Kenkyu* (Tokyo), June 1956.

FR26   Ritter, Richard, ed. *Two Fantastic Tales.* Diesterwegs neusprachl. Bibliothek, No. 7. Frankfurt and Bonn: Diesterweg, 1951.

FR27   Riva, Ubaldo. "Sogni e musica nelle liriche di Edgar Poe." *Ausonia,* IX (Nov.–Dec. 1954), 49–56.

FR28   Rivas y Calderón, Ismail. "La personalidad literaria de Edgard Allan Poe." *El Hogar,* No. 883 (Oct. 2, 1925), 23, 71.

FR29   Rizzardi, Alfredo. "Il mondo di E. A. Poe." *Archi,* I (Jan. 1950), 17–24.

FR30   Robinson, B. "Comparaison stylistique entre quatre histoires d'Edgar Poe et les traductions de Baudelaire." Diss., Paris, 1957.

FR31   Roddier, Henri. "Rev. of *Choix de contes,* trans. Charles Baudelaire and Roger Asselineau." *RLC,* XXXIII (Oct.–Dec. 1959), 594–97.

FR32 Rodriguez- Embil, Luis. "Sobre el autor de 'Las campanas.' (El poeta y el hombre)." *Cuba y América,* XIII (March 1909), 23–24.

FR33 Roehm, Alfred J. *Bibliographie und Kritik der deutschen Übersetzungen aus der amerikanischen Dichtung.* Leipzig, 1910.

FR34 Rojas, Armando. "Edgard Allan Poe en la América hispana." *Revista Nacional de Cultura* (Caracas), Nos. 142–43 (Sept.–Dec. 1960), pp. 152–61.

FR35 Rolland de Renéville, A. *L'Expérience poétique.* Paris: Gallimard, 1938, pp. 21–24, 95–99, and *passim.*

FR36 ———. "Une Source d'Edgar Poe." *NRF,* LVII (Jan. 7, 1942), pp. 41–62.

FR37 Roos, Vappu. *Dantesta Dickensiin.—Maailmankirjallisuuden suurimpien mestareiden elämäkertoja* [From Dante to Dickens. Biographies of the greatest masters of world literature]. Porvoo, 1962, pp. 478–490.

FR38 ———. *Suuri maailman kirjallisuus* [Great world literature]. Helsinki, 1965, pp. 369–370.

FR39 Rosati, Salvatore. "Edgar Poe." *L'ombra dei padri.* Rome: Ed. di Storia e Letteratura, 1958, pp. 50–54.

FR40 ———. "Edgar Poe in italiano." *Il Mondo,* VI (April 13, 1954), 9. Review of *Tutti i racconti* (1953). Reprinted as "Edgar Poe," *L'ombra dei Padri* (1943), pp. 50–54.

FR41 ———. "Letteratura inglese e americana." *Nuova antologia,* LXXXIII (Feb. 1948), 194–96.

FR42 ———. "La teoria dell'unità d'effetto in E. A. Poe e la sua portata critica." *Il Simbolismo nella letteratura Nord-Americana: Atti del symposium tenuto a Firenze 27–29 novembre 1964.* Florence: La Nuova Italia, 1965, pp. 161–68.

FR43 Rosny, J.-H. *Le Scarabee d'or.* Paris: Dentu, 1892.

FR44 Rossi, Sergio. "E. A. Poe e la scapigliatura lombarda." *SA,* V (1960), 119–39.

FR45 Rossini, Giuseppe. "Omaggi a Edgar Poe." *Popolo,* July 8, 1950, p. 3.

FR46 Roth, Georges [, ed.]. *Contes mystérieux et fantastiques.* Trans. Ch. Baudelaire. Prefatory note and annotations by Roth. Paris: Larousse, n.d.

FR47 Rousselot, Jean. *Edgar Allan Poe.* Paris: Seghers, 1953.

FR48 ———. "Edgar Poe était-il un initié?" *AgN,* No. 78 (Dec. 1952), pp. 30–40.

FR49   ———. "Le Roman d'Edgar Poe." *Hommes et Monde,* VIII (Sept. 1953), 53–65.

FR50   Royère, Jean. "Edgar Poe et l'esthétique de poésie pure." *Clartés sur la poésie.* Paris, 1925.

FR51   Rugiu, Antonio Santoni. "Una tragedia inedita per l'Italia: Il *Poliziano* di E. A. Poe." *FLe,* V (Jan. 29, 1950), 4.

FR52   Ruysdael, Johan. "Edgar Allan Poe: Fantastische vertellingen vertaald door A. Noorbeek." *Nieuwe Stemmen,* XI (1955), 99–100.

FS

FS1   Sacks, H. "Bemerkungen zu Marie Bonapartes Biographie des Dichters." *Imago,* XX (1934), 485–92.

FS2   Sadkowski, Wacław. "Spośród nowości literackich." *Wiedza i Życie,* No. 6 (1963), pp. 269–71.

FS3   Saeki, A. "Reference Books on Poe." *Eigo Kenkyu* [The study of English], Poe Number (Oct. 1949).

FS4   Saisset, Léon and Frédéric. *Les Histoires extraordinaires d'Edgar Poe.* Paris: E. Mafére, 1939.

FS5   Saito, Hikaru. "Death and Annihilation in Poe." *Eigo Seinen* [The rising generation], CV, No. 5 (May 1959), 8–9.

FS6   Saito, Takeshi. "E. A. Poe, an Essay." *Eigo Kenkyu* [The study of English], Poe Number (Oct. 1949), pp. 18–19.

FS7   ———. "Poe." *A Historical Survey of American Literature.* Tokyo: Kenkyusha, 1941, pp. 85–95.

FS8   Sakuraba, Nobuyuki, trans. "A Descent into the Maelström." With notes in Japanese. *Eigo Kenkyu* [The study of English], 1953.

FS9   Sano, Tetsuro. "Poe the Analyst in His Prose Tales." *Memoirs of Osaka Institute of Technology,* IV, No. 1 (1960), 14–20.

FS10   Santa Cruz, Mario. "Edgar Allan Poe." *El Libro y el Pueblo,* No. 30 (1957), pp. 38–40.

FS11   ———. "El genio de Edgar Allan Poe." *Repertorio Americano,* XIII (Nov. 20, 1926), 299–300.

FS12   Santamarina, Orvácio. "Edgar A. Poe." *Aspectos* (Rio), III (Jan. 17, 1939), 58–72.

FS13   Sanvoisin, Gaétan. "Edgar Poe célébré en Sorbonne." *Jour des Débats,* XLI, Part 1 (Feb. 2, 1934), 196.

FS14 Sato, Kiyoshi. "Wordsworth and Poe." *Current Thoughts in English Literature* (Tokyo: The English Literary Society of Aoyama Gakuin Univ.), XXII (Nov. 1949), 15–22.

FS15 Sato, Takami. "The Revival of *Twice-Told Tales.*" *Sylvan,* No. 7 (May 1962), pp. 58–67.

FS16 Saurès, André. "Edgar Poe." *Nouvelles Littéraires,* XII (April 7, 1934), 1–2.

FS17 Savelli, Giovanni. "Centenario di Poe." *Humanitas,* IV (Nov. 1949), 1084–91.

FS18 Savelli, Pietro. "Appunti su Poe." *Fle,* II (June 5, 1947), 4–5.

FS19 Sawa, Alejandro. "Crónica literaria (Poe y Baudelaire)." *El Cojo Ilustrado,* XII (Oct. 15, 1903), 608.

FS20 Schinzel, Elizabeth. *Natur und Natursymbolik bei Poe, Baudelaire und den französischen Symbolisten.* Düren: Max Danielewski, 1931.

FS21 ———. "Natur and Natursymbolik bei Edgar Allan Poe, Baudelaire und den französischen Symbolisten." Diss., University of Bonn, 1931.

FS22 Schleich, K. L. "Psychophysik des Humors." *Zukunft* (Berlin), XXV (1898), 374–93.

FS23 Schmidlin, Guido. *Hölderlins Ode: Dichterberuf, eine Interpretation.* Bern: Francke, 1958.

FS24 Schmidt, Augusto Frederico. "Páginas do galo branco." *Lanterna Verde,* No. 7 (Aug. 1943), pp. 23–25.

FS25 Schneider-Wittlich, Friedrich. "Edgar Allan Poe und E. Th. A. Hoffman: Zur hundertsten Wiederkehr des Geburtstages Poes am 19 Januar 1909." *Über den Wassern,* II (Jan. 25, 1909).

FS26 Schoenbach, Anton E. "Über die amerikanische Romandichtung der Gegenwart." *Deutsche Rundschau* (Berlin), XLVI–XLVII (1886), 420, 198, 206.

FS27 Schück, Henrik. "Edgar Allan Poe." *Poe, Valda noveller.* Stockholm, 1882, pp. iii–xiv.

FS28 Schuhmann, Kuno. *Die erzählende Prosa E. A. Poes: Ein Beitrag zu einer Gattungsgeschichte der Short Story.* Frankfurter Arbeiten aus dem Gebiete der Anglistik und der Amerika-Studien, No. 5. Heidelberg: C. Winter, 1958.

FS29 ———. "Die erzählende Prosa E. A. Poes: Ein Beitrag zu einer Gattungsgeschichte der amerikanischen Short Story." Diss., Frankfurt, 1957.

FS30   Schulz, F. O. H. "Poe: Amerikanische Dichterprofile." *Prager ill. Wochenschau,* VI, No. 1 (1944), 1–8.

FS31   Séché, Alphonse. "Notice biographique et bibliographique." *Edgar A. Poe.* New trans. Victor Orban. Paris: Louis-Michaud, 1908.

FS32   ———. "Notice biographique and bibliographique." *Poèmes complets; Scénes de Politian; Le Principe poétique; Marginalia.* New trans. Victor Orban. Paris: Louis-Michaud, n.d.

FS33   Semerau, Alfred. "Edgar Poe: Zum 50. Todestage." *Wissenschaftliche Beilage der Leipziger Zeitung,* No. 116 (Oct. 5, 1899).

FS34   Serravalli, Luigi. "Il 'Gordon Pym' di Poe." *Progresso d'Italia,* Nov. 1, 1950, p. 3.

FS35   Servadio, Emilio. *Stravaganze.* . . . Rome: Formiggini, 1929.

FS36   Servi, Lidia Rho, ed. *Racconti.* Turin: Unione Tip., Editrice Torinese, 1932.

FS37   Seylaz, Louis. *Edgar Poe et les premiers symbolistes françaises.* Lausanne: Imprimerie La Concorde, 1923; Paris Champion, 1924. Reviewed: W. Fischer, *Anglia Beiblatt,* XL, 79–82. F. C. Roe, *MLR,* XXII, 234–36. Y.-G. Le Dantec, *RLC,* IV, 164; X, 373.

FS38   Shelgunov, N. V. "Edgar Po." *Delo,* No. 4 (1874), pp. 276–85. Signed: N. Sh.

FS39   ———. "Edgar Po—kak psikholog" [Edgar Poe as a psychologist]. *Delo,* Nos. 7–8 (1874), pp. 350–66. Signed: N. Sh.

FS40   Shimada, Kinji. "Baudelaire, Translator of Poe." *Eigo Kenkyu* [The study of English], Poe Number (Oct. 1949), pp. 24–27.

FS41   ———. "Edgar Poe." *Life and Literature of America.* Vol. IV. 1958.

FS42   ———. "On Poe's Tales." *Shin Shosetsu,* Nos. 9, 10 (1947).

FS43   ———. *Poe and Baudelaire.* Tokyo: Evening-Star-Sha, 1948.

FS44   ———. "Poe and Mallarmé." *Shigaku* [Poetics], IV (Dec. 1947), 42–46; V (April 1948), 45–50; VI (June 1948), 33–41.

FS45   ———. "Poe, Baudelaire and Mallarmé." *Introduction to Comparative Literature.* Tokyo: Kawade-shobo, 1951, pp. 135–45.

FS46   ———. "Poe in His Youth." *Shigaku,* IV, No. 9 (Dec. 1949), 16–26.

FS47   ———. "Poe's Marriage." *Fu Setsu,* No. 8 (1948).

FS48   ———. "Researches on Edgar Allan Poe in the United States and Europe, a History." *Eigo Seinen* [The rising generation], CV, No. 5 (May 1959), 6–7.

FS49   ———. "A Talk on E. A. Poe." *Eigo Kenkyu* [The study of English], XLIII, No. 12 (Dec. 1954), 12–15.

FS50 Shinagawa, Tsutomu. "Poe in Japan." *Nippon Hikaku Bunga-kukai Kaihô* (Tokyo: Tokyo Institute of Technology), Nos. 1–17 (Jan. 1956–April 1960).

FS51 Siebel, Paul. "Der Einfluss Samuel Taylor Coleridges auf Edgar Allan Poe." Diss., University of Münster, 1924.

FS52 Silvio. "Edgar Allan Poe." *Wędrowiec*, No. 24 (1900), pp. 467–68; No. 26 (1900), pp. 516–18.

FS53 Smith, Charles Alphonso. *Die amerikanische Literatur: Vorlesungen gehalten an der Königlichen Friedrich-Wilhelms-Universität zu Berlin. . . .* Berlin: Weidmann, 1912.

FS54 Somare, Enrico. "Torna spaesato Poe a Nuova York." *Corriere della sera,* May 6, 1949, p. 3.

FS55 Soong, Stephen. "Introduction." *Anthology of American Poetry.* 2nd printing. Hong Kong: World Today Press, 1963.

FS56 Sorani, Aldo. "La malatti di Edgar Poe." *Illustrazione medica italiana* (Genoa), IX (1927), 53.

FS57 Spielhagen, F. "Amerikanische Lyriker: W. C. Bryant, E. A. Poe. . . ." *Vermischte Schriften.* Vol. I. Berlin, 1864, pp. 259–320.

FS58 ———. "Edgar Poe gegen Henry Longfellow: Aus meiner Studienmappe." *Beiträge zur literarischen Aesthetik und Kritik.* Berlin, 1891.

FS59 Staats, Armin. *Edgar Allan Poes symbolistische Erzählkunst.* Heidelberg: C. Winter Universitätsverlag, 1967.

FS60 Startsev, A. [Review of] "Poe, E. A. Izbrannye rasskazy [Selected stories]. Moscow, 1935." *Literaturnoe obozrenie,* No. 4 (1936), pp. 28–29.

FS61 Stefanile, Mario. "La conferenza di G. Baldini sul romanticismo americano." *Mattino,* Jan. 30, 1954, p. 3.

FS62 "Cronache letterarie: tutto Poe." *Mattino,* May 11, 1954, p. 3.

FS63 Strafforell, Gustave. "E. A. Poe." *Letterature americana.* Milan, 1884.

FS64 Streinu, Vladimir. "Edgar Poe şi Scriitorii Români." *Revista Fundaţeilor Regale,* II (1935), 620–41.

FS65 ———. "Poemele lui Edgar Poe in Româneşte." *Pagini de Critica Literară.* Bucharest, 1942.

FS66 ———. "Titu Maiorescu şi E. Poe." *Classicii Noştri, Casa Şcoalelor.* Bucharest, 1943.

FS67 Strobl, Karl Hans. "E. A. Poe." *Die Gesellschaft* (Dresden), XVII, No. 4 (1901), 194–97.

FS68 ———. "Eingeleitet." *Edgar Allan Poe, eine Auswahl seiner Erzählungen.* Vienna: Gesellschaft für graphische Industrie, 1923.

FS69 ———. "Poes Weltgedicht." *Die Nation* (Berlin), XXIII, No. 40 (July 7, 1906).

FS70 Strodtmann, Adolf. "Poe." *Amerikanische Anthologie Hildburghausen: Bibliothek ausländischer Klassiker,* 1870, pp. 16–20.

FS71 Stroer, Ernst. "Edgar Allan Poes Lyrick." Diss., University of Vienna, 1910.

FS72 Suarés, André. "Edgar Poe." *Nouvelles Littéraires,* XII (April 1934), 1–2.

FS73 Sugimoto, Takeo. "E. A. Poe in England." *Jour of Shiga University,* XIII (March 1963), 1–10.

FS74 ———. "Edgar Allan Poe and Sarah Helen Whitman." *Jour of Shiga University,* VI (Nov. 1955), 1–12.

FS75 ———. "The Essence of E. A. Poe's Poetry." *Jour of Hikone University,* IV (March 1954), 68–82.

FS76 ———. "The Horrible Element in E. A. Poe's Poetry." *Jour of Shiga University,* I (March 1951), 1–8.

FS77 ———. "On E. A. Poe's 'Ulalume.'" *Jour of Shiga University,* VII (Dec. 1956), 378–90.

FS78 Sukhonin, S. "Edgar Poe i odin iz ego 'uchenykh' kritikov" [Edgar Poe and one of his 'scholarly' critics]. *Vestnik vsemirnoi literatury,* No. 5 (1901), pp. 139–67.

FS79 Susanna, Francisco, trans. *Edgar Allan Poe: Poemas en prosa.* With preface. Barcelona: Editorial Apolo, 1946.

FS80 Suzuki, Shunji. "An Appreciation of Poe's Short Stories." *Osaka Literary Rev,* No. 7 (June 1968), pp. 105–15.

FS81 Suzuki, Yukio. "E. A. Poe and Japanese Literature." *Japan-America Forum* (Tokyo: American Embassy), XIII, No. 10 (Oct. 1967), 87–94.

FS82 ———. "A Fabrication of Poe's 'The Philosophy of Composition.'" *English Literature* (Tokyo: School of Letters, Waseda Univ.), No. 19 (Jan. 1961), pp. 239–46.

FS83 ———. "Poe." *Main Currents in American Literature.* Tokyo: Waseda University Press, 1955, pp. 47–50.

FS84 Szana, Tamás. "Nagy szellemek." *Pest,* 1870, pp. 36–56.

FS85 Szász, Károly. "The Works of the Late Edgar Allan Poe." *Budapesti Szemle,* IV (1858), 153–56.

FT

FT1   Tanizaki, Seiji. *Edgar Allan Poe: Man and His Work*. Tokyo: Kenkyusha, 1967.

FT2   Tashima, Hiroshi. "On Edgar Allan Poe's Essay on Literature." *World Outlook* (Kobe Municipal College of Foreign Languages), II, Nos. 2 and 3 (July 1948), 36–46.

FT3   Tasselin, R. "Un Poète américain: Edgar Allan Poe." *Bibliothèque Universelle et Revue Suisse*, IX (March 1881).

FT4   Tate, Allen. *Saggi* ["On the Limits of Poetry" and "The Forlorn Demon"]. Trans. Nemi D'Agostino. Rome: Ed. di Storia e Letterature, 1957.

FT5   Tello de la Piña, Raquel. "La necrofilia en Allan Poe." *Humanidades*, I (Dec. 1943), 101–13.

FT6   Terán Lomas, Roberto A. M. "Meditaciones sobre Edgar Allan Poe." *Universidad* (Santa Fe), No. 45 (July–Sept. 1960), pp. 141–48.

FT7   Thalès-Bernard. "Revue critique." *Rev Contemporaine*, XXIX (Dec. 31, 1856), 383–88. Review of Poe's *Works* (New York: Redfield).

FT8   Thibaudet, Albert. *Etranger, ou études de littérature anglaise*. Geneva: Ed. de la Petite Fusterie, 1925.

FT9   Thomas, John Wesley. *Amerikanische Dichter und die deutsche Literatur*. Goslar, 1950.

FT10   Tiempo, César. "El cuervo y las campanas." *La Sirviente*, I (1962).

FT11   Toporov, S. A. "Mrachnyi genii" [A gloomy genius]. *Sem'ia*, No. 42 (1899), p. 6. Signed: S. T-v.

FT12   Torelló, Bautista. "Prólogo." *Cuentos de lo grotesco y lo arabesco*. Trans. R. Lasso de la Vega. Madrid, 1946.

FT13   Torres y Prado, Pedro de. "Edgardo Poe." *El Mundo Pintoresco*, III (June 17, 1860), 174.

FT14   Torres-Ríoseco, Arturo. "El caso de Edgard Allan Poe, en la literatura hispano-americana." *Atenea*, XXVII (1934), 398–407.

FT15   ——. "La cultura literaria y científica de Edgar Poe." *Nosotros*, 1st ser., LII (March 1926), 242–46.

FT16   ——. "Edgar Allan Poe." *Atenea*, XIII (1930), 30–40.

FT17 ———. *Ensayos sobre literatura latinoamericana.* Berkeley: University of California Press, 1953.

FT18 ———. "Las teorías poéticas de Poe y el caso de José Asunción Silva." *HR,* XVIII (Oct. 1950), 319–27.

FT19 Toyoda, Minoru. "Edgar Allan Poe and Ryunosuke Akutagawa." *Thought Currents in English Literature* (Tokyo: Aoyama Gakuin Univ.), XXVII, No. 1 (Nov. 1954), 1–12.

FT20 ———. "Edgar Allan Poe and Ryunosuke Akutagawa: Lecture on a Comparison of Them as Short-story Writers." *Essays on English and American Literature for the Celebration of Professor Nakayama's Sixty-first Birthday.* Tokyo: Shôhaku-sha, 1961, pp. 1–12.

FT21 Tracy, G. M. *Les Amours extraordinaires d'Edgar Poe.* Paris: La Palatine, 1963.

FT22 Trompeo, Pietro Paolo. "Poe a Roma." *La nuova Europa,* II, No. 15 (April 15, 1954), 5. Reprinted in *Tempo ritrovato* (Rome: A. Staderini, 1946), pp. 53–57.

FT23 Tügel, Ludwig. "Nachwort." *Im Wirbel des Malstroms und andere seltsame Geschichten.* Trans. Carl W. Neuman. Reclams Universal-Bibliothek, No. 7626. Stuttgart: Reclam, 1950.

FT24 Tusiani, Giuseppe. "L'enigma di Edgar Allan Poe." *Nostro tempo,* II (June 1953), 8–10.

FT25 ———. *Sonettisti americani.* Chicago: Division Typesetting Co., 1954.

FU

FU1 Uhlmann, A. M. "E. A. Poe, der Dichter des Grauens und der Angst." *Börsenblatt für den deutschen Buchhandel* (Leipzig), No. 121 (1954).

FU2 Uitmen, U. [Whitman, W.]. "Znachenie Edgara Po" [The significance of Edgar Poe]. *Whitman, W. Izbrannoe* [Selections]. Moscow, 1954, pp. 264–66.

FU3 Ungaro de Fox, Lucía. "El parentesco artístico entre Poe y Darío." *Revista Nacional de Cultura,* XXVIII, No. 178 (Nov.–Dec. 1966), 81–83.

FU4 Usinger, Fritz. "Edgar Allan Poe." *Tellurium: Elf Essays.* Berlin: Hermann Luchterhand, 1966, pp. 7–19.

FU5 Usov, A. "Dekadentstvo. (Bodler i Po)" [Decadence. (Baude- laire and Poe)]. *Kratkii sistematicheskii slovar' vsemirnoi literatury* [Short, systematic dictionary of world literature]. St. Petersburg, 1906, pp. 135–43.

FV

FV1 Vail, M. "De la littérature et des hommes de lettres aux Etats- Unis." *RDM* (Sept. 15, 1841).

FV2 Valdés, Ildefonso Pereda. "Notas sobre Poe." *El arquero.* Montevideo, 1924, pp. 129–31.

FV3 Valéry, Paul. "A propos d'Eureka." *Variété I.* Paris: Gallimard, 1926.

FV4 ———. "La Situation de Baudelaire." *Variété II.* Paris: Galli- mard, 1930, pp. 129–55.

FV5 Valldeperes, Manuel. "El principio de trascendencia en la poesia de Edgar A. Poe." *Torre,* XIII (1965), 43–55.

FV6 Vallette, Jacques. [Centenary of Poe's Death.] *MdF,* CCCIX (May 1950), 442–54.

FV7 ———. "Chronique." *MdF,* CCVIII (Jan. 1950), 162. Review of *The Centenary Poe,* ed. Montagu Slater.

FV8 Vance, Thomas H. "The Symbolist Tradition in American Fic- tion: From E. A. Poe to Henry James." *Sprache und Literatur Englands und Amerikas.* Ed. Carl August Weber. Tübingen: Max Niemeyer Verlag, 1952, pp. 125–50.

FV9 Vančura, Z. "Z Nových Knih o E. A. Poeovi" [From new literature on E. A. Poe]. *Časopis pro Moderni Filologii,* XV (1928–29), 139–43.

FV10 Deleted.

FV11 Vapereau, Gustave. *L'Année littéraire et dramatique, 1858.* Paris: Hachette, 1859.

FV12 Varhia, O. "Kirjallisuuden taikuri [The wizard of literature]. Edgar Allan Poe." *Kansan Kuvalehti,* No. 40 (1949).

FV13 Varona y Pera, Enrique José. "Poe y Baudelaire." *Desde mi belvedere.* Barcelona, 1917, pp. 53–57.

FV14 Vasilisk. "Edgar Poe." *Rebus,* No. 13 (1883), pp. 118–20.

FV15   Vásquez, Angel Martín. "Edgar Poe restrepo; poeta de la muerte." *Universidad de Antioquia,* XXII (Jan.–Feb. 1948), 137–42.

FV16   Veer, P. van't. "Een bezoek aan Poe's cottage." *Literair paspoort,* V (1950), 80–81.

FV17   Vega, Rafael Lasso de la. "Edgardo A. Poe—Su vida y sus obras." *Estudio,* XXIII (Aug. 1918), 179–87.

FV18   Vendelfelt, Erik. "Edgar Allan Poe och Strindbergs drömspel." *Meddelanden frän Strindbergs-sällskapet,* No. 26 (April 1960), pp. 7–10.

FV19   ———. "Frödings dikt om Edgar Allan Poe." *Samlaren,* XL (1959), 77–87.

FV20   ———. "Fröding och Poe: Några anteckningar." *Gvensk Litteraturtidskrift,* XXIX (1966), 56–66.

FV21   ———. "Fröding upptächer Poe." *Ord och Bild,* LXIX (1960), 302–6.

FV22   Vengerova, Z. [Review of] "Neobyknovennye rasskazy [Unusual stories]. St. Petersburg, 1896." *Obrazovanie,* No. 10 (1896), pp. 94–97.

FV23   Verlant, Ernest. [Edgar Allan Poe.] *Rev Générale,* II (1888), 555.

FV24   Vern, Zh. [Verne, Jules?]. "Edgar Poe i ego sochineniia" [Edgar Poe and his works]. *Modnyi magazin,* No. 23 (1864), pp. 353–56.

FV25   Verne, Jules. "Edgard Poe et ses oeuvres." *Musée des Familles,* XXXI (April 1964), 193–208.

FV26   ———. *Edgardo Poe y sus obras; Noches de Torcuato Tasso.* Barcelona, n.d.

FV27   Vestdijk, S. "Bij de 100st sterfdag van Poe." *Vrij Nederland,* I (Oct. 1949).

FV28   Vinciguerra, Mario. *Romantica e decadenti inglesi.* Foligno: Campitelli, 1926.

FV29   Vivaldi, Cesare. "Un Poe universale." *Mondo Operaio,* II (Dec. 24, 1949), 12.

FV30   Vleuten, Karl Ferdinand van [*sic*]. "Edgar Allan Poe." *Zukunft* (Berlin), IV (Aug. 1, 1903), 181–90.

FV31   Von Ende, A. "E. A. Poe. Eines amerikanischen Dichters Golgotha." *Beilage zur allgemeinen Zeitung* (Munich), No. 74 (1898).

FW

FW1   Wächtler, Paul. *Edgar Allan Poe und die deutsche Romantik.* Borna-Leipzig: R. Noske, 1911.

FW2   Wainstein, Lia. "La letteratura americana in Russia." *SA,* XI (1965), 447–62.

FW3   ———. "La situazione limite di E. A. Poe." *SA,* VI (1960), 73–86.

FW4   Waldron, John. "Un classico del terrore spirituale." *Fle,* VI (July 8, 1951), 7.

FW5   Watt, Robert. "Biographiske Notitser." *Phantastiske Fortael-linger: Oversatte af . . . Watt.* Copenhagen: K. Vissing, 1868, pp. i–xi.

FW6   Weber, Jean-Paul. "L'Analyse thématique. Hier, aujourd'hui, demain." *Etudes Françaises,* I (1965), 29–71.

FW7   ———. "Edgar Poe, ou le thème d'horloge." *NRF,* LXVII and LXIX (Aug.–Sept. 1958), 301–11, 498–508.

FW8   ———. "Rev. of *Choix de contes.* Trans. Charles Baudelaire and Roger Asselineau." *NRF,* LXVIII (Aug. 1958), 345.

FW9   Weiss, Aureliu. "Propos sur la littérature fantastique." *L'Enseignement sécondaire au Canada,* Jan–Feb. 1967, pp. 44–51.

FW10   Wendel, H. "Einiges über E. A. Poe." *Magazin für Literatur* (Leipzig), LXXII (1903), 357–59.

FW11   Wetherill, Peter Michael. "Baudelaire et la poèsie d'Edgar Allan Poe." Diss., Birmingham, 1955–56.

FW12   ———. *Charles Baudelaire et la poésie d'Edgar Allan Poe.* Paris: A. G. Nizet, 1962. Reviewed: Austin, *MLR,* LXI, 139.

FW13   Whitman, Walt. "E. A. Poe." *Amerikanische Rundschau,* V, No. 27 (1949), 56–61. With four illus. by A. Beardsley of Poe.

FW14   ———. "Edgar Poe, Carlyle, Emerson. La Signification d'Edgar Poe." Trans. Léon Bazalgette. *MdF,* CXIV (March 1916), 35–44.

FW15   Wi, N. "Edgar Allan Poe—w 100-ą rocznicę urodzin twórcy 'Kruka.'" *Swiat,* No. 4 (1909), pp. 9–10.

FW16   Wildberg, Bodo. "Poe und seine Kunst: Zu seinem 100. Geburtstage (19. Januar)." *Westermanns Monatshefte,* II (Feb. 1909), No. 105.

FW17   Winwar, Frances. *Nawiedzony gród* [The haunted palace].
Trans. Maria Skibniewska. Warsaw: Państwowy Instytut Wydawniczy,
1961. Reviewed: Anna Gorazd, "Edgar Allan Poe," *Zycie Liter,* No.
37 (1961), p. 9.

FW18   Wittich, M. "Edgar Poe." *Neue Bahnen* (Vienna), 1904, pp.
382–83.

FW19   Woestyn, H.-R. "L'Extraordinaire Randonée d'Edgar Poe."
Figaro, Dec. 14, 1929.

FW20   ——. *Politian: Drame romantique inédit.* Paris: Emile-Paul
frères, 1926.

FW21   Wölcken, Fritz. *Der literarische Mord.* Nuremberg: West
Verlag, 1953. See pp. 15–50.

FW22   Wolff, A. L. *Tod und Unsterblichkeit: Das Leitmotiv von
E. A. Poes Werk.* University of Berlin diss. Berlin, 1937. Reviewed:
F. Schönemann, *Zeitschrift für neusprachlichen Unterricht,* XXXVI,
320–21; "A. B.," *Archiv,* CLXXI, 268–69.

FW23   Wyzewa, Theodore de. "La Correspondence d'Edgar Poe."
RDM, CXXV (Oct. 15, 1894), 936–46. Reprinted in his *Ecrivains
Etrangers* (Paris, 1896).

FW24   ——. *Nos Maitres: Influence de Poe sur Villiers de l'Isle
Adam.* Paris, 1895.

FX

FX1   "X. Y. Z." "Edgar Poe e il sou carteggio inedite." *Revista
europea,* May 1878, pp. 89–104, 318–43.

FY

FY1   Yagi, Toshio. *Destruction and Creation: Essays on Edgar Allan
Poe.* Tokyo: Nan'undo, 1968.

FY2   Yamato, S. "Parody in Poe's Poems." *Youth's Companion,*
No. 10 (1949).

FY3   Yamato, Yasuo. "Poe's Poetry." *Eigo Kenkyu* [The study of
English], Poe Number (Oct. 1949), pp. 13–18.

FY4 Yamaya, Saburo. "Poe, Hawthorne, and Melville's 'Benito Cereno.' " *Studies in English Literature* (Tokyo: Hosei Univ.), No. 4 (March 1961), pp. 21–32.

FY5 Yokota, Tadasuke. "E. A. Poe as a Man." *Jimbun Kagaku* [Cultural Sciences] (Gifu: Gifu College of Education), No. 1 (March 1953), pp. 17–21.

FY6 Yoshida, Kenichi. "An Explanatory Note on Poe." *An Outline of World Literature* (Tokyo), XXXIII (1959), 445–48.

FY7 ———. "On Poe." *Bungakukai* (Tokyo), July 1948.

FY8 ———. "On Poe's Poetry." *Eigo Seinen* [The rising generation], CIV, No. 5 (May 1958), 18–19.

FY9 Yoshida, Michiko. "Poe's World." *Language and Literature* (Tokyo: Aoyama Gakuin Univ.), No. 8 (March 1967), pp. 47–69.

FZ

FZ1 Zardoya, Concha. "La belleza de Edgar Allan Poe." *Cuadernos Americanos,* LVI, No. 2 (March–April 1951), 222–44.

FZ2 Zimmermann, Eléonore M. "Mallarmé et Poe: Precisions et aperçus." *CL,* VI (Fall 1954), 304–15.

FZ3 Zimmerman, Melvin. "Baudelaire, Poe and Hawthorne." *RLC,* XXXIX (1965), 448–50.

FZ4 Zimny, Aleksander. "Piewca trwogi i klęski." *Rzeczypospolita,* No. 327 (1949), p. 5.

Index

Index